In search China

David Kellogg
with Liu Fei & Tang Min

Edited by
Dorothy Stein

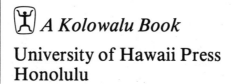

A Kolowalu Book

University of Hawaii Press
Honolulu

University of Hawaii Press edition 1991
91 92 93 94 95 96   5 4 3 2 1

First published 1989 by
Hilary Shipman Limited, London

Library of Congress Cataloging-in-Publication Data
Kellogg, David.
    In search of China / David Kellogg with Liu Fei
& Tang Min ; edited by Dorothy Stein.
        p.   cm. — (A Kolowalu book)
    Includes index.
    ISBN 0-8248-1403-7 (paper)
    1. China—Description and travel—1976-
I. Liu, Fei.   II. T'ang, Min.
III. Stein, Dorothy.   IV. Title.
DS712.K45   1991
951.05'8—dc20   91–10813
                                                            CIP

Cover illustration and design by Santos Barbasa Jr.
Typeset by Florencetype Ltd, Kewstoke, Avon
Printed in the United States of America

University of Hawaii Press books are printed on
acid-free paper and meet the guidelines for
permanence and durability of the Council on
Library Resources

Contents

INNER MONGOLIA

HEILONGJIANG

JILIN

Shenyang

LIAONING

Baotou. • Hohhot

BEIJING

Peking • Beidaihe

Tianjin • TIANJIN

HEBEI

Yinchuan

Zhongwei

NINGXIA

Xiji. Shunmishan

Lanzhou Longde

GANSU

SHANXI

Jinan Weifang

SHANDONG

Anyang

SHAANXI Luoyang

Xianyang . Lintong Sanmenxia Zhengzhou

Xi'an

HENAN

JIANGSU

Shiquan.

Nanjing

Suzhou. Shanghai

Zhuxi

Yicheng•

ANHUI

Chengdu

HUBEI • Zhongxiang

. Dazu

Qianchang• • Wuhan Hangzhou•

Chongqing

ZHEJIANG

Changsha•

GUIZHOU HUNAN JIANGXI FUJIAN

Gulyang Fuzhou•

Anshun Quanzhou,

GUANGXI . Liuzhou Meixian• Xiamen

GUANGDONG

Nanning Canton• . Shenzhen

HONG KONG

Zhanjiang MACAU

Halkou

Nada .

Hainan Island

This book is dedicated to the students and teachers of
China, especially to those who, in June 1989, voted
with their lives for democratic rights and for a socialism
which will finally deserve that name.

Acknowledgements

Liu Fei's *Pearly peaks in a dream* was first published in Chinese in *Xizang Wenxue* (Tibetan Literature) in April 1986. *Artists at home* appeared in *Xizang Wenxue* in March 1987 and in *Xiamen Wenxue* (Xiamen Literature) in June 1988.

Tang Min's *The mysterious miasma of Taimu Shan* was first published in Chinese in *Qingchun* (Youth) in February 1986.

Special thanks are due to 'Old Peng', who discussed the originals of the translated materials at length, swabbed tears with his shoulders, and provided instructive and timely quotations from Engels and Sandor Petofi.

Chinese names

It is only a slight exaggeration to say that over a billion Chinese people share only a 'hundred old names' as family names. The family name comes first, and is the one used by everyone except for intimate friends and family. Women do not change their names when they marry, and husband and wife may call each other by their family names, as when Liu Fei refers to her husband as 'Old Pei'. As one might expect in such an age-graded society, people often address each other in terms that reflect the relative ages of the speaker and the person indicated: 'Old Pei' if the speaker is younger, 'Little Liu' if older.

Names are open to a lot of punning and wordplay. In this book, this comes out in the occasional translation of names, such as 'Righteous Rebel' and 'Metal Mountain'. Personal names sometimes reflect the circumstances or emotional state of the baby's parents at the time of naming. For example, during the Cultural Revolution, children were given names such as 'Red Guard'. Thus when the battalion commander in Tang Min's story changed his name from 'Middle' to 'Loyal' during the 'Unswervingly Loyals' campaign, he was being opportunistic, but not as bizarre as the reader might think.

Foreword

Until very recently, China seemed to most Western countries a very distant and rather mysterious place, in David Kellogg's words, 'the closest thing to another planet on earth'. A vast and immensely populous country, with a culture at least as deep and rich as our own, but with far more historical continuity, it still appears – despite a vast amount of recent news coverage – somehow unknowable except as belonging to one or the other of two benighted categories on which an endless stream of travellers and journalists file reports: the 'Third World', with its immense problems of poverty and underdevelopment, and 'the Communist world', with a social and political system regarded as both alien and repellent. So it is not surprising that few Westerners write of China from the standpoint of anything but observers, with varying degrees of sympathy and affection for the Chinese people, and almost invariable hostility toward its regime. Nor is it surprising that in consequence the experience of China seems to have had so little impact on them. But what would it be like for a Westerner to become Chinese?

The experiences recounted in this book came about almost by accident, and yet paradoxically were prepared for from David's early childhood, when, for no apparent reason, he suddenly became fascinated by all things Chinese and by the even more exotic land of Tibet. As an adolescent, these interests led him to begin learning the Chinese language. At the same time, a strong and idealistic moral bent shaped the development of his social and political views. At the University of Chicago, where he studied

vii

Chinese, he joined the youth organization of the Spartacist League, a Trotskyist group. When the organization became enmeshed in an internal power struggle of which he was scarcely aware, he unwillingly resigned, left the University, worked as a welder, and then embarked on a trip to Europe in 1979–80.

This was not his first travel experience, since he had accompanied his parents to both Europe and India as a child. In the course of several sojourns in France, he had become fluent in French, and journeyed to other countries in both western and eastern Europe. In the final leg of his 1980 trip, however, he decided to visit the Middle East, where he had never been. While travelling through Syria, he was kidnapped and interned in a series of secret prisons. (The fellowship among the inmates of these prisons is implicitly remembered and compared sadly to the isolation of the young delinquents in the passage in this book describing his visit to a Chinese borstal.) More fortunate than many other similar captives, he was released after two months, and he returned to Europe and then to Chicago, where he worked again as a welder until the collapse of the steel industry in 1982 made him redundant. Thereupon, he decided to return to North Africa to take up a serious study of Arabic.

At the end of a year of intensive language training in Tunisia, he went to London to acquire a language teaching certificate, which he believed would help him to support himself while he continued his studies. Then, en route to Sudan, a chance encounter with a roving Australian turned him eastward, accompanied only by a portable typewriter and a cassette recorder and still dressed for the tropics, to fulfil his childhood dream.

Living and travelling in many parts of China since then, he still finds the 'human scenery', particularly that of the ethnic minorities, his predominant interest. And it is these special concerns, personal history and background that have shaped the fresh and unusual perspective informing the experiences, descriptions and impressions that are recounted here.

This book came about in a fashion almost as unpremeditated as the experiences themselves. The bulk of it consists in selections from a stream of letters, flowing almost without break, whether issuing from the Gobi desert, the mountains of Tibet, a cancer hospital in Peking, a science university in Wuhan, or the cosy domesticity of a classroom in Canton. The letters were originally meant for consumption only by family and friends. So too were his occasional attempts to capture his impressions and adventures in the form of recorded conversations and sketches. Eventually, however, his fascination with modern Chinese literature and his friendships with several young artists and writers whom he met in the course of his travels led him to try his hand at translating some of their essays and short stories, and then to want these to reach a wider audience in the West than that of his immediate acquaintance.

As these letters and sketches followed each other, they developed from a record of the exploration of a wonderful but alien world into a story of transformations of many kinds. The China into which David plunged eagerly in early 1984 was one in the throes of profound political and social transition, halfway through the 'reforms' that eventually triggered the current political and economic crisis, and the dramatic events in which this book culminates. His observations and conversations with peasants, teachers, students, doctors, writers, artists, truck drivers and shop keepers reflected the effects of reform policies on many aspects of Chinese life, and the hope, excitement, bewilderment and anxiety they entailed.

But perhaps the transformations in David himself are even more striking. Starting out on a journey that was meant to be 'only a detour', he carried with him a common youthful problem of emotional as well as occupational retraining: how to redirect a life in which it had become clear that he could neither participate in the mainstream of his own culture nor in the important events of history as he had hoped. It seemed the answer lay in building a 'little life' of mundane contribution to a country and people he liked and admired, and a system with whose aims, despite its bureaucratic and authoritarian distortions, he was basically in sympathy. As the months and years go by, the wanderer becomes a settler, a restless young man matures, high adventure gives way to professional responsibilities, and, most remarkable of all, an outsider comes to see another culture as his own, another country as his home. What starts out as superficial, if highly individual, accounts and descriptions of places becomes a record of development and change.

Integral to this story, David's translations and his acquaintance with their authors add another dimension in which to view the many layers of Chinese life. Although his own experiences and observations are not retailed without their share of humour, his accounts cannot aspire to the delicate satire with which the Chinese woman – even more than her male compatriots – may view her own society. Thus, Liu Fei's honeymoon journal presents, from the inside, a picture of young middle-class Chinese as tourists themselves in a culture different from their own, but one in which, very much like European expatriates, they live, and from which they benefit. Tang Min's ironic ghost story is a view of the legacy of the Cultural Revolution in the countryside, a view inaccessible to the 'big nose' passing through. At the same time, it shows the imprint of earlier Chinese fiction and its derivation from the storyteller's art. On the other hand, Liu Fei's sly portrait of her husband and his friend reveals much, not only about their male fantasies, but about the effect of the 'reforms' on the outlook and values of artists and writers, and the always tense relations between Tibetans and the ethnic Chinese who live and work among them.

Dorothy Stein

1 | A journey to the East

Budapest, 31 December 1983
Dear D & B,
Voilà, I'm in Budapest, trying to get a visa to go to China.
I'm not sure how you will receive this news. I suppose you
are grown used to my odd itineraries, but this one is further
off course than usual. On the other hand, you seem to think
that almost anywhere on earth would be better than Sudan.

Why now? Well, for one thing, because I have already
bought a train ticket, Budapest to Peking, round trip, with
indefinite layovers in Moscow and Outer Mongolia on the
return trip. I got it for about $80 with a student reduction, all
perfectly legit. If I get all the visas I'm asking for, I will leave
Budapest on the 23rd, get to Moscow on the 25th, leave that
evening on the Trans-Siberian, and arrive in Peking in five
days, 17 hours and 20 minutes. The dining car, I am told,
will be changed every country, so that one may at least taste
some of the culinary turf one is transiting.

Now one of my problems seems to be that the Chinese will
give me only eight days of visa, hardly enough to turn
around. This will not do. But I have it on reliable Australian
evidence (the Strines are the most amazing people: each one
carries a travel agency in his head and an outfitter's in his
knapsack) that by transiting to Hong Kong and applying for
a tourist visa there, I can have three months more or less
free. I have dreamed so long of China that I won't be able to
sleep if I have only eight days there. And I must do it now, it
seems so near and it will get another of my adolescent
longings out of the way. No? I almost feel like I've given
away some of its reality by blurting it out. But look at it from

another point of view, say, from Budapest, it's so close you can practically taste it.

It always sounds much easier than it actually is. I have already done the embassy stomp all this week, and I have another three weeks – if all goes well – to get it completely lined up. There are currency regulations, the works, and you even need a hotel reservation in Moscow before you can get a transit visa. But I gotta do it, I gotta do it, or I'll never be able to really settle down. You know, I've been getting ready for this trip since I was nine years old, and all of a sudden it jumps out at me from around the bend.

How did I get here? Well, I finished the translating gig in Paris, which ended up paying me about 5,000 francs in all. And I really thought I was going to Athens until the day after I left Paris when I met this mad Australian in St Dizier, and even then the whole thing sounded so mad – it still does – that I thought I'd better go to Budapest and see exactly what could and couldn't be done before I wrote you yet another letter full of maybes and ifs and ending as all mine seem to with 'I'll let you know when I find out'.

So then I hitched out to see Andreas in Germany. Hesse is a very pretty sort of place, just physically. The Oberstadt, where Andreas lives in Marburg, is thick with 13th century buildings, but you'd never really know it because they are still building with hand-hewn timber bones and mud flesh, with chipped and split slate all over, making the roofs kind of slithy and scaly, and the streets, cobbled in the usual fan pattern that sprays out from under the hood of your car when you're driving fast over it, are smooth and reptilian in the rain.

Nothing's parallel, all the floors sag and the walls bulge jauntily, and the land slithers around full of ducks and garbage, practically covered by Autobahn, and the mountains sail above it with veined sheets of rock rigged with mad tangles of chestnut and oak and maple and topped by the phallus that Kaiser Wilhelm built to commemorate the slaughter of the Paris commune, next to a kind of accordion cafe for featherheaded buffoons in lederhosen.

2

Once it was a terribly decadent Weimar *Kneipe* [bar] entitled the Spiegellust, 'lust for mirrors', as I like to read it, a hangout for the earliest Nazis in the region, who were indeed some of the earliest in the whole country. All the streets leading up into the forest are named Spiegellust. The burnt-down synagogue is now a park, and there are no Jews left, but there are blond lads like Andreas studying Hebrew down in the University.

It was really interesting to observe him in his natural habitat, it made some of his oddish behaviour in Tunis more explicable. He is, as I think I told you, an inveterate Kneiper, a fixture of filthy beer joints called 'New Wave' or 'Jazz Caveta' or 'Delirium', all catering to the same crowd, usually on the same night. 'Punk' or 'skin' or 'neo-romantic' are not even distinctions in dress in Germany, much less ideological distinctions; they are simply momentary moods. Andreas' only concessions to neo-romantic affectations are letting the fingernail on his left pinky grow the length of an extra finger-joint and occasionally wearing a lavender scarf. Otherwise he looks and rather acts like a Teutonic knight. I accused him of ideological muesli-punk one night, but I think I mistook him for Germany in general, a mistake he himself often makes. It's all ideological granola, no edges, put it all together into one big bowl and add milk until indistinguishable. And in fact the hippies and punks and wavies and neo-roms and the rest not only talk together and drink together, they have a very hard time telling each other apart. The Mood is the milieu and the medium and the message.

But under close beery observation by candlelight and neon lamp, the Mood is not utterly devoid of content, however vacuous it may be. The basic self-evident truth is light-minded pessimism, which does not even have a ring of sincere despair to redeem it. You don't even need the Gallic mournful look, although you must try to look serious without looking underfed. You plop yourself down in front of your Pils or Weizenbier with lemon, and, without heaving a sigh, you remark deadpan that maybe Europe has ten

3

years left, outside maximum. No one dreams of asking why, the statement is self-evident. You then fleck your listeners with foam and announce that basically it's no love-song, dig, no future in it. Maybe somebody nods; after all, it's adolescent to feel good about feeling bad, and anything that comes safely before adulthood can't be bad.

I really couldn't keep up with Andreas' Kneipe waltz, and some nights I just stayed home and did Arabic, or I tried to learn German by studying inscriptions on lavatory walls, the way people learned to decipher Egyptian hieroglyphics. That and eight days of listening to Andreas makes me something of an expert on Germany, or at least male student Germany.

On Christmas Eve, Andreas wanted to sing and dragged me to a kind of 13th century revival, sponsored by some order of Lutheran monks that believes in putting the Catholicism back in Protestantism, mumbo-jumbo, incense, candles, biscuits and grape juice, the whole bit. We had been kneiping all day and all evening and in the middle of the service I went for a piss under a flying buttress and didn't come back.

From whence I went to Vienna and spent two days, getting a visa for Hungary and eyeing museums, much more interesting from the outside than from the in. They wear their skeletons on the outside, mostly, red porphyry bones with creamy helical heads. The marrow is out, too, and flesh-coloured stone covered with ash from the lungs of the suburbs. All imperial cities give me the creeps, the idea of so many living on unproductive and accumulated labour. Hardly ever seeing anybody producing anything is bad enough, you get the feeling that it is all done by black magic, or from God, or that we are all busy dividing and redividing a finite amount of the earth's bounty, as you so dourly think. But in Vienna's case, all the accumulated labour and capital is long dead, a dead empire that in dying physically destroyed many of the Hungarians, Slavs, Montenegrins, Wends, and other slaves who built the pyramids. But inside the exo-skeletons things are still bought and sold, divided and redivided, and the plaster on the walls looks scrumptious.

Thence hence. Budapest is about as un-German as you can get. Lovable, but not exactly lovely, the facades that are supposed to make the rude brick look like stone were often shot off during the war, or maybe the revolution. No one has bothered to plaster them up, there are bullet holes all over the downtown area; a minimum of repair was done: there was too much new housing to build. The metro is a dream, of course, and the buses all seem to run on the honour system, which means nobody pays. I've only seen three people punching tickets so far, so why own a car? Yet many do.

There are little plaques with hooks for hanging wreaths, archives of this and that, National Museums of the Working Class Movement, the Hungarian Working Class Movement, the Communist Party, the Resistance, the Deportation, the Jewish archives – in an old Turkish mosque. Monuments all over. There is a monument for the 'victims of the Counter-revolution', well situated, for nearby there is a monument for the 'victims of the Working Class Movement'. Continuity all over. Why bother to bung up the bullet holes? Not exactly the Germanic way of living with the past. What do they really think of the monument to Lenin, though? Is it just another 'monument to the victims of the Counter-revolution'? Or just another place for public snogging, which seems to be something of a national pre- and post-occupation?

The original Uralic people from beyond the Don have apparently melted without a trace into the bloodstream of the Danube, leaving only their language, a knotty mass of verbs that end in 'enk', 'ink', 'ok', and 'el', depending on whether they mean eating or drinking, and 'gy' is pronounced sort of 'dy' on the lips of women who look occasionally Turkish, occasionally Scandinavian. I carefully studied the sculptures of the early Uralic conquerors for a clue to what Hungarians looked like before incorporating huge numbers of Germans, Croats and Rumanians, but they just looked like medieval kings, wasted faces, curly beards, sloping brows. Yet a thousand years is not very long, really.

It is New Year's Eve, and people are stalking the streets with huge horns, like green and red plastic Alpine tobacco pipes, all framping away. As it got darker, more and more adults joined in, and I was finally almost run over by a blind couple too busy honking to hear my footsteps. For my part, it's the traditional time for recriminations. Not sure why, what makes this particular relationship of earth to sun ripe for self-pity and regrets, except that it makes it possible, by memorable occasion, for me to remount the four years spent out of the Party.

Before then there are almost no memorable occasions. Since then there are the peaks and valleys of a 'little life', 'relationships', as they say, people who governed this or that six-month cycle like astrological signs: Alix and Holly, Sugar and Cecile, and places like Cairo and Tunis, Chicago and Oak Park, like observatories, where certain meaningless sightings were taken and results falsified. A regular Druidic calendar. I keep thinking that I have at last grown used to the idea of a little life, lived by the calendar, rather than a political life with a sense of direction, that at last I have ceased thinking of years AP, and at last given up the idea that I am destined that way again.

I am so bloody, bloody tired of it, yet I can think of nothing else. I once tried to tell an Algerian comrade, in Arabic, why I was no longer a member, and he kept demanding to know the political basis of the purge, what the issues were. How to explain that there were none? We all sat and listened to a tape of a punk rock song the organizer was fond of, meant to help us laugh at our executions, a kind of blindfold. They all spoke, and we were asked if we had anything to say. And then a list of the resignations thev wanted was read out. I was the last on the list. No politics at all, really. And now I remember the song Gene liked so much: 'What will it take – To whip you into shape – A broken heart – A broken head – It can be arranged – It can be arranged.'

6

Why then is this sense of waking up, of giving up, of abandoning all hope larger than life, always fresh and astonishing, and not quite credible? Why indeed? Enough of this self-pitiful self-hatred, impossible to get out of or get any sense out of anymore, and I'd rather be in China. I write all this only for ritualistic reasons, because I happened to be writing when the hour of the annual rite approached, and much as I respect your opinion on other matters, I have never been terribly impressed by your ability to make sense out of my own life. It is really asking far too much, since direct experience has always been the source of all my own insights, that you give me insights merely on the basis of my insights. Research is not exactly, as Burt says, the process of finding that there is no particular reason why you shouldn't hold your preconceived opinions, but it is curiously difficult to make sense out of someone else's records, isn't it?

Anyway, my itinerary, provisional of course, is, roughly, 23 January, leave Budapest, 25 January, arrive Moscow, 31 January, arrive Peking, check mail, spend maybe four days, 3-4 February, leave Peking for Canton, 8 February, arrive in Hong Kong, spend maybe a week there, depending on how long it takes to get an entry permit, and then go back through China for two months or so. Canton, Chengdu, Changsha, Wuhan (God, magic names, I don't believe in their power, or even in their geographical position, but . . .), Hangzhou, Shanghai, Xi'an, Suzhou, Tianjin, Peking, at least. Amazing, huh?

I'm really guilt-ridden about letting your letters rot in Athens, and I suppose this letter, which is more a long drawn-out literary postcard, since it can't pretend to be half a correspondence, is meant as penance. In any case, I will be back in Budapest within four months from today. And that's really all I can say right now.

Budapest, 16 January 1984

Just got, with somewhat tempered gratefulness, if not filial grace, your letters and enclosures. Thanks for all, especially for handling my mail from overseas, which you didn't offer to do. Sorry, Dorothy, I can't tell you more currently about my plans, because I don't have any. I really thought I was going to Athens until the day after I left Paris, but if you repeat a typo, you get modern poetry, and if you repeat a bunch of wrong notes and dissonant chords, you get music. My itineraries tend to operate on the same basis.

A stroll through any museum in Budapest will give you some really interesting slants on history. There is a real, sometimes rather overblown, attempt to get at productive relations, and even a kind of Braudelian view of how the workers lived. There is a mock-up of a mine next to the display of King Mathias' burial crown jewels; bracelets and what-not are shown as indicative of the level of luxury and culture, and symptomatic of certain productive relations. Real attempts are made to get beneath the surface, sometimes with rather laughable results: the Transylvanian nobility somehow come out as nationalist patriots fighting Habsburg absolutist reaction, in the interests of the bourgeois Hungary to be. The Turks generally get a bad rap, since they represent . . . what? But these are the questions that do concern me when I hit up museums, that's what I really think about when I look at crown jewels. How to get beneath the surface, how things are really produced, by whom, under what conditions? How many people were paid to sit around and think great thoughts in this society as a result of whose sacrifice, and by whose decision?

All around me, despite everything, things seem profoundly right here. Oh, not in relation to what they could be, of course. Hey, Burt, you've been here, do you know what I mean? It's not the streets named Bela Kun and Lenin and even Raoul Wallenberg. There are also plazas named Roosevelt and Rakocszi and Mezo Imre. It is the sensible public transportation, the concern for good housing, the absence of scroungers and bag ladies, the multi-nationality, the exuberant sexuality of the young people. A lovable place.

Cheap, too. Window-shopping Hungarians, intent on their quarry even though it's Sunday and everything but eateries

are closed, peer past their reflections to glimpse – me, my
cannibal fingers plunging into my pig-knuckle paprikash in
the Self-Service Restaurant, dribbling gore all over a book
I'm trying to read. (From the shattered looks coming
through the pane I gather this is not done.) But things
dripping sour cream and beet blood, yes, and cabbage and
potatoes, yes, but also ferocious spiced and pickled things
that open the nose and the sinuses. Combinations that never
fail to surprise, things that look sweet and taste salty, and
vice versa, candy bars that look like chocolate but taste like
apples right down to the crunch of apple flesh; nothing here
operates by the code whereby grape-flavoured things are
grape simply by definition, even though the real relationship
seems purely arbitrary. Noodles with ricotta and bacon fat
dribbled on, cakes with apple fillings topped with raspberry
whip made of pasta, sausages of blood and groats, cherry
soup, greasy, fleshy things swimming in red goo, just like in
Tunis, Hungariash Paprikash. So much for flavour.

Right, anyway, it has taken me 16 days to secure a Soviet
visa, and I won't really be sure of getting it until Friday,
which will give me two days to get a Mongolian one, and I'm
told that's the most difficult of the three. And that's all for
now . . . Write you from Moscow if . . .

Budapest, 21 January 1984
There! Really it was indescribably tedious, by far the
toughest time I've ever had lining up visas, and not over,
quite, although I'm due to depart in hours. None of the
embassies would agree on my exact time (not just date) of
arrival in their territory, and departure for the sovereignty of
another, but no one is allowed even a day's leeway.
Mongolia wanted eight dollars in cash, no traveller's
cheques. No-one could agree on currency regulations, no-
one would issue double entry visas covering the return, and
some assured me that a return visa would be unavailable in
Hong Kong or Peking, although I find that hard to swallow.
Moscow wanted me to reserve a room at the Hotel
Metropole, which I wouldn't use; I cannot take forints or

roubles in, and no change places would be open, so they say, in Moscow.

Finally, this morning, just when I thought I had it all lined up, the Mongolian consul pointed out to me that my Soviet visa doesn't become valid until the day after tomorrow, and I am due to leave tomorrow. Just now, though, I realized that the time difference between here and Moscow will validate my visa tout juste – with 27 minutes to spare! Similarly, if the Mongolian estimates of my transit time are right, and the Chinese are wrong, I will arrive in China with only four of the eight days allotted me to get to Hong Kong (it takes seven). Conversely, if the Chinese are right and the Mongolians wrong, I will arrive at the Mongolian border in darkest Irkutsk two days ahead of the validity of my visa.

It is always hard to determine what is a real problem and what is simply diplomatic obstruction meant to weed out hippies and preppies. Several times I was simply told, 'No, we do not give out visas. You've got the wrong country,' and I was reduced to standing plaintively outside the consulate in the driving snow, once for several hours. But if the trains are, hah, on time, and the Mongolians are right against the Chinese, I'm in!

I come from the library now, where I've been cramming Chinese and Mongolian history, Russian phrases, Lu Xun's poetry, and interviews with Qing idiot officials, trying to get back some of the Chinese that Arabic has elbowed out. I emerge with exactly the feeling I used to get reading Marco Polo, or Tibetan histories, or anything on China in Forest Lake: my thoughts thick with loess [a yellow clay soil found in China and the American midwest, fertile but easily eroded] and senses full of flood and famine and horror somewhere on the other side of the planet, really unable to concentrate on what is in front of me; my Hungarian seems to fly by like a radio broadcast in the back of my head, and nothing tastes right. Just like when I was a kid, and China was the closest thing to another planet on earth. Only a week . . . I really have to snarl out loud, and turn up my collar and yank my matching Lenin cap down the side of my head, because otherwise I'll be doing the *hora* all the way through Siberia. I still feel hopelessly unprepared, though maybe a week in the train will accustom me, at least in theory, to the idea of arriving. Maybe it's like puberty, you don't get prepared by the wait, just gradually pushed.

Anyway, this is really just to cry victory, and get these paintings off my baggage. They are all various degrees of failure. I still basically want to be a realist painter, at least while travelling, so it is all done in the style connoisseurs here know as Irrealism, or Incompetent Realism. I cannot paint what is in front of me, and I somehow feel as if that is almost a moral failing. It means that the hand tells the head what to do, that you have to adapt what you are thinking to what you are least incapable of doing.

I seem to proceed around the globe on roughly the same principle, and I would like to do a painting to illustrate it: a modern Odysseus, wandering somewhere in China with a huge wooden airplane propeller like an oar over his shoulder, followed by a huge crowd of children, which fortunately he doesn't notice, since they are Chinese and very polite, or he might misinterpret it, plant his oar, and sacrifice to the wrong god, in the wrong spot, himself in some avatar or other.

My one regret in this delirious ecstasy of a trip is newspapers. Maybe you could find something comprehensive about events in Tunis for me and send it. I haven't read so much as a want-ad or an obituary since I left Vienna.

Train to Moscow, 23 January 1984
Dear Old Man and Lady,

Just passed through Kiev, where the spunky young woman with a world-weary face and a mouthful of gold who shares this compartment caustically welcomed two young rustic-looking Russians to the upper bunks. There they proceeded to down half a litre of vodka with their morning tea, and then wolf down two chickens for breakfast. The Ukraine is going by in the opposite direction under a drifting white sky and a sprinkling of snow.

It is lunchtime now, and the two Ukrainians just came in with six bottles of lunch. The pretty young Russian woman is laughing at me from the pages of her Dostoevsky. I did a rather lousy water colour of her when we were stalled at the border and she was asleep, and she just found it in with my Chinese and Arabic papers. I am doing Chinese from a 19th century tome I got in Buda, full of interviews with fossilized Qing officials. The form taught for, 'How do you do, what is your name?' is, 'Have you eaten white rice, sir, and what is your precious and exalted name?' The answer is along the lines of, 'Sir, unworthy and presumptuous as I am, I have deprived you of your share, exceeding all propriety; my humble name, low as grass, is Wang.' What tremendous work the modernizers, like Chen Duxiu, have done on it! Arabic needs a Chen Duxiu rather desperately. But at least my Chinese, slowly returning, is taking back some of the turf the Arabic elbowed it out of four years ago.

Now the liquid lunch has begun – vodka, beer and champagne, all at once. Outside, people are zipping back and forth, mostly back, on cross-country skis. Giant furs looking like dogs, giant dogs that look like furs. And I have giant steps to take. I got a hilarous Intourist guide to Moscow that begins:

> 'Here we enter the socialist world of equality and dignity,' said a young Algerian girl. 'The city has no real estate salesmen,' an American businessman observed in surprise . . .

I have visions of Potemkin Village hotels with all Moscow flashing by in animated comic strip paintings carried by Intourist guides past the windows. Which is almost exactly what I will get, seeing Russia from a train window. On the way back, though, hopefully, I'll be able to see Moscow in my Sudan clothes without freezing my balls off.

Surrukh Bataar, Outer Mongolia, 29 January 1984
Surrukh Bataar was the national hero of the Mongolian People's Republic. He started out as an oiler or something in the Tsarist gun corps, and was drawn into the Bolshevik

revolution early on. Then, when Mongolia became a refuge for Baron Wrangel [the last of the White Guard rebels against Soviet rule] during the civil war, he managed to organize Mongolian resistance against him, which led to the Mongolian revolution. Mongolia is a country of only a million people or so, heavily diluted by vast spaces, and until recently almost untouched by wealth in any non-hoofed form. In fact, in Surrukh Bataar's time a third of the population, as in Tibet, were monks, and the rest had a birth rate so low the very existence of the Mongols as a people was in serious danger. Here one might think a bit of eastern Europe was transplanted to Central Asia, except for the old people in fleece-lined raw silk outer garments, Russian fur hats, fur boots and faces with rolling wrinkles, gaunt like the Gobi desert.

How different from Siberia, the whole of which seemed rather more densely populated than the upper Midwest, but I think that is simply because we passed along the populated fringe. There were cabins everywhere, often terribly heat-inefficient looking, with even worse-looking big-window bauhouses in places like Irkutsk and Omsk, and little villages of what look like large doghouses but were in fact *maisons secondaires*, dachas for Leningrad workers. There was ice fishing on Lake Baikal, lots of people without ice houses, just lying prone on the ice and dragging up fish almost too big to pass through the hand-hewn holes. Sunset at three in the afternoon; cities too smoky from pungent spruce-fired stoves to see the stars or moon, but lit with giant spotlights, providing a pleasant kind of motorway ambiance; food, mostly garlic-flavoured, with slabs of meat and dabs of sour cream, umpteen kinds of piroschki, pickled peppers and cabbage and beets, salted bread, now going slightly stale on this, the seventh day of the trip.

The border was almost immediately reflected by the landscape. The trees stop, you can go for hours and hours without seeing a single house or yurt. Very occasionally you see someone on a horse, or an understandably ornery-looking group of hairy camels, rubbing their gums raw on grass roots, an eagle circling overhead, or a shaggy group of horses looking too fat for transportation purposes. I have been looking avidly for signs of Lamaism, but all I can find is postcards in the restaurant wagon, where they will extort at least a dollar for the privilege of having this postmarked Mongolia.

Linguistically, I have been in China almost since getting on in Moscow, and, as Paul predicted and I doubted, I seem to understand almost everything said to me, though I still express myself with some difficulty on things like the taste of Tunisian camel flesh compared to Bactrian, which I hope to try in the dining car this evening, or the intricacies of Peking opera based in the early Han dynasty, which played over the radio, tuned to Peking since Omsk, last night. The night before they broadcast one about a city during the Warring States period, which was evacuated before an advancing enemy, and the hero general, Zhuge Liang, stood at the gate, inviting the invaders in. The enemy, suspecting a trap, withdrew. But of course there was none, and most of the opera seemed to consist of the hero calling out to the enemy, and the enemy, whom I seem to identify with rather closely for some reason, self-consciously hesitating on the basis that, well, maybe it wasn't a trap, but made to look like one, or maybe a trap made to look like a trap that doesn't look like a trap, and so on.

Occasionally I exchange a little French with the girl in the next compartment, who is half Chinese and half Russian. Besides her and her father, a mathematics professor, everybody else is more or less a Chinese functionary. Her father was exiled by the Sino-Soviet split, and is full of stories of the liberation, life under the Japanese, and student life. He went to school with some of the functionaries in the Forties, and is now returning to a country he knows almost perfectly by map and memory, yet he is quite unfamiliar with the human landscape. He imagines it as a Chinese Soviet Union, and some of his school comrades shake their heads and try vaguely to talk about the Cultural Revolution, or the Gang of Four, or the anti-criminal campaign. We three are the only really starry-eyed travellers, the ones who can't sleep at night, and we tend to talk and eat together a lot. I'm almost afraid to get off at the other end, when I think it is only beginning.

Alive, well, and deliriously happy, David.

2 | Odysseus wandering

Canton, 12 February 1984
Dear Old Folks,

Now then, I will try to do some kind of rough justice to my trip, without sounding like a travel writer. I left off in Outer Mongolia, right? Hairy camels, bloodthirsty non-violent Buddhist demons, hardly any people, but prosperity of a rough, Central European sort, in Central Asia. Yurts there were, but they were cement, with chimneys belching clean white vapour where the yak skin flap should be. There are maybe a million people in Outer Mongolia, all Mongols, while Chinese Inner Mongolia has more like 18 million, but mostly Hans. Hans are the Chinese of the ethnic majority, so called after the Han dynasty (206BC to 220AD). They have long been quite distinct peoples, the Outers and Inners, some say since Genghis Khan's brother Ogudai founded Karakorum in order to try to keep footloose young nephew Kublai from wandering down to the bright lights of Peking, which of course wasn't really Peking until Kublai founded it, but already exercised a certain gravitational attraction on the Mongols. The Inners are much more sinified, so much so they are virtually sinified out of existence. Unlike the Outers, who have a country, they have an 'autonomous region' that seems to be basically run from Baotou and Hohot, two new Han settlements.

Crossing into China was a really touching moment. Most of the Chinese on the train had tears in their eyes, and the two old women were jumping up and down like little girls, even though it was already dark and you couldn't possibly see anything different about the now Chinese Gobi desert outside. It was the first time I ever heard anyone say 'Motherland' like they meant it, like they were really related. Next to the sleeper I shared with old *Laodage* ('Big Brother', I called him, to his amusement) Wang, there were a Chinese math professor from the University of Leningrad and his daughter, who was my age and really, really pretty, in that funny Eurasian way, with an incongruous European peninsula of a nose stuck between Asian land masses of cheek bones. He was returning to the country of his birth, which he left at the age of 20; she was returning to a country she had never seen, but had studied assiduously in college when it was not exactly the most favoured of subjects at Leningrad. I remarked at one point that there were no cars and very few factories, although the desert was already behind us and Peking only an hour away. Père turned on me angrily and shouted that there were cars and factories all over, and Jeanne lowered her eyes and remarked in French, which Père did not understand, 'He's prouder of China than the Chinese'. But she and he too, in different ways, could not quite understand how the others could make such a fuss over such a motherland.

Because China is poor, really poor. It's a lot more, but to see that you have to get used to seeing poverty so brutal and universal you can't really imagine anything else, and you don't see it any more. Not even scrappy Algerian or scruffy Tunisian poverty, not slightly used-looking Eastern European poverty, but poverty like Indian poverty, massive and undiluted and overwhelming. I keep trying to imagine how this fact was hidden during that trip of Nixon's, when all we got was an image of China that was huge squares with a few professorial types peddling bicycles for purely calisthenic reasons, clean and spare and simple. Was it really possible to construct a whole Potemkin village for credulous Nixonians and 'Friends' of China, and populate it with shadows like a Wayang play? I can't imagine how; I've seen, barely 50 metres from Tiananmen Square, houses built of jerry cans, cement block monstrosities which even *Renmin Ribao* [*The People's Daily*] declared unfit for human habitation, open

17

sewers leaving open latrines, where the shit is still saved for fertilizer. I've seen plenty of beggars, some suffering from progressively debilitating diseases that look a lot like leprosy. I've seen people wandering in rags through working-class restaurants and getting spat on and ejected; I've seen people looking through garbage cans, and sleeping in streets in zero degree Peking. Yet they say it is much better now. God, what must it have been like before? I cannot believe that China has known no starvation since 1949. I simply cannot believe what was once the all-justifying myth, that the Chinese never go hungry.

I guess partly because of that shock, and partly because of the thermal shock, which gave me a terrible cold, much of Peking was wasted on me. Oh, I saw the Imperial Palace. It's there, and it's huge, really, on a scale that is terrifying in a crowded land-hungry place like China. The emperor apparently had to build big because he was terribly fond of open spaces. The Stalinists seem to be even fonder of them; they enlarged Tiananmen by a factor of four, and the response to the growing bicycle congestion has been to widen the streets rather than install simple traffic lights and pedestrian crossings, even though widening was at the expense of the old city walls, which were the foundation of the city built by Kublai Khan, torn down so that Peking could maintain its mad city-crossing style. Tiananmen is the ultimate monstrosity: big enough to house half a million people, right in the middle of the city, and it houses exactly one who's been dead for eight years and no longer fondly remembered even by those who got jobs from him. Tiananmen, to me about as impressive as an outsize parking lot, is a perfect symbol of the housing policy.

I didn't visit the palaces until about my third day in Peking. I spent the first day seeing *hutongs* [residential alleys] and slums, and the second, hitting temples. I spent a lot of time in the streets and in restaurants, where I ate enormous meals at ludicrously low prices – like a *dimsum* brunch for about 15 cents. My attempted splurge, a meal at a Sichuanese restaurant recommended by the *NY Times*, came to exactly a dollar and 65 cents. I keep thinking about what such low prices must mean in terms of real wages.

Then I took an express train to Canton, 37 hours on a so-called hard seat, which cost 17 dollars and felt like a bed after the hard seats of Egypt and the hard roofs of Sudan. I spent two days in Macao trying to arrange passage to Hong Kong, with the docks crowded with people trying desperately to get back to desk jobs there, after blowing their Chinese New Year bonuses in the casinos of that slightly ridiculous little enclave made up of two leper islands and one massive gambling resort, all done up in real eighteenth century Iberian, or maybe Midi, architecture. So I was a few days late getting to Hong Kong, and, though only months ago the idea of Hong Kong made my mouth water – a whole city like London's Chinatown – once I got there I was anxious to leave and soon did.

Oh, it had its moments, you know, when the sun set and the lights came up across the bay, the bars, the Suzie Wong joints and all-night Chinese groceries, Victoria Peak lit up like a great fat laughing Buddha, Kowloon prostrating its promontory before it, amidst all the ships waiting to unload and lighting up too, one by one, and on the waterfront you can even hear the oaths of the sailors, often in English, and the clatter of Mah Jong tiles across the water, if a tram isn't passing too close. And the Cat Street Bazaar and the Man Wo temple, where incense has to be constantly pumped out so the worshippers can breathe, and huge wads of coloured paper are carried through the temple, burning, to the incinerators outside.

It was all right, but it wasn't China, it was a big Chinatown, and I felt rather foolish wandering around and gawking at all the cutie-pie haircuts, pouty lips, surgically altered eyes, leather pants, smokey-glass decor, and white mannequins wearing the the Chinese equivalent of chinois-erie. Yes, McDonald's and Kellogg's and ridiculous prices for contemptible trinkets made in USA. Double-decker buses and double-decker trams with adverts nobody can read, but everybody seems to obey. Banks, banks every-

19

where, with other nations' money reproducing asexually, without cross-fertilization by industrial capital. And more absurd-looking young women, with wavy hair and drooping lips in what is supposed to be a Bardot expression, none of it tough and cynical, just vacuous and stupid-looking, without the excuse of poverty and naivety. All the cross-cultural pretension made my head ache after a while. Really, why hang around Chinatown when China is right across the border?

The south of China is richer than the north. I don't know if I would have noticed that if I hadn't known it, but it is so, and now I do see it. Also, I managed at last to see a little something besides poverty, through it rather than around it. There was a lot to see: Spring Festival, Tet, and Dragon and Lion Dances everywhere, pyres of firecrackers going off, leaving mountains of singed red paper and echoes that buzz in your ears. There's a mosque that everyone says dates from the lifetime of Mohammed, which is impossible, but which probably does date from the century after, with a minaret more like a circumcized penis than any I've ever seen, and a crazy leaning 16-storey pagoda where sacrifices are still made, though not as profusely as in Hong Kong.

I am trying very hard to learn the language, which is another reason why I wanted to get out of Hong Kong. Old men, full of memories and very fond of chat, are the greatest language labs ever developed. And best of all, there is an incredible street life here. About a block from my hotel is the food market where you may buy roasted pangolins (a kind of scaly anteater that is really delicious), live Chinese raccoons, owls, parrot-like blue and green birds with straight beaks, monkeys, soft-shell turtles of all kinds, skinned, dried and spiced rats, swans and geese, and, of course, dogs, usually split down the middle or hung by a hook through the throat. On my first turn down the dog aisle, my eye was arrested by the sight of half a dog emerging fresh from the charcoal, red and crispy and delicious-looking, and then being plonked down next to the other half, skin just torn off and guts still spilling out over the slab, lips drawn back to reveal huge teeth. I was a little anxious at the sight, I admit, not simply as a fellow carnivore, but also because cooking seems to make such an enormous difference, almost as big as death itself.

It took me several days to finally sit down and have a full-size dog dinner, but this evening I finally did. They give you a kind of unglazed clay pot and a little *kanoon* of hot charcoal. Then they put a layer of garlic and ginger into the pot, a layer of onions and cabbage and a few good-sized chunks of dog, already red-roasted, over which they pour a little soup. You wait for a few minutes, and the stuff starts to bubble about half way through your second cup of tea. You get a few side dishes of hot and sweet sauces, 'bean death' [hot bean sauce], and oyster sauce and some red stuff and a few others. Then you fish out your dog and greens, souse them in the sauces and plant them on some rice to cool. Even Millie [a pet dog] would wolf it down, and it only cost about a dollar 20, with salad, tea and *mao tai* [a strong liquor] for dessert. Next I will try the monkey, I think, although the dog is good in cold weather. The girl at the hotel, who has skin like the summit of Tai Shan, says that dog is very bad for the complexion. Pangolin, on the other hand, is supposed to be excellent, but it is summer fodder. The taste is roughly comparable to toughish but very lean dog.

On the way back I wandered around for a while among the street calligraphers, one of whom did abstract renderings of rather reactionary sentiments in several colours. I bought 'Dragon (traditional symbol for a male child) is bright, Crane (girl) is happy', because the characters for dragon and crane look like cartoon dragons and cranes, and I rather like the convergent strands of representative and imaginative calligraphy they expressed, since Chinese characters were originally meant, of course, as pictographic, while calligraphy evolved through a felt need to liberate characters from representation.

21

Canton, 15 February 1984
Dorothy and Burt,

I suppose much of what follows will sound a little like Beneath the Valley of My Further Disillusionment III. China is the greatest trip I've ever made, but, politically, it is one of the biggest shocks. Because it is so poor, but really, really great, and it is hard to maintain the right mix. When I first arrived in Peking I spent the first two days just walking around the hutongs, trying very hard to see through the misery, to see something beside it, to accept it as universal, like unfolded eyelids, and look instead for individual features.

It's going to take more than five days, but it is already a little easier. Canton is wealthier, for one thing; there is a lot of Hong Kong money here, lots of street bustle, plus remittances from overseas, and the good, wet land is hereabouts. In the north is the hungry winter, yellow sky and pinched faces. Here western clothes are all over, while Peking is all padded cotton and Russian earflap caps. It is not that Canton is equidistant between Hong Kong and Peking, not at all. I do not share the common foreign sentiment that says that Canton is a pale ghost of a departed Hong Kong. On the contrary, Hong Kong is a Cantonese Chinatown, much much more Bloomingdale's China than anything in China.

Dorothy, in view of how horribly poor this country is, of how terribly hard life is, particularly in the rural areas, I can't help but remember with a great deal of distaste your moralizing about how the Chinese were reintroducing capitalism by eliminating the communes, and how disgustingly rich the peasants were getting growing luxury goods. I think I said at the time that one mustn't take the smug crowing triumphalism of the liberal bourgeois press too seriously; now it really looks like a cruel joke. The commune system managed to be both decentralized and inefficient. By allowing individuals, rather than bureaucrats, to pocket or reinvest some of the excess, while guaranteeing grain to the cities, the government is basically changing nothing except the inefficiency, hopefully. Prior to 1980, everybody was organized into communes and paid according to bureaucratically determined workpoints; now everyone belongs to a production team and is paid a combination of wages and what they can scare up rather pathetically through busting their asses on the side. But before and after 1980, the real unit of organization was the village, and the real system of distribution was according to work. All that has been done is to alter some of the bureaucratic distortions, as far as I can see.

Industry has apparently proceeded in the opposite way, and some factories are now operating as 'communes' with their managers supposedly exercising discretion over reinvestment and the division of the profits. But of course, even if the state gives up some of its centralizing function in industry and increases it in agriculture, the main instrument of centralization is the Party; it decides reinvestment and profit, whether at the state or management level. Any more ambitious egalitarianism directed against workers and peasants seeking to better their lot and that of their children would be silly Pol Potishness – which I suspect was quite popular in China where there was little else, meaning capital, with which to construct socialism. Let the smug TV journalists crow. China has a great deal of primitive accumulation to suffer before there is sufficient capital for socialist production.

Not all of this suffering is necessary, of course. Coming here from Mongolia and the USSR, my biggest political impression is what a horrible stupidity, compounded by crime, lay in the Sino-Soviet split. From the Americans, they got a short list of pop-gun weapons and a few Coke bottling plants, now closed. They gave up maybe 20, 30 years of progress, dams, factories, and above all a reliable source of productive capital and technology. What a waste.

There is an extraordinary fascination with death and mutilation here. Huge posters and photography displays publicize the mass executions in every town. The crowds are enormous and enthusiastic, the victims barely adolescent in many cases. There are also enormous posters all over Peking allegedly warning against train accidents, with huge explicit pictures of mutilated corpses: a man whose head has been smashed by a train wheel, brains and blood splattered all over with bits of skull like sudden thoughts; a fellow completely shredded from the waist up, looking like a frayed mattress wearing pants, so unrecognizable as to be hardly sickening. These posters attract throngs of little old ladies and kids, who stare at them much longer than I would have thought possible, let alone comfortable. I thought the posters rather salutary, in view of all the industrial accidents I've seen, but, of course, as a friend of mine pointed out, the only real way to campaign for public safety is to revalue human labour, and do elementary things, like install pedestrian crossings instead of widening the streets, and railway crossings, and eliminate the cattle-car seatless passenger transports.

The other big campaign, now officially ended, was a campaign against 'spiritual pollution' from abroad – meaning us. You can still see the cartoon posters everywhere, showing the obvious and irrefutable link between lipstick, petty thievery, and arson, in one case; lingerie ads, wife-beating and rape, in another; dreaming of tall buildings, hot radios tuned into Hong Kong and murder, in a third. And of course it often targets young women, who are invariably guilty of loose morals. On the other hand, the birth control campaign, as well as the very strict enforcement of financial penalties, has been a considerable success. Everyone says *'Zhongguo ren tai duo le'* ('Too many Chinese'), and no one has more than one kid in the street. That, of course, is a precondition for real, as opposed to inflationary, progress, and I suppose that alone justifies the revolution, if you imagine such a mighty historical step requires moral or moralizing justification. But there is much that it does not justify, even if you imagine it can be justified.

Macao, where I spent two days, and where Wang Fanxi [a Chinese Trotskyist] spent much of his exile, is cooler, relaxed, perversely Portuguese, Mediterranean, with a little park of a peninsula crawling with dog-racing tracks, Jai Alai parlours, and casinos thronging with Hongkongers on their Bank Holiday. And then two tiny islets, once leper colonies, where a few old priests who were kicked out of China in the Sixties eke out a living on memories. I stayed in a really, really cheap joint, fashioned out of red paper and green wood, where you could hear everything in the whole *hospedaria*, which I thought meant hospice, and smell at least half of it through the incense that billowed out of the wallpaper. There were tin altars located on every floor, which made me a little anxious about ending up a burnt offering to somebody's remote ancestor, and a cat who snored in my bed, politely refused when I asked her to leave, and firmly returned when I forcibly ejected her. I didn't know cats snored. In the morning, I dropped my sleeping bag, which I use to fight lice and bedbugs, on the floor, and the floor bounced.

Macao is so tiny you keep retracing your steps stomping around it, but so rich in contradictions that it hardly matters. There is 17th century Iberian architecture, a leper colony on one of the two uninhabited islands connected by a causeway to a crowded peninsula, casinos bigger than the Cote d'Azur, Taoist temples, Portuguese signs and even a Portuguese newspaper that no one can read – both more European and more Chinese than Hong Kong. Cheaper, too.

No one spoke any *putonghua* [Mandarin] there, except recent arrivals from the mainland, and I suppose I cut a pretty odd figure, spending half my time in my miserable flophouse, typing and steadfastly refusing to speak English. Since leaving Budapest, that is, three weeks ago, during which time I am required, according to a time-honoured agreement, to write mum only once, I have written you twice, Paul twice, Alix twice, Kathy thrice, Cecile once, Sue once, Anna once, a friend in Paris once, a young Soviet woman I met on the train once, and two other letters to people in England and the US – no letter shorter than two

25

pages single-spaced. Naturally, I do not at all regret the enormous expenditure of ink and time, since my efforts receive such universal and warm recognition.

Anshun, Guizhou, 1 March 1984
Dear Old Man,
So, get out your atlas and let me tell you about some of the interesting little dots on the South China page. Some of the dots may be very hard to find; this one, about a 150 kilometres southeast of Guiyang, has about 50,000 people (tiny by Chinese standards), but I spent today and some of yesterday at a place that is not even marked on my excellent Chinese maps: a settlement of the Chinese 'Kabyles', the Buyi, colourful barbarians who slice mountains into paddies and dress their women like Hokusai prints and hate the rare Hans who cross their paths. (On the way back on the bus, one of these dainty little women, with chopsticks in her hairdo etched in a long swirl over to a little bun fastened with jade, hawked robustly at the sight of a Chinese man by the side of the road, and landed an enormous gob in his face as we zipped by. The whole back of the bus, swathed in peacock blue and headdresses just like hers, was paralysed with laughter half way to Anshun; the Hans on board pretended not to notice or understand.)

It took me maybe an hour and a half to travel 27 kilometres, though the tracks around are getting more beaten, partly because of Huangguoshu Falls, 20 kilometres in one direction at a place called poetically 'the Zhen Ning Miao National Minority and Buyi National Minority Self Governing County', and a really stunning series of spelunking caves, accessible by canoe if you keep your head down. They are called Long Gong, the Dragon's Palaces, and are about 30 kilometres in the other direction.

I look at China through Arab eyes, I'm afraid: the scenery is succulent and very tempting, but my love for the human scenery, the artificial, the revolt of culture against nature, is too strong. Nevertheless, when I paddled out of the caves after about an hour of watching weird dragon- and monkey-shaped stalactites, shifting like shadows, and saw this huge cliff, maybe 300 metres high, curving ever so gently over my head, so that the horizon appeared to be right where the noonday sun belonged, and it started snowing enormous flakes, I got a sudden pang of sympathy for that romantic revolt against culture in so much Chinese art, even in the artificial arts the Arabs revel in, like poetry. I remembered one of the first poems I ever read in Chinese, when I was about 17: 'Three million dragons of white jade are fighting, their broken scales cover the sky . . .' But it will never be a tourist trap, even if a whole naturally-occurring Disney world lay half a mile underground; the tireless efforts of CITS [the China International Travel Service] do far more to preserve it than any legislative or natural obstacle.

Tomorrow – actually I leave tonight on the slow train – I am headed for Kunming. Ah, but there are lots of little dots between Canton and here I must tell you about. The night I left Canton, I went to a Buddhist temple with some of my Chinese friends and atoned for my dog-ine feast by having a huge vegetarian 'Roast Duck' dinner, along with the 'Eight Treasures' dish that I like to make at home. In the morning I caught a slow boat to Hainan Island, off the coast of Vietnam. Travel in China is always extraordinarily comfortable, if leisurely and somewhat lax in hygiene. In *fifth* class, I got a comfortable spring bunk with a huge stuffed cotton quilt – in the hold, true enough. The crew made sure I ate enormous and delicious meals and got me into the ship's movies twice, free. One of them asked me, with a certain awe in his voice, why white people never got seasick. (He had apparently seen one other bloke make the crossing, a sturdy gimbal-gutted Scandinavian, and considered his empirical sample sufficient.) I do, of course, but the crossing was quite mild, which didn't prevent half the hold from retching all night. Well, I explained that Chinese food was too good to waste.

Getting around is always easier in fact than it is on paper, though with the aid of the nimble-fisted Travel Service it is never very easy. I was permitted to stay in Haikou, an incredibly poor and run-down city completely cut off from the minorities, the Li and the Miao, who live in the interior. Practising selective ignorance, I managed to spend about four days in a town called Nada, maybe 140 kilometres southeast of Haikou. Nada speaks an oddly comprehensible dialect, rather like the Guizhou dialect spoken here. Odd indeed, since the Hainan Hans speak a dialect of Cantonese unintelligible to Canton Cantonese, who are feared all over China for their ability to stir-fry fricatives and implode plosives. Apparently Nada was the place of refuge, or maybe exile, for the leaders of a revolt centred in Guizhou during the Ming dynasty, or anyway, some time in the indeterminate past.

Hainan has historically been the great gulag of China. Hai Rui, whose dismissal from office sparked off the Cultural Revolution after an interval of a few centuries, is buried in a tragi-beautiful grey *koubba* [grave] flanked by huge stone camels that made me quite homesick for the Maghreb.

A play about Hai Rui by a protégé of the mayor of Beijing was interpreted as condemning the dismissal of Peng Dehuai, the hero general of Liberation and Korea. Peng was of Hunanese peasant origins, uneducated but blunt. He was a brilliant tactician of guerrilla warfare, and defence minister from 1954 to 1959, but lost all his posts when he became critical of some of Mao's policies. In 1962, there was an attempt to rehabilitate him, and he wrote a now-famous 80,000 character letter of self-justification to Mao which was critical of the losses in the Great Leap Forward and the split with Russia. In November 1965, he was made deputy chief of national defence construction in southwestern China, but in December he was recalled to Beijing and imprisoned by order of Jiang Qing [Mao's wife]. He died in prison in 1974.

Nada is also called Dan Xian, or Zhanxian, and has a tribal name meaning the 'earring wearers'. Its streets are full of old Miao and Li women selling antler cheese with reputed magic powers, and exhibiting dancing monkeys on strings. I was taken in by a wonderful guy in his late forties, and I got my first taste of what real Chinese meals are like. By careful

28

observation, I have now figured out some Chinese table manners, so I won't always appear like a Uighur [a Turkic ethnic minority] wielding chopsticks. Eat slowly, stop every three bites and do something else: light a cigarette, spit, talk, stare out the window, urge your neighbour to eat. An empty bowl always means you want a refill, since it is terribly gauche to ask for more, so stop eating with a full bowl in front of you. Don't eat very much, your host is probably planning a month's meals around the leftovers even as you eat; the Chinese are not as noisily hospitable as the Arabs, but perhaps more profoundly so: they are under no illusions that Allah will replace the sheep slaughtered to feed the guest.

Once you get the hang of the rules, Chinese dinners are really great, relaxed, fun affairs, much more enjoyable than the face-stuffing one does in the Arab world. People drift in and out, the conversation goes round and round, people play drinking games and go to the toilet and come back, and the eating lasts from sunset until time to go to bed. My host, the innkeeper, presided over everything in the most incredibly low-key manner. Every topic, from the Cultural Revolution to everyday life, was discussed with me in my bad Chinese as if I had been in on the serial discussions that have been going on at the inn for all the years since the very beginning. It never occurred to me, as it later turned out, that I was the first foreigner he had ever seen, let alone met.

His wife, terribly pretty, intelligent and ravenously curious, somehow projected the same utter naturalness and total lack of snobbery of any kind, not only with me but with the Miao labourers and truck drivers who occasionally came home with me in the afternoon. Once, over dinner, they expressed anxiety that conditions there were too humble for such exalted guests as me and my truck-driver friend. (This was, of course, a formula, but I wasn't sure it was devoid of sincerity, so I wasn't sure how to react.) I laughed and said I was not a *ganbu* [Party official], but a *lao bai xing* (the hundred old surnames, the common folk) in my own country, and complained rather loudly that the Chinese seem to judge rank by the size of the nose (in Chinese, a big nose is *gao*, which also means tall or exalted). My first pun in Chinese, a language practically designed for it, and it was hugely successful. For a moment I actually felt at ease as the centre of attention, which is what I am wherever I go here, purely because of my appearance.

Now here I'm afraid I must do a kind of *passacaglia* on *xiang fa*, or the well-worn grooves of thinking in the psychological landscape. I have with me a kind of trendy China guide for the snide, supercilious, slightly footloose college student, purely for information on which rules are bendable where. It is full of this kind of crap, and manages to make China into a small place full of small minds. On the contrary, China is such a great place that any attempt to grasp details usually loosens your grip on the scale, and vice versa: you are hopelessly outnumbered. But without grasping a little of the xiang fa it is impossible to get a grip on the *gui-ding*, regulations and reregulations. And maybe, if it is done right, the xiang fa gives you a little glimpse of the image the Chinese have of themselves, and of the image the barbarians have of them.

Anyway, it turned out that Nada was a 'closed' town, and eventually the Nada police, who fortunately never had this problem before, wrote me out permission to stay, but asked me to return to Haikou to get onward permission. I nipped back to the mainland on the short ferry ride to Hai 'An, where little rosebud shrimp cost about 15 cents a kilo, and you can wolf them raw or dipped in about a million different sauces. Then I bussed down to Zhanjiang, a town that 'opened up' while I was in Haikou. By a stroke of luck, I was reading the paper in Chinese that day and got the whole list of 140 odd places just opened, some of them, like Dali the ancient capital of the Bai kingdom, falsely reputed to have been razed during the Cultural Revolution, just a dream on the lips of a few foreign residents while I was in Canton. But I've got permission to go and I'm on my way.

Zhanjiang was a little dull, but cheap, a centre for pangolin slaughtering and the illicit sale of sea-horses and sea-dragons (which look like sea-horses that have been straightened out) as medicine. I washed my change of clothes and caught a bus for Nanning, capital of Guangxi, via Beihai, before they were dry. The Snide Guide lists Nanning as utterly devoid of colour, but I found the market there even more gruesome and grisly than the one in Canton. The dog butcher specialized in whole puppies, which he would kill, eviscerate and skin right before your eyes. There were also scaled and skinned pangolins alongside live caged ones, sliced like so much dragon salami. (I wonder, by the way, or out of the way, what the relationship of the pangolin with the Chinese dragon is: did the dream precede the discovery, as the unicorn did the narwhal, or did the discovery precede the dream, as the manatee did the mermaid? And is the similarity the source of many beliefs about the medicinal properties of the pangolin, which even western-trained doctors here occasionally swear by?)

The first day, I tried to skin a beast called a *shui-gou*, or water-dog, for the benefit and amusement of some of the Zhuang trappers in the market. It was a rather bloody business, not even remotely related to unwrapping a cut of meat from Safeway, but if nothing else this trip has allowed me to get comfortable with the idea of being carnivorous. There was also a pretty good musical teahouse, a blind man playing the *erhu* – the two-stringed snake skin fiddle – and a marvellous market street for hawkers of magic potions and better mousetraps, including a Cantonese bloke who had invented some kind of spring thing designed to spring open in the mouse's mouth and catch it behind the teeth. All this was explained through a terrific mime, his cheeks bulging out while he repeatedly charged the crowd, only to be jerked back as if on a string. Sure enough, he had a huge string of rats, apparently freshly caught because still fat. His grasp of the local dialect was pretty rudimentary apparently, but he was doing a roaring trade.

Alright, Nanning was a little short on temples and history. The second day, I biked out with a few college students about 30 miles to a little lake plied by Zhuang tribesmen

31

fishing. I rented a boat from a fisherman so I could show off my Minnesota paddling technique. They were quite impressed with the speed I made, although some of the fishermen I passed, trying to scare the fish into their nets with jangling steel rings, claimed I was undoing all their work. Later I realized that the students' main purpose on such excursions was to find a place where they could have the kind of mindless *boums* [parties] we used to have as pre-adolescents in France, before we considered sex within the realm of possibility, with Kool Aid, horrible tape recordings, cookies, fruit, and unbelievably maladroit ballroom dancing. Most of these blokes were older than me, or my age. Stunted growth, suddenly as bloodcurdling as the old men's heads you see fastened on to infants' bodies behind the begging bowls in the market, and suddenly I felt an intense desire to be back in Nanning market skinning dogs. I'm afraid I had to use my Uighur manners licence, which I try not to use, to steal away. Barbarian from beyond the wall . . .

I like buses. Though they are usually freezing and agony to the ass, they are also the best way to get to places where you aren't supposed to go, and to get to and at least stop and eat in places where you are strictly forbidden to spend the night. The bus to Liuzhou, the coffin-making capital of Guangxi, broke down so often I was afraid I was going to spend at least one night in some village en route, which would not have amused the *Gong An* [police] in Liuzhou. The Miao of Guangxi have great-looking houses, huge and medieval and roofed with split rocks rather than ceramic tiles, with little imperial-style crescents in the pents. I also got to see a Buyi funeral, with all the participants in paper hats, including the deceased – all thanks to the maladies of our bus. In Liuzhou, though, I got put on a train straight for Guiyang.

Guiyang is one of the just-opened towns, and actually quite recently the police kept out people who had legitimate business and official permission to be there. Not only did I get in, thanks to a bureaucratic fuck-up combined with some selective ignorance, I got to live in a village about 20 miles out of town, Huaxi, a very ordinary sort of place except that some rich man tried to create a sort of mini-Hangzhou there in the last century, with some really gorgeous mountains like tin hats, and tall pagodas with exaggerated horns. The fuzz seem to think that makes it a good place to store radioactive foreign guests that are the waste products of their tourist industry. I stayed in a perfectly Chinese hotel, mostly with itinerant Sichuanese workers and some college students who were trying to program the Guizhou University Radio Shack computer to write Chinese characters. Their system was so terribly slow in setting up the characters, though, it took about ten minutes to do each one, and I doubt if there was room in the memory for more than a few hundred. (Has anyone else worked on this problem? I'm afraid *pinyin* [alphabetical writing] is really not a solution: no one uses it.)

Guiyang itself is a mostly medieval city, huge and stony and cold, with moats and drawbridges, where even the Mao statue stands as if dressed in armour. There I saw a little guardhouse with a horned roof made of green corrugated roofing stuff and a quite simple welded roof structure underneath, instead of the intricate system of support that was originally designed, according to Needham, to allow wood to take the extraordinary weight of all that tile, but was characteristically kept by them, long after it was rendered obsolete by metal and stone construction, as good-looking dead weight. Best of all, Guiyang was where I got permission to go to Anshun, and a few villages around, where white man never set foot.

And today, you probably noticed, I am 25. So I bought a copy of Sima Qian's *Records of the Historian*, the best history of China before Needham's, written two thousand years ago, so it misses a lot, but there is so much imagination and sheer incongruity in it, huge amounts of it are devoted to conversations, and such a profound sense of tragedy, one can almost fill in the blanks. It is full of convoluted, self-conscious nuggets, like:

Another time the duke of Sheh asked Tzu-lu his opinion of Confucius, but he did not reply. When Confucius heard this, he said, 'Why did you not say, "He is a man who never wearies of studying truth, never tires of teaching others, but who in his eagerness forgets his hunger, in his joy forgets his bitter lot, never worrying that old age is creeping on"?'

That's humility, or maybe senility, anyway, something to emulate when I'm old.

The scientific detail is even better, rather like Aristotle at his most imaginative:

What height can men reach? The Chiaoyao pygmies, three feet high, are the smallest. The tallest cannot be more than ten times their height, that is the upper limit.

Impeccable logic, no? Anyway, one old man to another . . .

Hong Kong, 13 March 1984
Dear Dorothy,

I spent a week in Kunming, capital of Yunnan, for two reasons, first because there was a lot of music there, and for some reason I have started recording a great deal of Chinese music, especially blind erhu fiddle players, street-singing in pairs, and Kunming is full of them. I also found this abandoned Buddhist temple in the Muslim quarter, now inhabited mostly by Xinjiangese. It had been turned into a teahouse where there is a kind of amateur opera serial based on the *Romance of the Three Kingdoms* being performed every night, never quite ending, always roughly taken up where they left off the night before, but with the most amazing erhu players, one bloke dressed in an army uniform, another in his early thirties dressed like a street vendor, with a huge cowlick on one end of his head and a cigarette dangling from the other. I made two tapes there, but only one turned out very well.

The other reason is that I met this French woman I have tagged behind back to Hong Kong. She has to go back to India, where she works, and I have to get a new visa and make arrangements to take the train from Peking back. Which means it's not too early to make plans for my return. Yes, I could get a job here, and I will if I can't land that one in the Sudan. But remember I'm studying Arabic now, and I still feel like I should be in the Arab world. This is, after all, nothing but a detour. Yet another.

Shanghai, 28 March 1984
Dear Old Man,

Shit, I was all dressed up for a night on the town in the only place in China where there are nights on the town, at a jazz joint reputed to have the best – and only – bebop in the land, from eight until the unheard-of hour of eleven. I put on my best bopping threads, slouch hat and chemise bretonne, I show up at the Heping Hotel for the first set – and there's this sign there, vaguely familiar from Shanghai's notorious past, saying that Chinese people are not allowed, that the room is reserved for foreign guests and Overseas Chinese, in both Chinese and bad English, as if to reassure the clientèle. I called the manager and said there was some mistake, this was one of the infamous signs the English had put up, and somebody forgot to take it down. He didn't get my joke, but thought it simply hilarious that a foreigner should express decent revulsion, and in Chinese, and he kind of minced and laughed in a particularly disgusting fashion: 'Heh, heh, well, you know, that was the old society, this is the socialist new one, right, heh, heh?' After about ten minutes of his kind of self-abasement, I left. With my chronic jazz deficiency.

This morning I went and stomped around the stomping grounds of the founders of the Communist Party, the young intellectuals and red students of Shanghai. My blood-soaked Shanghai, where nobody lives, and nobody remembers, except for rather mendacious monuments to people who disappeared either politically or physically during the late Twenties, in the back of the tiny two-room house where 12 or maybe 13 or maybe 15 people founded the Communist Party of China. I got into the house where it all happened, where the first meeting took place on hard wooden stools around a severe-looking table. It is a rather nice-looking house, at least from the outside, French Quarter, fleur-de-lis in red and black brick with a big brass-knobbed door, similar to about four others in the same street. The unrestored and filthy houses, absolutely identical, on the other side of the street give a somewhat better feel for the place.

No two of the books I've read agree on the exact date of the founding meeting, or the number of participants. The number was probably 13, plus two representatives of the Comintern, a Russian mediocrity named Podnesovsky and the Dutchman Sneevliet, known to the Chinese as Ma Lin, founder of the Indonesian Communist Party. His Party name was Maring, and he later died in a Nazi concentration camp. When you ask one by one what became of the founders whose photographs are posted, well, four defected to the KMT, two died before they were 25, one ended up teaching history at a university in Canada. Mao alone survived, rather like the curious longevity of Stalin. (This is what I find a real mystery: why was Mao there? He was a snot-nosed kid just out of Changsha Normal School, who had been living in Peking for two years. He had no history of activity in the May Fourth movement [the 1919 student demonstrations protesting the Versailles treaty award of Shandung province to the Japanese that paved the way for the founding of the CCP], and none of the Trotskyist accounts, including Maring's, mention him.) But the more I learn about Chen Duxiu, the real founder of the Party, the more admirable he seems. He is also, in a very real sense, the founder of modern Chinese literature, a kind of Voltaire and Lenin and Trotsky in one. He went slightly daft in prison under the Kuomintang, and developed some rather bourgeois notions of democracy.

Tomorrow I'm off to the Twenties' and Thirties' digs of Lu Xun, the great writer the Stalinists keep trying to make Mayakovskian mythology out of. Every grotesque statue of him they put up, rakish in his occidental hairstyle and moustache straight from a police poster, seems to start reciting his great poem 'In Mockery of Myself'. Shanghai is full of that kind of wry heroism for me.

Today I went for a nine-hour hike, from the French Concession down Nanjing Lu, past a restaurant once known as Chez Louis, now known as 'East Wind', but still world-famous for its Grand Marnier Souffle. I had ice-cream – I am still recovering from Millie's Revenge, a tonsillitis I developed after a dog dinner in Canton – at a little cafe once known as Sullivan's. It is now called the Donghai, and a centre for a funny kind of Chinese punk movement, with mods on bicycles instead of Vespas, sporting brush haircuts, but blue Mao suits instead of leather jackets.

And then I discovered this crazy old men's park, where, instead of storytellers who spin yarns loosely unravelled from Ming novels, they had stand-up comedians, usually old couples in their seventies, telling jokes about marriage, with a slightly ribald tinge, quite unthinkable for the repressed young, whose sexuality must be either off or all the way on. In the palace of youth there are big posters up advertising one of the new operas they are trying out to replace the old revolutionary ones that are now too embarrassing, co-productions of the Gang of Four. These new operas are sitcoms, with incredibly convoluted and insignificant plots, but lots of arm-waving and emoting. The captions are often sparser than usual, so I tried to imagine a plot that would fit them, Shanghai, and the sequinned costumes on the players in apparent imitation of Elvis's later years.

Down the street, back in real life, back out of my imagination, I watched an old woman vigorously pumping a bellows with one hand, and turning a crank attached to a steel bomb with a pressure gauge, rapidly rotating over a huge roaring coal flame, practically glowing with the heat. Suddenly she donned yet another pair of asbestos gloves, black with soot, seized the bomb, wrenching it from its armature, dumped it into a chamber covered by a layer of carpet, and shouted for everyone to stand back. We did, and there was a huge explosion. I jumped a mile and so did the carpet. The woman wrinkled in smiles, symmetrical gaps in her teeth sending out beams of gurgling laughter. Puffed rice! Really. I sat and chatted with her. She had a long memory, but could say nothing about the Twenties and Thirties except that people were pretty hungry then.

37

Then I went through the Chinese old city, where there is a really smashing Confucian temple, rather like something out of the Humble Administrator's Garden in Suzhou, white walls and stained wood, and none of the red and yellow overwhelmingness that most Ming temples try to swamp you with. Best of all, though, there is another Humble Administrator's Garden, this one in the centre of a wild market place featuring Muslim *dimsum* restaurants and duck eggs boiled in tea. Except, unlike the the one in Suzhou, this Humble Administrator went over to the Taipings [nineteenth century peasant rebels, followers of a mystical semi-Christian religion] during the rebellion, so the roofs are adorned with a kind of fascinating anti-foreign, anti-imperialist, pre-communist imagery: heroic younger brother of Jesus Christ attacking cowardly and treacherous puppets of anti-Christian Englishmen. But all done in black slate, in a very Chinese style. Really, so pretty you forget to smile at it, until you see the more modern propaganda added since.

I haven't had so much fun since I was in Kunming, as a matter of fact. Kunming, as I think I wrote, was a great place for music. And outside Kunming, there was this amazing temple, the Qiongzhu Si, or bamboo temple, from the Tang dynasty. In it there must be a thousand of the most garish, bizarre plaster monk figures you can imagine, sculpted by the mad Sichuanese monk Li Guang. Some had arms three or four times their height, reaching out across the room; one peeling the skin off his face to reveal another underneath it; one splitting open his belly with his fingernails to show a golden Buddha in among the intestines; several looking bored; one looking ravenously hungry, about to bite a peach, another selling newspapers; others playing instruments, singing, eating, looking at each other, picking their toes, looking very bored, an Arab, or maybe a Jew, a black, a fat old Amitabha with kids crawling all over him and sticking fingers in his navel – everybody except the serene-looking Buddha figures you see in India. China is a most irreligious place, even in its temples. Chinese tourists now flock to the temples to have their pictures taken by friends while pretending to pray to the deities, but very, very few are actually there for earnest mumbo jumbo. It seems as if no one has taken Buddhism seriously since the big repression against Buddhists in the Tang.

Then I went back to Hong Kong, via Hengyang and Canton, which seems a strange thing to do, even in retrospect. Partly it was to see off this French woman I met who was on her way back to India where she worked, partly it was to get a new visa. In any case, after a few semi-miserable days in Hong Kong I had to spend five fully miserable days in bed in Canton with tonsillitis, which I contracted lobbying for a bed in the Chinese part of the dormitory.

After that, I worked my way up the coast via Quanzhou and Fuzhou in Fujian province. Quanzhou was once the greatest seaport of the realm under the Song dynasty, from which the mad flotillas of sixty thousand men set sail to Somalia and elsewhere in order to collect tribute. It is also a centre for early Islam; there were Arab missionaries there more or less consistently from the ninth century to the time of Marco Polo, and they are all buried under Arab tombstones on a hill overlooking the city, one bearing a date only 200 years after the Hegira. There is also a Song dynasty boat, gigantic and in excellent condition, just excavated, and a mosque supposedly built along the lines of my favorite Damascene mosque, the Ommayad.

But, above all, Quanzhou is where I saw the most beautiful houses in China, with huge horned pents and eaves like Viking ships, with walls that kind of sweep up like red sails, incorporating incredible arabesques in the brick-layers' designs, which are sort of echoed with a rotation of forty-five degrees, because the bricks, glazed like porcelain, have diagonal slashes of lacquer at random intervals. The whole effect is quite brain teasing, but very, very charming. In one of these houses, I was taken in by a crab fisherman, and stuffed with crab meat.

I'm going to Nanjing, maybe tomorrow, and thence to Peking to arrange my return to Europe at the end of April.

That should give me four weeks, which is enough to hit Xinjiang in Central Asia. Kashi, or Kashgar, right on the Pakistan, Afghan, Soviet border, has just been opened to foreigners, and I am very anxious to go.

Baotou, Inner Mongolia, 7 April 1984
Dear Dorothy and Burt,
   It will warm your heart to learn that Marisa, the French woman I met in Kunming, gave me a full-length cotton padded Chinese army coat with fur collar, in which we both spent many cold nights on a train in the mountains west and east of Yunnan. After which she returned to the Indian side of the mountains, where she works. Besides being extremely heartwarming, this greatcoat gift seems to have triggered the arrival of spring, just in time for the northwestern leg of my expedition. It is possible I will look into a job when I get to Xi'an; Sudan is getting very hard to get into already, though it is really where I belong. In any case, I am staying in China at least another month, in order to see Xinjiang, Ningxia, Gansu, and Shaanxi, and possibly take in more of the Yangtze River route.
   I got letters from half of you in Hong Kong and Peking, and I checked the non-existent poste restantes in Peking and Shanghai for others. You are apparently missing a lot of my letters. The one from Ulan Bator is probably just late, but maybe some have been mislaid by someone. Typing kind of calls attention to itself here. My health remains sparkling and rare as white jade, and I can understand overheard conversations in some provinces, especially in the north, the northwest, and any area where Han settlers from diverse areas have taken to putonghua as a lingua franca.
   My real problems are neither medical, monetary, logistic, linguistic or thermal, but more bureaucratic. This morning, having little else to do, I went and argued with the police for two hours to secure permission to go to a town about two hours away, which they insisted was inaccessible owing to the height of the river. I pointed out there was a bridge over the river, and they countered there was another river I didn't

know about. Giving up in despair, I just went to the bus office and bought a ticket without an official permit. One is severely penalized for obeying the law here, and though I am naturally inclined to obey it anyway, I can only go so far. I do not, unlike most travellers, change money on the black market; I refuse to go through contortions to avoid the 75 to 300 per cent surcharge tacked on to everything for foreigners; and I will get permission from the fuzz when I can. But, really, a bloody two-hour drive, and it takes an hour and a half to go from here to the cop station. Anyway, as revenge, I pulled out a copy of the official announcement of open cities and extorted two cities in Ningxia (the Muslim autonomous region), one in Gansu, and one in Xinjiang. The town nearby I wanted was also on the announcement, but they insisted the non-existent river was too high. (The whole northwest, according to the *People's Daily*, has been suffering from a severe drought, and most of the water I saw on the way here was frozen.) So it goesn't.

I guess I last wrote from Hong Kong. After Marisa left for Calcutta, I returned to Canton, where I was refused hotel space, although the hotel I wanted into was half empty. I sat and lobbied for almost four and a half hours, really, constant unwavering hysteria on both sides, all in Chinese. 'This dorm is for Chinese only.' There is racial segregation in a socialist country? What about Japanese, Hongkongese, Overseas Chinese? 'Look, you can come to our country, can we go to yours?' And so on. All of the hatred and fear of foreigners occasionally come pouring out from behind the Stalinoid 'Friendship' facade, and it is a little bewildering. In the end I simply led a group of foreigners into the dorm and we sat in.

Racial segregation is something of an obsession in China, for reasons that are only partly politico-bureaucratic. The Chinese hate blacks and Arabs. Though they vary from genuinely humane to obsequious with whites, there is probably a lot of resentment of these creatures who come and pay a month's salary for a night's lodging. Now, for example, I am staying in a double room because I insisted on paying dormitory price, but of course the hotel was unwilling to put me in a room with Chinese or even Mongols. If you ask for an explanation, and I always do, you learn they are 'concerned for your safety', an answer that always infuriates me, involving as it does a terrible self-abasing slur on the Chinese people, and an insult to my intelligence – as if foreign hippies never rip each other off!

The next day I had to check into the hospital with tonsillitis, which was triggered, the doctor told me, by arguing too much. I was kept, naturally, in a separate room. (Chinese medicine, incidentally, is decidedly overrated, even according to Chinese doctors. Traditional medicine relies avowedly on the placebo effect; a recent study in *Le Monde de Médécine* tried to extend this to acupuncture, though how do you do open heart surgery with only a placebo anaesthetic? Western medicine, as practised in China, consists largely of sixteen different overdoses of antibiotics, available without prescription and over-prescribed anyway.)

After about five days I was well enough to leave for Quanzhou, a Fujianese town which merely has the best crabs and the prettiest cottages in China today, but in the 12th and 13th centuries was well known to merchants in Somalia, Zanzibar, Qatar and Port Sudan, or rather Suakin. From Quanzhou huge fleets of sixty thousand men, easily capable of founding colonies in savage ports like those of Europe, set sail under the Ming emperor Yong Le and touched southern Africa, where they apparently made contact with ancient Zimbabwe, for their porcelains were found in the Zimbabwean ruins, along with much older ware. In fact, the oldest porcelains extant were unearthed in Fustat, ancient Cairo. Quanzhou still has a huge stone 'pontoon' bridge built under the Song, as well as a gigantic cliff inscribed with sailors' prayers, and a few smashing monasteries.

Most interesting of all, though, are the traces of the Arab past; names in a cemetery that are inscribed in Arabic go back to the 10th century, but end mysteriously in the 13th.

There is a huge mosque, the biggest I've seen in China, built in 1008, allegedly a copy of the Ommayad – my favorite mosque in Damascus – where all the clocks tick to different rhythms, and where Saladin and John the Baptist slumber the ages side by side. (I can't tell if it really is, because the Ommayad has a huge covered bazaar all around it and is impossible to see from the outside except through a forest of legs and carpets, while it is impossible to get into the Qingjing mosque in Quanzhou.) How old is the oldest mosque in China? Most people agree it is the Huaisheng in Canton, but they give an impossibly early date for it, while some guidebooks say that the Qingjing is, but of course it is much too late. Arabs were settling in Xinjiang by then. My guidebook, another donation, petulantly insists on both improbable views, but does not dwell on them, being chiefly concerned with gastronomy, as a Gallic guidebook should be. Praise for crabs, not Arabs.

Continuing up the coast by bus, I came to Fuzhou, and finally Hangzhou, the Chinese newly-weds' equivalent of Niagara Falls, where even the dorm towels have 'double happiness' signs on them. As you might expect, it is mostly watching water, but I was primed by Polo's description of Hangzhou under the Yuan, a mad metropolis bigger than it is today, and by bloody tales of the sack of the Taipings' Hangzhou by the Qing and their foreign henchmen.

I think what I like best in Hangzhou, besides the Fenghuang 'Phoenix' mosque, done up to look like a Song minister's tea garden, what I really like best, were the place names: 'Observing the Fish at Flower Harbour' and 'Spring Dawn at Su Causeway' (the one built by Su Dongpo, the poet-governor). In the middle of West Lake is an island containing four lakes, one of which contains an island with a large basin. Around it are four large bronze-bellied molochs, which, when lit up, cast reflections rather like the moon on the surface of lake, lakelet, and even basin. The name of the island is 'Reflections of the Moon's Impression on Three Profound Pools'. One lake, you see, doesn't count, but no one will tell you which one. Perhaps one is not very profound, but there is also an intricate system of teahouses, with zig-zag causeways because evil spirits travel only in straight lines, so it is a little hard to count the number of pools. I like the perversity of having, in a lake, an island with a lake with an island in the middle, and naming the whole after the reflections in the water.

The whole thing was rather shockingly clean for China, and I was sort of relieved to take the great sewer, the Grand Canal, to Suzhou, after about a day and a half of peonies disgorging seated statues of Lu Xun. Suzhou was even more crude and vulgar and natural than Hangzhou, though it has been carefully sculpted into little artificial natures by various minor Song officials, only to have the most succulent parts gambled away by their creators' sons, destroyed by Mongols, rebuilt, destroyed and rebuilt, rebuilt and destroyed, and at last preserved, sort of, as put together in the 10th or 11th century. The most amazing rosewood and shaved marble furniture, in huge dark-stained wood and white pavilions, with sombre charcoal-gray paths, none of the reds and greens and blues and yellow tiled roofs of the Ming; this is a period of effete snobbery, handwringing and stately angst. And names like 'The Humble Administrator's Garden', or 'The Garden of the Politics of Simplicity', or 'The Garden of the Master of the Fishing Nets', or, simply, 'Lingering'. My favourite, though, was the 'Forest of Lions', a place where the landscapist had gone out and gotten some already Daliesque-looking rocks, and then cut them up and cemented them seamlessly back together in various surrealist shapes, and placed huge stone phalluses here and there suggestively. So much for the latest campaign against modern and abstract art.

Suzhou gave me the roughest time getting a hotel room I've ever had. You come in about 6am and they say it's all full, those who are leaving have left and their places are already sold out. You argue for three hours, then someone quietly suggests you take a few hours break to see the town and come back at 6pm, maybe someone will change their mind and leave late. So you take the hint and come hopefully back, but no, it was a ruse to try to get more money, or maybe just more begging and pleading out of you. Finally they let you have a room, for nine times what a Chinese would pay, which has been empty all day, except that you share it with two other foreigners and there are only two beds.

It looks like sheer sadism, but I think it is simply that I am a foreigner with nothing but money in a place where goods are distributed more according to *guanxi*, that is, who you know. I have a vile temper in such situations, and it is easy to see nothing but how China treats foreigners, after that extraordinary mixture of mendaciousness and servility. In the Arab world, it is worth considering rather carefully how Arabs react to foreigners; even if the foreigner provokes rather than releases the reaction, it tells you rather profound things about Arab society. In China it tells you nothing at all. Easily 80 per cent of the population live in places which have never seen a foreigner and never will. We who imagine that our passing is more than a source of hard currency and reflections rather less profound than the fourth impression of the moon, we are simply having what blacks in Chicago used to call 'a Chinese baby', making a big fuss over nothing.

Back via Shanghai. Then to Nanjing, by boat up the Yangtze. In Nanjing there was the tomb of Hongwu [the reigning name of the peasant rebel who founded the Ming dynasty], with some great stone sculpture, and a smashing Taiping Museum set in a garden easily as pretty as those in Suzhou. But it was not a very lively street kind of place, so I went back to Peking to get rid of my return ticket, and to extend my visa, and came here, where there is a huge lamasery, once the most powerful in Mongolia, that owned 500 slaves and a coal mine. The coal mine and the lamasery are still operating, but it is a little hard to get around, since the bureaucracy claims what the poverty of the roads leaves.

My days are pretty full here. Just getting around is a full-time job. Keeping my eyes open and language study are overtime. And I have hardly any time to do any painting or

45

sketching, especially since such things tend to attract huge and intimidating crowds. It is terrible because I see so much. But I am never alone. Once in a village, followed by a crowd of wide-eyed people of all ages, I ducked into a public toilet, thinking they would respect my privacy. Instead, all the men filed in and surrounded me, while the women waited outside. Ever tried to piss with almost a hundred eyes fixed on what you are doing? Yes, well, painting is even harder.

Yinchuan, Ningxia, 10 April 1984

While writing the last paragraph, I was thrown out of the hotel I was staying in and sent to another at seven times the price. *Gui-ding*.

Alix describes Mongolia, where she has never been, as 'empty and anything but'. Much of it is as desertic as the Sahara, rocky rather than sand, just as the real Sahara is, with sandy bits. But there are also high snow-capped mountains, and, north of the Chinese border anyway, grasslands. There are few camels south of the border, though lots of people wear camel. On my way out of Baotou, a bloke offered to sew what looked like the outer two thirds of a particularly hairy camel inside my greatcoat. I figured that the season wasn't right, and anyway, he wanted about 13 bucks for the job.

When they don't wear camel, they dress in rather silly synthetic Mao suits and stay indoors, in houses that look like either utterly out of place Chinese, or utterly out of place Arab, with walls all plastered with shit and mud and straw for insulation, no matter how fine the brick and tile work – rather like wearing long underwear over your Mao suit. Remember, out of the population of eighteen million, only about 10 per cent are Mongols, which still leaves more Mongols than in Outer Mongolia. The others are people who may have lived here since 1949, or even before, but still can't speak a word of Mongol and dream of opening restaurants with names like 'Suzhou Gardens' or 'West Lake'.

Ningxia is perfect, though. The whole province has just been opened up for the first time, no one has seen a foreigner anywhere, none of the cops know the rules. Yinchuan, full of new construction of a rather jarring kind, is also full of old Ming and Yuan ramparts. It has two huge pagodas that date from an even earlier period, supposed to be contemporary with the Spring and Autumn period – Confucius' time – when Ningxia had nothing much to do with China. Also there is a brand-new mosque, built on the Libyan model because all the old ones were destroyed during the Cultural Revolution. I did discover the West Gate mosque, though, which most people don't know or claim to not know about. A really gorgeous thing built at the beginning of the Ming, before the Imperial Palace made architecture all gigantic and gaga.

Tomorrow I will try to reach Zhongning, where, rumour has it, all the mosques survived the Cultural Revolution. In about three weeks I'll be in Xi'an.

Zhongwei, Ningxia Hui Muslim Minority Autonomous Region, 13 April 1984
Dear Old Man and others around,

Ah, the moon is up there steeping in sun-warmed, yellow and rather muddy air, the jasmine tea is steeping here in the pot, and I have just finished my nightly louse inspection. (I found two, one of which was the biggest I've ever seen, practically a tick; I hope he was simply having a comfortable retirement, and not on maternity leave.) Despite their humble salaries, lice share with policemen the distinction of being the only seriously unpleasant aspects of travel here.

I am not sure what you mean by adventures; I've seen much more on this trip than on others, but it has also been far more uneventful. Today for the first time I attempted a long-distance hike in the Gobi. I found a likely-looking bend in the Yellow River, Shapotou, where rumour had it that dunes several hundred metres high existed that allowed you to simply sled straight down into the water all covered with sand. I got ready, missed the train, shook the hotel police

47

agent, and then set out, convinced that the spot was only about 29 kilometres away, and that I could return by night following my tracks if I had to. I thought the route across the desert would bring me to an interesting bit of the Great Wall, unlike the cut stone and winding dragon-belly-scale steps of the famous bit near Badaling. Here it is just pounded earth and mud battlements, more than a thousand years older, dating from the dawn of unified China, when the omphalos was Shaanxi to the southwest. This bit of wall doesn't wind a jot, but lies straight across the desert like a lance, slicing dunes in half, and here and there being sliced in half by a dune.

My maps were wrong, of course, and my route across the desert a bit rougher than I expected, duney like the worst of the Sahara. About three in the afternoon, without water, I went back to the rough road along the river and hitched a ride with a commune truck as far as the Great Wall. The wall is so much mud crumbling into so much sand, distinguishable only for about half a kilometre's length, with dunes on both sides like a snow fence after a bad blizzard. Nowhere is it high enough to keep a camel out, and if I hadn't been looking for it all day under a sun-baked sky and breathing mud-caked air, I probably would have walked over it or through it.

Yet I sat there on the summit of one of the embattlements and had a good laugh, not only at myself. I was thinking of when Nixon visited Badaling, the Ming section of the wall, where they take large numbers of foreigners and confine them in small spaces in order to photograph them with the official wall in the background. Nixon was in his element, small-town boy with that peculiarly American breed of small-town petty meanness, mouthing a Great Thing for a Great Occasion in a Great Place. He had been lugging it around for three days, waiting to say: 'It is indeed a Great Wall.' Except of course the Chinese don't use the character *da* (great) to describe the wall, but only the character *chang* (long). So the *People's Daily* dutifully appeared the next day with the grinning small-town boy sententiously remarking,

'Gee, that's a mighty long wall', or something to that effect, which probably did not impress the average Ningxia peasant with the perspicacity of the American people. So, lugging around sententious phrases is even more pointless than carrying a typewriter through the Gobi, as I do. Nobody here knows the ringing phrase that Armstrong bungled upon taking the first stumble on the surface of the moon, but today one of the commune blokes, whom I was telling about the splendours of Badaling, told me proudly that, according to Armstrong, you can see the Great Wall from the Sea of Tranquillity.

From a town near the Great Rubble, or the Long Rubble, I hitched a ride on a donkey cart to Shapotou, where the dunes looked only about 150 feet high, with a few kids sledding down them toward some clear streams emptying into the Yellow River like drops into the ocean at the bottom. I sledded down once, and as I came down the steeper part at the end, where some of the sand was blown here and there into grotesque shapes, I heard the 'humming of the sands', a rare phenomenon apparently caused by shifting sand layers, that Thesiger mentioned. Thesiger reported that he could control the sound by putting his foot down and picking it up. I found I could control it by sliding on my bum and paddling with both hands. It sounded vaguely like a car engine starting, but slightly hummier, and caused absolutely no sensation of vibration or anything else. The idea of my tiny and rather bony buttocks ringing something deep in the innards of this enormous opera house of a dune was, well, it made me feel like the little springs emptying into the bend of the Yellow River, and apparently changing its course. In one of the little streams I found a small green lump of almost pure clay, perfect for modelling, and made, with a few other lumps, a statue of a camel to commemorate the event. I set it at the bend of the river, and then I hiked about half way back, and hitched the other half, to Zhongwei.

And where is Zhongwei? Zhongwei is a kind of crossroads between Gansu, Ningxia and Inner Mongolia. It's old and looks it, but things keep well in the desert. There is a fine lamasery done under the early Ming, in a very horned Chinese style, not at all like the Tibetan one I went to in Inner Mongolia. The town is built around a huge red edifice with crossing tunnels in the base, and three high horned roofs with chickens and other fierce creatures grimacing along the ridgepoles, also Ming and in better shape, since, adorned with Mao quotations and fitted with a chime that plays 'The East is Red' on the hour, the Red Guards saw no reason to gut it during the Cult Revolt, as they did the lamasery. But Gao Miao, the lamasery, is now being repainted and parts of it look really exquisite, like something from *The Dream of the Red Chamber*, with a dreamy green-scaled dragon roof curling above it like incense smoke. It is mostly a Han rather than a Hui town today, too, even though it is in the armpit, so to speak, of the Hui (Muslim) autonomous region. The market is full of pork, the pigs wander the street with impunity, and the opera singers that play and sing under the Ming roofs have thick Shaanxi accents.

There is one mosque, new and shabby. The old one was destroyed by party bureaucrats dressed as Red Guards. The Hui bring things to market driving two-wheeler engines that can be hitched to ploughs as well as carts, but are steered rather clumsily by long handlebars. The Hui tend to be very simple country folk, big in generosity, almost Arab-size, while the Hans here seem very un-Chinese in their rudeness, their nastiness to each other, the violence and aggressiveness of their interactions. Haggling, unknown in most of China, is here a cross between a brawl and a game of chicken; people laugh cruelly at any pratfall, any loss of face, any bad bargain, and make a point of insulting me in ways they think I do not understand, and which, in fact, I sometimes don't. Waiting in line is unthinkable, a sure sign of senility or feebleness; offering one's seat on a bus is absurd. One of the major pastimes of young punks is keeping people from using seats that are empty.

I wish I knew why they are so very un-Chinese and almost inhuman in their manners. They are not, like Turnbull's

Mountain People, cannibal poor. People live in mud houses, true, but they do not sleep in the street, and few even till their lands with their bare hands or by donkey or ox: every peasant seems to have one of those carts with a two-wheeled engine to pull it. Nor am I merely seeing a reaction provoked by a foreigner. I may well be the only foreigner officially here in the last 20 or 30 years; no one can remember any others, and the town was just opened legally only weeks ago. Anyway, they treat each other the same, only without the glee of being able to insult someone in a language you think he cannot understand. Odd and interesting rather than infuriating. They are far too pathetic and miserable to be infuriating. My theory is that many are forced settlers from Shaanxi, which is overpopulated; they are dying to go home, and have nothing to tie them to the land and still less to the people on it.

Now I will walk backwards as far as Shanghai, where I wrote you last. Yinchuan, the capital of Ningxia, is a long day's bus ride away. Yinchuan is bigger and older, but much like Zhongwei, huge Ming gates at the four walls that no longer exist, two pagodas that date from nobody really knows when, and the same fallen opera stars from Xi'an and Taiyuan. The countryside was criss-crossed with canals, whence the name Yinchuan, or silver streams, I guess. It looked very rich.

There were four mosques in the city, three of which only a few old men knew existed. I got to sit in on a class in Arabic grammar. None of the Hui would speak Arabic to me, although they were all anxious to hear me recite the Quran with the correct pronunciation. The central mosque of Yinchuan, a synagogue at one time, is a gorgeous grey-roofed Ming thing, with beautifully painted rafters and a thick wall in wood, hung with Arabic calligraphy done with all the elements of the Canton street calligraphies I had seen. Everyone was bitterly disappointed when I told them I was not a Muslim and would not join sundown prayers, and when I heard the call to prayer, as sonorous as the nightly call I heard in Tunis, I almost did.

51

I came to Yinchuan from Baotou, the biggest city in Inner Mongolia, where I spent several days, beyond the wall for the first time since January. I managed to slip out of Baotou on two long day trips, one to a Mongol village south of the Yellow River, the other, far more interesting, to a lamasery.

To get to the lamasery, I took a bus about 60 kilometres up a dry riverbed so uneven that once the bus came so close to tipping over that the driver had to bellow to all us standees to lean over the other way. (On the way back I hitched, oddly enough, very successfully.) There, amidst snow-pated, lama-capped peaks, vast like a desert propped up on yurt poles, was the monastery of Wudangzhao, once the most powerful in Mongolia, proud owner of 500 slaves and a coal mine, which still runs. Entirely Tibetan in design, art and construction, the monks still speak Tibetan to each other and burn yak and camel shit in little Franklin stoves.

The paintings were really mindboggling, psychedelic like the stuff in Kunming, with very little sterile serenity. One chamber of the monastery was entirely devoted to the fiercer cannibal gods. The doors were pleasantly painted with detailed and life-sized pictures of two flayed bodies hanging by their heels, and the huge, black sabre-toothed guardians of the faith drooled blood sipped out of skull caps. The rafters were painted with chains of human heads, and the treasury, behind the reliquary, was crammed with jewellery fashioned of human bone. I wanted to know if they still practised celestial burial, flaying the bodies of the dead and leaving them for the vultures, but the monks spoke rather poor Chinese and they thought I was being irreligious. I suppose the jewellery is all that is left of the monastery's slaves. The coal keeps Baotou's factories going, and many mud houses, those with fluted *kangs* [brick platforms heated from below] to eat and sleep on, heated by smoke, toasty warm in the bitter cold.

There is another lamasery in Qinghai I'd like to visit, also for the paintings, but I have mysteriously lost my desire to see Tibet. The rest isn't so interesting, and is a little hard to relate. I went to Peking from Nanjing and Shanghai, chiefly in order to sell my ticket, not for the Budapest price, but for the price of a ticket to Berlin, more expensive, of course, but still less than the Chinese price to Budapest. This will allow me to stay in China for another month, after which the money runs out. In the meantime I've had two offers of jobs for the summer, one in Peking and the other in Xi'an, which I think I will take, even though I should be somewhere working on Arabic. But this will allow me to stay long enough to really perfect the Chinese, and maybe make enough money to get back across the Channel to England. I know it is not really what I should be doing, but I can get Arabic material in Xinjiang, I think, and work on both.

You will be pleased to hear I am thinking of settling in Xi'an, which is also one of the most archaeologically interesting places in China and has thirty thousand Muslims and a huge mosque. According to Sima Qian, the unifier and first emperor of Qin had nearly a million people work on his tomb in Xi'an, as many as on the Great Wall. Under a huge hillock, he had a sky set in precious metals, with pearls for stars, and streams running with quicksilver, and scale maps of all the provinces of China crammed with their treasures. The army of terracotta warriors was only one of four buried to guard the four cardinal points of the tomb. Most of the workforce, all of the emperor's concubines and family, and even his horses, were buried alive in the tomb itself. The site is well known, but has not been excavated. It is also well known, and reported by Sima Qian, that the tomb was opened and pillaged by the rebel Xiang Yu only 11 years after its completion. The pillage itself is a matter of some interest, I should think. There is much else in Xi'an besides swine flu and the Qins: a Han town, and even a neolithic settlement, Ban Po, in almost perfect condition.

Urumqi, 11 May 1984
Dear D & B,

So much to tell. This time I really have put off telling it too long. Extenuating circumstances and constant motion, as well as good company. I've been down in Kashgar the last few weeks, right on the Afghan border, the very end of the end of the earth, much more Arab than Chinese, though in fact the folks there are Uighurs, a Turkic-speaking people, Muslim as hell and paradise, sunken eyes and hawk noses, foreheads like the empty quarter [of Arabia] and tattooed eyebrows. Arab coffee shops where hashish is copiously smoked and no words of Chinese are spoken.

I travelled there with a young woman who's been working as a doctor in Hong Kong, a vegetarian, which saved me from the endless shits I would have had from eating half-raw mutton kebabs and intestines stuffed with equal parts of pepper and rice. Last night we got sanded in about 40 kilometres from Daheyon; the wind was too strong for the bus to coast down the mountains into the Turpan Depression, which lies far below sea level, and the driver didn't want to waste fuel using the engine – and besides he was afraid the paint might be sandblasted off the side of the vehicle.

Today we said good-bye, down at the Daheyon train station, where a meeting was being held to display the latest condemned men. (I've seen several of these meetings already; even in small towns they are apparently bi-monthly, which is a lot of executions.) There we were, blubbering at each other, like the blokes up on the stage, who were trussed up like turkeys for the kill. Everyone, for once, was staring in another direction, and missed the horrible, surrealistic mush of our good-bye – thoroughly indecent by Chinese standards, Louise bursting into tears ('Zhang Qimin, Han nationality, 24 years old, to be shot . . .'), me being long-armed and very English, muttering about how much I looked forward to a nice sheep intestine, then, when the train pulled up, struck blind by one of my frequent pangs of self-pity, I blurted out something like 'Shit, I'm alone'. Louise, despite much phlegm one of the most thoroughly lovable and loving creatures I've ever met, practically dissolved in a waterfall of sentiment over a jagged rock of self-mockery. ('. . . Qin Wei, Hui nationality, 20 years . . .')

The patron saint of Kashgar is Xiangfei, the fragrant concubine, a Uighur princess shipped to Peking to join the harem of Kangxi. The legend goes that she steadfastly refused him and was finally ordered to strangle herself by the Queen Mother. She was buried in a hole in Peking, but her relatives here have a huge crazy quilt of a mausoleum, with some tiles green, some blue, some white, others of a mauve or yellow crayon colour, all jammed together without any design. Only seen from afar does it make any sense as a single building, though it is perfectly symmetrical and Central Asian, rather like the photos of Bokhara and Samarkand I've seen. Kashgar is a lot closer to Kabul and Tashkent and Alma Ata than to Urumqi.

The story is apocryphal and the tomb is actually that of her father, Abak Hoja, who was a well-known holy man in his own right. He was also an important landlord, and his tomb was supplied by 20,000 acres of land and quite a bit of rural industry. Xiangfei, whose real name was Teleshat Shanimo, was very homesick and returned to Peking for a visit, where she died. The Emperor was very grieved and gave her a handsome funeral.

Now I will mentally go backwards as far as Inner Mongolia, where I think I did write. I hitched to Turpan from Dunhuang, where the great caves of Mogao are. In the third or fourth century, when Buddhist feet first trod the Silk Road, the first cave at Mogao, near Dunhuang, was completed. Over the next fourteen centuries, the Buddhists passing through and those ensconced in the monastery there compiled a library of perhaps over 100,000 tomes in the 400 caves around Cangjing, the cave set aside for protecting scripture. These were pilfered around the turn of the century by an German named Aurel Stein, who was working for the British Museum, with the connivance of a Taoist priest who had discovered them. But the caves also had frescoes on their walls, about 45 kilometres long in garish, lurid greens and rosy reds and a kind of funny blackened cerise. These were horribly damaged by Baron Wrangel's men when they camped and built fires in the caves while fleeing Trotsky's Red Army. But enough is still there to dwarf the graffiti and make it seem thoroughly petty confronted with the sheer force of imagination of the frescoes.

The early stuff isn't really that great, thousands and thousands of of Buddhas in a cave, all the same, with faces blackened and noses and eyeballs left white, for relief if not perspective. The more involved murals usually show Jataka stories [about the life of the Buddha], full of karma and self-sacrifice, rather like the 'Die like him' campaign the Maoists ran when Lei Feng killed himself in an industrial accident. There are scenes of Sakyamuni cutting his flesh to feed the eagles, and Prince Sittha feeding his body to a famished tiger and her starving cubs and one does not even get the sense of compassion exuded by women feeding bread crumbs to pigeons. There is also a comic strip serial, so long and varied and cliff-hanging it is almost irritating, about a woman who goes on a pilgrimage and sleeps in a graveyard, where a snake bites her husband. Then she crosses a river with one son, and turns back to find the other has drowned. She arrives back at the other side to find that wolves have carried off son number one. Then she marries a handsome prince, but he turns out to be a robber, so both of them are condemned to be buried alive. The dogs dig her up looking for meat, and so on and so on.

The Buddhas all look rather stupid and expressionless after a while – and then, suddenly, the Sui and Tang dynasties happen, Buddhism is a mass religion, not an idea dear to a few converts. It has to deliver real people and it does. The cult of Amitabha makes its appearance, first as a kind of St Jude of lost Buddhist causes, then more like Jesus Christ. Finally, the walls are screaming the Amitabha-sutra at you like a toothpaste commercial. Elaborately captioned before and after pictures show you sterile women saying the sutra and getting knocked up; Silk Road merchants say it to subdue robbers, like a kind of instant Charles Atlas course. The cult of 'The Pure Land in the West', still very powerful in Japan, makes its appearance in the murals too, and some of the goings on in the Pure Land look like Jesse Jackson's Saturday Push meetings in Chicago. There are Buddhas with things dangling in their chest hairs, *bodhisattvas* who smirk and even leer, and in the death cave, the 'Reclining Buddha' resembles a fat and happy courtesan who has dozed off after a good screw, oblivious to the retinue of hysterically mourning Arabs, Turks, Tibetans, elaborately coiffed hill people and other barbarians, all plunging knives into their breasts to show their grief, figures distorted and faces grimacing.

I stayed almost a week in Dunhuang, getting into all the open caves and hanging out with the son of the curator, himself a painter and curator from the Imperial Museum in Peking, just rehabilitated after doing time during the Cult Revolt. He has a studio right at the caves, where he lives and where I stayed for a few days. His father, who was educated in France, suffered horribly during the Cult Revolt. He is full of bitter memories of riding home from Peking on coal trains to bring his father food, and spending about three weeks in prison himself, thinking up nasty things to say about his father in public meetings. On his studio wall is a poster of Mao in Red Guard uniform, which I thought was a joke in bad taste. He looked funny when I asked him, and said, 'To not forget'.

I travelled to Dunhuang in his company from Jiuquan, where we met outside another execution meeting, he embarrassed, me brimming with embarrassing questions, since several of the victims were from minorities and suffered from various rather vague accusations. Jiuquan was in all ways a rather creepy place, with the worst housing I've seen here, all post-liberation, like camping in a parking ramp, massive concrete walls, no heat, open sewers and outhouses. There were beggars hovering over your plate to finish off any scrap you might drop on the floor or leave, and lick the plates 'clean' for the restaurant staff. And over it all, the massive Jiayu fortress at the end of the Great Wall, still only hammered mud, since building stones of any size are rare, a snaky morass of slimy mud, wrapped here and there into knobs that once were guardposts, about which the Tang poets wrote things like, 'Once outside the Jiayu pass I can't help weeping, for before me lies the Gobi, and behind the Gate of Hell.'

I came to Jiayu and Jiuquan from Xining, in Qinghai, where one of the biggest shrines of Tibetan Buddhism still operates, the birthplace of Tsongkhapa, 'the Man From the Land of Onions', which means Xining. It was freezing and snow-covered when I was there. The monastery of Taersi is large, but curiously Chinese-roofed, and redolent of rancid yak butter, which is used to light, cremate, and sculpt mammoth and minuscule scenes of the life of Sakyamuni [the Buddha], in riotous melting colours.

Taersi is a thoroughly bizarre place, full of Tibetans pilgrimaging on horny-skinned bellies and turning huge creaky prayer wheels. It was a warm day at the temple, and the yak butter sculptures were getting spreadable and Dali-esque, not to mention odoriferous, in halls that were so dimly lit you could barely see the paintings under the accumulated grease. There was a ceremony that night lasting some eight hours in which a senior lama sat all lotused up above a sand painting, quite intricate and thoroughly temporal, and cast quantities of butter, rice, sticks and herbs into a fire, while the faithful framped and crashed on cymbals and alpenhorns. One monk explained ecstatically that his holiness was burning all the butter in the world, all the rice in the world, and so on.

I preferred the daily exercises, in which various young initiates, looking very fresh out of their Mao college uniforms, sat and seemingly tried unsuccessfully not to laugh or flinch as grinning and boisterous and utterly unwashed lamas slapped their palms and told ripping yarns. I later learned they were not trying not to laugh. This is a well-organized form of monastic debating, in which a monk stands and harangues the initiate on some point of Buddhist doctrine, and asks a question with the slap of the hands. The initiate is supposed to answer. They don't always take it very seriously.

The monastery lodge, normally full of pilgrims and now also housing two bearded West Germans, as well as an anthropologist and myself, was right in the middle of the festivities. The West Germans were gurunoids, or lamanoids, of some kind. Why Westerners should be attracted to this vulgar, violent, brutal and barbaric form of Buddhism is beyond me. It seems to Buddhism what the medieval Catholic Church was to Christianity.

In Xining itself I met all kinds of very hip young Tibetans with Mao suits and swarthy earnest faces, big drinkers and big talkers, less hidebound than most Chinese, but with a disturbing tendency to light up whenever the Dalai Lama was mentioned, no matter how political they were. Xining is full of them, studying medicine and English, dressed very hip, fluent in Chinese. Yet they still grab you by the arm and ask breathlessly if you have ever seen his holiness, you know, his hobby is sub-atomic physics, and he makes frequent trips to the US to discuss it with the experts. Anyway, his picture as a young man is ubiquitous, and 20-year-old vials of his excreta are still around. Tibet must be an altogether strange and unbelievable place. Most Chinese mention it with horror, and hardly anyone has been there.

From Zhongwei in Ningxia to Lanzhou. In Lanzhou I was on a bus returning to my hotel when a woman reported the loss of 20 yuan, about ten bucks, I guess, but half a month's salary. The bus was immediately sealed, and we were all driven to the police station, where we sat and stood, sweating and packed in as you always are in Chinese buses for about an hour and a half. When a few people had collapsed from exhaustion, the doors opened and a cop entered, glanced neither left nor right, and selected a likely-looking youth. Then we were immediately released. 'How did they know?' I asked. Shrug, smirk, 'History . . .'

I'm going to try to get a gig here in Urumqi, before I move on to Xi'an. Everyone thinks I am mad; there is a whole lot here, but not to most people's eyes. Here I can learn Uighur, and sweat in summer and freeze in winter, and go to Kashgar every term break, and work on Arabic somewhat more easily. There are no other foreigners, except 'travellers' who pass through on their way to Kashgar or Tianchi, where there is a fringe of Kazakh villagers, and no distractions of any kind. At the same time, there is an attenuated form of the tension I felt in Sudan, the tension of Muslim ways of life torn apart by people who desperately want to live otherwise, even if they can't imagine it very well. Without the danger. I really do think this is where I want to live. There are three places that might take me: the Marxism-Leninism Institute, the Agricultural College, and Xinjiang University, but they are all having struggle meetings for the next few days.

I'll be very isolated and lonely here, I suppose. There will be no more Louises or Marisas, social life will be even more 'among blokes' than elsewhere in China – though not as much as in the Arab world. Yet I'm sure it's worth it, and anyway, I have to have a place to stay put just to start painting again.

Now then, if I don't get a job, my visa will run out again on the 20th, and I'll probably be able to get another month, after which I absolutely must leave the country. I'm sorry, really sorry this time, that I can't give you a mailing address of any sort, or tell you when I'll write next. I know all this uncertainty seems highly unhealthy, but actually I think it is a fairly normal condition. You have been rather saintly about writing. I will try to settle down and answer some of your letters, and I think this is the place.

Urumqi, 13 May 1984
Dear Old Man,

I have been down in Kashgar for the last few weeks, far, far from China Proper, far closer to Afghanistan than here. I can't get a job and settle in Kashgar, but I think maybe I can here, and I'm going to try. Why? Because Kashgar is a kind of ante-China, more Samarkand and Bokhara than anything else I've ever seen, Muslim and yet pre-Muslim and post-Muslim as well, an amazing state of theological, cultural and social confusion.

You get there riding through the desert, of course, the Silk Road, which is more or less paved today, but not exactly silk. It takes maybe a week hitching, or four days on a bus, assuming no more than one major breakdown. It is about a thousand miles from Urumqi, but there's no hurry. It is just as wonderful as trucking through the Sahara in Sudan and Algeria, days spent crawling through a huge hot gravel pit, places where the wind is so fierce the truck has to stop to save its glass windows. Nights you prop up your chin with a wedge of melon, sluice down your sheep tripes stuffed with rice with a big dab of icy sherbet, hand-turned by a Uighur lad who tends to go limp-wristed at the crucial moment. A truck breaks down and everyone stops to help swear in sympathy at the Nanjing-made truck engine, a weak-kneed Han affair that looks like something out of the Thirties, with its gull-winged hood. They swear in a plethora of minority languages: Uighur, Kazakh and Russian, which the old people remember, and some villages still have as a mother tongue.

One day out of Kashgar, I climbed a carrot-topped dome of a mountain to get a good look at the trucks crawling in from Aksu for their last-chance breakdown. The ground was crunchy with laminated sand, almost crystalline. It broke off in beautiful boomerang-shapes under my feet, looking like sand roses curiously straightened out by some mis-step of the dancing dune. I saw a pale green girdle of creepers around one level of the mountain, with beautiful lady's-slipper flowers, so faint I first thought it was mineral rather than vegetable, but fragrant as lily of the valley. When I reached the top of the mountain, I looked immediately down at the oasis where we had stopped for the night, attracting dim shapes of trucks with the headlights off, as Chinese custom dictates. There was a huge salt lake behind it, with fish the size of small boats visible beneath the surface here and there. Red, red, red, like the Iron Range, the plunging sun hopelessly small by comparison, all was blood and iron and gore for miles, from the foothills of Tian Shan, faulted like great slabs of laminated sand, to the miles and miles of flat land we had crossed. Here and there the faults in the earth somehow produced a step up of a metre or two, after which the desert continued on as flat as before, as if nothing had happened. Turning around, with my back to the oasis, I saw there was a maraboutic koubba of some kind

61

right at my feet, with a crude red slab for a tombstone, not very old at all.

Love of the desert is peculiarly egoistic and very un-Chinese; it seems to go well with delusions of grandeur. I stumped back to the road and ran into a Uighur bloke I had met some 500 kilometres back, the day before, where I had helped him swear at his Chinese truck in its mother tongue. I am insufficiently humble to be Chinese, and insufficiently serious about grandeur to be Arab; maybe my Jewish grandmother was right in warning me that I had some kind of Turk's blood in my veins.

That was just getting there. Kashgar itself has the most unbelievable bazaar you ever dreamt of. I'm surprised the goggle-eyed Venetians and footsore Arabs didn't just turn around and forget about Chang' An [Xi'an], Dadu [Peking], and a few yards of wormy silk. Ha! What is mere silk compared to the yogurt they serve in Kashgar with crushed ice and a sweet sauce of honey, brown sugar and grape juice? Or walnut candy glommed up with some kind of sweet tree sap? Or the cold mare's milk you quaff at sundown, or the sultana and peanut blintzes in cream that fall apart in your fingers? Not to mention more durable goods like hand-rolled Uighur noodles, al dente, not to say half-raw and luke-warm, and rice with fruit and nuts and chicken, and sheep offal you never imagined might be found in the inoffensive bodies of the sheep you pass on the street every day.

None of the bizarre witch doctor stalls I described from Nanning can compare with the stuffed owls, bats, horseshoe crabs, pickled snakes, dried snakes, fried snakes, velveted antlers, pulverized antlers, lizard heads, etc., that Louise and I inspected in Kashgar. There was a medicine man selling an array of bears' feet, deer heads, snakes in every possible size, shape and state of desiccation, lizards with ribs flared out like wings, and various beasts you've never seen before: something like a trilobite with legs, and another thing like a seahorse, but shorter, fatter and straighter. Louise, the English doctor I was travelling with, was outraged that such things continue, and doubtless they do cost lives. One morning I saw a whole bear's foot on one of the stalls. I asked what you cure with a bear's foot and the medicine man assured me it was bound to cure something in you somewhere.

The women of Kashgar all seem to live by selling each other delicate little brass and garnet earrings, while half the men carry and sell huge arrays of flick knives, bayonets, brass knuckles, daggers of every conceivable size, shape, temper and price, with handles of tin, brass, silver, gold, rhinoceros horn and laminated plastic. Some of them say 'Tashkent' or 'Bukhara' in Uighur, and carry little Soviet flags in the arabesques on the blade. Every Uighur male has at least one, though I only saw one of them take it out – a ferocious-looking gent of about 80 on a bus trying to get his grandson or great-grandson to shut up by threatening to lop off his own ear if the kid didn't quit bending it. (The bus kept hitting huge bumps, and I expected to get the ear right in my lap.) Every male also comes shod with knee-high leather boots, over which they wear those little rubbers I was always so embarrassed to wear in elementary school. When they pray, they only take the rubbers off, and I wonder if their feet ever see the light of day.

The trinket-sellers keep trying to palm off old coins on you: Tsarist 50 kopek pieces, special money minted when Kashgar was under warlord rule 60 years ago, and silver Tibetan coins three centuries old, for about ten cents a piece. I had a pair soldered by a blacksmith into earrings for Louise; the seller was horrified by the idea. But listen to this: outside the mosque, there are old men with really old Arabic manuscripts, selling for a song. I saw three or four at least 400 years old, according to the Hegira date on the back page, and could not resist buying two *dala'ils* [prayer books], one three centuries old, and one only two. Both are illuminated in gold, green, pink, blue and red, with whole-page drawings of old mosques. It is very doubtful if I will be allowed to leave the country with them, though they are not technically Chinese antiques; still, it is worth a try, and in the meantime they are spellbinding bedtime reading even when I have to look up every other word.

63

Like I said, it is Muslim as paradise and hell, yet not so. Show me a Muslim country where women wear transparent stockings, knee-high skirts, don't cross their legs when they sit, and order their menfolk to put away the damn *duttar* [a three-stringed plucked Arabic instrument, like a banjo] and finish washing the dishes. The little girls have tattooed eyebrows, and a fringe of hair on their shaved heads from temple to temple to keep the sun off their faces. They play in the streets like little boys until past puberty. There are heterodoxish goings on everywhere you look, rams' heads hung on walls against the evil eye, lines of people bearing bread or sugar or water to feed to the sick, on which the faithful blow after praying (ugh!): *baraka* [blessings] as well as countless TB bacilli.

At night the cafes are full of raucous old women smoking huge cheroots of hashish (which is all over, despite official claims that it's been wiped out), and everyone has to take turns playing the *rebaba* [a bowed string instrument, also Arabic] whether they've ever played one before or not. In my favourite cafe, a joint that sold a kind of lentil curry after hours, there was one regular who specialized in transvestite dancing; he was 40 and unmarried, but no one insinuated there was anything odd about him. He knew his routine so well he could do it even when he could barely walk; he was also the biggest drinker in the place. All this went on gaily into the wee hours of the morning, except on Friday nights. Louise used to laugh at my spending every night out until four or five, but I often saw women alone doing the same thing.

Before Kashgar came Turpan, another stop on the Silk Road, or rather two stops: one was Jiaohe, a city on a pole, like Constantine in Algeria, maybe 1700 years old, where Xuanzhuang, the monk whose trip to India in search of Buddhist scriptures formed the basis of the great Ming novel *Monkey: A Journey to the West*, preached his most foot-stamping get-happy sermons. The temple is roofless, and the image headless today, but still there, and lying all around the ground are scads of pottery bits. That's nothing – at

Gaocheng, the Silk Road stop at the other end of the Turpan oasis, there are half a dozen tombs which have been opened but not really excavated, and in one there are two bodies, mummified by the dry air, which the local lads dare each other to touch. Around it on the walls are incongruous Tang paintings illustrating the four Confucian virtues: Man of Earth, who works and shuts up; Man of Jade, who does nothing and accomplishes everything anyway; Man of Stone, who always speaks his mind, mouth agape, teeth bared; and Man of Gold, kneeling, with his mouth gagged.

Nearby, there are some thousand Buddha caves, not quite as magnificent as Dunhuang to begin with, and terribly vandalized by Muslim iconoclasts, who, like Christians gouging out the erections of the gods of the Temple of Karnak, have hacked out the haloes, leaving rings that are merely uglier but no less suggestive. In fact, it somehow lends a Christ-like passion to the scene. A few of the haloes are intact: mad, psychedelic, Hendrix-style Afros in lightning bolts, mostly in red or cerise pigment that has turned a ghastly black through oxidation. And riding back along the Flaming Mountains with their painted-on valleys, you can really see where the inspiration came from. They are like those laminated sand boomerangs, but only as they must appear to an ant, huge shards of crystalline, ragged red, slipping down over each other into that perverse, flat, flat, step up, flat desert. Jaunty and jagged.

On my arrival in a Muslim city, my first action is always to nip out to the great mosque. I'm not sure how this got started, probably in Sudan, where there is little to see except street life. So on arriving in Turpan I dashed out to Sugongta. Not a very old mosque, only about 200 years or so, but really big and bizarre, with a barrel-shaped minaret bearing a dizzying array of brickwork geometrics, and two huge metal hoops to keep the cracks from widening. Off the main prayer hall there are a score of these tiny little chambers with domed roofs and moon-shaped skylights cut into them at various places, which gave it an eery, moonlit atmosphere even at midday.

I did a lot of sketching, but I soon acquired, as you always do in China, a sizeable retinue of kids, and I thought I'd head back. As I crossed the cemetery, the wind started, and I remember that practically the last thing I saw more than 15 feet away, was this stripy snake, looking very poisonous and battling the wind not very successfully. I was very nervous because my companions were a frisky lot, but as soon as they saw it they ran away screaming. And then I had to take shelter, because you could barely stand straight, much less walk, in the blast of hot sand descending from the mountains.

The next day I woke up bright and early, around ten o'clock, and it was dark, really dark, but reddish-dark, like the inside of a bottle of burgundy. It got so dark around noon – and this is supposed to be the place in China where the sun is most dangerously bright – that walking in the streets was next to impossible. You had to feel your way, like in a closet, among the rubble sidewalks and canals gushing with washing, drinking and disposal water. It was much darker than night when I was trying to eat my lungs and intestines down at the Uighur lunch spot. When I came back from lunch and banged at the locked gate, someone came out and told me gravely that it was impossible to leave the hotel. The hotel staff went slightly daft. Someone locked the gates with a huge padlock 'because the weather is no good', and another kept racing around to all the rooms every five minutes to anounce that the power was going to be cut 'as soon as the candles arrive'!

It was certainly impossible to leave Turpan for a few days. Like being snowed in at Christmas, it was quite festive, really. The red gradually turned yellowish, and visibility increased to about a hundred feet at sunset. The next day I hiked out to Jiaohe, about ten kilometres. But it was only an unfathomable collection of uninhabitable shapes bearing no resemblance to a city in that air, surrounded by a canyon that apparently had no bottom, just a kind of horizon at your feet. The day after, a small van arrived from Urumqi, a three- to five-hour drive away. They had done it in 20 hours, and the van listed from the gravel that had accumulated up to the window sills on the leeward side. There was not a trace of paint on the windward side, and not a single bit of unprotected windowpane anywhere. There were five passengers, all terrified, their faces scraped red and raw, and the door on the driver's side had dents that looked like they had been made with baseball bats.

Which brings me to the end of this letter and almost to Xi'an, where I will mail this and look around for a gig, not having found one in Urumqi. I am getting a little worried about having a job for next year. Bumming around is exactly what I'm doing, and while I seem to get something out of it, more than most I meet, I dislike intensely that rootlessness and shiftless feeling. It is not conducive to serious thought and the 'not unduly flexible' programme I am supposed to set myself for my degree in Arabic at London University. But, God, you should see those Kashgar manuscripts!

3 | Setting down

Bell Tower Hotel, Xi'an, 22 May 1984
Dear D & B,

I've got to get out of this joint before noon or I'll lose even more money paying for the fancy stationery, so I can't really answer your letters. I'll try that from Peking. This is just to let you know how I'm doing.

Not well. You don't just walk in and ask for a job in China, not even on the recommendation of someone you've never met. The purpose of most jobs, at least in the bureaucracy's view, is patronage power, rather than actual function, and jobs are kept open like hotel rooms, in case somebody important shows up at the last minute. There is a strong tendency for bureaucrats to not say no, even when they have no other power or purpose. They run you ragged with come-back-tomorrows, will-call-yous, and so on, and they send you on errands they think you cannot possibly accomplish. There is also a tendency not to admit they don't know the person or information for which you are looking; I've been told that the 35-year-old bureaucrat I'd been talking to the day before has now retired, and, on another occasion, that a famous doctor has fallen ill and been taken to another hospital.

Since I must leave the country in a month unless I actually have a job, my case seems practically hopeless. No one in Xi'an can really help me, most make only a pretence, hoping I will hang around a little longer. The hotel people think it is a big joke that I insist on trying to get into the cheap Chinese accommodation in order to make that possible. They imagine I'm being colourful when I tell them that I've spent, hanging

68

around Xi'an for a week, the money I was saving to return home in case of failure. However, I was stood up this morning by someone who had assured me that I actually had the job, and then left a note blaming me for being late (I was early). It is obvious that the money really is spent, and I really have failed, and I'm not at all sure why.

Yet, as you say, I am probably better off Shanghaied here than on my way back to Europe with no guarantee of getting the job I really want in the Sudan. It is just a little disconcerting that one can lose in a week, because of foreign affairs regulations, money that was supposed to last months, and there is nothing whatsoever I can do about it.

Now what? Now I will return to Peking, and then maybe try Wuhan, hoping for a miracle. The miracle will probably not occur, and I do not have the money to return to Europe any more. I was saving it in an envelope, but in order to stay in Xi'an for this 'assured' job in the Medical School, I finally broke down and ripped the envelope open. When my visa expires at the end of June, I will try to get to Hong Kong and wire for money there, if I don't run out before then. I suspect that if I get money in China it will be converted into Chinese currency, which is not much good. Anyway, I guess I will have to try Paul, since I'm not sure where you'll be. God, what a mess!

Please, please, send the letters from Michael and Marisa to the US embassy in Peking. Especially from Marisa. I am surprised and glad she wrote; we had a nasty good-bye, me sick, she guilty and angry, Hong Kong horrid and drizzly. More from Peking.

Beijing, 31 May 1984

This is more from Peking. More of the same, not more definite. Xi'an was a bit of a disaster really; after leaving the Bell Tower Hotel, I slept one night in front of the station, nearly got picked up by the cops, and finally went out to Lintong, the village near the tomb of the first Qin emperor, and talked myself into a Chinese hotel by claiming I was from a rare national minority in Xinjiang. This normally works for only one night; however, in this case, the man I took such pains to convince turned out to be a police agent, which meant I could have stayed longer, I guess. But the next day, bright and early, I had pig stomach and black garlic noodles for breakfast and caught, almost immediately, a truck which took me all the way to Luoyang.

Truck drivers in China live very close to the edge, and this bloke doubly so. His wife had been a teacher and he had made a career in the PLA [People's Liberation Army], but both lost their jobs when a second child was born after the 1981 law, and his wife was sent back to a commune all the way across China, while he had to take the trucking job. A friend of his had just lost his licence for seven years because of 'a bad lifestyle', which meant, in his case, letting his fiancée ride with him in the cab, which his work unit supervisor thought implied intimate relations.

Not likely, actually, from what I've seen of the hours these blokes work. I got the ride around seven, and we got to Luoyang near midnight; now this bloke had started out at four in the morning from a village maybe 100 kilometres west of Xian, so he put in a 19- or 20-hour day, of which I personally witnessed 16. The next day he had to drive all the way back. 'That's harder,' he grinned. 'The truck's full of oil then.' So why do they bother with the terror campaigns for road safety, the filthy gory posters of smashed heads with collapsed eyeballs and torsos shredded into a pool of motor oil for the entertainment of gawking grandmas and their child charges? Why do they try and sentence truckers for being involved in accidents? They are hardly accidents, they are scheduled events, determined by the murderers who draw up the work rosters.

My driver was a bit backward in a lot of ways, with his extra kids, and Stalin and Mao still his heroes. He raved about how the Soviet Union tried to rip China off for its pork production, and so on. Yet he had a good handle on his interests. 'We need two things, independent unions and the right to strike, first of all,' he said. That's a beginning at least.

We stopped frequently to break down. He explained to me that much of the private industry the West gloats about so much involves little job shops producing their own bolts and such. Most of these private bolts are crooked or stripped or simply not round, and our main problem did in fact seem to be that we were shearing the bolts that fixed the brake drum assembly to the axle plate, and the bolts that sheared were all privately made ones, without the yellow heads that the state factory puts on them. At one such breakdown, an old woman brought us tea and stopped to chat in a very musical but to me practically meaningless dialect. The trucker bloke asked, tongue in cheek, if she was out emulating Lei Feng at her age. She hooted through her non-existent front teeth and said she was much too old and selfish to compare to Lei Feng.

Lei Feng was a young idiot who wanted desperately to fight in a war and was disappointed because he was born into the one generation in the preceding hundred years of Chinese history to be deprived of the opportunity. Party leaders consoled him by telling him that helping little old ladies across streets and working Stakhanovite hours was just as glorious, and he did so with a vengeance that eventually led to his death in an industrial accident, while unloading a truck. He was eulogized by Mao in a famous article, 'Learn from Lei Feng'. The article was nothing compared to the cult it spawned, which runs directly counter to both the public interest and public safety. There are still moronic songs around lauding Lei Feng for everything. I have one ten-minute opera aria about how Lei Feng refused to eat a mooncake because he thought maybe somewhere there were soldiers defending the country who didn't have any. What a shithead!

At this point, I decided to see if I could understand anything she said, so I asked her if she had any kids. 'Na, no kids,' she replied. 'Only a daughter.' And the word she used for 'a' was *zhi*, which is for dogs, rather than *ge*, which is normal for children. The trucker saw nothing abnormal about this; after all, he himself had lost everything because he didn't get a son until the third try.

71

We rolled through a tiny hamlet, and there was a little kid tending geese. One of the geese was slow in deciding which side of the road to make for: where his fellow geese were, or where his gooseherd was waiting with a worried wrinkle in his forehead. My driver pulled up over the goose, and rolled down the window. 'Is this thing I've run over yours?' He drove off with a laugh. The goose and the kid were left behind in a cloud of dust.

And on we went through rural Henan, with its crazy cave cities with Gothic doors, and cultivated plateaus on top, and what appeared to be a cattle market in every town simultaneously, at last coming into a valley that wriggled down to Luoyang. We arrived at an ungodly hour, and the trucker bloke profusely thanked the roof of the truck that he would not be forced to sleep under it (where some bureaucrat might find him and force him to unload in the middle of the night). Instead he could go to some cheap filthy flophouse and flop. I couldn't, so I slept in the bus station on the floor, in Marisa's coat. I had a neighbour, who decided my ear was the one to bend with loud complaints about the nasty breed of cheapskate that blew in from Shaanxi to buy things and was too miserly to get a hotel ticket, so instead they came to this nice quiet bus station and kept honest hardworking sons of the Henan soil awake, doncha know? Round about five o'clock they woke us to sweep up, and just as I was drifting back to sleep a huge explosion boomed out from a locomotive depot, followed by intense hissing of steam. '*Gan mao le yige*', shrieked my gabby neighbour, 'One's got a cold.'

So did I. Actually, according to Louise, they are not colds but respiratory viruses centred almost entirely in the bronchial tubes, where all the sulphur dioxide given off by the burning of poor quality coal collects. It is a general and almost pleasant Chinese condition, afflicting you about two weeks out of every month, a massive sense of very un-Western social solidarity when you suddenly realize, draped over three chairs and a spittoon, coughing, or standing on your head with a clove of garlic in your mouth, that the

72

whole city is coughing up the same green sauce so they can all breathe without rattling like a haggis full of sheep's hooves.

I stayed in Luoyang about three days, counting the nights I slept in the bus station. I also met a young woman who was trying to write one of those *Rough Guides* for wayward Australians, mostly from the bowers of Travel Service hotels and restaurants. She was really too interested in China and the Chinese to think about the kind of daily pettiness such guides must necessarily occupy themselves with. She spoke Chinese quite well, with a Cambridge accent, and knew much more history than hitching lore. Quite, quite well read in Chinese, and somewhat excessively pretty in that peculiar English way that makes you look like you should be riding a horse, infinitely more interesting than the sluggish lumps of migratory fat she had to write for. Anyway, in Luoyang we did all the touristy things together, and I even allowed her to feed me a hotel dinner, which I later regretted, consisting as it did of a peculiar cuisine that claims to combine western and Chinese principles of cooking, and instead merely ignores both at the peril of the diner.

Some of the time I spent flat on my back sketching in the caves of Longmen, the great Buddha caves carved out of the stone along the river there. No rivals of Dunhuang, but there are some nice ones, like the medical prescription cave, which has nothing but old family remedies for malaria and colds and whatnot, many of them identical to those in use today. The caves have ironically weathered much worse than the mud frescoes at Dunhuang, though they were carved, unlike Dunhuang, of stone for the ages. The stone was porous and drippy, and, worst of all, sawable; many of the statues were decapitated by tourists in the 20 years before liberation.

After the caves, we crossed the river by hopping from sandbar to sandbar, and I snagged a fisherman for a little lunchtime chat. Cambridge Catharine had been shaming me by reading all the bloody medical presciptions in the cave, so I got a chance to shame her by conversing with this bloke when she couldn't understand a word he said. And from him I found out the best way to hitch north to Anyang and Peking, and then I did.

Peking is a very different city from the pinched, yellow-caked, painfully poor village I arrived in last January. Now it resembles Canton. It is very romantic; there was a young couple pawing each other on the bus yesterday – oh, not very daring gropes, really, and she was obviously less into it than he was – under the amazed eye of a grizzled provincial. The staid Pekingese on the bus, like hip Londoners, all managed to look a thousand other directions without locking glances.

Peking always makes me pissed off at foreigners. Even the really thoughtful, sensitive ones see only the looking glass, and work themselves into a lather about the bureaucracy that we foreigners (we foreigners! And the Chinese people?) must endure. This morning I watched a bloke cross Tiananmen Square in camera and college student regalia, talking tedious nonsense to himself out loud; the Chinese all stared at him, understandably, but he didn't notice anything, except that as usual he was being stared at.

This neighbourhood, right outside where the outer city wall used to be, a moat still flowing in front of it, was quite lumpen in January, being the place where all the peasants tend to get off. It still has a certain atmosphere. There is a whole family living in a burnt-out truck bed near the station. At first they tried to open a small letter-writing business, and then yesterday they managed to get hold of large numbers of broken packing straps from some factory, which they are now using to weave baskets that cost more than the reed baskets the new arrivals are used to. During the winter everyone is too busy trying to keep warm to do anything else, but now, suddenly, the whole standard of living seems to have changed, and China seems a prosperous country indeed. I am astounded that I could have compared it with India.

Is it me? It usually is. I need a job, I need to stay here. Travelling around, you are always anchors aweigh in a sea of

new images. You notice absolutely everything and absolutely
no variations within the phenomena; they all seem timeless
to you. This makes you a gold mine of the kind of useless
information that goes into travel writing and good travel
stories, in which, as Levi-Strauss says somewhere in *Tristes
Tropiques*, the desire to impress drowns the ability to
critically evaluate evidence by other than your own experience, or even to effectively use that experience. I think I am
warming to Levi-Strauss, precisely as a travel writer. Isn't
that slightly perverse?

Near here there is another quarter of Peking that I'm even
fonder of, the Muslim bit, one of the few that wasn't all
Minged up, and still gives you a feeling for what Peking was
like before it was a capital. There is an ancient mosque, built
under the Song dynasty, according to the imam who keeps
it, full of mad animistic motifs, huge steles done in Arabic,
and Quranic quotations put up where the Mings usually
installed little landscapes on the rafters and beams and
crossbeams. It has none of the very witty use of occasional
coincidences between disparate cultures that marks the
mosque in Xi'an. For example, there the well of ablution
was turned into a little rock garden, and the windows of
wood and paper lattice work include designs of arabesques
and stylized Arabic writing, and Quranic quotations are
done in a kind of 'grass cursive' style and put up on scrolls in
the prayer hall.

The mosque of Peking is a Chinese mosque, rather than a
Silk Road outpost. If it really does date from the Song, the
Muslims of the time were probably assimilated village
Muslims, not arrivals on the Silk Road, which closed after
the battle of Taras and the fall of the Tang, if I remember
right. In any case, Silk Road Muslims would have no reason
to go to Peking, which was not even the Mongol capital of
Dadu at the time. A woman in Turpan told me the reason
the Muslims are called 'Hui' [return] is that they were
marooned in China proper by the cut-off of boat trade, and
they were always trying to return by land; the northwest,
Gansu, Ningxia, and so forth, were the closest they ever got,

which is why they are so numerous there. I wonder if there might not be some truth in her story, though it certainly goes against conventional wisdom. Anyway, it is a pleasantly lazy thought that admits no excess baggage like evidence if you seek to pursue it, the sort of thought I like to entertain while wandering around Peking in the heat, going from one yogurt and ice stand to another, and packing my guts with halal food.

At first I was quite repelled at the thought of living in Peking, one of the few cities that actually has laws on the books prohibiting Chinese and foreigners from being lodged under one roof, and phalanxes of detectives to enforce them. Yet now I am not only resigned to it, I look forward to it. It is possible I will find out tomorrow whether this will happen or not, though indefiniteness and lack of tenses seem to be the general rule in business transactions of all kinds. I guess that's it for now. Don't write yet.

Beijing, 21 June 1984

Got your scare package some days ago; I've been replying to some of the well-aged letters in it. But the scare is over anyway. I'm gigged, at the Cancer Research Institute here, and the visa has been extended a month and is now being converted into a work permit. I got the job maybe four days before my visa ran out, i.e. one day before I had to leave. And I did get it through the notorious 'back door' from which all things boonful and baneful and bureaucratic flow. Just as you must go to Peking to get a job in nether Ningxia, you must go to Ningxia to get a job in Peking. The thing was arranged for me by an associate director of the Institute who I met in Yinchuan after being kicked upstairs into the most expensive hotel in an admittedly not very posh town. I looked him up as a last desperate measure, and within a week it was all arranged. Rather the way you might expect it would happen, innit?

It is really impossible for me to be cynical, though; the students are all amazing and admirable people. Best of all, I have one of the few jobs teaching English that is not simply 'pisser dans un violon', a reflection of the current fascination with useless occidental gadgets and the underlying mercenary alliance of the bureaucracy with US imperialism, and a distraction from the really burning issues of the enlightened strata, namely, translating things in sufficient variety and quantity and quality, and developing their own language as a tool for artistic expression and scientific communication, rather than wasting their time on the acquisition of something that is not much more than Latin or Greek to most of them, but merely flatters the bureaucratic ego and feeds the pretentious appetite. My people do have constant contact with people abroad; they are involved in finding a remedy for cancer 'by combining Chinese and Western methods', as Zhou Enlai directed before dropping dead of cancer. They really need English and will use it.

On Monday I am supposed to address a meeting of the Institute – in Chinese – on the general plan and problems anticipated in my course, which I have been inventing as I go along. I already have a very impressive-looking office, in which I read *Renmin Ribao* all day, not so very much slower than anyone else. True, I am slightly nervous on account of my big nose, the fact that all my students are among the most educated people in the country, the youngest is 15 years older than me, and my tendency to speak in the truckdriver Chinese I picked up on the road. But, actually, I am far more worried by the unsettling observation that foreign teachers in China enjoy prestige, status and salary, as well as critical feedback, out of proportion to the amount they actually teach. This is particularly true of foreign teachers of high prestige foreign languages. Will I fail? How will I tell?

My feet are dry, and I do not need your money, thanks, since I am now making my own. I look forward to a year of writing incredibly uneventful and maybe even perspicacious letters; there is much to see utterly unconnected with my feet and pockets. Having been faithfully reading the paper for the past week, I find it is far, far more eventful than the best Arab newspapers. Especially now since it is full of fallout from the purge last October, with the upper bureaucratic echelons busy denouncing the middle ones in the name of the lower ones. There are scandals of millions of yuan lost by this or that bureaucrat in the provincial government on the front page almost every day, and even more heart-breaking investigations of the autonomous regions. There are also 'heartbreak' articles like a recent one on the nationwide problem of the unmarried over-30s, on which the leading comrades of the party and the nation were asked to pronounce. They came up with this amazingly uniform three-point programme, to wit: 1) Thoroughly discuss this problem in all party branches to raise general political consciousness of it as a major social problem; 2) Carry out thorough and meticulous discussions in the mass organizations; and 3) Help certain comrades with the resolution of certain 'attitudinal and practical problems'. I think the 'attitudinal problems' refers to the fact that most of the problematic unmarried are women, because of the distaste for women of doubtful fertility.

The American election-year conviction that anti-Communism and pro-Chinese feeling are in no way incompatible has certainly caught on here. The paper is full of the most incredible, thinly disguised garbage, even on Chinese issues. There is a regular column devoted to trumpeting the economic successes of Taiwan as proof of the correctness of the 'One nation, two systems', which so far has not gotten any more from Chiang than the Xi'an caper did. [On 12 December 1936, Chiang Kaishek was caught at Xi'an and detained by generals Zhang Xueliang and Yang Hucheng, who tried to force him to agree to a 'One Country, Two Parties' arrangement in order to resist the coming Japanese invasion. Chiang agreed and was released. He then went back on his word, which resulted in great loss of life among the Communist forces. Yang was murdered and Zhang is still a prisoner on Taiwan.]

I have in mind to write something about being In Search of China In Search of the Capitalist Road. Westerners so like to flatter themselves that it is their fine example that

China is emulating, that the benighted heathen have finally found the road to Damascus and salvation. A Swedish punker with yellow and purple hair explained to me what a salutary effect he was having on Chinese dressing habits. When I appeared unconvinced, he spent the next hour trying to explain his Garfield-the-Cat T-shirt to the poor girl behind the long-distance phone counter. The Western media have been just as ridiculous in their treatment. Remember *Time* magazine gloating over the population campaign, claiming that the Communists were caving in to tradition by putting up posters showing male children? And the outrage this caused among Tunisian feminists? Well, it was all based on a hasty, superficial squint: easily 90 per cent of the posters actually show *daughters*, and there are even special posters put up to promote the idea that having daughters is just as good or better than having sons.

The same kind of gloating over economic reforms. I've been to several political study meetings, and read a lot of *Renmin Ribao* on the subject, and I'm convinced of the following: 1) That *gai-ge* [reform] is simply an attempt to introduce piece-work and destroy job security, identical to the measures Stalin introduced during the industrialization of the Thirties; 2) The main point of gai-ge is to increase productivity at no cost in investment capital; 3) Precisely because of this, it cannot be beneficial to the Chinese, or even in the interests of the so-called 'four modernizations'. China's labour productivity is indeed among the lowest in the world, not because the people don't work hard enough, but because labour is so plentiful and capital is so scarce it is a positive waste to make anything really labour-efficient. But the easier it is for the authorities to throw labour at a problem, to avoid replacing men with machines, to terrorize the workers and the unions, the worse it will be for the actual rather than the verbal modernization of industry, agriculture, transport, communication – even defence. 4) The only possible solution lies in independent unions, the right to strike, and higher wages, even at the expense of the food producers, and the realliance with the only possible source of real productive capital and useful technology – Russia. 5) The strengthening of the peasants against the workers, the strengthening of the rural areas against the cities, and the distribution of land and goodies to male heads of households all act against this. You may think that some of this resembles Hinton's nostalgic Maoism. Nothing of the sort. Wait till I get the figures together to prove it. I don't want to write some vapid thing about what I saw in China, as if that was of any importance. I think the main point I want to make is that gai-ge is still another tiresome plot on the part of the bureaucracy to blame the working people. And I think I should start out by saying that the West remains China's worst and falsest hope.

One of the reasons for the inexpressible feeling of relief I have in putting down my bags, even in a place like Peking, is that I feel no barrier, linguistic, cultural or bureaucratic, can be as big an obstacle to learning more – and getting any further than the 'hello, where you from, do you have any sons?' dialogue I have to do a million times a week, i.e. getting some kind of stable long-term relationships that permit more profound discussions – than this bullshit of being constantly on the road. It is impossible to get much more even out of the best, most intelligent, sensitive, articulate people you meet than a name and a glimpse of them disappearing into that black hole on the horizon where the rails meet.

Among the immoral and sloppy habits one picks up on the road is the assumption that one's own personal experience is the only thing worth making sense of, and that one is a statistically significant and representative sample. Being on the road is not only morally bad, because you develop a touristy, 'holiday romance' attitude toward relationships, exchanging addresses quite cynically knowing they will not be used, and eventually sleeping with people you really have very little to say to, and saying *n'importe quoi*, secure in the knowledge that you don't have to stay and listen to the response. It is also linguistically bad, because you lose the ability to discuss any but the most petty and pragmatic travel problems, which are the only things you have in common with the other roadies you encounter. Finally, it is bad for your powers of observation, because in the numbness induced by perpetual newness you totally let slip the slow and subtle variations over a period of time.

On this my third visit to Peking I am finally noticing things like which days are market days, on which days the parks are packed, what a difference the seasons make in the street life, and what kinds of peasants are camped along the garbage-strewn boulevard outside the hotel, the level of the canal, the presence of swimmers and fishermen, and so on. To let slip those things for the sake of 'going the distance' is obtuse and immoral and stupefying, and I don't want any more of it.

Peking, as Louise would say, is really frisky. Full of colour: sweaty workers stinking of garlic eaten whole and raw, wearing pink tank tops, women in glittery and practically transparent dresses, all dressed rather the way I do, without any regard for things like clashing and mirrors, but with a vague eye to the utterly inimitable. People slither underneath the rope segregating the men's part of the swimming pool from the women's without any compunction, and no one ever blows the whistle.

Maybe part of the lovable loucheness comes from the quarter of town I'm in. This bit is jam-packed with peasants fresh from the provinces, drifting in without work or residence permits. They camp by the road where I once did, weaving baskets, knitting jar-insulators that turn fruit jars into tea glasses, and filling out appeals to the housing authority from a tattered model copy making the rounds. They sell baby ducks to naked children, and wrap tiny snakes, caught in the muck of the canal when the water level went down, around their fingers. The blokes who work in the hotel studiously avoid them, though some of them are slightly louche themselves. One guy was sent here when his mother, a former opera star, heard him singing. Before Liberation, opera stars had a very low social status, for sexual and other reasons, and she still thought an honourable career as a hotel toilet cleaner would be better. He still does a great Zhuge Liang, with the besieger hesitating on the threshold of an empty city, his armies behind him. He performs from the hotel roof and today he read articles from *Renmin Ribao* in all the dialects of the regions mentioned in the stories. He's a year younger than me.

I agree that none of the drawings I have done here is as interesting as what I was trying in Hungary; that is because I cannot get beyond the sketch stage, being constantly overwhelmed by newness, and getting all my best ideas buried under newer ideas. When I first set foot here in January, with a few of the things I had tried to do with frozen water colours on the train, and sketches done with heating coal, I realized I would need a quantum leap in technique to be able to render any of the sacred architecture here. And to get your technique past the the sketch-exercise point you have to do a lot of sketching and exercising, none of which comes easy on the road, or anywhere stationary in China either, because of the crowds. One day I tried sketching while squatting in the public toilet with 20 other toilet-goers, all brilliant conversationalists; I thought maybe they would be too distracted to stare, and, anyway, fumbling with paper is part of the ceremony. But it's too awkward a position, and I was a little afraid someone might take offence, so I ended up just producing ass-wipes. I must have looked like some kind of scapulimancer, with paper oracle bones.

All of which is yet another reason why I am really pleased to be heading this letter with the same city as the last one, which I haven't done since Budapest. Maybe now I will shut up a little, write short letters, stop walking backwards on my hands and trying to travel-write all the time. And that is all I have to say, which is considerably more than 'any mother' is entitled to, even if occasionally less than you deserve.

13 July 1984
Dear Old Man and all the others,

Naturally, I have already developed a terrible crush on one of my women students, an elegant lady over 60 who is in charge of nuclear medicine and has put herself in charge of fattening me up. She even has a technician write down how many *liang* of rice or steamed bread I order in the cafeteria, and she is constantly bringing me *suan-nai* [a kind of yogurt], and dimsum instead of flowers. Ay, married women, they have no sense of romance!

But it is wonderful, not just to be a regular at a gig, but to have become a 'regular' at the public toilet near the bus stop. China has an extraordinary atmosphere of excretory egalitarianism, and a visit to a public toilet, which I deliberately choose every morning over the hotel toilets, which have partitions, is a great *bain de foule*, rather reminiscent of that scene in Bunuel's *Fantôme de la Liberté*, where all the neighbours sit around on toilets gaily conversing, and some horrid little brat complains he is hungry and is hustled off to a private locked cubicle to be fed. Public toilets here have very regular clients and the atmosphere crackles with conversation as well as flatulence; they would probably regard partitions between the slots as sure evidence of anti-social tendencies. There is a bloke in 'my' toilet who presides, as it were, from a kind of director's chair set over one of the slots, and with one of the canvas straps removed to permit evacuation. He's in there for hours every morning, smoking, reading the newspaper, and making sure no one gets too excited over the discussion that's going on.

Next week the Institute closes for summer vacation, and I'm off with my class to the far eastern end of the Great Wall, where it goes down to the sea. Doctors, and even scientists generally, I have noticed, tend to have a rather abysmal sense of history; I spent a whole lunch explaining that the bits of wall recently discovered in Manchuria could not possibly be part of the Great Wall, since Manchuria became part of China two thousand years after the Wall was built, precisely to keep out Manchus. And indeed Manchuria became part of China, or, rather, China became part of Manchuria because the great pass we are going to go swimming at was purposely opened to the enemy by a general of the tottering Mings, so that they could crush a peasant revolt. So I now have them at least half convinced that where the wall meets the sea really is the eastern end of it, and that it does not somehow travel under the Yellow Sea and re-emerge in Manchuria along the Korean border. I suppose it was all very, very long ago for most of them, and also huge quantities of history have been wiped out by political study, and sometimes actual politics. They have all spent the last ten years doing farm work in Tibet, or worse. When I try to drill the past continuous, I forget all about the grammatical structure of what they are saying, the content is so riveting. And they all make about half of my obscene wages.

The housing question is not quite solved. I have to obey Peking's Jim Crow laws and live in foreigners' housing, which right now means sharing hotel space with French hippies and whatnot, most of whom view China as a pretty stamp on their passports. I am tempted to join the peasants camped out along the boulevard, particularly now that the level of water in the canal is high enough to swim in again. They are streaming in from Shanxi with their exotic musical instruments, collections of carefully raised medicinal snakes and scorpions, and improvised parodies of classical opera.

It is a positive riot to run the gauntlet of these folks when returning home from work. They all know I speak Chinese, and are anxious to talk, though not particularly keen on listening. How pathetic we all are when we talk, obsessed with being understood, and so indifferent to understanding we are usually oblivious to the response we get. Of course, we big noses are by far the worst offenders: 'Tell me all about yourself, what do you think of me?'

We all measure this vast place by the length of our noses. *Time* magazine gloats on and on, week after week, about how soon *Renmin Ribao* will be as slick in its stupefying drivel as *Time* itself, and foreigners lecture me about how their presence is producing a revolution in China that will dwarf all hitherto known social convulsions in China's history. Last night this young punk with purple dyed hair and a Garfield-the-Cat T-shirt spent an hour trying to convince me that her haircut was a matter of historical significance almost as great as the coming of the Jesuit missionaries, at least for the women who saw her on the street. When I remained unconvinced she tried to explain to the reception clerk who Garfield the Cat was, in very approximate English, of which nothing was understood.* If I were to be asked what I admired most in Marco Polo, I think I would have to respond, paradoxically, his sense of proportion.

My next vacation is January sometime, when I will probably return to Europe to try to land a job in the Arab world (I'm supposed to be doing Arabic, remember?). Otherwise I would like to go back to Xinjiang, or maybe Yunnan. I have uncovered three more Arabic manuscripts from the 15th century – another dala'il, a book of science called *Source of Knowledge*, and a part of a Quran – which show that the area was more or less in constant contact with the Peninsula, despite the Buddhism of the Uighurs and the battle of Taras.

Well, Dr Zhang has just breezed in, with a new haircut that would look vaguely secretarial and stupid on anyone else, but somehow makes her look like a tinselled watermelon, gracefully ridiculous. She is brandishing a *suan-nai* and what looks like a bagel. I must run.

27 July 1984
Dear Dorothy and Burt,

Well . . . actually . . . I've just been on vacation, I'm ashamed to say. Already. The whole Institute got a week off in healthy respect for the heat of the Gobi, and I accompanied them to Beidaihe, where Peking's dachas by the sea all are, and to Qinhuangdao, from whence the Qin emperor sent his fleets, and to Shanhaiguan, where the Great Wall goes down into the sea. Having watched Chinese tourism, quite a new and interesting phenomenon, from without for five months, I suddenly find myself within it.

---

* Inconsistency in anecdote discussed in a later letter.

I had my picture taken literally hundreds of times blocking various heart-throbbing vistas in the Institute's holiday uniform of sombrero, swimsuit, and white lab coat, with the leg of a dismembered crab in one hand, and pincer of a disgruntled doctor's son in the other. I got up at ungodly hours to see inhuman, and often invisible, natural wonders, thankfully surrounded by thousands of other Chinese with the same idea. The sun, supposedly rising from the sea at Qinhuangdao, or steam rising from the mountains behind the Great Wall at Shanhaiguan, turned out to look more like clouds rising from the sea, and the sun broiling the already well-done mountain sides. But the company was good-natured and slightly self-mocking, and the whole thing was more fun than being in some parody of a Ming opera, *The Doctors*, plus maybe a little of *Monsieur Hulot's Holiday*.

Continuing my efforts to cap your impatient eruption of questions: yes, I think I will get a chance to work on Arabic. Like I said, I've got a load of manuscripts bought in Kashgar, and my teaching schedule is quite bearable. I teach three and a half hours a day, five days a week, and I hang around my office in the morning, mostly typing letters like this and reading, but also making myself available to correct abstracts and what-not. That is purely voluntary, because I happen to like it here, where there is far more going on than at the Foreigners' Zoo where I'm living. I have to live at the same old grotty hotel, packed with unwashed and completely amoral travellers, some of whom are Jesus freaks and others long-haired 'rebels'. Coming to work is a bloody breath of fresh air.

I wish I could live at the Institute. In fact, I only eat there. I think I rhapsodized over the iron regularity of my bowels in my last letter. One of the reasons why you shouldn't allow yourself to get Jewish maternal over me, Dorothy, is that the competition is too stiff. Under the guidance of 30 Jewish mothers masquerading as Chinese nutritionists, I am putting on large quantities of meat. I am also forbidden to eat at my favourite purveyors of *jiao-zi* [meat dumplings] and *zhu ti-er* [red-cooked pig's feet], who apparently also purvey hepatitis quite regularly.

My contract is purely verbal. This is not surprising, so is everyone else's. Written contracts are not a big thing here, perhaps even less so than in the Arab world with its omnipotent three witnesses. What is really important is 'good vibes', and for the moment mine are great. I get about 200 kuai [yuan] a month, plus all living expenses. The cash is of course in unconvertible funny money. I've opened a bank account for it all; maybe I'll use it for another expedition to Kashgar, or try to get to Tibet. Clothes are unnecessary, but could you arrange to get my grammar bibles – so imprudently shipped to you from Canton in February – sent back? English books are hard to get here because the best are all photographed and printed in facsimile in defiance of international copyright laws, and therefore do not exist for potential buyers with big noses. And even the best are not very good. Not good enough for my minions, anyway.

They are a motley crew indeed, insofar as language level is concerned. I have managed, through ruthless triage, to form them into roughly homogeneous sections, but the women are all far better at writing than the men, who are all far better at speaking than the women. All speak far better than they understand, rather like me in that respect, but all read far better than anything else. With one exception, a practically deaf-mute old woman, who writes impeccable prose, they are all quite useless at written composition, although they know far more ten-syllable words than I ever will. I have abandoned the reading and writing skills to their own initiative and their Chinese instructors, and have centred my course entirely on the spoken language, especially oral composition. This is also a great leveller, since, although the groups are not very homogeneous in any other skill, no one is really very good at putting together a sentence that says what they really mean.

I write all my own material for the moment, although I've found a good supplementary situational dialogue text, which guides me. They all seem to feel learning language is rather like going to medical school: you go around memorizing lists of words the same way you memorize lists of pharmaceuticals

and symptoms. I have managed to displace their memorization from words to phrases, which at least allows them to
speak intelligibly, rather than in the manner of someone
looking up every word in a dictionary. I wonder how to
break the news to them that the whole approach is
dreadfully wrong, that it is not so much a question of getting
outside information in, but of getting what is inside out, and
all the substitution drills and whatnot we've been doing
merely give them phrases that are as unconnected with the
nexus of language as the stuff they've been looking up in the
dictionary, merely enlarging the digression. They are all
very pleased with their progress; it is going to be a bitter
blow when they see how helpless they are in the face of life
instead of structural prompts. I tutor one of my students in
French; the authorities told him to learn English because he
is going to Montreal next year! He is in big trouble; his
English is not the greatest, and what little French I can
inoculate him with is in a hopelessly Parisian accent and
chiefly serves to confuse him in English class.

I had a horrid dream and a brush with reality recently. I
dreamed I was giving a class and these three foreign experts,
also teachers, I think, wandered in. For some reason I
thought my doctors should put on a special show. So I began
to put all kinds of pressure on them to perform. They oppose
being pushed around on principle, being twice as old as I
am, and twice as educated, not to mention twice as pushy, so
they broke out in a chorus of Chinese. I tried my usual
'What's this, Chinese?' grimace to no avail. So at last I
announced as a joke that the next good doctor with so much
as a syllable of the flower tongue on his lips, I would
personally *hong chu qu* (throw out). Naturally, someone
piped up, and I threw him out, hardly pausing to think
whether my threat had been a joke disguised as a threat, or a
threat disguised as a joke. Suddenly we were in one of the
Saturday struggle meetings they have here, and the three
foreign experts were criticizing my class. 'It was painful to
see you do it: the idea of discipline crossed your mind like a
gimmick, another aspect of make believe, and suddenly it

was far more real than what you were trying to teach, much more real than language, it was you putting on your show . . .' They were rather snotty and nasty in the manner of Fran and the others in my teacher-teaching class, but what they said was so true, I still cringe to think of it.

A few days later, I was putting the doctors through their paces, having them give me directions for getting from various remote parts of the building to others, and one of them was rather slow in coughing up directions from the Cellular Genetics Lab to the men's room. I began to twitch nervously in order to spur him on. I had the class so convinced that I really needed to piss that two of the students leaped up to show me the way, both women, of course.

There, I meant to write a rather newsy sort of thing, with lots of news about myself, rather than mere thoughts about myself, but I seem to have gone back to my lively old ways, under provocation, but still.

20 August 1984

I was just lapsing into the semi-catatonic state in which I usually attempt serious writing, as a substitute for serious thinking, when your latest outrage arrived. But I have also decided to get serious about my students' wanton use of prepositions, and I am designing some clothes to have made by the tailors in the free market of Guan Yuan, right across from Jiang Qing's old residence (now a kind of cut-rate kiddieland for workers). So it will have to wait for next weekend before I can take a good whack at your cretinous Gandhi-oid historical moralism on the peasant question, and your positively enraging remarks on the Russian question, and, last but not least, some very fundamental philosophical errors, which, since I am reading lots of philosophy, I noticed.

First, first. You want an explanation of gai-ge. It was a profound social change in the countryside, like it or not. The purge going on at the same time had nothing to do with it. Since then, by force of having nothing else to talk about during Saturday afternoon study sessions, and also because of certain frightening social forces dragging China inexorably towards the US, it has acquired a very programmatic character. A definition is therefore a bit more useful than a translation. In the cities, the gai-ge seems a relatively harmless species of trying to increase production by incentives for the petty bourgeoisie, piece-work for the working class, vast increases in the power of middle management, enormous opportunities for small traders, and, though of course no one says this, the creation of yet another level of management managers, to serve as yet another social base for the bureaucracy.

In the countryside, gai-ge is the death-knell of your fortunately non-existent homogeneously poor silent majority. It is a ruthless kind of Bukharinism, a get-rich policy that can only mean merciless stratification of the peasantry, and searing polarization of the whole countryside. Today another article appeared on the consumption of colour TV sets and refrigerators in the Beijing countryside. If it is rocketing near Beijing, it is already astronomical in Guangdong, the southestern province nearest Hong Kong.

Naturally, someone pays for all this. Not just the poor peasants, although you can bet they pay through the nose. Workers pay higher prices for handicrafts, for vegetables, for all the stuff that passes through the hands of the state, since the amount of goods the state now gets is of course considerably smaller. Even basic goods whose price has been fixed since liberation, that are bought with ration tickets – beans, rice and wheat – become dearer because scarcer. (The most ridiculous article appeared the other day purporting to discuss the question of protein in the Chinese diet. The conclusion was that, you see, the state subsidy on beans was too high, and if it were removed, bean curd makers would find it far more profitable to make bean curd, and consumers would find it far more economical to eat it. The one flaw in this, of course, is that removing the subsidy increases the price of raw beans by 10 per cent, rather than decreasing it, so this reform would have the opposite effect.

In passing, the article also remarks that 'another' reason for the high price of beans is massive export to Western countries in order to earn precious hard currency for the tourist hotels and Toyotas to be bought with.)

The longer the queues get, the more people are forced – forced, not invited – to go to the free market and pay higher prices. Above all, workers feel a terrible housing crunch that peasants do not, and this can only get worse as building materials, land, and whole building enterprises pass into commune, co-operative and private ownership, and the state spends less and less money on the cities. For the moment, though, things are very cool, there is plenty of money in some people's hands, and nothing to spend it on, so increased diversity is more important than increased prices. But when the markets begin to fill up with peasant produce that the cities cannot afford, watch out. People are already incredulous at the fact that their salaries are always going up and their savings always going down.

My students are all really great fun; yeah, they're a little older, but most of my friends are too, remember, and also Chinese women in particular seem to age very slowly. In some ways they are terribly adolescent until they get married, and then some, and they get married late. Most of them are happily married, and swaggering, and quite thoroughly domestic. None of them ever has anything but housework to report on Monday past tense drills; none seems to sleep later than six o'clock; all are inexhaustible sources of good recipes I have no means of trying out, thanks to my housing situation. But most of all, they are completely free from any trace of jadedness, or cynicism, or lack of enthusiasm. They all love work, unpretentiously and thoroughly. I wish I could learn from them.

We do all kinds of research here, in answer to your question. But traditional Chinese medicine has purely clinical uses, anaesthesia and so on, since its theoretical basis has long since been proved false. Have you ever considered how much the picture of Victorian medicine before germ theory resembles the much romanticized but equally deadly traditional Chinese medicine? It too has outrageous physical explanations (hepatitis, for example, is supposedly caused by 'liver essence' mounting to eye level, and the theory of 'five elements' much resembles 'animal magnetism'). Chinese traditional medicine not only had no germ theory, its knowledge of anatomy was far more rudimentary than that of Victorian body-snatchers. Thus kidneys are reproductive organs, spleens are digestive, and arteries, veins, and even nerves are practically unknown, but imaginary ducts for *qi* – an untranslatable term from Chinese medicine and Taoist philosophy meaning something like 'inimitable life force' or 'indescribable body essence' – are omnipresent. You can imagine how they got in the way of acupunture needles! No wonder Dr Sun Yatsen had it banned. But everyone, or almost everyone, in my class uses traditional medicine for incurable things like colds, since they are great believers in the importance of placebos, even for doctors.

That does not leave much basis for experimentation, besides which, the whole holistic idea is not readily adaptable to research on tissue cultures and mice. So they mostly do Western-style research, on a tight budget. But I think I mentioned that one of my students had adapted traditional Chinese pharmacology to Apple computer software, and another is working with ultrasound. Also, they do a lot of clinical work. One of my students specializes in sucking all the bone marrow from patients and then giving them massive doses of radiation and drugs that would normally shrivel up the marrow, which is then put back in. Another is concerned with growing large quantities of cancer in 'naked' mice, that is, immune-deficient ones, and testing various kinds of pickles for their ability to decompose into nitrates and nitrites, and recompose into nitrosamines. Another is studying the structure of cell membranes. He focuses a laser through a microscope and generates a tiny area of fluorescence using a photofluorescent drug. Then he increases the power until the membrane is destroyed and times how long it takes for the cell to repair the cell wall. By doing this he gets a very good idea of how long which cells take to repair the cell damage caused by oncogens.

Last Friday we discussed genetics and Lysenko, and half the class didn't know Lysenko was a quack, and the other half still thought Mendel's Law was reactionary. That I can do without, but not the extraordinary pleasure they seem to draw from a discussion of Ming novels, or a good meal, or just a good game of chess on a Saturday (Chinese chess, a real head-buster I am just getting addicted to). They are hungry and enthusiastic just the way I always am in the Third World, except they actually live here.

I spent the whole weekend making a tape of various bizarre accents for my students. Karen, the daughter of a Scottish miner, stars with her delicious brogue, but I also have a Liverpudlian, an Australian, and a New Zealander. One of the things I like to do on Sunday mornings is read *Journey to the West* over coffee and mooncakes [pastries filled with sweetened bean paste]. I think I told you about it, the story of the Monkey and the Pig and the Tang priest Xuanzhuang on their journey through the Flaming Mountains to India to fetch the sutras. It is like three solid volumes of *Alice in Wonderland*, complete with the most outrageous poetry and scatology. My favourite bit is when they turn themselves into Taoist immortals in order to devour a peach banquet, and then piss in the urns meant to receive the elixir of life. When the faithful quaff the chalices, one of them wipes his chin and says, 'Well, it's a bit off, innit? Like pig piss, really, innit?', whereupon he is squelched. Karen's favourite bit is when they cross over a river into Womanland, where no men have ever been, and drink some of the river, only to discover that the good priest has become pregnant as a result. The next three chapters have to do with the search for some way to induce an abortion.

Anyway, each to his own domesticity. I have to run along. Sunday mornings, you know, are best for housework.

14 September 1984
Dear Old Man,

No, I don't think I can make it to Hong Kong. The problem is that October 1st is National Day, the 35th since the founding of the PRC. And it's gonna be a really big wing ding, huge, in fact, and for some reason the government isn't big on letting people into Peking for it. It is virtually impossible for Chinese to travel here during the weekend, and the people in Hong Kong have stopped giving out visas. No train tickets in or out of Beijing are being sold, and I'm afraid if I left it would really be a problem to get back.

What's more, Tibet has been opened to foreign travellers for the first time in several thousand years. No kidding. On Sept 1 the government announced it was granting individual travel permits to Lhasa to practically anyone. It will be very easy to get one, and I am definitely going as soon as I have time. Even if I stay here for another year. Remember my fixation on Tibet when I was about 14? Strange, isn't it, I sometimes feel as if I'm living the dreams of adolescence, only backwards. Anyway, I plan to make a major expedition out of it, since I will probably be able to overland it. I am trying to learn some Tibetan, and saving my money. RMB [*renminbi*, 'people's money'] aren't worth much outside China, but inside a little goes a very long way, as long as you stay away from airports and tourist hotels.

Working in a hospital even here has little of the cameraderie I always got a kick out of in the factory: too competitive and gossipy, and there are moments when it is pretty grim. But I don't like living in the hotel very much, so I often stay in my office very late, and I've even spent the night a few times. I like walking around the wards, talking to the patients and doctors on duty, and I sometimes help out with things like emptying bedpans and mopping up blood. It's a very small hospital and the wards are everywhere. The terminal ward is a particularly pleasant place, with a little rock garden and pools, and metal fences in the shape of flying cranes, and a larger-than-life statue of two cranes snogging in a pool. (The crane is a symbol of longevity.)

Last week a bloke next to me began vomiting up whole litres of blood, obviously in the last stages of his liver cancer. They pumped a few litres back into him, but on Wednesday he died, to everyone's relief. Dr Yong, one of my students who does night duty in this ward, shook his head and said it was like working in the pig slaughterhouse in Shaanxi, where he sat out the Cult Revolt. There is a lot of liver cancer around these days; I think the Institute is doing a special series of experiments. Liver cancer, according to one of my specialist students, would kill other types of cancer, if we could just figure out how to give it to them: it is apparently one of the most malignant kinds.

What the patients lack in extroversion, they make up for in a kind of quiet warmth. There is a patient who plays erhu. It is used for Chinese opera, the latest of my painfully acquired tastes. He will probably be alive for only a few more months, so I have incentive to learn. Everybody is terribly good to me here, even when I've given a perfectly awful class, which occasionally does happen, and a really good one always makes me feel a star. And the food is bloody good. Last night Dr Zhang took me out to a Korean joint on the west side where they specialize in cold noodles and dog meat, with cut apple slices and a dollop of 'red death' laid on with an ice-cream scoop.

I'm back to painting and drawing again. I found some great graph paper, just the right texture, with the most interesting chromatic markings on it, in the lymphoscintillography department. I'm working on a collage of live human skulls in the shape of a party conference, done with over- and under-developed snapshots from the gamma camera. My students complain that I tend to the morbid in my listening comprehension tests, but I think my morale is quite high. I'm also writing a fair amount, considering how little time I have. The amount of material I've written for the course already amounts to 200 or 300 typewritten pages (double-spaced, though).

All of which I laid aside for about two weeks when Karen, a lass from Scotland, was around. She suddenly made it far more pressing to spend Sunday afternoons rolling jiao-zi into perfect moon shapes, and thinking up bits of chinoiserie to impress. She had just finished a two-year teaching stint at a borstal in Hong Kong, and she was bicycling back to Scotland via China, Russia, and eastern and western Europe – she was taking the Transsib because of no bicycling visas for Siberia – and was about the only young person I've run into here who has a little of my enthusiasm, which I'm dying to share. The Chinese, brimming with enthusiasm on other subjects, cannot quite share my enthusiasm for the soil under their feet; they keep confusing it with absurd patriotism and horrid politics.

Well, here I go. It is autumn, Peking's golden season, and I'm off to the free market to buy a *jing-hu* [a small stringed instrument] for the opera session tonight. Then I have to help my buddy Lida with his housework (everybody's home gets inspected for National Day, for God's sake). Tonight I'm nipping over to the Xinjiang for a Uighur meal of raw mutton and raisins. Yum. And lest I neglect the jiao-zi part of your person, and think you live by high energy physics alone:

Eggs jiao-zi. 1) Take 2 or 3 eggs, break them and stir with a fork or chopstick until you get a homogenous goo, light yellow. 2) Take half a pound of chopped meat, add some oyster and hot sauces, garlic, salt, wine, and so on, then mix. 3) Mince scallions and ginger and add them too. 4) Get a really big spoon and a really small one. Coat the big one with oil and put it right on the fire. 5) When it is really hot, pour a little spoonful of egg goo on it and roll around to make a disk. 6) When set, put a little spoonful of meat in the middle and fold the egg over it with chopsticks to make a crescent shape. 7) Cook 4-5 minutes more like an omelette, but on a low fire.

Ants Climbing a Tree. 1) Get some Chinese bean vermicelli. Cut it into 'trees' about 3-4 cm long. Fry them crisp in oil. 2) Chop some pork very fine and fry in oil with onion, ginger and garlic; then take off the fire and add soy sauce, sugar, salt, millet wine and MSG and mix. 3) try to get the vermicelli to stand on end (I usually stick them in a bit of steamed bread), and then pour the ant-sized pork particles on them.

2 *October 1984*

Dear Dorothy and Burt,

The situation here is much as it was back in Tunis. No one is allowed to grow up until they marry, and I, as with Munira in Tunis, often find myself made the pretext of somebody's adolescent rebellion. It means absolutely nothing, of course, but then a lot of what we do doesn't mean a whole lot more. Is it more noble to be wanted for your mind than your body? Suppose what is wanted is a western education that will earn lots of money, or a conversation piece for trendy dinner parties? I'd rather have a good meaty body, actually, but the problem doesn't stop there. Do I want to be wanted for something that really attracts the person in question, for whatever low and base reasons, or would I prefer something that is put on public display for the edification of friends? Moot point, you would say, since I have neither. What about being wanted for your big nose? For the violent reaction your big nose provokes? That is the worst of all worlds. And that is what is going on here, I know.

The other day I was walking down Xidan past one of those horrible dances the government now organizes in an attempt to marry off singles, when I noticed something rather like prostitutes walking around in front of the dance hall in red regalia and gory lipstick, denim corsets and so much make-up their beauty was kind of a tasteless stew, awash in sauce. All quite young, too young to get tickets through their work units who would give tickets to the over-30s, all waiting, rather obviously, for an old rich stag. Several lit up when they saw me; maybe I didn't have a ticket, but I was an enticing bit of jailbait.

Sure enough, the other day the technician Ah Ping came in practically drooling with excitement about a classmate of his sentenced to two years for sleeping with a foreign student. And a woman was just fired from the Cancer Research Institute, where she cleaned monkey cages, because, apparently, it was discovered that she was expelled from Peking Medical College some ten years ago for sleeping with a foreigner. Dr Jin, one of my students, tells me about another friend of hers who now lives in Tibet and has married a Tibetan, because she had had a child by a foreigner and could not find work in Peking.

So, yes, I am wary when one of my students, a woman so terribly self-conscious, particularly where men are concerned, that she barely opens her mouth in the presence of others, suddenly decides to confide in me. When I was discussing the 'social problem' of the unmarried and over 30 with her, she remarked a little breathily that many women were disappointed in love once, and decided never to fall in love again, lest they forget. She asked me what I thought. I, ever the mush-head, felt pretty awful about doing it, but replied that I thought it was pretty self-indulgent and childish. I didn't mean to scare her away, I think it right that she confide in someone, but I don't subscribe to the view in which mutual self-destruction is somehow the highest proof of love, or even basic sympathy.

Also, although Chinese women are everything I like, ferociously intelligent, serious, articulate, utterly devoid of world-weariness and cynicism, and burning with curiosity, and although I still think oriental women are the most beautiful on earth, before marriage most of them are children. Even the over-30s. Zhang Lin, who will be 33 next year, imagines that since I am permitted to, I must like disco, and make-up, and mushy movies. How to explain that it also permits me to dislike them? She will think I am saying that her parents, who are always wrong, are right after all, and of course that isn't what I mean at all.

Lida, my boss's son, is getting married as soon as he and she can find an apartment (meaning within the next three years), and I have finally managed to impress on him, but not on her, the importance of having some good ferocious fights before it's too late. I think she cannot imagine that living with someone involves more than resolving parental agreement and the housing crisis. Last night I met Lida and his fiancée by chance wandering around Tiananmen. He was trying to persuade her of what I said about fighting, and of course she was agreeing with every word.

These are not progressive times for China. We are, as everyone knows, in the middle of a severe labour surplus, which elsewhere is known as unemployment, and of course, labour surplus, thy name is woman. The papers have been discussing a recent proposal by all the women leaders of the Beijing Municipal Labour Federation that women be given *three years'* maternity leave at 75 per cent pay. They have also been lionizing women in the provinces who give up jobs to look after their children (and sometimes explicitly give their jobs to their husbands). The pet writer of the month, who is always the centrefold in *China Daily*, was recently a perfectly cretinous specimen of Françoise Sagan turned Total Woman: she specialized in books about highly educated women with happy professionless marriages.

It is the maternity leave proposal that is by far the most dangerous. As things now stand, women get six months maternity leave, provided they take the one-child pledge at the hospital, with full pay. Men rarely get any paternity leave. Nurseries do not take children less than one year old, so *ayis*, or nannies, are doing a roaring trade. Which of course privileges educated women and condemns ordinary working women, since ayis are too expensive even for many engineers, and far too expensive for doctors. But even six months is too long for many women, who find child-rearing horribly dull, especially with the kid's grandmother breathing down their necks, so many deliberately refuse the one-child pledge (a formality anyway, since two are illegal), and are forced to report for work in two weeks. You can imagine what the three-year maternity leave will do to this. I have foisted as many discussions on my class as I dare on this subject; not one so much as agrees with paternity leave, much less communal child-rearing – that went out with the Cult Revolt. But some of the young mothers agree that 75 per cent pay is too low for the women, and, as one of the few female leaders in the municipal government has pointed out, still too high for the state to afford.

Another thing I did recently was prepare a review of a syrupy play called *Romantic Duet* for listening comprehension. The wretched plot was about a shopgirl and a coal miner. The shopgirl loses her original fiancé, whom we never meet, because she is a humble, unpretentious shopgirl. Then she wins the love of the coal miner. But when she tells the poor bloke that her fiancé kissed her, he flees in embarrassment cleverly disguised as disgust. Dr Zhang pointed out to me that the coal miner was jealous, not so much of the fiancé as of the greater 'sexual' experience of the girl, and he disguised it as traditional morality. The fiancé, Dr Zhang says, must have been an ambitious intellectual. Normally, intellectuals prefer humble shopgirls; they are professionally servile and guaranteed uneducated. *Time* recently reported that seven out of ten illiterates in China are women, and the universities admit that only 24 per cent of students are female, figures that would be illegal in the US. And even this figure is going down. The reason is simple enough. There is no percentage in educating women as far as country people are concerned, and for city people, education is a terrible blot that can make it impossible to marry.

Last night the bureaucracy spent 80 million RMB; it was their 35th birthday party. That's about 20 million dollars. This seems unbelievably high, but it was what I was told. Several doctors at our Institute, including party members, wrote letters of protest at the extravagance to the Central Committee. Today people are sweeping the results off the streets and washing them down the sewers. I've never seen quite such a combination of money, preparations, and lack of enthusiasm.

First of all, the whole city was cordoned off, rather as if we were going to be attacked. Any place within two miles of Tiananmen Square was so packed with cops no one could go more than a block from his home without a special permit. This was to prevent people from attending the parade, which was reserved for bigwigs.

And it worked. I managed to escape the guard posted at the hotel and to slip through the barricades and finally reach the centre of town after seven hours. It was a really creepy sight, rows and rows of tanks and heavy cannons and missiles rumbling through streets practically deserted except for Chang An Dajie, the main drag. For bureaucrats only. I stopped to buy an egg from a bloke about a block away from the big shindig, and asked if he saw the parade. 'What?' The, you know, the *renao*, the commotion. 'Oh, yes, I watched on TV . . . for a while.' My sentiments exactly.

And then the fireworks. Even the babies were bored after the first hour, and hardly anyone stayed up to watched the end. Ugh. All that for only twice the price of a decent mass transit system, or a couple of dozen hospitals, or maybe a couple thousand housing units, just to mention some of the non-productive things you could spend it on. Such a deal.

5 October 1984

Yesterday my class was cancelled by the administration because supposedly there was too much work to do. In fact, the union committeeman distributed movie tickets to everyone, and we all shuffled down to see the latest bit of mush out of Shanghai. It was a truly dreadful thing, with all kinds of perfectly outrageous coincidences conspiring to inflame love between an imbecilic street tough and an even more imbecilic flapper, all revolving around stamp collecting. The stamps were pretty and very interesting, and made me understand a little better the national passion for stamps that everyone seems swept up in (rather like baseball or cricket fever). But I had to pay the price of putting up with the movie's heroine, who resembled so exactly the two-dimensional Chinese women of my age (with two expressions exactly: pout at the evils of society, and embarrassed giggle at the recognition of her invisible sterling qualities) that I kept getting shivers down my spine. Zhang Lin, who sat next to me, apparently thought I was touched by the film. I told her I preferred the cartoon, *Police Sargent Black Cat*. Anyway, it will be good grist for the rabid reviews that are rapidly becoming one of the favourite features of my class.

The 'reform' progresses with two steps back for every step sideways. In particular, the cadres are having trouble figuring out whether they are actually supposed to be setting up all these new co-operatives and individual enterprises, the way they usually do when there is a 'mass' campaign on, or only supposed to be cheerleaders for other people to do so. This is a puzzle because the idea of cheerleading is not ingrained in bureaucrats; they are used to cheerleading with a pistol. The result is that today the front page drools over a 'collective' shipping company in Chongqing set up by a member of the political committee of the highest legislative body in the country, the Standing Committee of the People's Consultative Conference, while the editorial page sternly warns: Cadres Must Not Join Businesses. Chaos.

I am busy, busy, busy these days, writing material for my next class series, trying to finish a Ming dynasty novel (my first major project in reading classical Chinese), painting, and finally trying to draft an article about my wanderings out west. In my spare time, I practise jing-hu, a kind of snake-skin bongo drum on a pole that is the main fiddle for Peking opera, and try to sing opera. It is an acquired taste I have now firmly acquired.

My visa runs out on the 20th of January, and the possibilities for renewal still do not look good. I long to make a trip to Tibet, and I will definitely do so, even if I have to go to Hong Kong and get a tourist visa for the trip. But after that, it will be time to return to Europe and prepare for definitive settlement in the Arab world; I am still hoping for Sudan. But I think I will be infinitely richer for having made this detour.

28 October 1984

Things are not going well at work. I'm about to punch a hole through all the paperwork I'm bent over, and I'm trying to have a crisis of conscience about the teaching method I have fallen into. My people really deserve better than I give them. I am only teaching them what to say, not how to say what they want, and the fact that they are pliant and Chinese makes it both easy and inexcusable to carry on this way. So in the middle of the week I found myself frantically trying to catch up with the text book I discarded some weeks ago. I seem to have dispensed with only the useful things in the book – the illusion of finiteness, progressive difficulty, and, above all, continuity – and used it only as a source of stultifying one-liners which I mutate in substitution drills that are supposed to be a substitution for thinking about grammar. The result is quite awful and confused, my casualness is simply scatterbrainedness and carelessness, and they know it.

Worse, I've begun weekly lectures on grammar and American life, which I detest. The first, about how children learn grammar and what this means for 50-year-old doctors, was a raging success, and ever since then I've been chasing after rising expectations. Now at last I have definitively begun to fail. This hurts a lot, not because I imagine myself to be a born pedagogue, I know by now I am not a born anything, but because they really are very, very good people, the kind of self-sacrificing, hard-working, modest, intelligent people I would like to be, and they deserve better.

For example. Dr Deng, who has been studying very hard, first Russian, then English, and who has been assigned to spend a year studying ultrasound diagnosis in, where else, Montreal. He is transfixed with the problem of using ultrasound to diagnose thoracic tumours. He is convinced that with practically no money and only a little basic anatomical knowledge he can bring down one of the major pillars of the high urban death rate. He was one of a generation of heroes who graduated 20 years ago, was given a list of terrible outbacks that would cause suicides among today's young doctors, and simply scrawled 'Send me where people are sickest' on it and handed it back. He describes arriving in Qinghai, the prison state just north of Tibet, on horseback, and how the commanding officer just shook his head when he asked to be sent wherever life was hardest. He laughs at himself a little, too, but not the way the loutish *ochiana* laugh at his generation today. ('Ochiana' is a great Russian word I just discovered. It means 'no belief', and is used to describe the young punks devoid of will and purpose common in post-revolutionary Russia.) He rigged up an operating theatre using shaving mirrors and bed sheets for light, and proceeded to save entire towns full of lives. He is still terribly modest and attributes most of it to the hardiness of the Tibetans. He describes how he saw people recover from meningitis after their spines were so full of pus they clogged his biggest spinal tap needles. He never drained appendixes before whipping them out, which is essential in urban patients to avoid the risk of peritonitis. The Tibetans considered him a bit of a minor *bodhisattva* [Buddhist saint]; he laughs a little and says this is probably because he could sometimes tell the exact size of a liver, and it would be confirmed when the body was ripped open for sky burial. And occasionally he would revive people who had fallen off their horses drunk during the Tet celebrations, and gone into exposure shock.

Gradually he became more and more interested in the problem of echinococcus, a liver parasite that Tibetans often get from their dogs. I can imagine him prowling around the town dogs and the distended abdomens of school children with exactly the same kind of good-natured astonishment concealing his dogged thoroughness and practicality. He figured you could off it with the most basic of antibiotics, because, unlike the rest of China, Qinghai hasn't flooded itself with antibiotics and antibiotic-resistant strains of disease. Sure enough, he gave some of his most egregious cases tetracyclines, which are prescribed as a placebo elsewhere in China, and found the parasite dead when he operated on the liver.

Since the cyst was too big to be broken down by the body in the later stages, the problem then became finding the disease early enough. So he invented a simple blood test, and tested the whole primary school, and found, to his astonishment, that a third to a half the kids were positive. He then decided that the war had to be taken to the dogs' bodies, and dreamed up a three-part clinic: a ward for children, a ward for adults, and an experimental ward for dogs and sheep. When he couldn't get the money for it, he threatened to return to Peking, and found, after nine years, that his threat was eagerly accepted. Nobody took his place.

I don't begrudge anybody their place in Peking or their trip to America. On the contrary, it is wonderful that it is Dr Deng, who doesn't particularly care for the bright lights, who is going, and not one of the ochiana. And I believe Dr Zhang is right when she shakes her head over the years she spent in nether Shanxi sewing up this and that: 'I went there thinking I was a revolutionary; I realized, though, that I am a biochemist.' Yet even being a revolutionary is a meticulous, and not simply a well-intentioned sort of business. I am a little anguished that there is no one to take their places. It is the sort of thing I wanted so much to do when I was younger, and I find instead I am in a position that practically forces me to patronize these people.

The Central Committee just had a plenum and ratified the urban half of the reform. The extent of the reforms, coupled with the bizarre scheme of 'one country, two systems' [referring to Hong Kong], makes everybody wonder if we can call China socialist still. Yet whatever it is, it is not capitalist yet. But the commanding heights of the economy will in fact be ruled by prices and markets if the reform works out. There will be major price rises soon, and people are rather moody about it.

17 November 1984
Dear Old Man,

As you once noted, I find it difficult to get along with any powers that be anything, so it looks as if my job may not be renewed in January no matter how hard I try. I will miss the gig, because I enjoy it more than any job I have ever done in my life, and I have learned an extraordinary amount from it, not just Chinese, but medicine, pedagogy, linguistics, and even some of what I am worst at, getting along with human idiocy in its most organized, malignant forms. But I must get to Tibet, and a winter expedition seems particularly inviting since everyone assures me it is thoroughly impossible.

Following that, I have several offers for other work, although I would prefer to be here.

I am doing some very interesting translating work as a sideline, and am now in the throes of translating a paper to be given in Geneva next month about the use of natural neurotoxins as analgesics in advanced, which is to say dying, cancer patients. Apparently cobra venom and an even more lethal extract from *fugu* fish livers are more effective than the usual opiates, and not at all habit-forming. Why this latter quality should be a consideration in a patient you are just seeing off is one of the mysteries of the profession, but I don't think even I would like to die stoned out of my gourd.

I am never sure what is Chinese and what is medicine, since I am marginal to both worlds, but I am slightly shocked at the routinism and inertia of death here. First of all, considering the proximity to their patients in which the doctors here live, thanks to the Beijing housing shortage, the lack of rapport between patients and doctors is a little surprising. But there it is. I have seen even the best doctors send patients outside air-conditioned labs to wait in sweltering halls for test results while they chuckle and joke over them. The technicians sometimes handle them like meat, the doctors examining them like camera fodder, and occasionally the only interest shown in the non-physical existence of the subject is whether or not he is sufficiently illiterate so that the results of his test can be scrawled on the envelope.

Patients are rarely if ever told of their fate. The doctors explain that such is the Chinese psyche that if you tell a patient he has another six months, he will probably croak in five just to spite you. It is true that no one believes in life after death here. This fuelled a raging discussion during one of my Wednesday lectures. I brought in a tape of a dying cancer patient facing her fate quite bravely. The resulting argument was so heated, that an iron-hearted mortality statistician left the room in tears.

On one level, I am outraged that dying patients are considered minors by their children and even their doctors. On another level, I am more interested in understanding

106

than in finding another outlet for righteous indignation. This is a society of intensely familial people, who not only live in families but often delegate certain aspects of their own consciousness to other members of their families. It is enough that your children know you are dying, at least in the eyes of the doctor, in the eyes of the children, and even in the eyes of the patient sometimes. Dr Deng, a man who represents a kind of paragon of Communist humanity to me, has just found out his mother has breast cancer, and has been assuring her it is only a mild case of tubercular armpits. He has just left Peking to go to Canada for two years. She will be dead long before he gets back. How did he manage to say goodbye to her?

I too have a hard time talking to the patients, though the nose barrier is so big that the class barrier is insignificant in my case. I occasionally play *xiang qi* with one of them, and I played jing-hu and sang songs one night with another. Some evenings I stay around here until very late just to savour the atmosphere. It is transient, of course, few will be around in six months, but it is not at all the filthy transience of the hotel where I live.

I go home at night to record some little story in an Australian or Kiwi or Lancashire accent, and the foreigner, if I am lucky enough to find one willing, wants money for his bloody voice. I'm not even asking them to think, just read. Why are foreigners so relentlessly solvent and so emotionally bankrupt, so selfish, so useless, so venal and backward, so ignorant and incurious? I know, of course, they are not all like this, and the ones who are are simply helpless dumb animals in a foreign country at bottom. We are the scum of the earth, we 'travellers', we are an oily film, ever present and ever shallow.

The political study class is about to begin. This week's topic is the coming rise in prices, so I think I will attend. The sessions are occasionally interesting, actually, though it is surprising how homely and conventional they make them, rather like the scout meetings in Forest Lake I had to go to. (Bet you didn't know that was what you were socializing me for!) They remind me of when I met Jim Veneris, the American airman who was shot down in Korea and decided to become Chinese; I was impressed by the fact that he was obviously not at all a Maoist revolutionary, as I had imagined, but only an ordinary Chinese man who happened to be born in West Virginia. I was horrified at how the success of a revolution apparently turned everything that was a matter of will, free choice, and struggle into a kind of blind, banal convention. Looking back, this 'insight' was really mere prejudice; after all, it is better to be Chinese than Maoist, now that I know what each really implies. Nevertheless, the idea of everything I consider subversive and wonderful being later on conventional and creepy is unnerving. Makes me think I have less time than I thought.

Thanks for the stuff on wave-particles, but you seem to have answered none of the questions I asked, and answered one question which, although interesting, I didn't ask.

21 November 1984
Dear D & B,

Just over the Wednesday hump. The rest of the week is always downhill, and consists largely of pleasant moments like this one, sitting in my office with my Xishuangbanna 'cannon' tea and Sichuan oranges, watching the snow fall on pinched Peking. The oranges are a fringe benefit of lending my office out to the union for their orange sale, the tea is yet another gift from an embarrassingly grateful and slightly grating student, and the snow is warming things up considerably.

So my last letter was emotional profligacy? Not at all. It is the Chinese way to do things, no matter how routine, by highly discombobulating campaigns. Brushing your teeth without the necessary motivational hortatory display is a sure sign of lack of sincerity, and will probably lead to tooth decay. So I too have campaigns. When I wrote last I was in the middle of a radical redistribution of my teaching method, which, after half-digesting some Chomsky, I had decided was too obsessed with performance and insufficiently with competence. As a result, I was visited by the spirit of Chomsky present, with decidedly more of suet than of communicative spirit about it, my students astutely managed to assimilate all of the new uncertainty without touching any of the new material, and all present seemed to be making each other nervous. I am not yet on solid ground, but you will enjoy my musings on technique later.

My next campaign is already on the drawing board. I think this business of the continuous campaign, the constant shifting of emphasis is destructive to the teacher, but it is in the nature of teaching. Classes simply never finish up with the same kinds of problems that they begin with. My incompetence as a teacher comes from my inability to get out of my head and into theirs. I simply do not react quickly enough to bring the new emphasis in on time. What I most dislike about teaching is that apparently one of the most dangerous things you can do is permit an awkward silence or a feeling that you don't know what to do next. It destroys their confidence in you, and in themselves too. The other day I lost three pages of notes and had to ad lib for half an hour, and, although I often depart from my notes for an hour or two at a time, the knowledge that I must act, and act convincingly, paralysed me. I adjourned the class early and went to dinner. Wasted time.

But the class remains a knottier problem. How to teach people not to just repeat. I have introduced several new techniques based on this felt need. The first is that I talk about my dreams a lot, and I often tell little stories that must be carefully listened to in order to decide whether they are really dreams or not. The second is that I often have drills along the lines of 'repeat if it's true, change it if it's not', and I thoroughly ridicule replies that are merely English and not truth. But of course this has the effect of limiting imagination. I think I will soon have to introduce 'if'-clauses and conditionals, if I want to break my own monopoly on absurdity and lies, a very important part of language. The problem is, of course, that I will simply be introducing another, yet another, form of performance, another way of

109

saying things right, another battle in the war on Chinglish. And, after all, what they really want, what they really need to do, is not love the language the way I do, but buy their bloody groceries, take planes to conferences, not get mugged and ripped off, and come back to China safely to continue their research with only their illusions about Western technology broken.

One of the best teaching aids you could send me, actually, would be some good riddles. Preferably, they should be rhyming, since this helps fluency and pronunciation and allows me to present a lot of language without any writing. (I have practically banned writing from class, and intend to produce at least one fluent, illiterate student.) Riddles have become a kind of obsession in the Institute since I introduced them. I have been writing them myself, and I find I am running out. Also limericks, as in:

A doctor of pathology
Liked to write in the passive, you see.
Sorry, said I,
Could you please tell me why?
She said, 'Why is not known by me.'

As you can see, I am far more style than substance, as my students can see as well. I need to learn to be less flashy and more consistent, or I will never come to anything, not even an Arabic degree, much less a Chinese one on top of it.

I generally change the names of all the people I write about. During the Cult Revolt, all letters sent abroad went through some office in Qian Men, and my typing makes my letters particularly tempting. A too-frequent mention in a too-long letter may make things, as my leader says, 'inconvenient'. Life is already pretty bloody inconvenient. The *ling dao*, the leadership, cracked down on my social contacts one day when I didn't show up to a department meeting, and my only invitations to my students' houses are on the sly. The *ling dao*, of course, reserves the right to invite me to his own house, but I have begun to snub him. Anyway, Chinese surnames are all 'Smith'.

29 December 1984

Today I taught my last class; next Thursday I will leave
Peking definitively. Why? Well, of course because I've been
dreaming of the trip since I was ten and all, and just planning
it this afternoon gave me some of the exhilaration I felt in
Budapest while planning my China trip. I think Tibet
seemed as remote one year ago as China did two years ago,
yet here I am, almost there again, the air already seems as
thin as shaved ice, and travel plans as brittle.

Why now? Well, to tell the truth, I lost my job. It is a little
mysterious, but I'll tell you what happened, and then what I
suppose really happened. On Thursday I came back from
the British Embassy with some films. (I have inaugurated a
BBC film series in lieu of Wednesday lectures; I showed *The
Ascent of Man* and *The Voyage of Charles Darwin*, and I was
all set to show *Pride and Prejudice*.) And there was Dr Eh,
my benefactor. Dr Eh was the acting director when I was
appointed; I was a little nervous when the actual director
came back from America, but he turned out to be even more
enthusiastic about my class than Dr Eh, suggesting that my
salary be doubled and my visa extended. Just the day before,
Dr Eh had told me about this decision, and suggested, or
rather agreed with my long-standing suggestion, that my
class be opened to more people and reorganized with new
materials provided by the British Council (including some
excellent materials on medical English). And suddenly on
Thursday he was telling me that I could not have a visa
extension – something I had been counting on – and my
salary was being cut from the budget immediately. He said it
was due to budgetary considerations.

In fact, the Institute budget just got a big boost, because
we unexpectedly came out so high in the yearly tour of
inspection. I moved to a real pad in North Peking about a
month ago, and because of my move I was costing far less
than before, even including my doubled salary. Nevertheless,
I reiterated my long-standing offer to take an ordinary
Chinese salary, like my students. I have always considered it
unfair that I should be paid extra because of the size of my

111

nose. He said no, it couldn't be done. During the next few days, I checked several places that had been dying to hire me just a few weeks ago; all of them told me that it was now impossible. Yet it is precisely this season when teachers are usually most needed, because large numbers go home for Christmas and don't come back.

I think that it is simply circumstances beyond my control, namely, my big mouth. Only the fuzz could produce such a dramatic turnaround in my fortunes. This has since been confirmed to me by rumour, although practically anything can be proved in China by rumour. So it is obviously time, as the Institute Party Secretary explicitly told me, that I left Peking. I agree, actually. Peking is a tight spot for a big nose. I want some place really, really small. Where no one has ever heard of Foreign Exchange Certificates, and no one gives a damn what I think about the fighting with Vietnam. Furthermore, I am not convinced that I have been indiscreet; an English teacher who places as much stress on free conversation, and is naturally interested in politics as I am, cannot help occasionally touching controversial subjects, and whenever I did so, which was not so very frequently, I found the small risk amply compensated by the extraordinary interest I generated. Honestly, I have weighed my behaviour carefully, and I have no regrets. I don't think I could take regrets on top of leaving the best gig I've ever had and the best people I've ever worked with.

As if to underline that it was not budgetary considerations, I was given a great big going-away banquet at the most expensive restaurant in town, where the corrupt old Empress Dowager Ci Xi used to dine, a place that specializes, among other things, in 'Dragon and Tiger' (snake and cat meat) so I am leaving the gang with heartburn as well as heartache.

At the banquet, Dr Zhang remarked rather ruefully that the later classes got not only better books but better techniques than the earlier ones (she was one of my earliest students, and I borrowed her office one day in order to conduct the telephone unit over the telephone with the class downstairs). True. A great deal of credit belongs to Dr

Zhang herself, and also to Dr Tan. Funny, at first I really didn't get along with Dr Tan at all; she struck me as being quite narrow and selfish, and her obviously unnecessary presence and constant demands for attention placed a burden on the less advanced students. Yet after a while she became not just a very close friend, but somewhat indispensible to the whole class. She is not at all a leadership sort; she is bitchy and cantankerous and extremely sharp-tongued for a Chinese woman, but she is somehow very catalytic for a class. I think Dr Zhang and Dr Tan were both barometers – knowing them very well allowed me to do what I couldn't do before: judge the mood and speed of the class sufficiently accurately not just to know what exercises to prepare, but which ones to table and which ones to use when, right on the spot.

There are other good-byes, too, many of them patients. The other day I got a New Year's card that read:

Dear David, it's a pity that I couldn't hear your lecture on Wednesday afternoon. Because my liver function test is abnormal. Two months ago, I asked you when you will leave China. At that time, I thought you would come to my home to have Christmas dinner. But now I am sorry it can not be realized. Wishing you merry Christmas and Happy New Year!

Shu-jun

Which I guess means something like, 'Goodbye, I am leaving too.'

This letter has got to end soon. I have to get my apartment into boxes and take it over to another friend's place to be suspended in a hammock over the loo. The place itself is abominably ugly, the buildings are just like the barracks in Auschwitz, but the company is congenial, largely African students here to study medicine for five or six years. I cringe when I see how horribly they are treated by otherwise decent Chinese, these people who, utterly unlike us whites, have excellent and completely selfless reasons to come to this country, and are making tremendous sacrifices for their people. The intellectuals are by far the most abominably

113

racist. The workers and shopkeepers in the area like the blacks quite well, but even Dr Tan, for example, insists that they smell awful, drink too much and ogle Chinese women (all accusations more accurate about whites, who are constantly lavished with praise for the alleged sacrifices they are making for this country, ha!).

I will be taking only clothes and my tape recorder to Tibet, I'm afraid, so this may be the last legible letter you will get. There is no point in fixing an itinerary I may not be able to follow because of the weather. One of my plans, given the money, is to buy a horse in Qinghai and try to ride to Lhasa from the north. Sounds mad, doesn't it?

31 December 1984
Dear Old Man and Jan,

I am leaving for Tibet, although not directly. I am going out to a small place in Shandong province to see about a job, if not now then when I come back from Lhasa in half a year penniless. Then I'm hitching down through some even more microscopic places in Jiangxi and Anhui provinces, where my great heroes Peng Dehuai and He Long fought the Kuomintang. Then to Hong Kong, where I have to get a new passport and visa. Then I plan to go north to Wuhan, and catch a boat for a place called Emei Shan, about five days upriver in Sichuan province. Emei is one of the five great Buddhist mountains in China, the site of the world's largest Buddha, and a centre for Tibetan pilgrimage, in addition to having the most infernal hot pepper pig tripes ever to make it into the upper worlds. From the summit of Emei, you can see Tibet, and I think there are two roads which may be clear enough, provided the winter is mild, to travel as far as Kham, the eastern part of Tibet. If there are any Tibetans making the pilgrimage, it should be possible to travel with them as far as Lhasa. But the weather tends to shut down large portions of Tibet for large portions of the year, and it is quite possible the roads are not usable right now.

The north road goes almost directly to Chamdo, the capital of Kham. Even in summer it takes almost three weeks to go from Emei to Chamdo; it is one of the roughest roads on earth. A friend who travelled it five years ago described it as 'an animal track'. The south road skirts Chamdo by about 100 kilometres and continues on to Lhasa, but it too is rumoured to take weeks. In addition, the Khampas are supposed to be the wildest of men; they had a pre-liberation history of slaughtering people from Lhasa because they were 'foreigners'. If there are no trucks or buses travelling either road, I may have to buy a horse. The alternative is a huge detour, up through Xining to Golmud, which is the end of the rail line in Qinghai, the desolate 'prison province' to the north of Tibet, where I was last April. From Golmud there are often trucks going south to Lhasa, crossing the Changthang plateau. This would be the least interesting road, but the surest, and even that will take some weeks. I cannot fly, I don't have the money, and anyway I think the sudden change in altitude is not very healthy, nor very scenic.

Money may be a problem, and if a serious gig crops up on the way, I will take it. I have saved 700 yuan, and I have 200 dollars and a little Hong Kong money. I was expecting to work another four months or so, amass about twice the capital, and make the trip in the spring when conditions are not quite so arduous and wouldn't necessitate things like horses. But, as going-away presents, I got 100 yuan, some silk stuff, and over a hundred pounds worth of All-China ration tickets for rice. Don't laugh, they are going to be very useful; with the abolition of internal passports they have become the main means of controlling internal travel, so hard are they to get, and not having them stamps you as a foreigner. I forgot to mention that one reason I want to travel in winter is that with my cold weather mask on it is now impossible to tell I am not Chinese.

But now there are so many good-byes to say, and so fast. I'm not very good at them, and neither are they. Old Dr Zhang, with a face crusty like fresh bread and a voice warm like an oven with jaunty gold teeth set in the corners; Dr Wang, whom I always call *Lao Taitai* [old lady], with a face that always disappears in a mass of wrinkles and a voice that disappears in a mass of giggles whenever you talk to her, thoroughly fascinated by any idea you put in front of her, at least until the next idea comes along; and my alter ego, sharp-tongued, quick-tempered Dr Tan, who was my best friend at the Institute. Despite repeated warnings from the party leadership, we would meet secretly over half-raw Mongolian hot pot every week, and she would tell me with great gusto how her menopause was progressing, and how great it was to be 'almost a Buddha'. And Dr Tao, who lost her husband in the Tangshan earthquake, and hasn't smiled since. And Dr Wang, whose husband went mad and committed suicide during the Cult Revolt, and who has done nothing else since, and is rumoured to be remarrying someone younger than she is.

About a week ago I went wandering in a 'Freedom Market' in the North Peking suburb where Peng Dehuai spent the last years of his life. I maybe drank too much beer with my bean lunch, and some peasant managed to sell me a huge dog skin, for, 'tis true, the very low price of five yuan. When I got home I wasn't sure what to do with it. Some friend had told me that a dog skin should be sniffed to see if it was tanned well, so I did, and immediately realized why I bought it. I remembered when Felicia finally acquired the joie de vivre to go with her name, and used to lie down in the grass out in the Olsons' swamp and had no objection if I lay down and rested my head on her ribs. We never really bathed Felicia, but somehow she kept herself reasonably clean, smelling doggy, but also like straw, woolly and warm. The skin I bought had the same colour and smell. I wondered where Felicia wandered to when she set off to the North, as I imagine, to die an Eskimo dog's death in combat with some polar bear. Given her doggedness, she may even have ended up in some Manchurian dog-catcher's trap. Anyway, I cut the skin up and sewed it into a beautiful straw-coloured fur vest, the first clothes I've ever really made from scratch, with hidden clasps, Chinese-style, and no obvious way of getting into it, so it looks grown on. I had a little fur left over, so I made myself a little ear protector for each ear, the kind old Chinese men wear. They were warm, but peculiar in appearance, because of the white fur. As soon as I was spotted by a couple of children, they both chimed in with a little poem that is often the first one Chinese children learn to say:

Xiao bai tu, bai you bai
Liangge erduo shuchulai
Ai chi luobo, ai chi cai
Tiaotiao bengbeng, zhen ke ai

Little white rabbit, white as can be,
Two long ears growing out free,
Likes his carrots, likes his vegs,
So lovable, on his hopping little legs.

So I'm just hopping off now.

4 | Speechless in Lhasa

Sanmenxia, Henan Province, 8 January 1985
Dear Old Man and Jan,
  Wait. I've changed course again. As usual, there are extenuating opportunities rather than circumstances. For reasons I cannot fathom, the Peking fuzz smiled on me and gave me a three-month renewable residence visa. This is an extraordinary chance – it not only makes it possible to reach Tibet, it gives me a good chance of finding a job there. I don't have to convert my status like I did in June. So I left Peking not really sure what to do with this good luck, and just as I was bracing myself for ensuing misfortune, my second ride out of Peking was with a truck driver named Metal Mountain Wang, heading all the way to Xi'an. Practically half way to Lhasa, albeit the easy half.
  Metal Mountain has huge succulent lips, half a moustache, and an imitation leather jacket that comes down to his knees. He is distributing leather-processing machinery to remote sheep-tending communes in Hebei. We drive till late at night, keeping each other awake by telling stories. He would tell a ghost story from the Qing classic *Liao Zhai*, and I would try to remember the Japanese fairy stories from a book I had as a child. During the day, we talk of other things.
  'When I was a kid, *Lao Di*' – this means 'venerable younger brother'. In fact, he is about five years more venerable than I, but he is married, and the proud father of a son; he seems to imagine that his genes have been magnified, and not simply multiplied. 'When I was your age – no, much younger – I read everything. Old stuff. And

118

then modern literature. But as I went on to the modern stuff, I got the feeling they had it all ass-backwards. The closer it got to the present, the more dead and lifeless it all felt – full of, you know, big things, and devoid of feelings. Now,' – he downshifted the four-ton Nanjing truck and we hurtled around a gritty corner – 'Now I never look at a goddamn book unless it's at least 200 years old! Take *Dream of the Red Chamber*. Shit, I've read each volume four times! And gotten more out of them than any other twelve books.'

I considered bluffing. I hadn't really read the classics, but then I suspected he hadn't really read the moderns. I'd seen the opera made out of the book, but the language cluttered up the characters, and the characters muddled the plot, and the whole plot seemed pretty minimalist anyway. This guy falls in love with a poor cousin and gets married off without his knowing it to a rich cousin, by switching brides under the red veil. When he finds out, the poor cousin dies and . . . no.

'Four times? Well, maybe you can tell me . . . what was it about?'

'Ahh!!' he roars through his twirling moustache of an upper lip. 'I'll tell you! Light me a cigarette!' I light a cigarette and pass it to him. It is the first time I've tasted tobacco since I was about 13, and something in the flavour tangs of coffee, male bonding, and internal combustion engines. Metal Mountain is grinning like an emperor's grave and we thunder over some Song bones.

'It's about the decline of the old feudal family. The younger ones, see, perceive the plot as a struggle against grandiose traditions and dictatorial expectations! The elders, though, see it as a fight against the creeping mediocritization and effeminization of their values!'

'Who is right?'

'In reality – it's about the end of the world! Pfft!' Metal Mountain smokes hungrily for a moment. 'There are people who make a living writing articles like that, you know. Our Dream-of-the-Red-Chamber-ologists. The most famous one, the one I liked best, he did 20 years during the Fifties and Sixties. "A capitalist roader", as we said back then. But me,

119

hell, I would have liked to have had his job anyway. Spend my days in the red mansions of Ning and Rong and only come out to collect my paycheck.' He hawks up a lump of tobacco tar and mucus thick as axle grease, and sends it curving majestically out the broken wing vent of the truck. 'Problem is, Lao Di, I got out of upper middle school and had to get to work . . .' His voice idles down to the pulse of the engine, but I know from the curve of his lips he is muttering his favourite expression: 'Step out your door, and you start suffering.'

We've been stopping in some really hard-core rural villages to unload machinery and spend the night. First night out it was a little production brigade in Li County, Hebei. When we arrived, the children were all watching black and white TV in the village square, where a huge aerial, the tallest thing for miles, was rigged. We unloaded the machines and sat around discussing ancient Chinese history. Metal Mountain, I thought, must be an expert, but there was another peasant there who was at least his equal at drumming up the names of emperors and prime ministers, and rattling off dynasties to the beat of chopsticks and the clink of glasses. Finally, after midnight, we crashed on a clay kang heated with burning cotton stalks.

The next day out we made it as far as Anyang, in north Hebei province. The road was bad and the beast kept boiling over in the freezing wind. I finally noticed that Wang had the radiator covered and the water level low. In Anyang we had a small feast of Muslim mutton noodles, which opened my bowels at last. You cannot imagine the enormous gratification such matters provide on a trip like this.

The following day we made it to Zhengzhou, where we saw the ruins of the Shang dynasty city of Ao, the oldest urban ruins in China, maybe 4,000 years old. We stayed in an old opera theatre, with the trucks parked out in the stands, and the beds on stage, in front of all those headlights. In Peking, at least there are coal stoves, but here you get nothing but a padded quilt. You always have your clothes on and you get so filthy you itch after a few days. I

120

am dressed in a curious sandwich: two sweaters, leather jacket, dog skin, rabbit skin, PLA great coat, plus padded baggy pants. Warm but filthy.

Next day was a record slow day. We stopped to see the tombs of the Song emperors, the great caves of Longmen, and the tomb of Guan Yu's head, which was cut off by one of his enemies and sent to the great intriguer Cao Cao in order to inspire a vendetta against Cao Cao's family. Cao Cao, however, gave the head a glorious burial and had Guan Yu made into a god of war, which he remains to this day.

By nightfall we had reached Sanmenxia, near the Shaanxi border. It's a good spot, high in the hills around the Yellow River valley, so this morning we are recuperating, and we will probably make Lintong, where the Qin emperor is buried, today or tomorrow. The Qin dynasty lasted only 25 years, and included three rulers, of whom only the first is admired for his gifts of organization. He died in 207 BC.

I have hitched this way before, last May, so I am serving as an unlikely Sherpa guide. The roads are terrible, though, and the bridges worse. The main bridge over the Yellow River to Zhengzhou, a huge city, was a one-track railway bridge 'converted' to road traffic by sticking a few flagstones between the rails. You have to line up for hours to pay four yuan in order to be allowed to cross, single file, first a few going south to north, then a few going north to south.

I have decided to try the north road first; conditions on the east roads are supposed to be impassable. When I was in Xining last year a snowfall kept trucks from travelling for two or three weeks. Wondering what the snow will now bring, I will probably be snug in some nice warm cave tonight.

Xining, 19 January 1985
Dear D & B,

Now I really am half way. Yesterday I saw my first yaks, freshly trimmed, so they resembled long-tailed, spiky-headed cows. This morning I had my first meal of *tsampa* [roasted barley]. And I think I have a headache and a certain

121

loss of appetite from the sudden change in altitude, so I'm taking it easy for a few days. Then I will set off for Golmud, the 'gateway' to Tibet.

Let's see. I last wrote from Zhengzhou, a little over a week ago. After Zhengzhou, Metal Mountain slowed down considerably. On the road to Luoyang, we passed the tombs of the Song emperors; Metal Mountain stopped and we went on a wild goose chase after his favorite Song, Baozhang. ('A great, kind man, but he listened to the wrong people, I guess,' says Metal Mountain.) We turned up many tombs and found lots of wild rabbits, but finally gave up and asked a passing peasant. ('Never ask a woman peasant. Women don't know what's outside their doors, or if they do they're ashamed to say so.') Sure enough, Baozhang was sleeping a few miles away, in a place inaccessible to huge trucks. I consoled Metal Mountain by escorting him to the Longmen caves. The Buddhist sculptures left him pretty cold but he was quite taken with the curves of the modern Longmen bridge. It is a very pretty bridge, though hardly a wonder to Western eyes, rather like the Franklin Avenue bridge in Minneapolis, but smaller.

I liked the hot springs, where all the locals were doing their washing, and derived a vicarious thrill from watching them, not having washed myself since Peking. Disconsolate still, we visited the tombs of Guanlin. We were really hungry at this point, and just scouting for something to eat, when a cop pulled us over for 'crossing the centre'. Actually, there never is any centre, and even if there were, it would be impossible to keep from crossing it, because the side lanes are packed with people, animals and commercial practices. The cop obviously wanted money and shamelessly bargained with us, even after I displayed my nose. He assured us the alternative was impounding the truck for a month. We bargained him down to five yuan, a day's pay for Metal Mountain ('A day worked white!') and paid up. Now he really was desolate: Chinese history was a monumental plot against modern truck drivers.

The road we had to travel, linking the two capitals of the Han dynasty, was the worst yet, and it was late, late, late when we made it into the village of Sanmenxia in western Henan. Metal Mountain had *wai shang*, which are sort of nephews or nieces, I think, in an Army base near there, and he unfroze the engine and drove off to see them while I sniffed around town, eating things, mostly. It was a rather Alpine sort of place, set in the grasslands that layer up to the yellow Shaanxi plateau, richer than the cave cities, and full of heaps of dead rabbits, brought in by peasants as yet too poor to be growing chives in plastic sheet greenhouses during the winter. I bought two hoops made from rabbits' ears to keep my own ears warm.

By late afternoon, I had finished eating and ambling, and Metal Mountain had finished mothering his wai shang – who turned out to be a skinny little 17-year-old kid who'd already been in the Second Artillery Division for two years. (Metal Mountain had loaded him with cakes and woollen things and money.) We poured another 20 gallons of boiling water into the radiator (there is no anti-freeze in China, so this is how you start a truck), and drove off. Coming into Shaanxi by thumb is always a surprise. You drive along what looks like an endless plain, until suddenly you are at the top of what looks like a bottomless valley. You go down and come up, and then you're back on the table top again, as if you never fell off. It's a little creepy, as if the whole earth's crust were hollow, and split here and there by carefully sliced and tilled vertical barley and millet patches. The crust gets yellower and poorer, until finally you're in the cradle of revolution and, incidentally, civilization. Rejuvenated, Metal Mountain told me ghost stories, and we drove all the way to Lintong, the tomb of the Qin emperor.

The hotel in Lintong was the sort I stay in, not the better-class trucker's hotel Metal Mountain always chooses. It was inhabited mostly by trinket pedlars who made a living selling plaster statues and such to tourists. One of them showed us how to make plaster casts of little girls, laughing Buddhas and whatnot. He said we could make five or six yuan a day (a good wage for China), but of course we would have to spend two or three for food and accommodation. Metal Mountain

123

seemed fascinated by every aspect of the job, as if he were ready to give up trucking and buy a bag of plaster instead.

And then we had to say good-bye. I didn't want to get soaked for hotels like I did last spring in Xi'an, so I moved out to Xianyang, which is technically a suburb of Xi'an, but is historically just as interesting. It was old Qin's actual capital. The road to Xi'an is more or less planted over the ruins of his big palace, Epang-Xianyu. Liu Bang, who is buried under the northest corner, turned it into a pleasant cornfield in just 40 days, a much more thorough job than Scipio did on Carthage.

I spent most of my time in Xianyang in the shower, but the third day I went west to a bustling village called Xingping, and sat eating pigfeet in a tea house overlooking the village square. It was so twee and arti-idyllic, I never made it to the two pretexts I had set up for the trip: the Han tomb of Wudi, the third Han emperor, who fought the Huns so successfully, and the tomb of Yang Guifei, the favourite concubine of the Tang emperor Xuanzong, whose execution was made a condition of putting down the revolt of An Lushan and allowing the Tang dynasty to continue. (This measure was supposedly really aimed at the court eunuchs, who were too powerful to be attacked directly.)

The next day I returned to finish off the ears and snout of the pig, and to trek to the Han tombs. 'Lump of dirt', as Metal Mountain would have said, but there were some great caricatures of the Hun invaders in stone around the base of one of the generals who was carried off by disease early in the campaign. One showed a minuscule Hun grimacing under the hooves of a huge horse; another a Hun wrestling with what looks like a teddy bear. Maybe a midget giant panda. Then I did, at last, trot out to the tomb of Yang Guifei. The tomb-keeper took a fancy to me, and led me around declaiming the verses etched in the steles in his unintelligible Shaanxi pronunciation. As he pointed out, Tang Chinese was certainly nothing like putonghua, probably more like Cantonese, rich in closed syllables, and the 'corruption' of the Shaanxi dialect is probably the only Tang twang left in the north. He had an incredible set of tobacco stains on his teeth, like sunspots, some of them; they seemed to grow as he talked.

It was late, and I took a little trickle of a road north to Qianling county and spent the night on a peasant's kang with four other men. I got up before dawn and watched the sun rise from the huge pyramid of the long tank of Gaozong. There was nothing much else to see, actually, except two brawny stone lions, teeth and claws rippling in the sun, much more fearsome than the roly-poly Qing and Ming ones. Then I hitched northwest.

I learned from a trucker that one of the Great Buddha temples swept by Xuanzhuang in *Journey to the West* lay just northwest of Bingxian, so I went and had a look. A Great Buddha it was, too, being restored in gold paint and fluorescent orange that made it look a little like a dime store incense burner, but recognizably beatific under all that uglifying make-up. Best of all were the two bodhisattvas, one of whom had a curious expression of unfathomable pity, or lechery disguised as naturalness and naturalness disguised as lechery. Anyway, that sort of bodhisattva. I had just climbed a cliff to get a better sort of eyehold on the expression when the cops busted me for the first time (I had been going through closed areas almost all along, and have not spent a night in foreigners' housing until I got here). I assured them I was returning to Xi'an immediately, and then ran around a corner and flagged down a truck.

The truck was bound for Xiji, the poorest, most backward bit of Ningxia, the place I tried to reach last year from the north and failed. Two young Muslims, Jade Gate, 22 and very together, and Worship Peace, a little slack because he had been married since he was 17 (she was 14), but given to a joviality that Jade Gate eschewed. We shopped our way north, stopping whenever we saw something you couldn't get in Xiji, and soon the truck dangled cans of pears and bundles of canes, and the water bidon was full of persimmons. Jade Gate even blew his month's wages (400 yuan) on a cheap Sony tape recorder, against the advice of both Peace

125

and me, and that night in our hotel room in Pingliang he kept sitting up and looking at it, blinking to be sure it was still there, with the kind of extraordinary satisfaction that comes from something you are certain will really change your life. The next day, Jade Gate chain-smoking and Peace nodding off almost constantly, we made it to Guyuan, the administrative center of Southern Ningxia. There I got off, and there I really left the map.

When Jade Gate picked me up outside the Big Buddha of Bingxian, he remarked offhand that he had heard of a Big Buddha out in the desert in Ningxia, but had never been there and didn't really know where it was. I asked around in Guyuan and found out there was indeed one, unmarked on any map, at a place called 'Sumisa' (Shunmishan), which some said was on the road from Sanjing to Lijun, about 45 kilometres north of Guyuan, a hamlet maybe four hours by tractor west of Sanjing. I didn't really expect to find it, but the pull of the desert is pretty strong sometimes, and I hitched to Sanjing. In Sanjing, I walked about four kilometres into the desert. Finally a two-wheeled walking tractor came by, pulling a cart-load of people, and I jumped on with a laugh.

The cart only went on for about two hours, though, and then stopped right next to an elementary school. Soon I was surrounded by a mob of staring kids, and it was impossible to work on the tractor, which had lost all its transmission oil and locked up. We wrestled it up onto the cart, and then I walked out a safe distance into the desert with my mob of kids to talk for a while and let the others make the tractor fast. One of the kids had such an unflappable grin it was impossible for her to look serious, and the others treated her as a bit of an idiot. In fact, she was just jolly, lacking in cool, incapable of being supercilious, as far as I could tell. After a while I began to stare at her, and she didn't feel uncomfortable, but stared back and laughed with all her teeth bobbing. Then I got this creepy feeling that she was really beautiful, and I ran back to the tractor. The desert. It can change you into an Arab.

We cranked up the second tractor and set out. Now it was about five, and the desert was getting swollen and inflamed by the sunset. Big and red and jagged, like Xinjiang but with rushing brooks and even waterfalls frozen in mid-air by the sub-zero weather. Caves began to peep out of the bleeding cliffs here and there. I pointed, 'Are those Buddha caves?' 'Sumisa!' laughed the peasant, and then I saw the Big Buddha, carved in red stone, holes where his toes should be and very little below the waist, cruel crescent eyes, unforgiving and horrible in the red light. There was no place to spend the night, so I simply stuck with the tractor, getting off to look at the caves, and then running to catch up with it, which was pretty easy, since we had to push it up the inclines, and once we had to get off and inch it across a frozen brook.

We arrived in the hamlet of Lijun well after dark. There was no electricity, or water, or even two-wheeled tractors. The peasant who took me in lit his house by vegetable oil and ploughed with a wreck of a cow. I hadn't eaten anything since Guyuan, but I couldn't bear to eat the potato and lump of bread they offered me. Instead I just fell asleep on the kang and set out for Shunmishan again on foot before dawn.

There are hundreds and hundreds of caves around Shunmishan, some connected by tunnels, others accessible only by climbing chains hung far above. The caves have been thoroughly looted, so obviously someone at the British Museum knows about them. But once in a while I came upon a beautiful patch, a beaming, benevolent Buddha elbow, or a snarling demon's foot. While I was sketching, my gloves blew away over a cliff into a canyon, and I had to head back to Sanjing or risk frostbite. It was so cold the air seemed to stick to your face like metal.

Sanjing is on the road from Yinchuan to Guyuan, so it was easy to get a lift – a brand-new Toyota truck full of sunflower seeds, bound for Shanghai from Yinchuan. The driver was very xenophilic, and kept offering me apples and sparrows' eggs, which, since I hadn't eaten for two days, I did not refuse. I went as far as Longde, on the road to Garan and then crashed. The next day, two trucks got me to

Lanzhou. I spent most of my time in Lanzhou eating, just as I'd spent most of my time in Xianyang washing. Then, my bowels rejuvenated, I made for Qinghai, my final 'rest' before the Tibetan leg. Got a late start, though, and I only made it as far as Ledu.

Ledu is a Muslim place, but Tibet is felt. I got in very late and had dinner at a 'private' restaurant, since the state-owned ones all close at night. Two surly Hans muscled their way in and asked loudly for pork, but the Muslim owner just laughed at them. Then the neighbourhood drunk walked in. He was a young tough, and mock-saluted me in a rather provocative way, but the owner obviously liked him a lot, sat him down and had his whole family come out to greet him. Then he sat there pouring tea into him and talking endlessly lest he get up and try to do something violent. At one point, he took out an empty bottle and began waving it around, but the owner didn't bother to try to get it away from him. I expected a lecture on the evils of alcohol, but all he said was, 'We Muslims don't drink. Don't drink, don't smoke, don't eat anything but the five meats [sheep, cow, fish, chicken, and deer], but he after all is a Han!' I was impressed by his bar-room manner.

The next day I went out to Qutansi, which is a very old lamasery near Ledu, very big but in bad condition. The Qing paintings are all of goblins right out of the nighmare I had as a lad after reading *Japanese Fairy Tales*. All those blue, very muscular goblins, with fine-haired beards, trying to winch up Sakyamuni or steal his magic bottle. A huge demon with arms reaching out of his eye sockets, and, because it was an officially closed area, all the copulation paintings were uncovered. The curator, a fellow my age who had taught himself apparently everything about Tibetan Buddhism, told me he had no trouble explaining such things to me as long there were no women present. 'Why? Don't you think women do it?' Actually, Tibetan pictures of sex are probably painted by people who never actually do it; not only was the position difficult and the view impossible without the aid of a mirror, the expressions were entirely wrong.

Enough of this madness of detail. I have to shave and wash and get ready for the road. I've been reading some wonderful books. In addition to *Teach Yourself Tibetan*, I also picked up in Peking a marvellous history of the Muslims in China, which I can actually read, except for extracts from the Tang dynasty writers. One particularly puzzling extract turned out to be an account of a trip from China to Persia in the eighth century. I finally realized that the indecipherable characters were just place names, and when I looked up the modern equivalents, I realized the author merely followed the same route I did last spring: Lanzhou, Dunhuang, Turpan, Kuche, Kashgar and so on.

I also got a hilarious book put out by the Sichuan Peasants Bureau called *How to Do Marriage Things*. It is mostly about who to invite and how little money to spend, but there is a little about birth control. I guess I am very pleased with myself. I am still a 'traveller', but at least a literate, if not a thinking, one. This trip has been the most exhilarating and beautiful and mindbending one yet. But then I always say that, don't I?

Lhasa, 7 February 1985

Well, where was I? I last wrote from Huangzhong, or maybe Xining, where I spent a few days getting used to the altitude, and then set out west. I was picked up by Righteous Rebel, a young PLA soldier with an excited young kid's way of cussing, but a firm if slow hand on the wheel. It took four days to get as far as Golmud, but the scenery was worth lingering over. We stopped by Qinghai Lake for a day, to break down, freeze over and invest in ten *jin* of Huang fish, which we ate for every meal and never tired of. Four days of Huang fish and yak meat noodles later, and we were in Geermu, or Golmud. Which is not saying much; it is just the last stop on the railway, and so a centre for trucks on the way to Lhasa.

Golmud is about the same altitude as Lhasa, and the desert around there is of a funny kind, the clouds and the horizon unnaturally close, with no points much higher than one's nose to be seen, and the clouds seeming to whiz by over your head. I spent the night there, and the next morning walked way out into the desert, and got a lift from a truck bound for Lhasa.

My trusty trucker, Little Zhao, decided I was good only for donkey work, and had me hand-crank the truck engine every morning. Not only was the cold ferocious, but you remember I lost my gloves in Ningxia. I kept meaning to replace them but never found any good ones. The air was so thin, I would turn the crank once or twice, and then feel as if the crank was holding still and I was spinning. The energy drained right out, like heat, because the truck battery was practically worthless, and it got harder and harder to start. The cold was so bad, we couldn't stop for more than two hours for fear the radiator would freeze over, and then only away from the wind, and preferably on a hill.

The road climbed mercilessly. We did less than ten kilometres an hour much of the time, and slept for only one and a half hours at a time, sitting up in the freezing cab. This went on for two days and two nights. Worse, when our rest break came around, Little Zhao would insist on a little drinking party, the sort Metal Mountain was always fond of, except he could sleep it off, while we had only 90 minutes nodding over the steering wheel before I would have to step out with the crank over my shoulder and my sweater pulled over my hands to turn over the stiffening motor.

Little Zhao insisted that he was Sichuanese, and really did speak with an impenetrable Sichuanese accent, cursing me when I didn't understand (I cursed him back in South Chicago Jive). But in fact he grew up in Lhasa, in a family of truckers originally from near Chengdu (unlike three of the other truckers in our convoy, who were sons of disgraced Party members). Chengdu was still for him the city of dreams and good food, and he excitedly told me of a married woman he and his mates knew who would lay them for ten yuan a night. He was exactly my age, and even looked a little like me, with a face that looked slept in, the butt end of nonchalant, spendthrift destitution stuck to his drooping lower lip. No matter what happened, his expression said that worse had preceded it and worse would follow. The universe was a kind of big Jiefang truck, and obsolescence was something that occurred in manufacture.

Here I should say something about Jiefang [Liberation] trucks, since they were such a big part of my life for three or four weeks. Jiefang is just the name given to a Chinese copy of a 1930s or 40s Soviet truck. No more modern truck, except for the marginally better, but also too small, Dongfeng, is produced in China, so the age of any particular one is inscrutable. Some are brand-new but look 45 years old. They carry a maximum of four tons, although it is standard practice to overload them by at least one ton, and the main chassis beams are made of wood. The engine is a straight six with coil ignition and adjustable baffles for the radiator, which fluctuates wildly in temperature. The Jiefang's appearance is ungainly in the extreme, gull-wing hood, frog-eye headlamps, running board and so on. Chinese drivers are not overfond of the Jiefang, particularly since under the new reforms they are expected to pay for petrol and on-the-road repairs, which usually consist of their own labour and expensive parts – as we were about to find out.

The coil kept blowing out our distributor. I thought this and the cranky starter were bad symptoms, and said so. Little Zhao glared at me and replaced the distributor. There was too little oxygen to have a proper argument, despite our sleeplessness; we were in Tanggulashan Pass, right on the Tibetan border, on the night of the 27th of January. Tanggulashan is 6,000 metres above sea level, almost twice the altitude of Lhasa or Xining, a place where even Tibetans get headaches and vomit. I felt pretty awful but said nothing. Little Zhao looked awful, and said nothing.

Sure enough. Coasting down (to save on petrol) from Tanggulashan Pass we had big troubles re-igniting the motor, which did little but backfire when you stepped on the gas. In the flaying wind, Little Zhao whipped out the distributor and replaced it, but the motor still wouldn't restart. I practically collapsed at the crank, and finally Little Zhao came snarling out to have a turn. I was oddly relieved when he collapsed in half the time – we were stuck, but at least on equal terms. The battery was dead as a doornail and we waited four hours for the other trucks in the convoy to show up, by which time the radiator was completely frozen.

Little Zhao's mates pushed him off the road in disgust and told him to stay put for two days while they went ahead to Lhasa and sent back help. It is the truckers' code not to help those who are broken down unless they are in the same work unit, but in that case, not to move on without him. Still, there was nothing else to do, so Little Zhao put up with a family of yak herders. I was very tired by this time and a little worried about being a further burden on the irritable Zhao, so I took one of the other trucks on into Lhasa.

I never found out the name of the driver who took me next. He drove me down the road to a truck stop in Damxung, my first real truck stop in Tibet. I was so filled with wonder at the writing over the restaurant door, and the expensive and very poor-quality food, and the exotic and incomprehensible language – Tibet at last – that I barely listened to the grim discussion of what to do with Little Zhao and his truck. It was the driver who had taken me who finally stood up and proposed we go on to Lhasa (about six hours away) and leave the bastard to cool his heels for a few days with the herdsmen. He asked me to come in his truck, and I didn't refuse, though I expressed regret at inconveniencing him – after all, he had not originally agreed to pick me up. He replied in very upper-class Chinese, and I got very curious about him.

He explained as we left Damxung that his father had been a cadre in Sichuan who took a fall in the Cult Revolt and came out here and did menial work. The father's gone back, but the son, well, he said, 'I grew up here. I love it. I hate it too, sometimes. I remember 1969, when all our people out in the countryside were killed by Tibetan nationalists. Murdered. Mostly teachers and technicians, you know, but a few ordinary truck-driving blokes on their way from here to there. We all stayed in Lhasa, afraid to leave. The country-side was full of them, plus bandits, and ordinary murderers.' I asked him how he felt about Tibetan independence, and he looked a bit wary, like he didn't have very strong feelings, only very deep thoughts. 'I'm Chinese, me. I love my country. But I sometimes I can't help thinking, you know. They, the people here, they . . . love a different country.' He talked on and on, and the race issue was there, underlying almost everything. He told me about the Tibetan drivers, how they had their own sub-convoy, how they never joined the convoy of the Hans, even though they were in the same unit. He also told me about the other drivers, the books they read, the talks they had, and about Paul Robeson and American history, and various things he had learned listening to Indian radio. It was obvious he belonged to a different nation, not only from the Tibetans, but from Little Zhao.

We stopped at Yangbajain at almost midnight, and had tea. The three other drivers appeared and sipped tea, too, waiting for the decision of my driver. Would they spend the night at Yangbajain, or try to make it to Lhasa and a hot shower? Hot showers, you see, were to be had once a week in the unit dorms, and tomorrow was the day; if we didn't get in early in the morning, they might be out of luck. The dogs outside barked up a storm. My driver stood up and indicated we would make Lhasa that night, and the relief of his fellows was palpable. I fell asleep sitting up, something I tried not to do, because I know how soporific that can be for the tired driver, but he laughed and told me to sleep well, he'd wake me up when we got to Lhasa.

He did. He let me off right in front of the Dalai Lama's palace, the Potala. Hard to describe the feeling I had, at four o'clock in the morning, ten below zero, rubbing my eyes and wondering if I hadn't been dumped off in the middle of nowhere, in the stench and the dirt of the road. And then, looking up, seeing the Potala, with a few paper windows lit by candle flame, far, far, far above, like a medieval skyscraper, but huge, pouring down the mountain on all sides of it, like an artificial mountain in red, white, and molten copper. I couldn't believe it. I walked around the thing for at least four hours, carrying all my bags, oblivious to the early morning pilgrims. And then I was so exhausted I checked into a hotel at ten o'clock in the morning, and checked out that evening to move into the Snowland, and I remember absolutely nothing in between. I must have been utterly mad. Maybe it was the altitude.

I've been speechless in Lhasa for a little over a week now, studying Tibetan and stomping through monasteries. What can I say about Lhasa? All the religious stuff is here, all right: the most eye-searing colours I've ever seen, the ground shaking with a thousand pilgrim prostrations. Yesterday I hiked up to Pronka, the temple where King Songtsen Gampo became the first Tibetan to learn to write, taking lessons from a Sanskrit teacher. I am also learning to write Tibetan, for four or five hours a day, so I thought it would be a worthy pilgrimage.

Pronka is high in the mountains, a cell under a huge rock topped by a fortress, and carved with images of Sakyamuni, a yak-headed demon whose Tibetan name is Djigje, and a Maitreya [the Buddha of the future]. My communication with the lama was all in Tibetan because he didn't speak Chinese, which is rare in Lhasa. There were eagles overhead and streams clear enough to drink from underfoot, the kind of Tibet I saw a bit of up north, not at all urban and secularized.

But Lhasa is just that. First of all, anyone who has been here agrees it is the filthiest place they've ever seen. The streets around the Jokhang are troughs of frozen urine, lined with frozen shit. No sewers, not even open ones. The shit from the hotel lavatories simply pours out on the street, where it freezes and is trod down into a kind of sidewalk. It is hard for me to believe any Tibetans live past 14 in such conditions, much less 40. Yet even the diehard anti-Communists (an overwhelming majority of the population, even the Chinese-speaking population, which is all I have access to) say that conditions are much better now than they were. Indeed, it is one of the few places in China where there is new housing everywhere you look. Before 1959 I would have seen only the Potala, the Jokhang, and heaps of shit and corpses trod down by pilgrims in between them.

Then there is the Norbulinka, the summer palace the Fourteenth Dalai [the present one] built in 1954-6, *after* liberation. The walls are adorned with traditional paintings showing the history of Tibet up to the visit of the Fourteenth to Peking, and then showing, traditional style, the Fourteenth in between Mao, Zhou Enlai and Zhu De. He is a modern sort of monarch. Norbulinka has the only western loo in Lhasa (for his mother, actually; nevertheless, the pilgrims all kissed the floor). There is also a modern Avalokitesvara [the god of mercy, of whom the Dalai Lama is supposedly an incarnation], obviously from India, and a huge stereo that Nehru gave him.

I've been through the Potala twice, and each of the major monasteries once. There is so much painting to look at here, I feel I could spend fourteen lifetimes, like the Fourteenth. Instead I will probably stay until I am completely out of money, maybe one or two months. I realize this is rather foolish, but I have never been anywhere so pleasurable and overwhelming with things to learn, so I'm planning to stay at least until Tibetan New Year, and my five-kilo sack of tsampa runs out.

Funny how I am about knowledge, though. I must acquire it myself, or I simply cannot digest it. I studied Chinese for two years under the masters and did not learn anything. But once on my own, I was suddenly practically fluent. Two days ago some smart-ass grad student moved into the hotel. After talking to him for two minutes, I realized he had answers to all the questions I've been raising about Chinese Islam: what happened to the southern Muslims, the mosque at Zhongxin, why Tibetan Muslims speak only Tibetan, when the Silk Road opened. But what a smug, supercilious manner, so lacking in any curiosity, so unwilling to pose any questions that might alter our roles of master and student, even though his knowledge was ridiculously specific and narrow. He knew no foreign languages except Chinese, and little of that, nothing of middle-eastern Islam, and less of Tibetan Buddhism. So I dried up. I will have to find out about Chinese Islam myself.

Pali, 4 March 1985
Dear Old Man and Jan,

Post-birthday greetings from the highest inhabited place on earth, a village on the Tibetan frontier with Bhutan, invisible on your map, but in the county of Yadong, which is the finger separating Bhutan and Sikkim – 5,300 metres above sea level. I am taking time to write because it is one of the few activities that require little oxygen. Go slowly, oblivious to human bustle, like a yak.

This is a village of, well, jagged toothy mountains and jaunty dung and twig houses; filthy kids and natty yaks; wooden buckets of teeth-achingly cold water and rivers of barley wine; raw meat and beer for breakfast, tsampa and yak-butter tea three times a day. A temple completely levelled in the Cult Revolt next to a bunker probably left from border clashes with Bhutan, which is literally the other side of the village. Mountains, mountains, the molars, incisors and tusks of the cannibal clay.

I stayed in Lhasa over a month. This was rash because it's an expensive place, but it is also extremely beautiful, filthy, wonderful and horrific. A pageant of painted sex and violence, real goitres and chancres, beggars and lamas, bandit Khampas and soft-spoken monks. I also met Elizabeth, a young Canadian linguist who works in Shandong, and is one of the few I seem to be able to share at least my horror and astonishment with. Horror and astonishment of this degree are not easily shared, I guess. She went back to Jinan, and I am using these few weeks travelling with Nick to decide if I want to take a gig nearby and see more of her. It is a decision that will make itself, I suspect, because when I get back east I will be too broke to choose.

It's worth it, though. This is the sort of wild dream I had when I was a kid. The gory, sexy, lurid paintings are kind of an addiction. In Lhasa I used to feel a kind of physical hunger if I didn't visit a monastery every day, a hunger which, for me anyway, is simply not satisfied by the gorgeous scenery we have been travelling through.

In Gyangze, however, four days after we left Lhasa, I finally got my fill. There is a gorgeous lamasery enclosed by a hump-backed running red wall with a white parapet like the Great Wall. Inside, the walls are crawling with embroidery, and there are mountains of barley cakes and lakes of melted yak butter, my kind of scenery, presided over by painted panthers, yaks raping naked men, scenes of hell and strange scenes that keep recurring in the crowded margins of other scenes. The mountain of impaled bodies, an elephant carrying a monkey carrying a rabbit carrying a bird, the Sixth Patriarch with a peach, and many, many scenes from India: Krishna, entwined bodies, yogic postures, Garuda [the Indian eagle god] devouring a corpse, Ganesha [the Indian elephant god], and many more. India is close, but so far.

But who is this Nick bloke? And what am I doing near Bhutan? Nick is an English painter who gave up exhibition life at Riverside in Hammersmith to walk across Asia with a grant from the Winston Churchill Foundation and Fuji Film. He hoofed across Turkish Kurdistan, Iran, Afghanistan, Pakistan, and into Xinjiang along the Silk Road by camel and donkey, and at last south into Lhasa, where I ran into him. He speaks Turkish, Persian and Uighur, but no Tibetan or Chinese, so he is taking me into the wilds to interpret. As it turns out, we have been doctoring and physicking and consoling each other so much we seem to have forgotten who is sherpa-ing whom. So, after travelling alone for many months, I have an affable *compagnon de route*, and even official permits, since I am supposed to be an interpreter. Tomorrow, hopefully, we will get permission to go briefly into Bhutan. From there we will continue to Yadong. There we will try to get animals for the ride to Sakya monastery in Outer Western Tibet, the oldest in the country.

Speechless in Lhasa

Sakya, 21 March 1985
Dear D & B,

Bearing a five-pound bag of tsampa, fresh ground and pungent, with another pound ground into my army coat much to the hilarity of the villagers, I just came back from the Berwick Street of Sakya, a water mill by a rushing stream behind the giant temple that dwarfs the village of miserable yak herdsmen and snot-nosed kids. The millstone kept stopping, slipping its clutch, and dusting me. But your Camisa's coffee has no fragrance like freshly ground tsampa kneaded with hot yak butter tea and brown Nepalese sugar. Yum!

Sakya is the biggest single temple in Tibet, though it is the centre of one of the smallest sects, the Red Hat Delougpas, who were practically exterminated in the 17th century by the fifth Dalai Lama. The walls of the place seem to predict its downfall with masochistic relish; they are cluttered with scenes of torture, pornography and burning temples. A man having a sword thrust up his anus, garlands of heads tied with intestines, an old woman being raped, heads boiling in blood, a black Buddha spanking a man, another woman being raped on a pile of bones. Giant mandalas, with a kind of 'group theory' motif, based on four elements. Directions? Seasons? They were actually doors, with the colours in different places, and with different animals pictured as drawing vehicles in front of them. There were some mystical crossword puzzles, too, in which letters were rotated, all of which were varied as much as possible without repetition:

1 2 3 4
2 3 4 1
3 4 1 2
4 1 2 3

And so on. Mad maps of hell, wheels of life, always with the same vile pornography: women having molten metal poured into their genitals, people being sawed in half, skulls retching blood, and on and on. Then, suddenly, a huge serene sand painting of Sakyamuni, done by a special

138

lama. The relief, the contrast alone, is enough to persuade you.

But the most horrifying thing about it is the fascination of it. While practically falling into a mammoth mural of 60-foot mandalas, I had to agree that this was some of the best painting done in the world in its time, 900 years ago, the top in trompe-l'oeil art. The mandalas were not simply painted but gold filigreed, the bottom lost in a forest of silver and brass stupas. Never have I seen anything like it, medieval and mad like the Musée de Cluny, but far, far more varied and distracting.

I'm not really supposed to be here, but that's a long story. I spent Tibetan New Year in Lhasa, getting blessed, that is, bashed with a sanctifying instrument I had read about many years ago in an account of Tibet by some French missionaries. It is kept in Lhasa's Sera monastery and displayed only once in a lifetime by the head lama. It took 45 minutes waiting on line to get into Sera. Outside, monks were selling *khada* – white scarves – to the waiting pilgrims. Fifty yards on, other monks collected the scarves, which were then resold. Once inside, I was in due course pushed up in front of the head lama, who looked at me, laughed, and hit me over the head with the stone. It was later explained to me by Tenzing, the owner of the Snowland Hotel, that the stone had flown to Sera from India, and that being hit with it constituted a blessing of great significance. Also, as is traditional, I devoured huge quantities of tsampa, raw meat and *chang* (barley beer, of course), some of which was supplied by a movie company making a newsreel about us few big-nosed folk in Tibet.

Then I set out from Lhasa with Nick, without waiting for official permission. We set out at a snail's pace, because we stopped to do circumambulations at every temple we found, and took four days to reach the city of Gyangze, maybe 260 kilometres from Lhasa – by foot, hoof and tractor, because all truck traffic had stopped for Tibetan New Year. Gyangze is about 4,000 metres in the air, but it is the prime barley land of Tibet, and the chang is particularly good. That and a stupendous multi-niched stupa induced us to lay over a week.

Each niche on the stupa seemed to have a cave with a kind of theme on the wall, mostly sex and violence, but male fantasies of other kinds, too. Here two half-naked women embracing, there a beautiful sinuous woman in a yogic posture, with barely noticeable fangs in her mouth. Around the temple there was a huge vermilion and white wall with a washed lime parapet that had failed to defend the monastery against the conquering Yellow Hats. I did my circumambulation on the moonlit parapet, walking off a dose of chang, to the irritation of the monastic dogs, who were too lazy to climb up for a bite of me.

Thence to Pali, reputedly the highest historically inhabited spot on earth. Somehow I always manage to put my foot in it. That is not a complaint, actually, it is one of the few ways I can tell dreams from reality. Upon arriving in Pali, we were escorted to the house of the village head by an honour guard of children. Once there, we wolfed down the *kupza* (which is a kind of twist made of piecrust dough and fried) as soon as they came out of the fat. We hadn't eaten all day, and one of the children remarked, 'They can't be Chinese'. Then, as I stooped to reassure a yak calf who was nosing around me, he raised his tail in greeting. The lady of the house grabbed for his tail in panic, but too late. The calf shat on my foot and half way across the whole room as it fled. At that I fainted, though it was probably altitude more than mortification. All I remember is Nick suddenly pounding my legs into my chest and the Tibetans asking if I was drunk.

The next day we hiked up over the mountains into Bhutan. Since this is illegal, we didn't stay very long. But it was well worth it; we got to see a huge amount of the country, if only from above. Snaggle-toothed horizon of the Himalayas and fiery-looking mosses underfoot. The smell was very like Mt Ranier in the spring, but there was yak dung and antelopes visible all around us. We stayed a day and hiked secretly back into Tibet at nightfall; on the road we met a gaggle of Bhutanese tennis-shoe smugglers. The

Bhutanese are natty folk, unlike the Tibetans. They have a kind of dressing-gown they hitch up around their knees so you can admire their long johns, and a dagger and lots of jewellery. They also wear a slightly incredulous air I can heartily sympathize with.

We spent three days in Pali and then moved south to Yadong, or Chomo, as the Tibetans call it. Chomo is woody, not at all barren like Tibet; in fact, it is rather like Switzerland. It is quite Braudelian how the tree line utterly changes the material civilization of the Tibetans; it rather made me want to rewrite Tibetan history from the point of view of the effect of wood on people's houses and stores. Suddenly the Tibetans appear as prosperous chalet dwellers, and there is even wood instead of yak shit to burn. No tsampa to eat; the Yadongites eat rice, potatoes, and huge quantities of goat and sheep. They even take hot showers!

Undated

Dear Old Man and Jan,

In Yadong we got to take a shower at last (in Tibet, you shower once a month if you are persistent and very dedicated). We discovered that the water was heated by a little old lady who split the wood for the fire and looked as if she would split herself if it wasn't for all the knots in her flesh. So we stepped in to spell her, and within a few minutes Nick and I had forgotten the shower and were racing to see who could split a cord first. After about three hours, Nick won. (God, all that wood-splitting in Forest Lake was wasted on me!) Then we showered and got a very late start.

Which didn't matter a damn, because the road we'd planned on travelling, a spur that skirts Sikkim, Gamba, and Dinggye, and deposits you at the foot of Mt Everest, turned out to be untravelled, although not completely untravellable. We made about 45 kilometres the first day, and, miraculously, came upon a set of hot springs at nightfall that permitted us not only to spend the night outside on the heated earth, but to bathe for the second time in one day, and the second time in a month!

But the problem was food. We had very little tsampa left, no meat, a smidgeon of butter, and no prospects of a village for three days at the rate we were travelling. An old man came to bathe in the hot spring and gave us some roasted *tsema* (which is kind of like a juniper berry), but we had so few prospects we decided (that is, Nick decided) to forgo the evening tsampa. As Nick has noted, I become fairly despondent at the thought of missing a meal, and mildly suicidal if I actually miss one. So I got up at dawn and went hiking to see if I could find something to eat, figuring (correctly) that Nick would stay in bed another four hours.

I finally came on a small settlement of herdsmen, but they offered me only enough tsampa for one meal, which I felt unfair to sleeping Nick, and they refused all money ('We can't eat that!'). Several of them became quite rude, and one offered us a full dinner if we would provide firewood. I thought hungrily of the two cords we'd cut in Yadong; here there wasn't anything growing higher than your ankle. One of them finally told me where I could find an army outpost. I was a little nervous at that because we had been told *not* to travel this road because of bandits in Yadong, but an empty stomach is a terrible void and nature abhors it. In any case, I figured the army would catch us eventually. They looked me over and told me to get my friend, and we would talk business. I was overjoyed, because they were clearly talking corruption, and would therefore not try to report us.

I went back and got Nick. They sized us up and asked how much our bags weighed – and finally proposed 40 kilos of tinned mandarin oranges! I insisted that we buy some as security against denunciation, so we ended up with maybe six kilos and some dried rations, and left splitting our guts with laughter.

Now the bags were really heavy. The road went mercilessly uphill after each bend, and I almost had a hernia because there wasn't room for the rations in Nick's bags. We stopped every kilometre or so, and skipped not one but two meals. At last I whipped out a tin and swore I wouldn't carry it any further, at least not on my back, but it would carry me instead. Nick looked at me and said, 'I'm going to be an asshole about those oranges' (which he had not even wanted to buy). 'We will eat only one can a day, starting tomorrow.' I looked at him, and at the cliff behind him, and said, 'No you're not, and what do you mean "we"?' After that, I got my rations.

That day we hiked about 35 kilometres – up! We kept walking and walking. We found an abandoned *daoban* [road maintainer's hut] with a stream nearby, but decided not to stay as it was too early. At nightfall, we came to a sort of village and asked if we could stay, but we were refused permission at one house, and then had to walk about eight kilometres more to another. This is bandit country, and people were very suspicious. We kept walking until it was pitch dark, and we really couldn't see if there was anything worth walking on for, but, on the other hand, it was so cold and we were so hungry and exhausted, we were afraid of dying of exposure if we stopped to rest.

Finally, I thought I made out some caves in a cliff by the road, and Nick took a sort of pocket flashlight and went off to investigate. I was too exhausted to move, but I was afraid to sit down since I thought I might not be able to get up again. Eventually, I tried to follow Nick, almost lost him and thoroughly lost the road. Meanwhile, Nick found only a few shadows, much too far away to be of any use anyway, and finally found me stumbling around after him. We somehow managed another four kilometres to a daoban, and knocked on the door. The 'Benbula' [daoban keeper] was terrified out of his wits, thinking we were bandits, but our groans were so piteous he put away his rifle and let us have two sheepskin coats to spend what was left of the night in an abandoned shed. The next day we could barely move. (Well, *I* could barely move; Nick was bouncing around and trying to ride a fucking horse.) So the Benbula took us by horsecart to the army checkpoint at Gala.

From there we made a brief foray into the desert to try to reach Dinggye and Tingri the next day, but we were forced to turn back; we are going the long way around. So here we are, in sight of Mount Everest, Nepal and India. Everywhere we meet lamas secretly going to India, but no one else seems interested in going there. Nor am I. This really is the place I was dreaming of all those years.

But I'll be back in China proper within a month or so, I promise. I need the job as well as the illusion of regularity. Also the crushing effect of rural boredom is starting to bother me, not so much directly but through the people I meet, who seem obsessed with the contents of my bags.

Undated
Dear D & B,

Gala was a place of dust storms so regular and so fierce even the little kids could be seen looking anxiously at their watches and adjusting glacier goggles as the hour approached four. At a little after four, Tibet disappeared. It was simply impossible to keep your eyes open in the hail of grit and pebbles. We wrapped ourselves up head to tail in skins and waited. After nightfall, we went to an army base and spent the night. They too tried to sell us tinned rations and a part of a roast dog, and they overcharged us for miserable lodgings.

The next day, though, we got a truck to Gamba, and this was a historic occasion for us and for Gamba, for the truck was carrying, not just two big noses, but a man who said he was the highest lama in Sichuan, the 'Kongji Lama', who had come to bless the village people. When we arrived in Gamba, we were seated on the throne next to him, and the whole town sang and danced for some six hours. Then one by one they came up and gave one of the lama's minions butter, wool, or sometimes gold, silver or cash, and had their heads knocked down and a few words mumbled, hands and a white scarf laid on. Then they were pushed away and the next victim dragged up.

Suddenly a woman shouted, and the line stopped moving. She had paid double and she was pointing to eyes clouded with cataracts. The lama hardly glanced down; he simply blew into her eyes and she was shoved out. By nightfall, he had a whole four-ton truck full of loot, and a huge bolted metal strongbox of money, gold and silver.

And the next day it was time to move on. We made it to a small village about three hours away with a huge old ruined fort like a giant tooth bathed in gory red light, but the last few kilometres to Dinggye were completely impassable, and we had to backtrack and go the long way around via Xigaze and Sakya. Back in Gamba, fortunately, we met the lama, who had just finished loading his loot and was looking very satisfied, beaming a greenish light through his dark sunglasses. He took us as far as Gyangze and regaled us with the roast antelope he had acquired by 'art'. In Gyangze we paid for the trip by a corvée of unloading all four and a half tons of loot, but I was relieved, overjoyed, to be rid of the lama (and maybe he wasn't one; the place he said he was from later turned out never to have heard of him, and the temple had been sacked years and years ago).

Then to Xigaze, where we were underwhelmed by the second-rate monastery of Tibet's number two lama, the Panchen Erdeni. While we were there, we also made a trip by cart to the Xialuo temple with an artist and his wife, a writer, whom we'd met. They were on their honeymoon, and usually live in Lhasa.

.

5 | Pearly peaks in a dream
by Liu Fei

25 March

We left Lhasa this morning, already full of blossoming flowers and springtime warmth. Here it is still a world of snow and ice. These last two months, the hurried engagement, the hasty marriage, would have been enough to wear anyone down, and the whole way I've sat lazily listening to Pei go on and on. But now, out in the countryside for the first time, I can see everything with my own eyes.

We are at Xuegelashan, 5,300 metres above sea level. Not far off, the tallest peak of the jagged Nianqing-tanggulashan range stands cool and aloof, casting a long, lonesome caricature of a shadow in the sunlight. Down the mountain lies Majiang, the first stop of our journey. It is nothing but a few shacks with corrugated iron roofs, looking as if no one had stopped there for a century at least. Up on the surrounding mountain peaks there are pillboxes here and there to remind you that not everything in the Land of Snows belongs to the Buddhas.

The 'restaurant', black as the bottom of a wok, is draped with trophy banners dating from circa 1976 AD, chiefly self-awarded. A few big yellow dogs saunter nonchalantly back and forth beneath the table, as if to indicate they'd be willing to share our two-yuan plate of potatoes and fried beef bones. There is also tea with milk and sugar for a *mao* [one tenth of a yuan] a glass, and if you smile a bit for the dark red-faced cook, you can even have a bowl of clear water for nothing.

The army-operated loudspeaker in front blares forth the howlings of Brother Lunnong: 'No, we are not so badly off

146

. . .' In the yard there is a big crowd of people. I crane my neck for a look, and see that it is the Khampa from our truck selling Tibetan medicines, five yuan for ten pills. The customers all wear trusting, even reverent, smiles. It must be good for what ails you.

We go to the toilet, our truck fills up on petrol, we cross the Yarlang Zangbo, break down . . . I fall asleep.

26 March

In the middle of the night I hear someone weeping, but I can't tell if it's coming from next door or the next world. Then I have a whole string of nightmares. In the morning I am painfully awakened by Pei, use the terrycloth pillow cover to hastily wipe my eyes, and we hit the road, mouths dry and tongues furry, off to see Tashilhunpo monastery.

At the ticket window, my eyes fall on the Chinese characters for 'Welcome' spelled out in the cobblestones. There is something incongruous about this. We enter the main prayer hall and scarcely get a glimpse of the Qiangba [Maitreya] Buddha when a lama appears to shoo us away, possibly because, despite his smart red jacket, Pei had walked on through without offering up a bundle of Foreign Exchange Certificates to 'Buddha'. [1] The lamas continue to dog our steps, incessantly telling us to 'move on, move on'. In front of the burial stupa of the fourth Panchen Lama, we have only time for a quick glance into the eyes, narrow as stitches; we dare not linger. Maybe they're afraid our gaze will corrode the gold plating, or that we will somehow absorb the jewels and carry them back to Hong Kong.

Growing more and more suspicious, the lama calls over a man in a blue uniform to escort us out. Pei says that for some reason the lamas of Tashilhunpo have always been like that.

1. Because of Pei's jacket, the lamas apparently assumed that they were Hongkongese or Overseas Chinese, and expected them to make donations in the form of Foreign Exchange Certificates that the Bank of China exchanges hard currency for. They are nominally worth the same as an equivalent amount of 'people's money', but there is a black market in them, since certain items can be purchased only with these.

They have their own generator, their own water tower, and many other privileges that other monasteries don't have. [2] But Pei seems to accept all that, leans against a red wall and stares vacantly. Then we have to pay out tips and tolls every step of the way. What is going on here anyway?

The towering breasts of the 'Four-nosed' Guanyin [Goddess of Mercy] have been smeared with butter and plastered with coins. The walls are festooned with *thangka*-like silk weavings from Hangzhou, and there is a Chinese-style Laughing Buddha. Old Emperor Qianlong is there in person,[3] amidst a vast array of burning joss sticks and butter lamps. We sit in the courtyard of the scripture-reading hall and have lunch: a canteen of water, a few bits of army ration biscuit, and a load of complaints. A lama standing in the doorway wants his picture taken, so I pull out the camera and walk over. He hides his head in his cassock as if to ward off a demon. 'No, not a woman!' He gestures to Lao Pei that he should take it. I shout, 'Who do you think you are, still throwing your weight around? We've seen everything already!' I practically throw the camera at them.

30 March

We return early in the afternoon, driven indoors by one of Xigaze's dust storms. We roll a stone against the door and Pei sits on the bed putting his things in order while I am at the table writing my diary. Pei's room-mates are also driven

2. The first Panchen (or Tashi) Lama was supposedly the teacher of the first Dalai Lama, but there is a long history of Panchen Lamas, whose base is Tashilhunpo, attempting to use the China card against the Dalai Lamas. Because the Panchen did not participate in the Dalai Lama's revolt in 1959, he was never dispossessed of his monastery and his summer palace, and, more recently, the Panchen Lama, who was politically a supporter of the Chinese government, received a number of privileges which he has passed on to his monastery.
3. Emperor Qianlong of the Qing dynasty reigned from 1736 to 1796. Like many of the Qing emperors, he was a patron of lamaism, and his images and inscriptions appear in many temples. All Qing emperors were revered as incarnations of the Buddha in their own right.

in by the storm. One of them is a handsome American who looks like the lead in a cowboy film. He is studying mountaineering in Nepal, where he lives with a Tibetan family, and he can speak Tibetan. He takes out some yellowish jade and tells me it was a gift from his Tibetan foster mother. He is leaving for Kathmandu in the morning.

There is another American, David, and Nick, an Englishman. I am thinking of saving money, and I say to them, 'We want to rent a cart to go visit Xialuo temple. If you like, we could share it.'

'How far is it?'

'Twenty kilometres.' The two look at each other. 'Only 20? We can walk, we've walked lots farther than that before.'

David takes a bag of tsampa and a tin lunch box from the bosom of his jacket. The box has a slot in it, just big enough to admit a pair of chopsticks. He has a huge tear in his trousers, and you can see flashes of flesh through it. Nick is wearing a kind of Afghan gown that is so dirty you can't tell what the original colour was. David has a mouthful of fluent Chinese; he's been in China a little over a year, teaching English at the Beijing Institute for Cancer Research. He's been hanging around Tibet for over two months now. Nick is a painter, but unfortunately knows only one bit of Chinese: *xie-xie* [Thank you]. We would very much like to see his paintings, but all he has with him is a drawing he did in Istanbul, a line drawing in the classical style.

In the course of conversation, David mentions that he is a communist. He joined up in the United States. This is the first time we have ever met an American communist, and Lao Pei's interest is immediately aroused. He says a great deal we've never thought about, much less heard. Some of the words he uses make you think of some middle school text books you haven't read for years and years, or else a speech from some film epic. Actually, we are more interested in him than in his ideas. Lao Pei cautiously interjects a comment: 'You must be at least 40!' David smiles. 'How old do you think?' 'Forty-five.' 'And him?',

149

indicating Nick. 'Probably 50 or so.' David translates for Nick and they both burst into gales of laughter. Nick takes out his passport for us to see. Date of birth: 1958. For some reason I am distressed. Lao Pei is the oldest person in the room.

31 March

We managed to rent a horse cart for the trip to Xialuo for 17 yuan, plus five yuan for chang for the driver. Our bizarre brigade – me, Lao Pei, David, Nick and Little Gesan – all huddled together on it attracts a huge crowd of onlookers. All through the journey, we never lack an audience. Muleteers, donkey-cart drivers, horse-cart drivers, before an hour has gone by, the mighty escort is already a *li* [one third of a mile] in length. I stand on the cart, so excited my hands are dancing and my feet tapping. Without even waiting for it to come to a complete stop, I jump off and run over to a donkey rider, shouting to Gesan, 'Gesan, please tell him, he's welcome to ride in our horse-cart; I'd like to try riding the donkey!'

The rider agrees, but I am not too nimble about mounting, and he has to push and pull me up. I pat the donkey's head, 'You and I are good friends now, right?' Before we go many steps, he gets a pebble caught in his hoof and my hair looks stir-fried, but otherwise the road undulates smoothly beneath us. Soon our paths diverge, and it's time to part.

The rest of the trip is lonelier. Bare mountains, with narrow meandering trails. The whole way, David and Pei carry on an animated discussion. Three and a half hours later, a Yuan dynasty tile roof emerges from the desolate horizon. The Xialuo temple. Our spirits, depressed by the cold, immediately rise a notch. A shortish lama comes out to welcome us. I'm starving. I gnaw at the flatbread that Gesan has brought along. David takes out his dented lunch box, pours some tsampa from a bag, and, using the buttered tea supplied by the lama, he mixes it up with the finesse of an old hand. He and Nick gravely eat the result. I taste a bit.

Delicious. No wonder Nick wants to buy a millstone to take back to London; otherwise he'll have to do without his tsampa altogether.

This is the poorest of any of the temples I've ever visited. That much you can see by the vegetable oil in the butter lamps. After the scriptures are read, most of them are extinguished. Most pilgrims don't even know the temple exists, no wonder it is so poor. Why don't they put up a billboard on the highway?

There is an exquisite Huanxi Buddha image: a nude male god holding several nude female figures, and trampling another set of naked women, who nevertheless seem graceful and even joyous under his feet. Gold-plated and covered with delicate-looking, finely inlaid jewels, it is about half a metre or so in height. The room is so dark we are afraid the photos won't turn out, so we ask the lama if we can't move it outside to take pictures. He calls over two strapping young lamas, who finally succeed in wrestling it out of doors. Pei starts shooting like mad, afraid the lama will change his mind. Nick also takes advantage of the opportunity; ordinarily this *Lao Wai* [foreigner, lit. 'Old Outside'] wouldn't be allowed to take pictures. Only David seems completely uninterested in all this; he stands out in the sunlight, propped against a column, lost in thought.

We haven't seen many thangkas yet, so we ask the lama if there aren't some others around. He says to ask Kanbu. Kanbu is a gap-toothed and hare-lipped but very lively old man in a brown robe and a little knitted cap that looks like a ball of loose yarn. When the storehouse door is wrenched open, a cloud of dust emerges. Kanbu takes the thangkas out of an iron chest. Pei opens them for a cursory look, putting aside the better ones for a more detailed examination later. But Kanbu doesn't let him take them; instead he strides out cradling two of them in his arms. At the foot of the steps, he hands one to Pei and unfurls the other horizontally, his legs spread apart with the look of a conquering hero. We are convulsed with mirth. Maintaining the integrity of his pose, he calls on everybody to hurry up and photograph. Pei readily takes his cue, bowing gravely like an obedient houseboy. At the moment the shutter is snapped, Kanbu lets out a great bellow. 'Waaa!!' The lamas in the courtyard have probably never seen him quite so merry. Everybody (even the great thinker standing out in the sunlight) has a good laugh. What a character!

Then Kanbu asks Pei and me to come with him. We go into his bedroom expecting to be shown some rare treasure. Instead, we are offered some junket of uncertain age, and some biscuits and sweets. I eat a sweet and Kanbu pats my face: 'Pretty.' Without waiting for my reaction, he takes my head in his arms and snuggles up a bit closer. 'That-that-that lunatic! Pervert!' My husband stands dumbstruck on the sidelines.

The return trip seems to go much more quickly. The sun gradually declines in the west, melting into dimness. There is more conversation along the way, and David sings a revolutionary song in Arabic: 'The landlord has taken away my . . .'

In a field by the roadside two yaks are fighting, trampling the freshly tilled soil. The owner stands by shouting helplessly. Pei charges into the heart of the fray, and I run over too. Then another pair of yaks, dragging a plough, start coming for me. I stand behind a tree making faces at them. Then I return to the cart to wait for Pei.

The wind has mussed up Nick's hair, exposing a thick layer of filth on the scalp. His face is sunburned, especially his nose, which is sloughing off huge pieces of skin. A disgusting sight. 'Wait till I get back to England, my own mother won't recognize me . . . Come on David, and you, lady, let's get off and walk a bit,' he suggests.

I say, 'Not me. I want to save my strength'. David is scrawny and small-boned, and Nick quickly leaves him behind. He disappears into the distance, only the baggy Afghan pants visible, blowing in the wind. The mountains melt rapidly into the yellow-gold dusk.

When we dismount, they take out their money to pay their portion of the fare, but we refuse, and make them stuff it back into their pockets. They absolutely insist on taking us to dinner at a Muslim restaurant. David studied Arabic and lived in Arab countries for two years, and Nick too trekked long distances through that part of the world; they both agree we simply must sample the fine products of Islamic cuisine.

At the restaurant, David wants me to pick the dishes. I have no experience at this at all, so I simply choose at random. Over 'Islamic' tea, we discuss the day's experiences and our own reactions. David loses no time in starting to flog his revolutionary theories again. I don't want to hear them, so I chat with Nick.

'Travelling in the East must be very cheap.'

'Yes, depending on where you go.'

'Which country do you think was the cheapest?'

'Oh, Afghanistan. I only spent $27 US in one month.'

'That's really incredible. Seems like only enough to pay for a car and a hotel for one day. Is that because the exchange rate is so low?'

'That's not the main reason, I'm afraid. The thing is, I didn't stay in hotels or ride in cars. I walked more than 2,000 kilometres.'

I try to get Pei, sitting next to me, to listen to this tale of travel hardship, but he is utterly absorbed in the other conversation.

'Although I'm not particularly famous in England, I was lucky enough to get a world travel grant from the Winston Churchill Foundation, and the Olympus Camera Company of Japan also helped me with a camera and a large quantity of film. I'm supposed to travel along the old Silk Road, and publish my pictures in their magazine. They've offered me six pages at $6,000 per page. But now I don't think I'll give up the photographs.

'I set out from the great water metropolis of Venice, and first visited the very source of Western civilization, Greece. Then I went to Turkey, the Arabian peninsula, and Persia, and from there I entered Afghanistan.'

'Did you run into any fighting there?'

153

'Oh, practically every day. You might say I was running for my life at least half the time. Why the Soviet Army once razed two whole villages in order to get me. I often came face to face with death.'

'Why? Did you blow up their tanks or something?'

'You've got to be joking. No, I think it was because they didn't want me to live to tell people about the real situation there. I am the first Westerner actually to enter Afghanistan. Of course, I did it illegally. I couldn't possibly have gotten a visa from the Kabul government.'

'How did the Afghans treat you?'

'Amazingly well. Like a king, you might say. In many places, you know, they had never seen a European before. There were days when all I had to eat was one piece of bread; food was really precious. But no matter where I was, if even a little bit of good food was available, it was offered to me first. It was the most amazing place I've ever been. I don't know how many people lost their lives under Soviet fire because of me. Countless numbers risked their lives to protect me. Once an old Afghan was guiding me to another place when the helicopters arrived. There was a tremendous blast, and the old fellow was gone. If I'm around today, it's because of all the people who died for me.'

'From what you read in the papers, I guess the Afghan resistance is very strong, though. There are always accounts of Soviet convoys being wiped out and such.'

'Actually, it isn't very strong. A lot of Western reporters go on and on about Afghanistan, but they've only been to a few specially selected places. All they get is rumours and hearsay.'

'I thought you couldn't speak any Afghan. Didn't you have any language problems?'

'Well, in the beginning I couldn't speak a word. But after a month I was completely competent.'

'What? A whole language in a month?'

'Well, when a man is in an utterly hopeless situation, with literally no other way out, he can learn a language extremely quickly . . . I'm writing a book now, you know, but this book won't really be about me. It will be about the people, especially about those people who gave their lives for me.'

'And after you left Afghanistan?'

'I entered Xinjiang via the Pamirs. Very lucky, really. Again, I was the first foreigner to enter China that way for many, many years. The funny thing was, as soon as I heard the Uighur language, I found I could understand it easily. Uighur contains many words that are identical or at least very similar to Afghan words.[4] Then I travelled to Dunhuang, and then to Qinghai, and finally came here. I really consider myself very lucky to have managed to come to Tibet before the changes have become too great. In a few years, you know, this place will have changed so you won't recognize it.'

'Well, as a tourist, I too hope Tibet will retain some of its special medieval flavour. But from the point of view of the people who live here, I suppose the changes are necessary.'

'That's why I say I'm lucky.'

'Here you go! Five bowls of *Zhang* noodles!'[5]

I raise a chopstickful of noodles to my mouth. Horrors, they positively stink! The mutton is like something dug out of Mawangdui.[6] I really feel like being sick, but I'm afraid Pei will call me squeamish and finicky and not let me go to the countryside with him again. I force myself to gulp some down, and send a lot more surreptitiously to the floor.

4. The Afghans mostly speak Pushto, and some Farsi, a Persian language. But Uighur is a Turkic language that has nothing to do with either Farsi or Dari, the languages spoken in Iran.

5. These are mutton noodles that have been pulled out by hand, using an elaborate system of pulling, twisting and doubling, until the dough simply falls apart into noodles on contact with a hard surface. It is a joy to watch as well as to eat. The meal was really quite delicious, and I can only attribute Liu's disgust to the general revulsion many Han Chinese have for the strong flavour of mutton.

6. In 1972 the Han dynasty tomb of Li Cang, the Marquess of Dai, was discovered at Mawangdui, near Changsha in Hunan province. The tomb is renowned because the corpse of the Marchioness, who died around 160 BC, was in an almost perfect state of preservation, with plump but firm flesh.

I suppose everyone has a desire to confide, and that goes for Nick particularly. He seems to be the loneliest of souls. David is tirelessly sharing ideas and exchanging points of view with Lao Pei and Gesan, but Nick doesn't know any Chinese.

'Look,' I say, 'their conversation's really getting lively. David is an interesting fellow. You can't say his ideas really suit people very well, but he certainly makes you think. And you can always learn something new from listening to him.'

'Yeah, it's your own loss when you don't listen to others. Like that American in our room yesterday. As soon as he heard that David was a communist, he immediately despised him. He's really an idiot, though. He told us Sichuan used to be part of Tibet, and that there used to be three million Tibetans before liberation, but that the communists killed more than half of them.'

'Well, that's probably what the Tibetans he lives with told him.'

'And he believed it. What an idiot! We told him that didn't quite square with the facts, and he said we were just dupes of communist propaganda. So we showed him this book. It had a map that showed Tibet clearly within Chinese territory. He said it was all communist propaganda. So then we showed him the flyleaf: it was written by a Frenchman in the 19th century. Of course, I don't believe in communism either.' Suddenly he turns to David. 'David, can I use your real name in my book?'

'Suit yourself.'

'To tell the truth,' Nick continues, 'There are a lot of policies of your country I don't agree with either. I don't approve of all these imports of Japanese cars. It's only the top leaders who get to use them. And how is it that in a small town like this every shop is crammed full of foreign tape recorders? How can it be that China can't manufacture such things herself? You have satellites, hydrogen bombs, and a pretty respectable defence capability. Why can't you use it to raise people's standards of living? Yes, you do want to attract foreign technology, but not foreign products . . .

156

And, another thing, the bureaucracy here is just horrible. Why, in order to get a permit for this place, I had to wait around for a whole week! Still, I guess it's a good thing Tibet is open at all.'

'That's a very objective way to look at it.'

'I have a deep respect for the facts.' I have to smile. No matter what he says, Nick gives the impression of absolute sincerity.

'No, you're all wrong. It was Trotsky who truly applied Marxism-Leninism in the Soviet revolution . . .'

'But conditions in China are very different from those in Russia . . .'

David and Lao Pei are starting to bare their teeth and redden their knives. Little Gesan sits on one side, nodding, but I can't tell who he agrees with.

'David, what are those steamed bread things they sell here called?'

'*Hua juan.*'

2 April

As soon as it gets light, we take all our luggage down to the side of the road. There we run into an Englishman we met in Lhasa, who tells us he's headed for Kathmandu. Lao Pei says it's easier for women to hitch rides, and before any trucks even appear, he is pushing me into the road. It's the first time I've ever done this sort of thing, and I'm very embarrassed. I come up with all kinds of excuses to get out of it: one moment I need a drink, and take the canteen to fill with tea, milk and sugar; then, I'm trying to find yesterday's driver to try to get our money back. When I see a car from the Department of Transport, I start rushing around even more frantically, terrified I'll be recognized. Finally, I give up even the semblance of trying. I sit on a stone putting my diary in order, but fortunately, Pei is more thick-skinned than I am and eventually a truck appears. It's going to Lhaze, about 20 kilometres from Sakya. Hurray! We can do the 20 on foot. The foreigner climbs into the back of the truck wearing a sheepskin coat.

157

The mountains are stark naked; the rainfall here must be about the same as the Sahara. Lao Pei talks about the structure and composition of the mountain ranges the whole way. He flings out a hand, pleased with himself, and his cigarette flies out the cab window.

'Careful! Couldn't your butt get blown into the back and start a fire?'

'No.' He is so sure.

We are still far away from the nearest village when we notice people waving their hands at us. From the urgent expressions on their faces, they don't look like a welcoming party.

'What's up?' My God, the truck's on fire! People come running up with pails of water.

The fire is not very serious, and quickly extinguished. Only when they are actually climbing on board to put out the flames does our Englishman wake up.

'What's going on?'

'A dress rehearsal cremation ceremony!'

Fortunately, there is nothing but grass and rice in the truck, and only some packing material caught fire. But there is nothing but a single leg left of Pei's only good pair of trousers.

At the 33rd daoban on the Nepal-China highway, our driver pulls over. As usual, he needs to give a friend a lift to somewhere in the mountains. But it's a good chance to get out and stretch our legs. We stuff our hands in our pockets and coolly inspect the daoban. It is an abandoned daoban, to be precise: a now-forsaken cluster of broken-down shacks, currently occupied by some of the locals, a few piles of dust-coated firewood with a big rock on top, a cock strutting around with a flock of sparrows, his chin jutting out, and a big sign by the side of the road that says 'Chang Sold Here' in Tibetan. A big, burly chap is sitting at a sewing machine turning out Kadian covers.

We spend four yuan on a silver dollar bought from an old crone. Lao Pei says that the Tibetan government once issued a bunch of silver dollars in defiance of the Qings, but the issue was quickly outlawed, so their value as collectors' items has soared. Now each piece is worth upwards of 150 yuan. We can't read Tibetan, so we can only hope that ours is one of the rare genuine ones. The more Pei talks about it, the more excited he gets. If this turns out well, he might get into the privileged ranks of Lhasa's old coin collectors.

We wait for a long, long time and no one appears. Lao Pei eventually emits a cavernous yawn and curls up at the foot of a wall for a nap. Only after a time do I notice that underneath his inert body is a pile of yak shit. I try to pull him to his feet, but he just grunts and pushes my hand away, tuning in for the next episode of his nap. Well, let him lie. Anyway, yaks eat grass, so their shit can't be that dirty.

At two in the afternoon, a crowd of people finally show up and start loading cardboard boxes into the truck. I rouse Pei and drag him to the truck, but the driver calls out: 'We're not going anywhere today.' His younger brother is getting married tomorrow and he has volunteered to take the bride over, but she has decided she won't be ready to go until tomorrow. Obediently, we climb down, and Lao Pei suddenly sees the light. 'We've been marooned!' 'Don't move!' I click the shutter: 'And this frame is entitled "The Forsaken Hitchhiker" . . .'

The Englishman indignantly seeks out the driver to get his money back, and finds him installed firmly behind the chang counter. He fiddles with a calculator for a moment and then announces that he can refund the Big Nose only three and a half yuan. We swiftly unload all our luggage and camp at the side of the road.

Five-thirty in the afternoon. The sun goes west and my stomach is rumbling. Pei herds the locals together and poses them elaborately for a black and white shot with our brownie camera. The consequence is that each of us receives a bowl of tsampa and a portion of buttered tea. Lao Pei attacks his so hungrily, I offer him mine on the pretext of having no appetite. After our meal, I recline on the pile of firewood to write my diary. After a while, Pei comes and lies down sluggishly beside me, and, with an uneasy conscience,

159

tells me how well I am roughing it along with him. People get so gentle and pleasant when they are almost asleep.

The burly chap at the sewing machine must have put at least 50 litres of chang into irrigating himself today. Every 15 minutes he goes off for a piss. It serves as a kind of makeshift time piece. I sit huddled close to the foot of the wall, but it is difficult to find a clean spot. There are traces of excreta everywhere. Fortunately, I am near-sighted.

Towards evening, the temperature plummets. Even in my down jacket, I can't stop shivering. The master of the yard absolutely refuses to put us up for the night; if we sit out here and freeze, they'll just have to send us to the celestial burial grounds in the morning. Nothing to do but throw ourselves on the mercy of the Benbula, the chief of the daoban. We plan our attack: histrionic tears if necessary.

The old man's house is so crowded there is practically no place to put our feet. It is just as he says, there is simply no place to put us up. Then I hear him muttering to his wife in a corner. Our hearts are in our mouths, and finally we hear: 'Quilt. One. We lend.' He carries out the best quilt in the house, plus a blanket, and asks his eldest daughter to get us a pillow. The young woman then leads us to a mud-walled room, black as a cave. With a flashlight, we discern a pile of uncarded wool in one corner, next to a bicycle without wheels. We call the Englishman in, and Pei makes the bed, saying, 'Tomorrow you'll probably be crawling with lice.' 'Well, it's better than freezing to death.'

Before the bed is finished, the Englishman suddenly blurts out a torrent of words directed at Pei. They make a dash outside and I follow. There, far in the distance, is an approaching 'Liberation'-model truck. The driver says he is going to a village only about ten kilometres from Sakya. Of course, if we pay for the extra ten kilometres of fuel and a surcharge on our fares, he agrees to take us all the way to Sakya. In the end, it comes to 28 yuan. We know we are being fleeced, but we are a captive market. When we leave, Lao Pei leaves all his cigarettes with the Benbula who lent us the quilt. The poor Englishman will have to stick it out until tomorrow.

160

There is a friend of the driver in the cab already, so we can fit in only one more person. Lao Pei courageously volunteers to sit on the petrol drum in the back. I don't like the idea; by the time we get to Sakya, he'll have frozen like an ice lolly. I tell the driver that I can sit on Pei's lap in the cab. The driver seems shocked. I stick my neck out stoutly, 'He's my husband!'

The mountain roads are rugged and steep, and the driver drinks chang the whole way. Pei sees there isn't much left in the jerry can, and declines the drink and offers it to the driver. What a moron! Pei talks about all the accidents he's seen on the Sichuan road. Before he got into the Sichuan Fine Arts Academy, he worked for a few years as a mechanic on that route. I don't know whether he's trying to sober up the driver, or just to frighten me. By the time we get to Sakya, it's already past one in the morning. We find a place to stay and I fall asleep as soon as my head touches the pillow.

3 April

There is a flock of pigeons in the doorway, making a pleasant 'Gu-gu, gu-gu' sound. I break up a piece of steamed bread with my fingers and put it on a piece of wood to see if they'll eat it.

Sakya temple is more than 700 years old, and looks very different from all other temples. In the middle of the courtyard there are poles streaming with prayer flags, clustered in rough thickets. Lao Pei wants to take a picture, but a lama comes over and says in Tibetan that photography is forbidden. 'Not even outside?' I put in.

'If the master says you can't photograph, then you can't,' says a middle-aged man next to us. 'Where are you from, anyway?'

I have a small notebook on me with a number of Tibetan phrases jotted down, and I'm wondering if I should dig it out.

'I am Gela, this is the County Committee Secretary,' the old lama says.

'How do you do. We have a letter of introduction for the County Committee. We were afraid there might not be anybody in your office today, so we thought we'd come here first and then try to find you later on.' As he is talking, Pei takes out the letter, on which is written:

Comrade Pei Zhuangxin of our gallery and his wife Comrade Liu Fei are on a visit to your county for the purpose of gathering materials for our exhibition. Your help is appreciated.

Just before we left, Lao Pei got a whole stack of letters of introduction signed and chopped [7] by the officers of the gallery. Before they did it, they had demurred for two hours. 'You two are just going on a honeymoon, aren't you? Why do you need an official state introduction?' Pei was very patient. By experience he knew that everything here depends on directions from above. Even people belong to the state, how can we do without a state introduction? In Tibet, you can hardly go to the toilet without a letter of introduction.

When Secretary Suolang has diligently read the letter, he translates it for the old lama. 'Well, can we help you with anything? Are you all fixed up for room and board? The County Committee has its own restaurant . . .'

'Thanks, we're well fixed. This is my wife; she's an interpreter. They're planning to open Sakya up and put it on the tourist circuit, you know. So we'd like to see as much as possible and in as much detail as possible, so as to be able to deliver a complete report to her unit.' You tell them, Lao Pei! He didn't even blink when he came up with that stuff about 'putting Sakya on the tourist circuit'!

'I'm particularly interested in the *Jianguo* [mandala murals].'

Secretary Suolang translates this, and the old lama nods, but then he says that the Jianguo are specially protected and there are some murals that are simply off limits. 'But we've come all this way precisely in order to see how they are being

7. That is, stamped with a 'chop' or carved stone seal dipped in red ink.

protected,' I hurriedly tell Pei. 'If it's not done well, the upper echelon leadership will levy a fine and order a restoration project. But we have to do a thorough inspection first.' Our expressions are dedicated and conscientious in the extreme. I don't know what Secretary Suolang says to the old lama, but in the end he tells us, 'Gela will take you'.

4 April

Sakya means 'the white ashes'. The ashen walls of the courtyards and alleys make a kind of greyish checkerboard out of the hillsides. Children with their faces caked with grime trail long, long strings of snot from their noses. At the head of a dun-grey troupe of pack animals marches a single yak, its tail dyed bright red.

The adults have gone off to the fields to work, and the village is very quiet. Only the children and old people cluster around us. Everything we are wearing or carrying is stroked with wonder and incessant controversy rages over each and every article.

I used to think that the people here were really to be pitied. All they ever get to see in their lifetimes are films in languages they can't understand and strange cars and trucks from somewhere else. Their most extravagant form of self-indulgence is a New Year's donation to the temple of what little they've managed to save up over the past year. They use only the most primitive implements in their struggle to satisfy only the most basic needs. Yet it seems I was totally ignorant.

Pei came here the year before last to do a few paintings. One of them, of a little girl, later got published on the cover of a magazine. I asked Pei why he hadn't brought a copy of the painting to give to the girl. 'What for? I don't want to destroy the harmony and tranquillity of this place.' Only then did I really understand why, with all the works he has done in the nomad areas of Tibet that have been published, he has never once taken them back to the tents where he did them. He told me the way it really was. Sometimes a herdsman would look at his paintings and could not imagine

163

what use they might have; they would certainly never ask to have one.

7 April

A truckload of pilgrims from Sichuan. The driver agrees to take us at a price based on public bus tickets. There are already 20 people or more on the truck. They all speak Chinese, but they stare at us balefully, 'No room!' 'We rented this truck; you should give the money to us.' Amidst all the hubbub, Lao Pei hears an old lady next to me complain of a headache. Immediately, he digs out the medicine kit from my bag and hands her some aspirin. And suddenly the truck is full of patients 'I've got a cold.' 'I'm coughing.' Anybody want some athlete's foot powder? By the time our medicines are all spoken for, right down to the bag they came in, our seats are secure. 'We're from Kangding in Sichuan.' 'I'm from Chengdu.' It turns out we're all from the same region.

The benefits from our pills are immense and far-reaching. The old lady next to me has benefited most and is most expansive in her friendship. I can barely fit my behind in between her and the petrol drum. A particularly well-padded and imperious-looking fellow proceeds to plump himself down on our big bag. The two old bronze vases we paid so much for will have to endure a bit of reworking under the pressure of two buttocks we simply cannot afford to offend.

I am a bit worried about Pei. He is standing on the petrol drum, one hand wrapped around the steel frame of the tarpaulin over the back of the truck, the other holding the camera, snapping the scenery we missed during our night arrival. The truck climbs to the crest of Cuolashan and everyone lets out a big roar.[8] Pei refuses to be outdone, and tries out his coloratura male soprano version of 'One bright day' from *Madame Butterfly*. However, at least now

---

8. It is customary to bellow in order to dispel demons when going over a mountain pass.

164

he takes a rope and ties himself to the frame. As for me, I have already been tied in knots by a very pleasant old man pressing me from behind.

The 33rd daoban! I shudder vigorously. The burly chap is still pedalling his sewing machine; when he hears the truck he raises his head and stares as if stupefied. Lao Pei offers me the canteen. There is a bit of tea left, and I offer it to the old lady first. She hesitates, a bit embarrassed, and immediately hands stretch out from every corner of the truck. 'Thirsty, thirsty.' The canteen is empty.

A big foot in a gym shoe bores its way from some unknown origin and begins to trample my knees impartially and without malice. All the daily grind of the pilgrim's life is impressed upon this shoe, not only in its shape, but in its pungent and distinct odour. The old lady bellows in pain on my behalf.

When we at last arrive back at Tashilhunpo, I sit there quite unable to straighten my back and get up for a long moment. We stay at the same hotel. A little restaurant, a bowl of noodles, and I can feel all those layers of filth on my body. 'Comrade, could you add some more green vegetables, please?'

9 April

Pei is trying to make me jealous. In fact, the young woman in question is very nice, but she cannot arouse my jealousy. I am quite confident I can hold his affection, but I am a bit tired of talking, and at first I chat only out of politeness. She is 21 and has a child one year old. I ask a string of questions about young Tibetan women's attitudes toward love and marriage, their place in the home, etc. In her halting replies, my vague irritation vanishes without a trace, and gradually she confides in me as if I were a close friend.

She was born in the countryside. When she was 13, she came to Lhasa with her older sister, but she received practically no education, and returned to the country to be with her mother when she was 15. Then, when she was 17, she was told by her family that she was ill and had to go to Lhasa for treatment. She didn't feel ill at all, but her mother's firm conviction prevailed. When she arrived back in Lhasa, she learned exactly what 'illness' she suffered from: 'They had married me off. I didn't know the man at all.'

Her husband had been a year older than she was. A very handsome fellow, but that meant nothing to her; she got no pleasure from it. Her husband ran around with other women and fooled around all day long. When he came home drunk, he would shout at her, or punch and kick her. She was a servant in her own home.

She ran back to her family in the country, and poured out her troubles. Her mother understood, but was more concerned that her in-laws might say she had a shameless, lawless daughter, and they a demon daughter-in-law. So the answer she got was the same that has been handed down in such cases for a hundred thousand years: 'You are his. You do what he says.' Be a good, docile, obedient wife. The rest of the family considered her behaviour disgraceful.

Her in-laws simply wanted a daughter-in-law who would throw herself into the domestic chores. So, when she had been married less than a year, she left: 'I had no home.' Eventually she found a low-paying, temporary job. But no matter how often her husband sent people to threaten or try to abduct her, and no matter how her mother and sisters wept and cursed her, she refused to bend.

She used the money she'd been saving for festivals to buy brushes, paint and paper, and learned to paint at a woodworking society, studying Tibetan-style cabinet painting. That was how she met her present husband. He was nine years older than she was, and not very attractive. 'He was not good-looking, but he had a good heart. He treated me well.' I can understand what she means; I have not had it all smooth sailing in my life, either. Anyway, they got married very quickly. She was then 19, and their son was born the following year. I hoped she was very happy now.

'Did you come to Xigaze to visit your relatives?'

'No. To paint, I'm helping somebody do some cabinets.'

'I hear most people are unwilling to let women paint, and those that do pay only half the wages they do to a man.'

'Mm.'

'I guess your husband must really like your painting and give you a lot of support.'

'No. He doesn't let me paint at all. I came here this time because we had a fight.'

'I don't understand. The money you get painting is good supplementary income, at least. Is it that he doesn't he want you showing your face in public, or something?'

'Doesn't want me going out. Wants me to stay home.'

'Making meals? Looking after the kid?'

'No, my son's home with my mother. My husband's a truck driver, he's always away. But he never takes me.'

'I guess he doesn't care about the money. But then I suppose you don't really either.'

'Mm. I just want to work, but nobody wants me. I've got no residence permit, no schooling. I'm a "black" [i.e., without a work permit]. If I had a job, I'd do it even without pay. But my health isn't too good, and I often have to go to the hospital. The doctors in the hospital are really nasty, though. If I were a doctor I wouldn't be nasty. Or maybe I could sell stuff in a shop. I wouldn't fight with people all the time, like the others do.'

She squats down, saying that her back hurts. We haven't really walked far, and she has to stop and squat frequently. I rub her back and ask her what's wrong. 'Three days after I had my kid I had to start working around the house again. Since then it's always been like this. When I had the kid there was no one around to look after me. My husband was useless.'

'So what are you going to do? You're only 21.'

'I don't know. Life is such a bore, not really worth living. What can I do? I'm a black, utterly dependent on my husband.'

'You could go to school. Study. Write about your experiences . . . If you want to study painting, come to my place. My husband will teach you really well. Maybe in two years you could get into the Academy of Fine Arts.'

'My husband would object.'

Pei calls to us. 'Come on over. I want to take your picture.' She carefully fixes her hair and smoothes her clothes. 'No, don't take it, my hair's a mess.'

I help her smooth down a few mussed locks. 'Is your son a good boy?'

'Terrible brat. Just like his papa. Should my collar be in or out?'

'In is better. Do you believe in the gods?'

'Yes. I use the money from painting cabinets to buy butter to offer to the bodhisattvas. But when I'm really depressed, I don't believe so much.'

'Which god is that?' I indicate a figure on the stupa. She gives me the name in Tibetan. 'What's he in charge of?'

'Mmm, he . . . he is, well, after a person dies, if he was no good, he kills him, with a knife, cauldron and fire.'

'If you believe in the gods, aren't you ever afraid?'

'No. I haven't done anything bad, and my heart is good.'

'What's your name?'

'Quzhen.'

We leave Baiju temple and hike up the trail leading to Zongshan. Quzhen's back is very painful. I lend her a shoulder to lean on as we go along, stopping frequently. We had decided to climb Zongshan, but now we can't. Finally, Quzhen can't even stand upright. With difficulty, I help her over to a telephone pole to rest, and kneel on the ground rubbing her back. Pei goes up the road to try to hail a truck. Finally, we get two young people crossing the road with a bicycle to come on over. Pei manages to lift Quzhen onto the bicycle.

Before we part, Quzhen is full of apologies because we never got to climb Zongshan. But I'm not at all sorry. If we must talk of embarrassing things, well, I live in Tibet, alongside countless Quzhens. I love it, but today I realized I don't really understand it. What I've seen is simply the rough, uninhibited wild beauty of the Tibetan people, the pervasive brilliance of the religious art work, but I've never really considered the people who created it.

6 | Contracted abroad

Weifang, Shandong, undated
Dear Old Man and Jan,

In Sakya, we also did some hiking, hoping for our first glimpse of Everest, but no luck. So on the third day, we loaded up on salt pork, tsampa, and butter, and snagged a mail truck bound for Dinggye to the south.

The road to Dinggye was really rough. We broke through the ice three times crossing rivers, and even the two lamas we picked up were terrified and began mumbling mantras. Actually, those two didn't seem to know what they were doing. They gave the driver way too much money, and when they were deposited, as they had requested, at the foot of a mountain in the middle of nowhere, they seemed heartbroken. They had said they were looking for an old 'living Buddha' who lived up there, but from their questions I gathered they were trying to reach Nepal, and where they got off was three hopelessly arduous days from a crossing into hopeless arduousness, practically at the foot of Everest.

We stayed on, and the truck pulled into a dry river bed and got stuck, and almost sanded in. Visibility was zero, but when we finally arrived at Dinggye, we washed and hit the peaks. Then Nick surprised me. Four or five hours out of Dinggye, he made an obvious misjudgment of our route, and shouted at me to follow him. I refused, and continued, reaching the base of the final climb one and a half hours earlier and fresher than him. The last bit was straight up, over a pile of pure, treacherous rubble. Nick gave up and sat down, but I continued and caught up with him on the way down. That was the only time I ever outclimbed Nick, and I felt hard as nails when we reached the village much too late for dinner.

The road to Tingri was untravelled, but a truck was leaving for Sakya, and we took it. As the truck pulled out into the dry river bed where we had got stuck before, we suddenly saw what we had done all that vain climbing for: Everest, a very rare view of the most treacherous East Face, a huge white pyramid, unlike the rather unimpressive ridge view one sees from the north and south. It only lasted a few seconds, and then it was gone, but it was unmistakable, and when Nick's camera shutter had stopped clicking we could hear our breathing over the sound of the motor.

At the junction of the two roads, Tingri to Xigaze, and Sakya to Dinggye, we were loaned a small house for two days while we waited for a lift from some militiamen who were supposed to be guarding the bridge, but instead ran off to spend the night in Sakya. There was lots of firewood, and we still had lots of food from Dinggye. It was one of the nicest nights we spent in Tibet. Later on, some drinkers drifted by on their horses and got us very drunk, but not as drunk as they were. They were so paralytic they couldn't even try to steal anything, and we and one of the soberer ones packed them all into a horse cart. 'Don't worry about me,' he said. 'The horse knows the way, and my wife and son can unload the cart.'

The next day we made barely 20 kilometres to a wretched place called Lhaze, where I ate a can of pork and was sick as a dog for three days. The hangover didn't help, either. But from Lhaze we made it to the two Tingris, Old and New. New Tingri, strangely enough, has a huge fortress on a rock so steep the walls seem to be merely a continuation of it. Old Tingri was a miserable (in the French sense) village with a nondescript little ridge poking its nose over another non-descript ridge – impossible to know it is Everest. We tried and failed to find horses for the trip to the base camp, Rongbu Temple. Tibetans are very covetous of their horses, particularly when it comes to strangers, for some can remember the Chinese press gangs for *oulu* [impressed labour] and yaks. So we turned around and went back to Xigaze, and, after another week, returned to Lhasa.

Jinan, 15 May 1985
Dear Dorothy and Burt,

Here is what happened. On my return to Lhasa, I applied for a permit to travel to Shannan, where the last remaining relative (female) of a prosperous Kashmiri family lived in a broken-down mosque unused for 40 years. Nick and I had become friends with the Xigaze Muslims and they told us we would find interviewing her very interesting; I was still curious about the exact date that Muslims came to Tibet from Kashmir, and at what time they lost their Urdu (which they now use only as a religious language, and some seem convinced they are speaking Arabic). We were denied permission, my passport was confiscated, and I was asked to pay a fine for not having returned directly to Lhasa from Yadong – as I'd been told to do – but instead continuing to Xigaze, where I was granted permission to accompany Nick to Sakya and Tingri.

I refused to pay and was told I'd be deported to Nepal at my own expense within ten days. Every morning we would go sit in at the police bureau, and in the afternoons spend time with Liu and Pei, or see the sights all over again. The money, of course, was running out, but I refused to budge. And then my wallet was stolen in a Muslim restaurant, reducing me to about $80 and some loose change. I called the American embassy at Peking at my own expense (reducing me to about $60), and was asked, 'What do you want us to do about it?'

Finally I found a friend in the Bureau of Foreign Affairs, and the fine was negotiated down to 20 yuan, which I paid in one mao notes, just to peeve them. Then I was ordered to buy a plane ticket to Chengdu, which is unavailable to ordinary dogs and Chinese, but available to foreign big noses on condition they pay triple price, about $180. Instead, we slipped out of Lhasa before dawn and began hitching east.

172

The road from Lhasa descends slowly into a kind of giant wooded ear, where the same atmosphere as at Yadong prevails, piney and cedaresque, only with prayer flags where you would expect the Swiss flag to be. From Linzhi you climb steadily over a really horrifying mountain pass, the other side of which is slick as a frozen stream, with a wall on one side and half a kilometre's drop on the other. The truck skidded constantly, and once I was really on the point of jumping out, but when I reached over Nick for the door handle, I noticed he was asleep. By then, of course, the skid had stopped and we were almost at the bottom.

The first day, thanks to a really fast ride and keeping going until three in the morning, we made over 400 kilometres, which is unheard of in Tibet, all the way to Bayi, where the Dongba minority live, they of the enormous earrings and casual marriages. There we finally slept in an abandoned daoban.

The next day, around noon, a mad truck rented from Chengdu and full of Sichuanese pilgrims on their way home with a five-ton load of pilfered firewood, prayer rugs and rancid butter came roaring, chanting and singing up, and crammed us aboard. There were 35 of us in all, which is well over the legal limit, besides the stolen firewood, leopard skins, amulet boxes, silver and gold swords, yak hides, fox hats, butter and flowers, which were regularly replenished, as they wilted and their petals were whipped off in the wind. At times it seemed there must be far more, because they were always pinching, pouring water and feeling each other up.

All the way down it was a little like one of those long car rides I used to suffer as a kid, where boredom relentlessly turns everyone in the back seat into intellectual and emotional infants. The pilgrims were so jolly in their childishness, though, it was impossible to resist, and soon we were joining in the water fights, the merciless pinching, and even some of the chanting. Of course we eventually became the butt of many jokes, some of them quite, quite nasty. At times, most of the time, we were severely punished for the

173

slightest movement, and farting was punishable by mass excoriation. Nevertheless, the atmosphere dwarfed every discomfort. They were all fabulous singers, and devastatingly beautiful.

We did get to stop at every important temple on the way down, including Chamdo. We also stopped at the giant print shop of Degge, just over the Sichuan border, where the illiterate pilgrims all stooped to drink the ink, knock their heads on the printing blocks and carry away bottles of the print block washing water for their sick children. Was it Hume who wrote that scriptures necessarily democratize a religion? Only if there is also literacy. I wonder, if the Chinese successfully carry out their literacy campaign in Tibetan, will it Calvinize the religion?

We would halt to patch a tyre, and stay four hours drinking tea, boiled up while we were working. Once we were stuck a few days while they dynamited the road. The pilgrims, who were after all Khampas – regarded kind of the way we regard motorcycle outlaws – 'sowed terror throughout the region', and everyone sighed with relief when we left. The whole road seemed to twist and turn between larceny and pilgrimage, hysteria and serenity. We stopped twice at hot springs to bathe under the still falling snow, once in boiling water, for the water boils at less than 80 degrees Centigrade, which is not comfortable, but bearable. Tibetans are among the cleanest people on earth where there is water to wash in.

Sichuan is everything Tibet is not, and the transformation takes place in less than a day. Suddenly you are low, warm, in pouring rain, and the earth is a fountain of chlorophyll. Vegetables are cheap and people are surly. Not a yak or a temple or a blade of beaten silver, not even those beaten-red-iron mountains, bold and ferocious, on the horizon. We stopped two days in the house of the driver in the suburbs of Chengdu, to shake the bends – really, it was a little hard to get used to the thickness of the air!

About two days before our arrival in Chengdu, serious tension developed between Nick and me. I am pretty tough to live with, I guess. Nick is a man of such tolerance, however, he seems practically without fixed principles beyond a constitutional English niceness. His conversation is a mish-mash of trendy leftish opinions and sly male chauvinism. I think, however, what really disturbed me was not so much having to translate his pretentious and, to me, highly offensive stories about Afghanistan all the time (although I believe he should have been imprisoned for what he did, instead he will get a lot of money and fame); rather it was that his presence was a constant reminder that I am a foreigner, that I am not Chinese, which, when I am alone, does not come up very often.

I like acting Chinese, and it is no use telling me that I am not. Acting Chinese helps me, not just with the language, the day-to-day affairs, the bureaucracy and regulations. It also eases my mind enormously, keeps me in serious conversations, and nourishes my intellect far better than the curiosity that Nick's rap always arouses. It makes me feel at home. There was always a place for me among ordinary Chinese in hotels and restos, while Nick had to be treated like a famous writer and painter, and constantly made himself the centre of attention. I was left reflecting more often than I would like on the past, while what I really wished to think about was the post-Tibet, post-Nick future. (Elizabeth, among other things. It is true that she is Quebeçoise and not Chinese, but she is at least a resident.)

When I had decided that this was the real source of the rather petty arguments we would get into – for someone who had walked across Asia, he was hopelessly dependent on my opinion, which I found myself withholding rather spitefully – I told him. He was very upset and promised to part ways in Chengdu, but, actually not really against my will, since it was only a question of a few more days, he continued way out of his way with me, to Chongqing and then Wuhan. Until then, Nick's presence was like a rambunctious member of the audience, constantly leaping on the stage and shouting, 'But wait, you're really Michael Redgrave, you're not King Lear at all!' I wanted to scream,

'I know I'm not, that's not the point!' I wonder if he would have understood.

Where was I? Crossing China in the spring, I felt a burst of nostalgia, it was so different, so new again. Cherries bobbing up and down over our bobbing heads, and green, green, green, sloshing down valleys and rolling right into the unruly but sedate towns. After leaving our truck driver, we made for Leshan. There we saw the biggest and ugliest Buddha in the world, and I bought the opera version of the Qing dynasty version of *Pride and Prejudice, Dream of the Red Chamber*.

It was impossible to buy boat tickets, so we hitched out of town, got on a boat at a small stop, and made our way to Chongqing past sandbars like sleeping whales and amidst gorgeous gorges (which I ignored – after Tibet I was pretty well gorged) and big bogs of bamboo. All this time we had to sleep rough, having no money for anything but food, and, of course, the opera. In Chongqing we went to a smashing fine opera, and then paid for it by being bitten by rats and mosquitoes among the rotten food in the nearby market where we slept. A rat came up and bit my finger very hard while I was sleeping, and I was really frightened, but stayed well. At least, no dogs. There are more dogs than people in Tibet.

In Chongqing there is a concentration camp set up by the Americans, where 4,000 communists were systematically exterminated in about one and a half years in 1946–7, when the Yanks were supposed to be negotiating a 'coalition government' with Zhou Enlai. The photographs and artefacts were just like a small version of Auschwitz Museum: torture techniques, crematoria, and so on, just smaller, and the torturers looked a lot like the teachers you had in physical education in high school, flat top hair cuts and lantern jaws, piggy eyes secreting petty, small-minded, small-town American meanness one would hardly think capable of rising to the challenge of mass murder. Never say never again, as they say. It *has* happened *here*.

Another three days on the boat, and we arrived in Wuhan. Nick left at last for Xi'an, and I went off to be fed, lodged and clothed for a few days by two of Paul's students, who teach there now. Right now I am alive and well and at the address with the long, unpronounceable Russian name in front of it. She is diminutive and dark and her eyebrows meet decisively with a handshake right over the bridge of her flying nose, over yawning depths of enormous Jewish eyes, framed neatly by slavic cheekbones and Karl Marx's chiselled forehead. A pencilled mouth declaims from the pedestal of a chin, mostly slings and arrows, but occasionally I get the most beautiful flowers, usually wrapped around a rock. She has a discipline and consistency that appal me somewhat, given the periodicity of her temperament. I should stop writing about her, because this is her typewriter.

It is pretty hard to stop thinking about her, mush-head that I am. I think I was thinking about this moment all the way down on that skull-shattering truck ride from Lhasa to Chengdu. And yet. She seems to be engaged today in the most ridiculous kind of morning-after long-armedness, the sort of thing you do when you have successfully carried out a risky rip-off and you are counting your change frantically to make sure it was really you who came out ahead. What is all this about? Why does she recoil like those little Tibetan children who had such a horror of my monkey beard and my death's head eyes?

I've got to make myself more livable. Elizabeth is as irascible as I am, yet I've got to make some kind of future with her. She's going to be a big part of me. I hope to hang around her forever, or at least for the next six months in China.

Weifang, Shandong, 1 June 1985
Dear Old Man & Jan,

On the way here I finally stopped in Wuhan and looked up Zuli and Yao Kailun. They were very glad to see me for reasons I can't quite figure out, since I was an unwashed stranger. Chinese gratitude works in strange ways; its objects may be heritable. Anyway, I sat around listening to and saying good things about you for three days, and got around Wuhan with Yao to boot. They both seem really great, although they are terribly severe with their wonderful, sardonic daughter, who satirizes them mercilessly when they are not there. Yao remarked that my presence was a boon for little Yao-Yao, who usually had no one to talk to in the evenings. Given my rather horrid manner with children, I thought this was a rather sad reflection on the overrated parental qualities of the Chinese family.

Ah, but now I am in a bit of a jam. The same thing as this time last year, except I now have two trumps: I speak Chinese and have a resident's visa, indefinitely renewable. Ideally, I want to work here in Weifang, small, far from Peking, and very near to Jinan, where Elizabeth lives. (There is also a kite festival every year, the biggest in the world. I just missed it.) But the comrades are being pretty slow about settling up the details of the job, and I am getting pissed off.

Henan and Hubei, 14 June 1985
Dear Dorothy,

My 'sure' gig in Weifang was as unsure as anything else in this country. I received instructions to wait in Jinan with Elizabeth while they did the paperwork, and above all *not* to look for other work *or* to go to Weifang to inspect the site. This last instruction struck me as unreasonable in the extreme, so I went, got them angry at me by sleeping in the train station (oh, but they don't give a shit if I sleep in the train station in Jinan or Peking), refused to answer their prying questions about my friends in Peking, and then, when, after 13 days they had still accomplished nothing, I did the same thing again. Both sides were now angry in the extreme.

Worse. After I came back from Weifang the first time I spent a really hard week with Elizabeth. For all the right reasons, she didn't want me hanging around and said so. She now feels she was too cruel and threw me out gratuitously after I had lavished much kindness on her. That is not how I see it; I think she acted as any ferociously independent

178

woman would once a passing acquaintance moved in out of dire need and then announced intent to stick around. Although I was pretty upset that she withdrew from conversations unilaterally, I respect unconditionally her right to keep her distance, nay, I even approve it, given that I am male and hungry, so I thought I would find a gig that gave me time and distance and removed dire need, at least, from the agenda.

It was not to be. I left Jinan for Peking, but found myself too bloody depressed to disturb my self-pity by calling on friends. Anyway, I slept in the street for a week and returned to Weifang again where they sent me back to Jinan, with strict instructions to 'don't-call-us-we'll-call-you'. By what right do they inflict me on Elizabeth, whom they have never met? I couldn't face her yet, so I slept in the station and spent the day sketching. But the next night, when I called to tell her the situation (Weifang was supposed to get hold of me through her in three to seven days), I asked could I stay in her spare room for three to seven days and occupy unobtrusive corners of her waking hours? But during this period, the folks in Weifang who should occupy centre stage were strenuously doing nothing. The three to seven days turned into eight; the extra day was added by Elizabeth, so we could see an opera we both wanted to see. And then I felt obliged to *do something*. Not this time to save our relationship, for now that we both understand what is going on it seems that questions of dependence and dire need no longer bear so heavily, at least not on her.

Nevertheless, I dream of having an apartment and a steady job again, and actually doing something during the day. I think her presence is both a short-range reason to do nothing and a long-range reason to do something. Next year she will be in Wuhan, where she is organizing a language centre for a joint Sino-Canadian hydro-electric project. By coincidence, Paul's two graduate students who work in Wuhan have told me I can get a job there. I discussed it with Elizabeth, and she no longer feels particularly menaced by me following her around. But I am

179

really terrified that I won't be able to get a gig there either, and then where will I end up? I now owe Elizabeth 150 yuan, and have no immediate prospects of paying it back.

Next year in Wuhan? No one is expecting me there, where I will arrive later today. But at least I am not following her around the house, shouting questions at the top of my lungs. She was pretty upset when I left, after forbidding me to be mushy, but we have at last managed to stop cramming both our feet in the same shoe, and proceed our separate ways each with the shoes of the other securely on the wrong feet.

Yet in spelling out things that are not exactly written on the wall, I lose the opportunity to describe in more detail the first real harvest season I have spent in the countryside. I am writing this letter at a junction where two grain-loaded trucks tried to pass too closely and sank into the shoulder, thus cutting north China from south China for the next 24 hours. Before that we were bobbing south on a kind of amber Hokusaian wave of grain. Since the division of the soil, the peasants have stopped using any communal threshing equipment, and instead try to do everything individually, which means fighting frantically for a place on the public highway to lay out the *xiao mai* (little wheat, a knee-high variety, as opposed to the shoulder-high sort) to be threshed by the wheels of passing cars, after which they toss it up, fork by fork, to be winnowed by the wind. The demechanization of agriculture, inevitable since Mao refused to try to control population and attempted to collectivize without agricultural capital, is in full swing. During the People's Commune Movement, collectives were set up with no capital at all, and peasants sometimes killed and ate their animals rather than see them collectivized without compensation. Today there is more capital available, and collectivization might be beneficial, but the well is poisoned and no one wants to discuss it. As always, Deng's policies are simply the land taking revenge on Mao's moronic stunts.

All this individual threshing is technically illegal, and certainly dangerous for all parties; nevertheless, it is not simply tolerated, it goes on even in the major intersections of largish cities, a maze of grain, bicycles and truckers in grudging symbiosis with the peasants, who occasionally sell them produce at less than exorbitant prices. The shock of the price hikes in May has not worn off; on the contrary, the food hoarded in April is starting to run out, and the Chinese consumer, always anxious for a back door out of his predicament, is discovering a new tolerance for the peasantry. Who are discovering a new arrogance quite becoming to them. The proud *Lao Touzis*, [old men], cooked brown and cracking with wrinkles in the sun, sometimes force trucks to go around them rather than stop their winnowing on the centre line. Young peasant women are coming to work in blue jeans, and I can imagine them wearing a little bit of make-up, though it would melt after the first 14 hours of work in the broiling sun. Elizabeth gave me a denim salopette to wear, which is the envy of all the peasants I talk to. One of them pinched the inside of my thigh so hard he left a bruise, but he was only interested in the material.

Shandong is one of the coastal 'open' provinces, and it knows it. Henan is everything Shandong was, poor and overpopulated, but unconscious of both. Even young people love opera in Henan, and the Henan dialect is full of phrases that come from it: 'Blowing your lead singer's beard' means getting angry purposefuly; *da bar* means to go for a stroll; and 'Zhang Fei's beansprouts' are small things ennobled by gracious care, like children and ten-year-old bicycles. Henan is one of the provinces I know best, and thus like best, because I have seen it in three seasons. Now, for the first time, I am hitching across it from north to south, and there is as much variety as there was from east to west, more, for the food and speech already tang of the south. What a place! What people! And you want me to hold forth on non-existent plans instead?

Wuhan, 26 June 1985

This is just to tell you that my troubles are all over, at least for now. I've taken a job teaching this summer here at the mammoth Huazhong University of Science and Technology, probably the most prestigious such place outside Beijing, at an outrageous salary and 'foreign expert' status. That will last the summer; then I want to leave and work someplace a little more modest and closer to the real China. So I am considering offers from several places, especially the Academy of Sciences and the Hubei Medical College. Suddenly everyone wants me.

The present gig is a summer programme for teachers and TOEFL [Test of English as a Foreign Language] test-takers, which I will be sharing with about seven other foreign teachers and maybe a hundred Chinese. It will last until mid-August, and I will begin my new job, either at the Academy of Sciences or HMC on 1 September. (Really! Both offers are here on my desk. I have only to sign one.) The salary is much too high for my taste – 540 yuan a month, about ten times the average Chinese salary – but it was take it or leave it, and actually I no longer had the option of leaving it because I had insufficient funds to reach Hong Kong. My next gig, though, should be better (but how to explain to HUST that I'm leaving because my salary is *too high*?).

26 June 1985
Dear Paul and Janet,

Liu Zuli and Yao Kailun got me a wonderful job at their work unit, so my troubles are essentially over! I plan on transferring to something more modest in the fall (but when I tell the administration that, they just threaten to raise my salary again).

It really is all over, the pressure, the worrying, the scraping for money. I only have to work, and I am more than ready. I taught my first two classes and they were both raging successes with the students, although a bit ragged in my eyes, as first classes are wont to be. The students are extraordinary, ferociously bright, and they attack English the way the Olympic team attacks volleyball. I'm really, really grateful to Zuli and Yao.

Elizabeth arrives today!

7 July 1985
Dear Dorothy and Burt,

Yao brought your letter by last night. In contrast to the previous months, this one is full of reassurances and respectable horizons, and that is largely thanks to Yao. As I wrote before, I am teaching a crash summer course to Huazhong University teachers, mostly engineers. I took the lowest class, because I am bored shitless by the new breed of young Chinese who don't really give a damn about English, but are dying to pass the TOEFL and go to America. And the lowest class is always the older types, who have so much to say, although few means of saying it, the most promising possible teaching situation. André, the other 'C' teacher, shares my view completely, but we are both seen as slightly eccentric by the other teachers, really more because we refused to sing during their obscene Fourth of July celebration: snapshots of suburbia and Disneyland, carefully calculated to leave the impression that Americans all celebrate $40,000 plus salaries. I wanted to scream, and André, who is black and from Newark, kept wanting to ask, 'What country is that?'

I signed a contract with the Academia Sinica [Chinese Academy of Science], which will give me an even better gig next year, plus $600 to visit England with. Hubei Medical College, where I would have liked to have gone, wanted me to work without a contract, but Elizabeth pointed out that, given the political situation and my big mouth, this was not really a brilliant idea. I did ask the Academy to reduce my salary as a precondition for signing the contract, and they eventually obliged, reluctantly, because they consider it a first sign of madness.

My current job takes a great deal of classroom time and very little preparation, since it involves a lot of repetition and few of the freer exercises. So I will try to get this word in edgewise while the teachers are touring Hankou, another of the three cities that make up Wuhan. [HUST is in Wuchang, which is where the revolution that began the Chinese Republic started in 1911. The other one is Hanyang.]

Meanwhile, the students are supposedly 'self-studying' under the gaze of their 'monitor'. (Contemptible system; my students are adults and they are treated far worse than Montessori kindergarteners.)

Elizabeth stayed a week, but she was working pretty hard the whole time, and we had only three evenings alone at home (her home, she has two apartment suites near Wuhan University, and a car to drive her around. It is with little difficulty that I can persuade her to leave her fucking car at home, but she feels uncomfortable without her turf under her feet; as she says, 'I need a door I can slam in your face'). We spoke bitterness the first day, mostly because I found her too obsessed with her gig to pay any attention to the really essential matters at hand, namely me, Wuhanese opera, the new lychee crop, two Buddhist veggie restaurants where they serve things like veggie salami, and myriad cemeteries of revolutionary martyrs. Yet I do admire her ability to sit down and do a good job, shutting out the extraneous, even where essential to my mental health. After the first day, though, her presence was not only tonic, it was electrifying.

Before she left for Kunming, I paid back the money I owed her. She's going to knock around China for two months while I work, and then go to a conference on linguistics in Taiyuan. After that, we'll meet up in Canton or Macau in late August and spend ten days in Hong Kong and Fujian, then come back and get to work. I am counting.

15 July 1985

I wrote you not long ago, but will dash this off again as well, in celebration of regular correspondence, one of the chiefest of the considerable pleasures of my new life.

Yes, the propitiators of the jealous gods who guard my career are indeed Zuli and Yao, but actually I feel far more grateful to Elizabeth, who put me up, put up with me, and bent her considerable network to try to find me a gig, even as far away Xi'an or Beijing. Also, although I don't like to think about this, she stood to lose by helping me, and she probably did not want me in Wuhan, at least not at the beginning.

184

As for my current high salary, I did play briefly with the idea of giving money away, but that is really not the point. The point is that it shouldn't be my money, and 'giving it away' obscures that considerably. Anyway, I am very happy now with the wages the Academy of Science has agreed to, since they are roughly the equivalent of a good Chinese wage. The real reason behind my apparent fit of futile moralism, or moral futilism, is, I think, the sound trade union principle that everyone in the unit should be on a rough par with the most advanced workers. I have, as I told you, a hard currency allowance, which I accepted, and technically I am also entitled to change half my salary into hard, but since the exchange rates are obscenely favourable to the American dollar, that would be utter madness, as well as minor treason.

One of the other teachers is also a professor of theoretical physics, and she is teaching me something about wavicles and so on, but there is really precious little time for anything but English. My students are so wonderful, I'd rather spend all my time with them, and I usually shoot the breeze with them in the afternoon for four hours, when I am supposed to be preparing class and they are supposed to be self-studying each other. I have three wonderful, resilient older women, the sort that always enchant me so. One of them, Ms Wu, just dropped by with a new breed of watermelon she says was just invented; she has already discovered how to choose the best ones by knocking them on the lower dimples. Indeed, it was an excellent watermelon, particularly after I whacked off the top and poured in half a bottle of Qingdao cognac, and then shared it with Ms Wu and her daughter.

One of the best-loved features of my class is the songs I translate into English, following the example of the well-loved Chinese singers who sing things like *Jingle Bells* in Chinese. Another popular feature is chants, which I do instead of dialogue memorization, setting the chants to rhythms that I sometimes beat out on a prayer bell from the Buddhist temple in Hanyang. And then there are limericks. Mine spawned a host of imitations from my

185

students, some of which I find pretty good, though not exactly limericks:

> Wuhan, Wuhan is a fiery stove
> All the wind stop and the temperature stay
> But *bing-gao* [Chinese ice-lollies] and beer are all over
> And you can bathe many, many times a day.

And then:

> Damn! the rain again
> Damn! the rain again
> I curse this nasty rain
> It rain without end.

I refined a few of these and had the class chant them. Particularly the last one, which I said, in deference to the modesty of the student in question, came from the middle acts of *King Lear*.

Sometimes, though, they get pretty carried away. In order to clarify the difference between exciting and dangerous, I asked them to use one of the two to describe various experiences: smoking, Shanghai, airplane travel, dreams, movies, the Cultural Revolution. It was surprising how many considered that an exciting time; Mr Peng, my journalism-professor student, tells me it was the only time in Chinese history when true freedom of the press existed, because everybody everywhere was publishing something.

By the way, I have started to read the illegal or semi-legal private press here, whose appearance took place shortly after my arrival in China. It is absurd and sensationalist, with a lot about Jiang Qing, Liu Shaoqi, and so on, but more on the level of gossip than politics.

17 August 1985

This last week kind of fell in on me. I hate giving exams, especially here, where their significance is practically religious; they are no mere metaphor of success. In addition, I had a two-hour lecture to give, which I had less than no enthusiasm for – I did a comedy routine on 'Jews in China'. (There is a good book by Sydney Shapiro by that name;

there were some Jews in Kaifeng until the Jesuits came. But that had nothing to do with my talk, which was about Jewish jokes.) Last but not least, of course, I have been living in a constant state of heightened emotional terror, thanks to Elizabeth.

Exams are a ridiculous business anywhere, but this was a parody on a farce: two completely parallel exams, at least one of them totally useless, whose only function was to demonstrate once again the (often justified) lack of confidence on the part of the administration. My myrmidons, who had scored the lowest initially (23/60), rose to 'A' level (45/60), which is an increase so phenomenal I can only attribute it to the arbitrary idiocy of the exam itself. My own exam shows a more modest phenomenal progress, especially among the older students I've been rooting for. I've been sitting here on the train to Hong Kong trying to convince myself that I am merely relieved and do not feel patronizing pride in people, who, after all, are all much more experienced teachers than I am, when they are not my students.

They do not easily lend themselves to my patronizing, for the matrons are all busy matronizing me, apparently convinced that I cannot manage the slightest detail of my personal life. They gave me two days of going-away parties – even though I repeatedly protested that I would only be away for ten days – and a heap of pricey presents, including a jade chop [personal seal] and a Jingdezhen china vase. I bought a few presents in return, and made my now infamous *mi-ba* water buffalo meat burgers in yellow wine as a symbol of international confusion.

Last night we held a ghost story session in English. I thought it couldn't possibly last as long as the opera session of the week before, but it went on until three in the morning. My only young woman student was so terrified she kept her fingers in her ears for two hours. Women my age are terrible spectacles of emotional retardation due to repression. Many of them play with dolls and are afraid of the dark. Their company, for all their grace and beauty, often leaves a distinct feeling of disgust. Not at them, though.

187

Contracted abroad

I too am recomposing myself, just back from Mad
Confusing Elsewheres. Two solid weeks of incomprehensible
emotional excoriation with Elizabeth in HK and Macau.
Then two days of raiding the British Council in Beijing for
books, tapes and something called Realia (this is not a
country far removed from Albion, but a kind of show and
tell technique in teaching English). Elizabeth, as usual, has a
better idea. With characteristic chutzpah, she is teaching her
classes of physics professors physics classes in English,
making them correct her mistakes, so I suppose she is going
to be dragging in bunsen burners and rolling around chunks
of plutonium and Abstralia.

In Peking I once tried to explain to old Tan, my Chinese
Jewish mother, why one was inherently suspicious of
affections contracted abroad, why one cannot help wondering if they would survive the increased competition and
diffused attention of the native soil. She said, 'Yes, well,
some people get married to avoid that, you know'.

Desperate males. Dire straits. Restricted choice. That is
of course what Dr Tan really meant when she said that some
people choose marriage rather than expatriation in order to
end the romantic frictions of youth, which she basically sees
as caused by too much freedom. She calls me an 'animal'
because I sleep with women I am not married to; I explained
to her that animals were unfamiliar with the use of birth
control, not to mention inept at masturbation, but, rather
like her, narrowly preoccupied with the procreative aspects
of things. She protested that all she ever thought about
during sex was cell division. A wonderful lady, but even
more intolerant than I am.

I really do appreciate your advice, Dorothy, which I
would qualify as comradely. Of course you are right.
She needs more space and I need less need, or anyway,
less ostentatious needs. You are so right that it sounds
a little bit banal, the sort of thing I would try to put in
Italian and set to music. I am trying. But it is really not so
easy.

188

Space. I came to Wuhan with precisely that idea. I didn't take a job in her unit, even when I was desperate. I got my own flat, my own money, I gained weight so that she wouldn't feel so bloody responsible for me. I have shaved off my beard, because I only grew it to please her, and now I find she is displeased by my doing things to please her. I vowed not to see her on weekdays. When she said she wanted to be alone in Hong Kong, I told her I wouldn't go unless she wanted me to; then she wanted me to. I arrived in Hong Kong and took a room of my own, although she asked me to share hers, just in case. I think of her a lot, and I do not find it difficult to be considerate, but sometimes it is my consideration she finds overwhelming; last week she burst into tears because I went to get two bottles of hot water for her which the maid didn't get. 'You're not my servant! I do perfectly well without you!' To which I wanted to scream, 'She's not your fucking servant either!' But that would have been the end, because it is precisely my opinions on things like tips, maids, high salaries and so on she finds most threatening, and anyway beside the point, which is my apparent threat to her independence.

In Hong Kong she made a point of being unbelievably beastly to me; she never spoke to me unless to cut me down, she refused to walk next to me on the street. Constant, constant humiliation. It was so ridiculous I kept ignoring it until I was ready to burst into tears. I tried simply shouting, 'God, let's shout about it, let's talk.' But of course in Hong Kong it was impossible, we were too busy getting lost and trying to find vegetarian restaurants, and having all the usual quarrels instead of the quarrels we really needed. She still wants to end the relationship. I still don't. She resents the fact that the decision is now entirely up to her, and she doesn't want to think about it. I realize, of course, that she doesn't really love me, or she couldn't possibly treat me with such cruelty. But the idea of her shopping around China for a better lover is ludicrous, *pace* Dr Tan; you can't even get the brand of toothpaste you want normally. That is not smugness, that is just a fact of our lives.

27 September 1985

My strings with Elizabeth are broken. No, I didn't threaten, or issue any ultimatums, or anything. But we both know she doesn't want or feel capable of what I want and feel capable of, so it is an exercise in hypocrisy to go on sleeping together.

We cannot make love, but we can't really stop seeing each other either. We are both the only foreigners in our units, we both have no other friends in Wuhan; we depend on each other for everything from Hainan island coffee to Mozart operas to mooncakes to texts, cassettes and video-tapes. We can't really afford to hate each other, gloat, or wallow in self-pitiful pits.

If the above sounds unrecognizably mature, I assure you it is the result of a long and considered tantrum. I stopped seeing her for two weeks, during which she came by my place several times on business. I cannot now remember what she looked like, what she was wearing, or what her business was, only that she was here and that I didn't see her. I hated her intensely for spitting on my affection, for her petty enviousness of my pettier talents, for her sulking when I spoke Chinese, and her insufferable self-abnegation when I did a little intellectual posing. Above all for her despair and her lack of guts. I felt totally shut out, since it was obvious that her kindnesses were more between her and her culpability than between her and me.

But the day before yesterday I began to consider that in fact it really is all my fault. Of course it is. It is really the same thing that has occurred with all the other women in my life. I know how to be 'friendly and considerate' and not threatening and exigent. But I didn't do it. I could only think of expressing what I felt, and not of how it would be received.

This is the kind of crappy romanticism to which the Chinese are prone, the idea that it is the thought that counts and there is no need to try to phrase it in a non-destructive way, in fact, quite the contrary. I do not subscribe to this, any more than I subscribe to the long-armed coolness of

190

travellers you see all over China making love with their back packs strapped on and one hand on the Indian pouches holding their travellers' cheques. And I don't accept, gracefully or otherwise, the notion that loneliness is a kind of normal condition.

But except when wallowing in self-pity, I do not admit that my position is 'poignant', and if I lack some of the defences of real men, well, I think much of the problem stems from the fact that I have developed defences against which the women I meet have not developed offences: hyperanalytical madness, unpredictable and sometimes incomprehensible humour, and a bizarre notion of 'the adult thing to do' which corresponds to no adults I have ever met.

My classes are really a hell of a lot of work. Especially teaching composition, because I have decided I can really do a good job. I now have a huge stack of other people's writing to look at. It is rather enjoyable, really. And starting tomorrow I'm going to an opera every night for a week (we have a week off to celebrate National Day). Alone.

8 November 1985

I'm really very fed up with my foreign colleagues who imagine they don't have to prepare their classes. Elizabeth is, among other things, the only teacher here I really respect. Unlike me, she can give classes in which she hardly says a thing, and her students chatter away madly. She is also supremely organized, and her exercises always produce not simply right answers, but right emphasis; you find students really concentrating on interpretation rather than mere decoding, paying attention to speech features like tone of voice, special stress, and so on. She is really great.

She has turned me on to the rather little-known field of linguistics known as discourse analysis. It's really great fun, but almost impossible to describe. An attempt to put linguistics on a statistical rather than a merely theoretical basis, by giving large chunks of real discourse, rather than artificial, abstract samples, for analysis. It is horrendously complex, and obeys completely other laws than linguistics

191

proper, rather the way epidemiology is different from anatomy, but one has the impression of really doing something rather than merely saying something, with language. I'm reading her PhD thesis now. I wish I had someone to discuss it with; she refuses to talk about it.

I'm not sure what to do about her. I remain perfectly mad about her, though I imagine things will never be quite the same. I no longer find her very dangerous, but I still love her. And, after all, we are alone.

I have bought an oven, and I am baking a lot of bread according to Burt's ancient recipe. Also listening to a lot of opera. We got five complete operas in Hong Kong, and we are revelling in them. Nevertheless, the rarefied and personalized culture feels creepy some evenings, and I find myself frequenting grotty Chinese operas and swigging beer in filthy jiao-zi joints along the highway. But China is still wonderful.

3 December 1985

Briefly and quickly. I'm off work on the 25th of January and begin the new quarter on the first of March. My vacation is a bit longer than most other work units (considerably longer than Elizabeth's). Huazhong University's break is quite a bit shorter: they go back at the end of February. That is why it would be best for you to deliver your lecture then. At the end of January, people will be sitting exams and packing their bags and rolling Chinese dumplings. However, if you really can't stay that long, it can be arranged, malgré tout.

I couldn't tell you this sooner, because no one knew. The Spring Festival is determined by the lunar calendar, which is normally the province of the emperor, and, since the emperor's eclipse, has been rather uncertain. An extra month is interpolated here and there without any warning, by no one knows who, when the lunar and the Gregorian diverge too far, but this is quite arbitrary and unexpected. It may seem incredible to you that a country can be run this way. But far more incredible things are in store for you, I assure you.

10 February 1986

Only a week has elapsed since you left Xi'an, but already many bridges have gone under the water. I suppose what follows will not surprise you as much as it did me. But I'm going to recount it at maddening length anyway.

There was almost no traffic on the road from Xi'an, and I was really very worried that E would take a vacation and take off without me (she had been suitably vague on the subject previously). Besides, I had bought a huge bagful of junk, a pottery rhinoceros, a beard, and a whole set of opera face paints (today I took out the face paints and did the rhinoceros up to look like the Monkey King [the hero of *Journey to the West*]), and a collection of art books (very cheap here). So I gave up hitching after the first day and took a train. The whole train had apparently been booked up by some air force cadets from the academy in Xi'an who were by one of those ridiculous coincidences that is taken for granted in conversation, all from the same tiny suburb of Wuchang and on their way home to spend Spring Festival with their families. We stayed up the whole night talking politics with our breath visible:

'No one on the Central Committee can really talk, no one!'

'Deng is the only one who even knows how to think.'

'Yeah, but Zhao Ziyang at least knows enough to keep his mouth shut!'

'Crackdown on corruption again, according to my mate in Beijing!'

'That's a diversion – they have to pick up on it before the anti-reform faction does!'

'Yeah, well, they're going to be all the more tough for being insincere; they want executions and they want them high up!'

'My friend writes me from the Laoshan front line [the Vietnam border] that the fighting is getting tougher, but going well!'

'You moron! Ask him which is it, getting tougher or going well? I'm going out there next year!'

Then there was a discussion of the demonstration in Xi'an over the trade deficit with Japan:

'Yeah, but look, so small nobody saw it but the police!'

'You kidding? It was right in front of the train station!'

'Shee-it, half of them was just hustlers trying to scalp off their work-unit train tickets home, so they could spend the money drinking in Xi'an! I know, 'cause. . .'

' 'Cause that's what you were doing, weren't you?'

'Anyway, soon as the scalpers saw they had no money, they backed off soon enough; there wasn't even 200 demonstrators.'

'Back off in front of the train station and you get trampled to death. Besides, you know how it is, whenever people are standing in line, you figure they must know something you don't!'

'Smart thinking, really . . . how can you tell a demonstration from a queue for platform tickets?'

'Easy, you just arrest any line that starts moving!'

So anyway, to make a short story long, I got back in the afternoon and waited obediently until evening to phone (she finds all surprises unpleasant, but particularly pleasant ones). She was there and sounded very glad that I was. I went, we had a good laugh, and the usual strained gratitude over all the junk I bought her (not that I had chosen badly; she has Hindu ideas of prestation, you see, all is power relations thinly wrapped in coloured paper).

We talk about her work – she is very happy with it. I like hearing her talk about her work, even when she is not happy with it. And she likes talking about it – but suddenly she covers her mouth and remarks that she had decided before I came not to talk about it. (Shit, how unscripted our conversations are sometimes – you'd think we were real people speaking French, and not English teachers.) Is she glad to see me? She suggests pleasantly that I have three weeks left in my vacation and that I should get out of Wuhan. (This is a gentle manipulation. I recognize the thin edge of the hedge.) I smile and say I want to stay here. I have things to do and I want to be with her.

194

'But I wouldn't be at your dispensation!' she cries.

This is a high-class power struggle, and he who gives the first shit loses the trick. I consider replying as in the past. But I don't.

'But I don't want to dispense you!' I flee into the ambiguities of my command of French – I mean 'dispense' in the English sense, but of course what I have said is that I will not give her a dispensation. I laugh. She is unsure whose trick it is. She remarks rather smugly that I'd go anywhere with her if she had two weeks vacation, instead of four days, that my 'things to do' are only pretexts. Well, of course, and all this poker-faced crap of pretending not to give a shit is only a game. Does she not realize I am simply playing? Or does she relish even the illusion of detachment as a confirmation of her power? I see nothing particularly shameful in that (nor anything particularly honourable in the illusion of detachment I am conceding her), and I admit it gleefully. But she should know better than anyone how decisive pretexts can be, how inescapable the power of rationales over even reasons in sustaining decisions when people are looking on (I am still here in Wuhan 'doing things' a week later!).

She says she doesn't want to be obsessed with me, that she has been obsessed and does not like it very much. She even flatters me at great length on my allegedly obsessing sexual qualities. I laugh, and she accuses me of not taking compliments with my customary grace.

'But I want to savour it later, in private.' I touch her. She doesn't respond at all, and fortunately the hot water comes on at this point, so I ask if I can take a bath. 'Men are all alike. If you say you find them sexy, they think you'll go to bed with them.'

Actually, I'm just thinking of going to bed, with or without her. I've been up all night, and I'm not feeling sexy at all, particularly after what she has said. Another power game, I suppose. I am also rather weak from hunger, but my stomach is too upset to eat. I get into the water.

In the past, when I said I did not offer love expecting immediate returns with interest, I suppose I was sincere enough. But actually, I ignored the whole issue of her emotional convenience, and her desire, real or imagined, to disengage; I expressed my own feelings and didn't worry much if they interfered, constructively or destructively, with hers. And did the most extreme violence, incidentally, to my own feelings, which now border on murderous rage rather than unrequited love. Plus, I am fed up with this ridiculous make-believe that I am somehow above the battle simply because I am more conscious of it than she is. It is hypocritical of me to pretend I have not the slightest shred of macho honour worth saving. I must come to grips with what it means to be 'Elizabeth's inconvenient friend'. Come out of the closet. There is really nothing I can do that will make her forget, even momentarily, the whole game of dependence and convenience, the strategy of withdrawal she is pursuing, the balance of terror between us. But I try. So I tell her this long story, from my adolescence. I suppose it is an oblique attack on her solipsism, but above all a justification for what I am about to do, using her professed wishes rather than any guesses about her motives as the basis for action. And that is why, I says, I am taking your demands into account and getting my ass out of here without making love to you. Thanks for the bath, says I, and gets out.

Stay! She is near tears. I had thought my story to be more amusing than polemic. Perhaps I over-emphasized the bit on adolescence. I kiss her forehead and ask what is on her mind. She wants to know what demands she made that I was going to take into account. I tell her that I mean her request for an end to our relationship, of course, for her 'independence', her solitude. She does not remember having spoken of ending it. I am amazed. It is not the sort of thing one forgets having brought up. I quote a few of her phrases. She recognizes them suddenly and miserably. I don't understand. Can she really have forgotten? She obviously really did! Then she is only half-conscious when she plays these ridiculous games with such consummate skill! How can that be? Has she forgotten that there is a distinction between feeling and speaking, has she lost track of all distinctions between herself and the world? I can see her thinking, 'I am not a good person'. I know some of the agony of guilt that will follow my departure.

I ask if it will keep her up very late if I leave. She says, rather childishly, 'If it does, it does!', and then denies it, saying she will be asleep as soon as her head hits the pillow. I add a rather childish 'Na!' to ridicule her tone of voice, and we laugh. I leave. But only I know I will not be back.

Suddenly, I realize I have forgotten my gloves, and go charging back. As soon as the door opens I realize they are in my bag, crouching like dead rabbits at the bottom of a game pouch. I haven't forgotten them at all. For once, she is really confused. Me too.

She is alone. Because that is what she wants. And I am alone too, which gets me back to those mysterious 'things' I was going to do in Wuhan, while Elizabeth was not dispensable. Pretexts, she said, yes, but pretexts do live on long after the end is moot. Part of what I wanted to do is done. I have been working on Arabic, finished the plays of Guan Hanqing, finished Burt's book, finished the Sci-Tech Report, did some typing for next session, caught up vengefully with my correspondence. Started painting a little, too, though the results are not very gratifying (not counting the rhinoceros, which is standing here grinning at me). And I was going to write more about China, and less about me, but this letter is long enough.

7 | Passing through

Wuhan, March 1986
Dear Dorothy and Burt,

I feel a lot better. I got things done before classes started: wrote a long letter to a local sex education magazine about female orgasms and male masturbation (it was about eight pages long, by far the longest bit of composition I've done in Chinese; true, it is a subject at which I am an old hand); followed the news every day on the Voice of the UAE from Abu Dhabi, and read selections from the Quran in a bilingual Arabic/Chinese edition; read three books on discourse analysis; and went back to Beijing briefly to weep on Dr Tan's shoulder.

Dr Tan was typically nasty. She called me an 'animal' again, and told me I thought I had problems! It appears that after we had left, some foreign teacher of her daughter-in-law came by with Canadian relatives. The elder of the family got a headache, and, apparently with the daughter-in-law's permission, took off his shoes and lay down on her son's bed! Can you imagine? Such a horror! Foreigners are really scarcely human!

I got to see Dr Eh too, though Lida, his Chompie (Chinese Outwardly Mobile Professional) son is now studying in Roswell Park, New York, at last. As I had no money, Dr Eh put me up. As he had no extra bed, we shared his, a 60-year-old hospital director and an unwashed English teacher. He saw nothing unusual in the offer: 'My wife is away at a meeting in Chengdu; she's not using it.' I went by the Cancer Institute and saw all my former students. Some of them practically wept when they realized I was still in

198

China. I told them I wasn't going anywhere! I couldn't help reflecting what a terrible injustice I have done my Chinese friends by concentrating all my attention on a foreigner.

My conversation class is – extremely extreme. The good students, whom I never like very much, are very good indeed; the bad students, whom I prefer, are very bad. And there is hardly anything in between. Nevertheless, it risks being a very lively course: the material is really excellent, and the better students have ample opportunities to exercise their teacherly tendencies.

The composition class is hopelessly unwieldy, as predicted. In desperation at the thought of correcting 70 compositions a week, I have resorted to 'self-correction' sheets. I usually put together a 'typical error' composite of several sheets, with instructions on how to correct them, and then leave them to do it themselves. All assignments will receive either 100 or 0 this quarter, under Arthur Rubenstein's formula: either you can do it or you can't. The result is not a substitute for a real manageable class, but it is 'mangeable' at least.

The truly redeeming feature, of course, is the students. I have an ichthyopathologist, an expert in nuclear magnetic resonance, a specialist in edible algae, and a flourishing crop of agronomists from my favourite region, the far northwest. I think I will stay here another year, and then move to the northwest. Maybe to Xining, where I can study Muslims and learn Tibetan.

March 1986
Dear Old Man,

Thanks much for your letter, particularly for the physics rap. I have, in addition, some terribly distinguished-looking grey hairs from you for my birthday, one in my reddish beard, which makes my mug look kind of middle-aged and smoky, after a lifetime of looking adolescent and inflamed. I am savouring middle age with appropriate restraint, and look forward to as distinguished an appearance as my father.

Passing through

It was a birthday more like any other and unlike the one I passed a year ago in Tibet. Elizabeth, from whom I am now definitively unstuck, asked me over for dinner, and presented me with a silver ring from Xishuangbanna and a set of pictures of the Potala. Looking at the reflecting pool at the foot of the Potala, I cannot help reflecting that my expectations of a quieter life have been fulfilled beyond my wildest dreams, and, more surprisingly, so have my expectations that I would enjoy it more. Nevertheless, I would like to try to get back there this summer.

Halley's comet is a very big deal here. I have organized several classes around it, and we listened to the destruction of the Giotto cameras live on the BBC during one of them. Elizabeth went all the way to Indonesia to get a really good look at the comet; I haven't seen it, and I don't suppose I ever will. Equally big is the American space shuttle disaster, so Ken's letters are a fascinating source of copy for my exercises in composition.

I have been undergoing various kinds of revolutions in my teaching style, and, in addition, have undertaken to present a series of full-length feature films at the Academy, a business that requires some eight to eleven pages of written exercises, in addition to tape and discussion work every week – almost like bringing out a small newspaper. That leaves me little time for much else; my Chinese is suffering, not to mention my Russian and my Tibetan. Nevertheless, I feel I am getting something done, which I hardly ever feel about my language studies, and never felt about my 'American Culture' lectures. And, finally, I am learning a great deal about discourse analysis.

18 April 1986
Dear Dorothy and Burt,

Terribly sorry I've let you go this long, and I really have to let you go a bit longer. At first I thought I would put you off until I had a proper chance to write at length, and I wanted to type up my conversations with Metal Mountain Wang, as promised. But now it looks like I won't get a proper respite until May Day, when I really will sit down and write properly.

Anyway, I'm actually quite a bit prouder of the exercises I construct to accompany the film series I'm showing. They are not simply reading exercises; they are painfully worked-out attempts to develop predictive and other skills, going from reading, which is the students' forte, to interpretative listening and even discussions of intonation. Perhaps if you knew how many sleepless nights went into this weekly production, or perhaps if you saw how much my students make of the films we show – they laugh at the jokes, they talk about them for days, they await the next worksheet with something very like anticipation – you would understand why I prefer this kind of hack writing.

In addition, I've been putting out a weekly oral exercise tape with worksheet of one hour to an hour and a half in length, as well as preparing my next methodological revolution: classroom simulations. I decided, to put it briefly, that my teaching had become much too formalistic, which prevented me from structuring classes so the same vocabulary can be approached with 'everything the students have', reading, writing, listening, speaking, even talking about language. It also prevented me from organizing activities in which the same vocabulary is used under varying conditions: briefing, preparing a plan, carrying out a plan, criticizing, debriefing, etc. This kind of approach is so obviously closer to what happens in life, so obviously closer to what I do in my own language learning, and so obviously a healthy reaction against the hideous specialization of language learning at our institute, I cannot resist it. I must find some way to tap it. The films are an obvious beginning, but they are passive. What I really need is a play, like Dario Fo's, with audience participation. That is where the simulations come in.

And I have a new lover, who is a teacher over at Hubei Medical College. She's a funny kind of survivor, rather a mirror image of Elizabeth, that is, everything that she wasn't, and not anything that she was. She reminds me a lot

201

of Karen. We spend a lot of time reading together. What can I say? She's a *mensch*.

4 June 1986

Well, the last week of the term is closing in; I have finals to prepare, etc. Let me just fill you in on the questions you ask.

Elizabeth is still here, and has been pretty miserable, which I imagine makes her very happy. I had hoped to remain friends, but she so tires herself out doing me favours, and then gets bitter and resentful when I thank her only for the favours, or when I find the favours too enthusiastic to be of practical value. I am always conscious that she has something more on her mind, and that makes forgetting and friendship difficult.

What is Barbara really like? Actually, she is of working-class origins, orphaned at 13 and all. Well, leftish in a not very leftish way; she was a member of DSA [Democratic Socialists of America, a wing of the Democratic Party] at Kent State University, where she did a huge thesis on Employee Stock Ownership Plans. A little too quiet and uncritical, totally lacking in self-consciousness and egotism, but firm enough in defending her own interests; she has been known to tell me to fuck off. She is serious about China and Chinese. We will not see much of each other this summer, because, much as we enjoy each other's company, she wants to work on Chinese.

So do I. But the main thing I want to do is go to Tibet. I thought I would make the trip by bicycle, either from here or from Lanzhou in Gansu Province. It is a common, well, not very common, undertaking among patriotic-minded young Chinese intellectuals, one of whom may accompany me; but as far as I know, no foreigner has ever attempted it. I plan to leave here around the 30th, reach Lanzhou around the 15th of July, and Lhasa about two weeks later.

I am a great cinema-goer as well as opera-goer these days. And every single film I've seen in the last three months has been in some way a glorification of the family as 'the fighting unit of socialism'. By far the most nauseating was *Juvenile Delinquent* which was the subject of a national campaign of promotion. It was made by inmates of the Shanghai reformatory, who also wrote and sang the songs: *Mama, Far from Home*, etc. The story concerned a woman sociologist who becomes interested in doing a survey on inmates of the reformatory. She discovers that all of them had unhappy family lives, and especially bad mothers, and attempts to mother them all, to the dismay of the prison guards, who know their job better. She gets many people hurt with her meddlesome permissiveness, and then returns home at the end of the film to discover that her own son, left in the care of her mother, has been arrested and is being led away as a juvenile delinquent. There is something very sick about a society where this and *Rambo* are considered the epitome of cultural 'healthy thought'. On the other hand, a really great film I saw, *The Golden Dream*, in which a young woman tries to become a dancer to the dismay of her husband, who is a great pianist, has been roundly denounced for inciting young women to divorce their husbands.

Anyway, as part of the promotion campaign around *Juvenile Delinquent*, we foreigners were all rounded up and taken to a model prison. I remember behaving myself quite well, but some people say I asked some embarrassing questions – I asked about the suicide rate; I asked why they had a 'tracking' system, and pointed out that their system tracked 'unintelligent' people into farm work, while the more educated ones were sent to work in a glass factory, whereas in fact the mental operations required in farm work were far more complex than those required in most factory jobs. A large majority of the women were there for unspecified 'sexual' and 'moral' offences. I asked about the definition of the 'sexual' crimes of the female offenders, and why they were all tracked by sex instead of by ability: they were all seamstresses.

I got some interesting answers: the suicide rate is low, but not that low; no one ever thought of the 'tracking' system as a way of improving the prisoners, it was a matter of increasing production (?); there were too few women to justify a tracking system. Creepiest, I think, was the inmate who told us that no inmate ever talked about why they were in the clink. If true, it implies that they never make friends or trust another inmate. I met the same inmate on the street shortly after his release. His hair had grown, and he was much more open and smiling, but he confirmed what he had said. I am trying to weigh in on this debate with an article in Chinese, which will probably meet the same fate as my piece on female orgasms. (Dr Tan has kept a sullen silence on this last; I'm afraid I may really have damaged our friendship.)

More later. After finals, I mean, from on the road.

3 July 1986

I got, with gratitude, both books and your letter of 20 June, the former right before I left for Sichuan with Jan and Paul in tow, and the latter upon my return yesterday.

As for *Daily Life in Ancient China*, just forget it. I wasn't looking for any particular passage, I was just interested in a 'Braudelian' account of life in the Tang period. My own rediscovery of *Pride and Prejudice* owes much to a student who pointed out certain strong parallels with *Dream of the Red Chamber*. And much of the wonder of *Dream of the Red Chamber* comes from the worm's eye view of 18th century China you get. In one scene, Baoyu [the hero] and a cousin are initiated into the deep mysteries of spinning thread by a country maid. The cousin is mostly interested in the girl and doesn't understand that Baoyu is genuinely interested in how cloth and rice are produced. In another scene, the main characters, who have been searching heaven and earth for classical allusions to cabbages and kings, are confronted by a pawn ticket, and must send for a worldly servant to find out what it is, despite the fact that the pawn house itself is run by the family. These scenes fascinate me, not so much because of the characters' ignorance – as the author obviously intends – but because of my own ignorance. It is really like reading *Pride and Prejudice* or sifting through the ruins of Pompeii.

My finals were a brilliant success. I used simulation, as well as my usual interviews in pairs, and we all graded it together watching a videotape of the proceedings. The next day some of my students saw us off for a trip up the Yangtze, and we left Hankou in a downpour. The first day was mostly spent chatting in fifth class (one of my bunkmates was transporting cormorants upriver to fish), and coughing in the sickbay (where I had to go to get injections for my bronchitis). There were 'river pigs', a kind of river dolphin, surfacing all around us, and great turbulence. Around midday, we passed two floating pigs and a human corpse, apparently a common occurrence, according to the anchor boy; sometimes fishermen net fish that are too big for them, and their boats capsize.

The second day featured the great dam at Gezhouba, and a night visit to Yichang. The third day brought the really spectacular scenery, the gorgeous gorges where many of the characters of *The Romance of the Three Kingdoms* [China's first novel, by Luo Guanzhang (1330-1400)] came from. On the fourth day, we passed a few temples and made Chongqing, which was every bit as charming as I remember. Ferociously hot, with little dofu restaurants in deep caves in the stone of Pipa mountain. Jan and Paul stayed in an expensive hotel, and I got to sleep in the street with the market vendors, after nodding off in a teahouse.

Then we got up bright and early and took a bus to Dazu, where the incredible stone carvings are. There is nothing remotely like it anywhere except Dunhuang. There, in the interstices of the Buddhas, was a lot of the material civilization I'd been looking for: wineshops, with the prices listed, carved alongside herdsmen and women looking after babies, stones carved into the stone to look like rock gardens, two- and three-storey houses. Much of Dunhuang is, alas, concerned with depictions of nature. But Dazu, Dazu looks like a refuge for very homesick exiles from Chang' An [Xi'an], which is what it was in the early Song.

Anyway, from there to Chengdu, which is one of my least favourite cities in China. We stayed for cheap in a kind of atomic bomb shelter, which had been converted into a kind of hangout for hipsters called 'The Black Coffee'. I ran into a friend of a friend in Lhasa, a sculptor who was putting up a monument to the twelve martyrs of 1949 [suspected Communists who were captured by Chiang Kaishek, forced to dig their own graves and buried alive], and we had a good long pretentious art discussion. Then I came back here. I have much to do to arrange my trip. I hope to leave in two or three days.

PASSING THROUGH – A SKETCH

6 July

The boat up the Hanshui is such a country bus, it practically bumps upriver. Blunt and tubby, double-decked with no fore or after deck, a greying olive-green with metallic polka dots, it has to grind and shift gears and grumble whenever it hits turbulence, and it has no very obvious schedule or stopping places. Sometimes, out in the middle of the rice plants slipping by in the opposite direction, a few people hail us with their straw hats and we put out a plank, embark a cow or an old woman, or some fellows carrying giant baskets of ducklings suspended from a carrying pole, or discharge some Sino-Japanese TV sets destined for a guesthouse being built in a county seat some kilometres away. At other times, there is a barge anchored and used as a boat stop, with children on it catching tiny fish to feed their cats, or playing with live green flies tied to the ends of threads like model airplanes. My bicycle is locked to a pole in the middle of the baskets of ducks, and uncomfortably close to the rather messy cow.

'Where are you from?'

'Wuhan.'

'But where is your old home?'

'Well, I was born in America. Where are you from?'

'I'm from Anhui province. Can you understand my dialect?'

'Yeah, a little. We'll see how it goes . . . those ducks yours?'

'Yeah, 2,000 of them. Five mao each. That's a thousand kuai. And we make this trip about twice a month.'

'To where?'

'Tianmen county. The State buys them to raise there. Five mao each. Sometimes more.'

The man looking after the TVs has finished moving them away from the animals. He comes back and asks how much they see of it every month. Chinese conversations tend to get right down to business. Names and news are exchanged only once that has been established. The duck man, in a clean cotton T-shirt and polyester pants rolled up past his knees, white zigzag stitches showing, grins a gappy smile at the TV gent.

'You an administrator?'

'Yeah, three guesthouses. We're connected to the textile factories in Yuekou and Tianmen. You know, we export.'

'So you're State-run, are you?'

'Yeah, I get maybe 90 kuai a month, counting my bonus.'

'We get pretty close to that. A co-operative with 13 hands. We set up only last year, though. Pretty good, huh?'

The TV man scratches the red, blotchy neck emerging from his grey polyester safari shirt, Mao-suit material made up into one of those big-lapelled affairs with plastic silver buttons on the epaulettes. He takes the thing off and smiles agreement. He looks a lot younger in his cotton T-shirt. I notice a flash of silver in his smile and ask if his dental work is paid for by his work unit. 'Yeah.' The gap-toothed duck man looks interested.

'Listen . . . can I ask you . . . a rather difficult question . . . about America?' The duck man looks away. He was rather struck by the size of my nose, but is unimpressed by talk of foreign countries. 'Are there doctors there . . . who can cure this skin rot on my neck?'

I look. The flesh on his neck is suppurating, leaving a big depression at the base of his skull. 'Have you seen a Chinese doctor?' 'Yeah, nothing!'

As I drop off to sleep, I hear them comparing notes on the number of boat tickets they had to buy to ship their produce. Each TV costs half a ticket, and the 2,000 ducks cost six tickets. 'But look at that cow. I bet that cost five or six tickets right there.'

7 July

I disembark in the morning. With my spokes whirling shafts of sun in my face, I cover the 20 kilometres of canals, soaking water buffalo, and ripening rice between the port of Yuekou and the county seat of Tianmen, which is really not much bigger. Fishermen expectantly dip huge square nets suspended from wooden crosses that are almost as wide as the canal. Spokes of corn and rice radiate from points on the horizon, and the road squeezes out between them. A neat mossy fog down by the Hanshui, and a maddening, headspinning sun overhead. A young fellow in a black sleeveless T-shirt and grey hot pants with metal rivets above knee-high black fishnet stockings pedals up.

'What sort of person are you?'

'I'm from Wuhan.'

'Oh. I thought you were one of those foreigners in the movies.' He pedals away again. I wonder which film he means. He pedals back, and gestures at my bags. 'What are you selling?'

'I'm not selling anything. I'm having a good time.'

'So am I', he says ferociously, 'I'm having a wonderful time.' He pedals off towards a roadside popsicle seller and a watermelon stand. He is about my age, and I suppose he is unemployed. He has money, though.

I stop in Tianmen for lunch. A restaurant near the post office is serving frogs. This surprises me a little, for frogs are protected by law, since they are a good control on the mosquito population. In Wuhan they are sold in long strings on street corners and in alleyways, by country people with hushed voices, but they are not offered in restaurants. I have a big plate of them, cold but peppery, for a kuai and a half. In the middle of my meal, another youth in riveted hot pants

208

sidles up to me. 'Got any silver?'

'Beg your pardon?'

'Silver. Silver. Got any silver to sell?'

'No. Do you buy silver?'

He disappears. Later on I pedal up into the hills and find a place called Qianchang [Silver Field] near the ancient site of a neolithic village. I stop to fiddle with my bicycle seat and drink a few sodas in the sweat-boiling shade. A crowd gathers to comment on my fine Shanghai mount (it's a good make, and they are almost impossible to buy), and my stupidity in riding around alone when I could be touring in a bus with friends and a camera.

'Is Qianchang much further?'

'Quite a ways. And the hills are steep.'

Something tells me he does not mean it. I have often gotten on buses to be told they were hopelessly broken down, stood for hours in queues when everyone in front and behind was saying mournfully that the ticket window was closed for the day, and watched the pessimists' stoic acceptance of the confounding of their predictions. I think I understand the logic of it – the world is a giant conspiracy to prove you wrong, so you must place yourself in a position where this is to your advantage.

'Why is it called Qianchang? Is there silver there?'

The soda seller laughs and waves the money I have given her. 'Not for many dynasties now. It should be called "Wuqian"!' (Wuxi, or 'No Tin', is a famous Han tin mining town where the tin ran out. Wuqian, or 'No Silver', can also mean 'No Money'.)

'Why are you bicycling around in this heat?'

'Bicycling is great. When you want to stop, you stop. When you want to go, you go.' Off I go, and they laugh and clap in my wake. I almost expect to find Qianchang paved with silver.

The rice is ripening deliciously. Some of the strains have keen yellow-edged blades, and the plump grains, straining the chaff, pour out as if through tobacco-stained fingers. Other fields are a season or so behind; the blades just stand there, drinking silently, while the sun grinds stonily away at them. Here between the Yangtze and the Hanshui the land is unhelpfully flat; there are few irrigation streams and no water-wheels. If you haven't got a pump, you have to paddle the water up to the thirsty blades by hand. You stand and turn a wheel using two arm levers of bamboo, and the wheel turns a continuous belt of jute ropes and wooden paddles to quench the green thirst. I remember telling my composition class to write about some great Chinese inventions, and getting a good, detailed description of this 'ancient machine for irrigating'. Now I wonder if the writer had had to use one for six to nine hours on end. Today there are far more pumps than paddles in the fields.

Jiukou, where I stop the first evening, is paved with ruts, but there is a main street of cement slabs, about 50 centimetres above the muddy sidewalks, being laid down the centre of the town. I eat a huge dinner, rub my aching thighs, and ask if there is a place to swim. They direct me to a muddy reservoir where the water buffalo are wallowing; they look sullen and pachydermous as I strip down and splash in. The water is warm and the bottom vague and indefinite, squishy and unpleasant.

On the rutted street back to the cement slab main drag, there is a magnificent stone lion. Tied to it is a fat black hog, folded into huge fatty wrinkles as it buries its squashed snout into the similarly squashed snout of the lion. They both look like they'd been backed into by a drowsy water buffalo. I stay at a small 'private' hotel called the 'New Wind'. The name is redolent of the 1960s and the Lei Feng cult. The owner does not appear to find this incongruous at all. 'We set up only last year. Pretty good, huh?'

In the evening, everyone goes up to watch TV on the cool cement roof. I watch the old tile rooftops of Jiukou breaking over each other in the fading light, the cascade of tiles held in neat rows by square-shaped bookends which themselves have upward sweeping prows, like ships. There is a yellow ferret corpse on the roof. A young Sichuanese medicine seller is drying it. 'I come here for a month or two at a time,

210

selling my medicines. There isn't much to do back home. The medicines are made by our national minority people there. Very effective. But very expensive.'

'Do people have more money here than in Sichuan?'

'There is the same money, but fewer people.'

Sometime in the early 1950s a Professor Ma Yinchu drew a line on a map of China, from Heilongjiang near the Russian border to Yunnan near Burma, and pointed out that 90 per cent of the people of China lived east of the line, that is, on 30 or 40 per cent of the land. Of the land west of the line, practically nothing was arable. He then argued that doubling the amount of arable land, which was the stated Party policy, would be wasted effort if the population was allowed to double as well. Mao replied that more people made a stronger nation, and an 'anti-Malthusian' campaign ensued. Today, China has accomplished a truly futile miracle. It is the one modern nation where doubling the amount of arable land has done nothing to improve per-capita food consumption, which has actually slightly declined. It is the one modern nation where real per-capita income (since industry has gone from nothing to something very substantial in that time) has had almost no effect on the quantity or quality of the diet. It remains what it was.

Pigs and rice. I read somewhere that pork and rice are the meat and grain that require the least land input for the greatest caloric output. You can buy a piglet with a 'sawed-off' snout for around eight or ten kuai, and resell it in a year or so for more than 100. Many people do, not just farmers. Since pigs eat garbage and not grass, they require little land. You can do it as a sideline, almost anywhere. Pigs are an ever-present intermediary between a burgeoning population and the overworked fifteen per cent of the China's surface that is arable. Ninety per cent of the meat eaten in China is pork, mostly huge chunks of fat with small rinds of muscle attached. This diet has granted to most Chinese lives long enough to worry about arteriosclerosis, high blood pressure and heart disease, the leading killer here as in the West. But two Chinese dieticians recently concluded that only when the fat-to-protein ratio in the diet is completely reversed, will the Chinese live as long as the Japanese, who depend on fish and the sea. The Government has tried to promote the consumption of dofu to replace pork, but dietary preferences die hard.

8 July

Early the next day, I cycle to Zhongxiang. There is an ancestral temple built by Jiaqing, one of the most woebegone of Ming emperors, in the declining years of the dynasty. Far from town, hopelessly overgrown and unimpressive, lies the mammoth walled tomb of his parents and sister. A young boy takes me around it after I buy him a soda. Together we climb up to a decrepit Tibetan pagoda dating from the Kangxi reign in the Qing dynasty. He helps me read the tablet sticking jauntily out from the mossy bricks, and we talk about Zhuge Liang. In a train, a few weeks earlier, I overheard two young workers discussing his exploits for four and a half hours on end, and I borrow some of their stories to seem knowledgeable. It is no good. Not yet out of high school, he is already well versed in the *Romance of the Three Kingdoms*. What will he do with his knowledge when he graduates, I wonder. Appreciate kung fu films more critically, perhaps.

I cross the Hanshui and pedal across the sandy bank, through villages made grumpy and prosperous by rural' industries, to Shuanghe, where I camp. There are two lads there, with eight or ten little piglets in baskets. They are selling them, practically door to door at this little truck stop, as edible pets. One of the restaurant keepers comes over and buys one. They weigh it on a vegetable scale, tying it to one end of the balance by a leg, and off it goes, squealing, to a diet of restaurant scraps, a Faustian bargain of a year's duration.

In the morning I receive my first visit from the police. They examine my documents, register me as an 'Overseas Chinese', and point me in the direction of Xiangfan. The people I talk to mostly speak the marvellous dialect of

212

Yicheng, which contains a beautiful trilled 'r' that sounds rather like Edith Piaf at her best, and gets attached to everything. I can't understand a word, but it is music.

I stop briefly in Yicheng. There is a troop of children sitting in the road, oblivious to the five-ton Dongfeng trucks thundering by. They play a kind of noughts and crosses, where the noughts and crosses are movable, and sing a popular song from the opera *Ji Gong*. It is kind of Robin Hood tale about a Buddhist monk who goes around avenging the wrongs of the poor. There is a chorus of children in the recorded version, rather like the children's chorus in Pink Floyd's *Brick in the Wall*, and children all over China have taken it up as a kind of anthem, stretching it out of recognition, and bellowing it at their parents:

> Shoes all worn, hat all worn,
> My monk's robes are torn,
> My paper fan ripped in my hand,
> Laugh at me in scorn!
> Nanwu Amitabha, Nanwu Amitabha, Nanwu. . . .
> Heey! Hee-eh-eh-eh!
>
> Pointlessly go here and there,
> Aimlessly go everywhere,
> Walk and walk, talk and talk,
> But where there's trouble, I'll be there!
> Where there's trouble, I'll be there!

In Xiangfan I stop for cold noodles. I have an inexplicable craving for salted eggs, and eventually find some at a sesame-paste-noodle stand. I talk to the young woman selling the noodles.

'You speak putonghua so beautifully! Better than we Chinese do!'

'Nonsense! Anyway, my listening comprehension is terrible. I can't understand a word that the people around here say to me.'

'Yes, that is *tu-hua* [ground talk]. We Chinese have a hard time with it, too.'

213

'Well, but I'd like to learn it. I want to understand what ordinary Chinese say to each other, not just what they say to foreigners. Besides, in some of the places I've been, you know, they understand putonghua, but they can't speak it! You walk into a shop to buy something, and people tell you, "There isn't any! Don't try to threaten us with your putonghua!" And in some places they speak so pretty, but pretty hard to understand.' I try to say the word 'bicycle' with a trilled 'r' at the end of it, the way I heard it in Shuanghe. She laughs in immediate recognition.

'Oh, that's the dialect of Yicheng. I can't understand what they say, either.' Yicheng is perhaps 45 kilometres away. China is a whole country full of Chinas. 'The heart is everywhere, the centre nowhere.'

'What sort of person are you?'

'Well, I'm American, actually. But I live in Wuhan now.'

'Oh. Your country is much richer and greater than ours. Our country is so horribly backward.'

'In some ways. In science and technology, I suppose. But that is a small matter of a century or so. Soon China will catch up with the whole world. On the other hand, look at history and literature . . .'

'Yes! In history and literature, the rest of the world will never, ever overtake Chinese civilization.'

9-10 July

I picked up some pig-ears in the market and left Xiangfan to spend the night in Zhonglong, the former residence of Zhuge Liang. I arrived around six, and saw the Zhuge temple: hawkbilled roofs over red-lipped images of Zhuge Liang and Liu Bei, the Prince of Shu. The temple is in great shape, and mostly dates from the Qianlong reign of the Qing. A television crew is shooting a popular Chinese opera, *Seventh Rank Sesame Seed Official*, a satire on a bumbling, lower echelon Song Dynasty official.

After dinner I go for a swim, and wash clothes in the pond. Two women are there washing clothes, too. 'Look at him. He doesn't know how to beat them properly. Besides, he's stirring up the mud!'

'Be careful! You'll lose your sock in the whirlpool!' The reservoir empties into the rice fields below.

'Tell me, do you think it will rain this evening? I'm going to camp right here.'

'Go ahead, it'll be fine.' Of course, it pours.

I am awakened by a big rat nibbling at my sleeping bag. I bike out to the main road, squat under the downpour, and eat a pig ear for breakfast. The horizon looks manic-depressive, jagged and grey-green. Uphill and downhill. On the uphill bits, eveything seems to go wrong with the bicycle, and I am obsessed by details: the bags must be rubbing my rear wheel, I should stop and grease the chain again . . . When I try to think ahead, my mind spews out ridiculous sentences. My head is turning like a sprocket, and the topography is pedalling it. On the downhill stretches, though, my bicycle is a brilliant black blur, an asphalt buzz, and I myself think like a minor genius. Of course, I do most of my stopping, drinking and fixing during the uphill stretches, and the soda seller, and his daughter, the straw hat seller, and the little girl who sells bicycle parts look at me as if I were mad or a terrible crank.

A snake seller. He has a huge blue snake in his hands and is offering it to passers-by.

'Is that for medicine or for eating?'

'For eating! Buy it! It's delicious! Look how fat it is!'

'Isn't it poisonous?'

'No, not this kind. There are a lot of them around here. There are poisonous ones, too, though, so you'd better watch out.'

'How big do they get?'

'Three metres or more!'

11 July

My knee is hurting terribly, so I lay over for one day at the Taoist temple complex of Wudangshan. I leave the bike in Laoying, and take a bus up to the Southern Crag, where one of the temples is chiselled into the stone. The canyon below is a green riot, and the clouds dash around like animate beings. At the very peak, there is 'Golden Hall', a 'wood' building actually made from gilded bronze, with gilded bronze beams and 'bamboo' pillars in which lions and dragons are etched. In it sits the Zhen Wu emperor, a semi-mythical figure from Taoism, plump but grim, with a turtle's head rising obscenely between his legs. A man with his face caked with a kind of blackish growth hobbles up and kowtows. The *bonze* [priest] does not look up from his *Dao De Jing*, he simply bashes the gong three times. The visitor asks if he can throw firecrackers from the peak. 'Give them to me. We'll do it for you.'

Below the peak, there are several people painting. One of their subjects is a tousled bonze – long hair, bells, T-shirt – a caricature of a hippie. He is very friendly, and admires my Tibetan jewellery.

'Where are you from?'

'From Shaanxi. Most of us bonzes are from Shaanxi.'

'How many of you are there?'

'Over 100.'

'What? You all live up here?'

'No, there is a monastery down below. We come up here in shifts.' Another youth comes up and starts tugging at my jewellery. The older bonze tells him to be more polite. 'He just joined us. Many young people today, you know, they can't find work, they read a lot of kung fu stories, so they want to join. It will take a while.' Then I remember. Wudangshan is a kind of Taoist version of Shaolin temple, famous for its own particular variety of kung fu.

On the way down, two teachers from a village in southeastern Hubei try to speak to me in English. They have some trouble, and I am on vacation, so after a while we continue in Chinese.

'Tell me, in Wuhan we also have a Taoist temple, but the figures are all of Laozi and the Three Pure Ones. I thought that Zhen Wu was only a fairy tale figure. How is it that here there is only a statue of Zhen Wu, and no Laozi or Pure Ones?'

216

'That we don't know. That is all superstition. We only come here for the scenery. Why? Are you religious?'

'No, I don't believe in religion,' I reply. 'I'm a Communist.'

It is rather as if I had told them I was a Rotarian.

'Tell us – you see, we don't often get a chance to ask – what do the foreign papers say about our reforms? Do they mention it at all?'

'Oh, yes, but foreigners don't understand this question very well. What do you think of the reforms?'

'Well, of course, we think they are essential for the modernization of the country. Do the foreign papers say that?'

'No. Mostly the foreign papers gloat about the reforms. They think it shows that they, the capitalists, were right all along, and the communists now recognize that. They are very happy to come here and sell their products, but they are not very interested in modernizing your country. Why should they be? Then you wouldn't buy their stuff, you'd just make your own!'

'But the reforms – they have raised production enormously. Look. Meat! Everywhere! When I was a kid, during the "black years", the early Sixties, you couldn't even get steamed bread!'

'That's true. But the weather has been good, and most policies work well when the weather is good. Last year the weather was bad, and there was a huge shortfall in grain. Pork was rationed, remember?'

'No, that was only in the cities.'

'Well, I am a foreigner, and know little about it. But I think that the pro-American part of the reforms is wrong. The Americans have been friendly with China for 13 years now, and they have only tried to sell their products and make money. Where are their bridges, factories, hospitals, schools and railroads? They are imperialists, and –'

' "Imperialists"!?!' They laugh hilariously. 'Do you still use words like that?'

'Most people don't. But it's still true.'

217

14 July

The next day I pass along the banks of the Hanshui to the more mountainous region of Hubei, stepping up to the Shaanxi plateau. At nightfall, I reach the town of Hujiaying, perhaps 18 kilometres from the border. The tiny restaurant has nothing but noodles and eggs. I eat, then push my bicycle down a trail to the beach, where I camp on the firm-fleshed sand. In the middle of the night, a cigarette bobs toward me in the darkness.

'Where are you from?'

'Wuhan. Where are you from?'

'Around here. This is a good place.'

'Yeah. I thought I'd make it to Shaanxi tonight, but when I saw this place, I figured I'd stay the night.'

'A good place. Come aboard my boat and have a drink?'

'Thanks. I'm really knackered, though. Did 120 kilometres today – uphill. That's like rowing upriver.'

'No, it's not.'

'You fish?'

'Hell, I don't do anything. I graduated from school seven years ago and I can't find work. Just catch fish and eat 'em. I got enough to eat, but – really, it's boring.'

'Yeah . . . well, it's a good place.'

The next morning I get up, strip, and dunk myself in the Hanshui. He is gone, but I look at his footprints in the sand. He was pacing back and forth for much of the night, just pacing along the beach like a tiger in a cage.

15 July

Into, or up onto, Shaanxi. I cycle into Baihe right across the border, and ask about a road to Ankang. The direct road is impassable, I must go south, back into Hubei, and cross west to Pingli and Ankang. Baihe is built like Chongqing, on a promontory over a bend in the river. It is a murderous, winding battle up the 1,200 metre pass of Gali back into Hubei, and takes me most of the day. At night I camp at the fork of the roads leading to Zhushan and Zhuxi.

The next day I pedal through more prosperous land – melons everywhere in cool red and orange wafers, dogs fighting with pigs over scraps, little two-wheeled walking tractors that make possible mechanization without collectivization in every home. Some of the houses still bear the marks of the Cultural Revolution, though they have obviously been redistributed as private dwellings. On trestle bridges and dam works, government workers have obliterated each other's graffiti, resulting in odd conglomerations like: 'Beat down the four . . . wise leader Chairman Hua . . . straight ahead.' On every door there is a red paper poster, with a legendary character from an opera, like the King of Wu, or a tutelary god with a giant distaff, or the patriotic kung fu fighter of the Twenties, Huo Yuanjia, flourishing his fists like fly whisks. 'Mobilize the whole party behind the policy of taking agriculture as the basis!' 'In agriculture, learn from Dazhai!' 'Put politics in command!' 'Learn from Lei Feng, found a "New Wind" society!'

A kid in a yellow T-shirt, speaking putonghua in a kind of effeminate voice. 'What sort of person are you? What national minority?'

'I'm American. Aren't Americans the most beautiful minority people?' (The character *mei* which stands for American, really means 'beautiful'.)

'No.'

'Well, not all Americans are as ugly as I am.'

'That's not it.' He brandishes a 'thumbs-up' before the poster of Huo Yuanjia on the open door, and dips his arm like a pike. 'The Chinese are the most beautiful, the most intelligent, and the most righteous people on the face of the earth!'

16 July

The last shady kilometres of Hubei undulate by me in an orderly fashion. As the hills start to rise, I pedal furiously after a Dongfeng walking tractor hitched to a cart, and, grabbing the tailgate of the cart with one hand, allow my bike to be towed up to the pass on the border. At first the driver frowns, then we have a bellowed conversation.

219

'Pay attention to your safety, now!'

'Don't worry! I will!'

'What country are you from?'

'From America! Are you from around here?'

'Yes! We're from Chang'an!'

'So! There are two Chang'ans in Shaanxi!'

'Nonsense! Our Chang'an's a little village! Can't compare with *that* Chang'an!' (Chang'an, in addition to being the name of a large county near Xi'an, was the old name of Xi'an when it was the capital under the Han and Tang dynasties.)

'How much does one of these things cost?'

'Walking tractor? About 3,700 kuai now!'

'What? That's what a whole truck costs!'

'If you are in one of those fancy work units that can get one, get a truck! If you're a peasant, get a tractor!'

'But you don't have to wait for one?'

'No. You just save up. With a bit of land and a bit of luck, you can get one in five or six years. Sooner, in some places.'

We reach the top and I coast down into the Shaanxi plateau. We leapfrog past each other for several kilometres until I get embarrassed at so many goodbyes and stop for a drink.

After my drink, I adjust the seat and start off again. A young peasant, his wife behind him, pedals up to me. His name is Shen, and he has land in Hubei, but relatives in Shaanxi, whom he is going to see.

'I just got married, you see.' His wife looks much younger than he does, and he's only 20.

'Do you have birth control, too, over there?'

'Yes. But voluntary.'

'Here, no. Only two children allowed.'

'What? I thought – In Wuhan it's only one. Are you of a national minority, or something?'

'No, we're Han people. You can have two children if you want. But they fine you a bit for the second one.'

'Really, how much?'

'About 300 or 400 for someone poor like me. But if you're

rich, of course, you could pay up to 1,000. In Guangdong, I
hear, they pay 10,000 or more.'

'But that's nothing. You can earn that much on the extra
land the state allows you for the child. Not to mention the
extra labour you get out of him when he's grown.'

'Well, but they don't allot land for children after the first
one. The second one is landless. Still, you're right in a way.'

'What about a third kid?'

'Oh, they really get you for that one. 2,000 or 3,000, I
expect. If you can't pay, they just break up your family and
keep you from working for two or three years, something
like that.'

'How about you? You gonna have one kid or two?'

'We'll have one.'

'Why?'

'We can't afford two.'

'I heard that in Guangdong they sometimes let you have a
second kid simply if the first is a girl.'

'Yeah. We have that sometimes, too. But you have to
know the right people.'

China is a signatory to several 'human rights' declarations,
so cannot have a national one-child policy. Instead of a
single law, there is a patchwork of arbitrary policies carried
out by local committees.

Shen has a flat, and we stop to fix it. A real comedy of
errors. We whack off his tyre, whip out the inner tube, and I
give him one of mine. It's too small, so we send the other
one down the road with his wife to get repaired, while we sit
looking at pumpkins, corn, tomatoes and *mo you* [a tuber
used in making dofu].

'Is the land better here or back in Hubei?'

'Each place has good land and bad land. You've got to
have an eye.'

'How many *mu* [one sixth of an acre] of good land in this
field, do you think?'

'Maybe two. I've got almost two mu of good land back in
Hubei.'

'Is it enough?'

'Yeah. For a family, one and a half or two mu. If you don't eat much.'

17 July

Another mountain pass, and it is raining. I walk the bicycle uphill, since my tyre is leaking rather badly. A jeep full of police stop to talk. They congratulate me on my Chinese, on my bicycling, on my 'determination'.

'Forward ever, backward never! That's what the Red Army said.'

'Are you from around here?'

'We're from Pingli. We've just been to Ankang, and we're headed back. This road is pretty rough. You know, it was built by Wang Jingwei during the Anti-Japanese War. He had American help then. Hasn't been worked on much since.'

I ask about roads to Gansu. They advise me to take the southern route through Hanzhong. We talk of Zhuge Liang, since Hanzhong was one of his battle sites. There are temples to him in Chenggu, Hanzhong and Mianxian.

'Well, it's getting dark. Wet, too. Goodbye.'

I spend the night in a little daoban – one of the road builders' stations. The man who runs it was looking after a madman. Something in the gentle way he treated him told me they were relatives. The madman giggles a lot, and the daoban keeper sighs. 'He's a child! His mind is in ragged crotchless trousers.'

18 July

I cycle downhill thinking my genius, elated thoughts, and stop for breakfast in a spot just past the prosperous town of Pingli. As I pull up, two young fellows mock me by speaking Chinese with a foreign accent. One of them is dressed in mock-foreign clothes, and the other has a 'curly boy' mock Hong Kong haircut. It is hard to tell where the mockery ends and self-derision begins. I answer crossly and they are immediately crimson with apology. Not so tough after all. One is a local lad, in yellow shorts. He runs the restaurant.

The *baozi* are delicious, and the egg and tomato soup tastes of fine mushrooms and garlic.

'We set up only last year.'

'How is it doing?'

'Pretty good.'

'Mostly truckers, I bet.'

'That's right. Big spenders, since they're usually on expense accounts.'

The other fellow is flashier: black nylon shirt open to the navel, and those riveted hot pants in fatigued green denim.

'Say, I know Wuhan. I was there last year.'

'On business?'

'Bought wood ears [edible fungus].'

'Don't they have them here?'

'Oh, we've got 'em. Really expensive, though.' He pulls up his chair confidentially, and I'm sure he's going to ask me about sexual liberation in America. 'Tell me . . . what are softshelled turtles going for in Wuhan these days?'

19 July

I stop for the night in the smaller town of Hanying. Two big stone bridges span the Hanshui here. The next day, I cycle to Shiquan before lunch and stop to grease my bike. That finished, I look for a likely lunch spot. As I cross the centre of town, a policeman steps in front of my bike, salutes stiffly – and busts me.

The policeman clacks his plastic sandals on his glass-topped desk, swings his cigarette like a censer, and exhales demonically.

'Why, just why did you want to go to Tibet by bicycle?'

'Well, um . . . I've always wanted to go to the north-west by bicycle. I suppose it really has to do with the Cultural Revolution . . . See, I teach two very different kinds of students in Wuhan. Some are my age . . . our age . . . or maybe a little older. The others are quite a bit younger, not yet married, and just too young to have gone to the countryside as the older ones . . . as your generation . . . did.'

223

Clack. 'Eeehm.'

'It makes a big difference. The younger ones are . . . younger. They like dancing and making noise, dislike their jobs and learning English. They have very little to say in English anyway, they can't cook, clean their own clothes, carry on reasonable arguments with each other, or even do their own shopping, because all their lives their mothers and fathers have been grooming them for exams. The older ones, the older ones, have so much to say. About the Chinese classics, about Mozart and icthyology, about whether children should be beaten, Halley's comet and Japanese imports . . . They went to the countryside believing they were revolutionaries, and came back . . . when they found out they were something else . . . scientists and technicians. But they never have much to say about the countryside itself, when they talk about it. They say it was poor, and that they suffered terribly for two years, and people were backward and stupid and died a lot. That's all.'

'So you were out to see how backward our country is. Now, they live well in the countryside . . . better than we do.'

'No, actually, that's not it. I was passing through. To see if . . . they were still there.'

8 | The mysterious miasma of Taimu Shan by *Tang Min*

Up in the mountains there was a man who turned into a cow. This story was told to me by my friend Ah Lu, but the whole business was witnessed by thousands of people.

I told you that Taimu Shan had a militia company commander. He was a tall, beefy sort of fellow with a flat-top haircut. He had veins that popped out of his temples, looking like sinews, and long wispy eyebrows that seemed to hang from them. Actually, he looked the very image of one of those martial male falsettoes in a Peking opera.[1] He liked to knit his brows all the time, so he had two deep trenches between them, like a pair of parentheses, or the third eye of the god Erlang.

Now, this company commander liked to stand out and be noticed. He thought the militiamen under his command were the toughest in the whole area, so he called them a battalion instead of just a company, promoting himself to battalion commander. He took over a room in the headquarters of the production brigade[2] for stockpiling rifles and ammunition, and he nailed a wooden board reading 'Battalion Headquarters No Admittance' to the door.

---

1. Peking opera excluded women performers for most of its history; however, some of the male roles, as well as the female ones, were sung in a falsetto singing style, particularly those of young males. The martial male falsetto roles are known as *wusheng* and are noted for their manly appearance, which contrasts with their voices.
2. The People's Commune movement of the late Fifties and early Sixties abolished the terms 'village', 'township', and 'county', and replaced them with 'production team', 'production brigade', and 'commune'.

225

Unfortunately, he was an only son, so he couldn't join the real army and become a real battalion commander.[3] Nevertheless, he was a real he-man sort, quite unmoved by the charms of women, and he could hold his liquor like an ocean. The more he drank, the clearer his face seemed to get. By his own account, he was a gambler whose skill was surpassed only by his luck. 'The key is to have a cool head', he said. 'Win or lose, you don't get excited. You wait until everybody else gets muddleheaded, then you deal out the cards a bit sloppy, see. See them all clearly, figure out how to play it, get the trick!' The thing was, nobody ever actually saw him gamble. 'Me, I've got will power,' he said. 'If I say I won't gamble, I'll never gamble again!'

The battalion commander was fond of attracting attention. He would march his militiamen back and forth through a village like a dusty little whirlwind. When there was a production brigade meeting, he would always get there very, very early, and, when he took the floor, it was always at the top of his lungs, filling the place to the rafters with his voice. All he needed were a few words of encouragement from some leader slightly higher up, and out he'd run, raising hell and fearing neither heaven nor earth.

But, for all that, he was ill-starred, getting on in years, and still unable to join the Party. Whenever Party meetings were held, he'd be left outside like a hungry cat, murmuring somewhere down in his poor sore heart that outsiders like himself had no one at all they could turn to. For, you see, he was not originally from Taimu Shan. He really came from the coast north of the mountain, on the border with Zhejiang Province. There is a natural deep water port there, Shacheng Harbour, and our battalion commander was originally from there. Back in '70, when the fishing people were all being evacuated from the coastal areas during the war mobilization, he volunteered for transfer to the mountains, and brought his wife, son and daughter with

3. Only sons are not permitted to join the PLA, since they are their parents' sole means of support.

him, leaving an old mother to look after their run-down little house in Shacheng.

The wife of the battalion commander was just as tall as he was; in fact, they were a bit like brother and sister in appearance. However, Madame Battalion Commander's real flesh-and-blood brother was the commune Deputy Party Secretary at the time, and that was truly awe-inspiring. The battalion commander had been putting out his own brand of hard-working enthusiasm for ages, and still hadn't managed to join, but when this elder brother-in-law showed up, *he* managed to convince the production brigade Party branch to admit him at last. They say that on the day he joined up, the battalion commander's eyes were brimming with tears of excitement. That was what he liked best, actually. Everything he did had to go with sound and colours. Usually grand, tragic colours.

What he despised most of all was greed. For example, Ah Lu. He really despised her. Madame Battalion Commander had once asked her to buy her some material for summer trousers, the light, thin, wrinkle-resistant stuff that city folks wore. Ah Lu got someone to go up to Shanghai and get it at a special wholesale price, 30 per cent off the retail market price. Its colour was a dark, bluish-grey, very smart. Madame Battalion Commander crumpled and creased it in her hands, but it wouldn't wrinkle. She kept praising it over and over. Then she took out her money and tried to pay Ah Lu for it. Ah Lu replied, 'Oh, no, we'll settle it later.' Madame paused a moment and flushed, 'Oh, no, no. That will never do!' She took out 10 or 11 yuan, and insisted on settling up then and there. Unfortunately, Ah Lu was foolish enough to take the money.

When the battalion commander got home, as soon as he heard that over 10 yuan had gone for this flimsy material that was only good for two useless little pairs of summer trousers, he really blew his top. First he tried to unload the stuff on someone else, but no one in the village seemed to want it. They said that such light stuff would hardly stand up to two vigorous washes, and anyway you couldn't wear it in winter.

Some of them even remarked sourly that such fashionable stuff should be left for city folk to strut around in. Madame Battalion Commander was made thoroughly uncomfortable. Her husband was livid and wanted to toss the material right in the brook, but since they were running out of money even for daily necessities, they could hardly afford to sacrifice 10 yuan for nothing.

The battalion commander earnestly turned over in his mind the callous hearts of city folk. 'Only capitalism could make people so calculating and clever. Ah Lu is pretty shrewd, but ruthless at heart. How could she ignore the fact that we're going through some very tough times? How could she accept the money? That's our own sweat and blood! We're not like that old man of hers, getting bundle after bundle of banknotes every month!'

As a consequence, the battalion commander set about undermining Ah Lu's good name. And, with an opportunity to 'use live ammunition against a dummy target', people started to criticize her in public and give her a little taste of the more bitter fruits of greed. Ah Lu hadn't the slightest idea how her reputation had sustained this damage, being too absorbed in other experiences and feelings.

If only she hadn't taken the battalion commander's money that year, if only she'd made it possible for him and his wife to revel in a little bit of finery, given them a bit of city luxury, what a great contribution to their lives it might have been! Compared to human life, what's 10 yuan or so? But now it's too late for that kind of wisdom. The battalion commander is dead.

Samsara – the transmigration of souls in pain
The death of the battalion commander was sudden, strange, and, in the end, pathetic. Ah Lu didn't actually witness the scene. She had left Taimu Shan more than five years earlier, but when her godfather's real daughter came down to the city, she paid Ah Lu a visit. Chatting casually with her godsister, Ah Lu asked about all the various inhabitants of

Taimu Shan and their affairs, and eventually came around to the battalion commander.

'What battalion commander?' asked the godsister.

'I mean Wang Lianzhong, of course!'

'Oh, he got assigned to be a cow,' said the godsister.

Ah Lu didn't understand, so she asked again, and only then did she learn that not only had the battalion commander Comrade Wang Lianzhong passed away, but that Yama, King of Hell, had apparently sentenced him to reincarnation as a calf. And because his death has acquired the status of popular legend, his name has at last become known throughout the Taimu Shan region, never to be forgotten.

He had been promoted to rice depot deputy chief, and, simultaneously, chief of the transport team. Now, these were the best, most profitable posts available. The whole of the commune's grain was husked right there in the depot, and all the goods bound for Panxi Town were shipped by the depot team. Compared to peasants who go around all year with their faces to the yellow earth and their backs to heaven, he was sitting very pretty indeed.

Then along came the reforms, and the setting up of the contract system. The battalion commander and a few others managed to get the rice depot contract, while his wife went to work in the co-operative medical station nearby. So husband and wife managed to be head and shoulders above everybody else.

The battalion commander was in excellent health, and his capacity for work was enormous. But he also had power, and those who had contracted along with him invariably ended up with a feeling of having been wronged. For whenever a job was profitable, he was always out there in front, valiantly plugging away. But if the job was not so much fun, he would invariably let the others have their turn. Particularly when it came to getting up early in the morning to fuel and maintain the husking machine, and that sort of thing. That he never did.

At that time, they had just started setting up this new

'specialized households' system.[4] People in Taimu Shan really started getting their hopes up, and some even looked forward to leaving the co-operative organization altogether and going it alone. But the leaders somewhere up above seemed to hesitate a bit about it. Actually, what the commune and production team cadres were really worried about was something entirely different. Some said the Sichuan communes had already been abolished, the names changed back to county, township and village, and a lot of those who had been excused or partly excused from production duties had had their 'rice bowls' smashed.[5]

But the first new spring tea crop had already been picked and processed, and people's messy, itchy minds were already turning toward tomorrow. That night, the battalion commander was feeling in a particularly good mood. He and some of his mates had a potluck and boiled up some ducks to eat. Everybody was talking of ways of making money, their brains lighting up like little light bulbs. The battalion commander was drinking little and thinking a lot. To the others, he looked as he must have in his gambling days, perfectly cool-headed, calculating how, basically, to get rich. Well, we don't know exactly what he was thinking, but we do know that when he at last opened his mouth, he said to his busily bragging mates: 'You need to have real know-how. Making money takes real know-how. Only then can you get it rolling into your pocket. Real know-how.' And then he went home.

He said to his wife: 'As soon as we have money, we'll build a proper house here.' His wife laughed, but he told her sternly, 'I'm not joking. I'll tell you tomorrow. I've got a

4. This was a reform which allowed some peasants to give up producing low-profit staples for sale to the state and to concentrate instead on vegetables or cash crops or even rural industry, which gave the households increased income and much more independence.

5. The bureaucracy had been excused from production tasks in order to carry out political duties. For this they were guaranteed a state stipend, or 'rice bowl'. Hence, the cadres were concerned that reforms might mean the loss of this guarantee.

scheme.' With that, he dropped soundly asleep, and the night passed in silence.

Now, the battalion commander had a paternal uncle who had gone up into the mountain and put up a little thatched meditation hut. He wasn't really a monk who had renounced the world, nor was he a lay Buddhist; he was kind of a 'Vegetarian Gentleman', somewhere in between. While the battalion commander was eating boiled duck with his buddies, his uncle was doing his nightly sutra-reading. And some time after the commander had fallen asleep, his uncle abruptly sat up in bed awake. As soon as his head had touched the pillow, he had had an unusually distinct dream: that his nephew, whom he hadn't seen in years, was wrapped in the coils of a black snake and being squeezed to death.

The old man, awake with a start, thought, and thought again, very ill at ease. There was shrieking somewhere up in the black-daubed mountains, but when he stretched his hand out he couldn't see the five fingers in front of his face. He waited until the fifth watch,[6] and then left hurriedly for Panxi Town as soon as he could make out a glimmer of light.

The battalion commander had slept peacefully until four, just before dawn. Then he woke up. He thought that was a bit odd; how could he have woken so early? He lay on the bed, unable to get back to sleep, his head unusually clear and alert. This burst of clarity felt good, a kind of mental continuation of the previous night's exhilaration. Around half past four, he got up. His wife stirred and asked: 'So early? What are you going to do?'

'I'm going to have a look inside the rice depot,' he replied. 'Today we have to husk the rice.' And then his heavy footsteps went peng-peng down the wooden steps, waking up the landlord downstairs.

The landlord was a bit astonished to hear the battalion commander, who usually stayed in bed until the red sun was all over his wall and he couldn't miss it, getting up so early.

---

6. Traditionally, the Chinese divided the night into five two-hour periods, called watches. The fifth watch is at dawn.

How come? He listened to the unmistakable footsteps, heard him noisily bang the door, and listened to the footsteps gradually, gradually receding. He was irritated. He'd been meaning to have a talk with the battalion commander to try to get his room back. The upstairs room was really very nice, and it had been rented out for a good many years now. The rent was next to nothing, practically zero. Upstairs, Madame Battalion Commander started snoring loudly. 'Just like a man!' the landlord thought. Then he, too, went back to sleep.

That morning, Ah Da, who was supposed to fuel up the rice-husking machine, overslept. When he woke up, it was already six o'clock. His old lady was in the kitchen, cleaning the slop buckets. The sound of burbling water came to his ears, and that meant the *congee* [rice gruel] had already been scraped out into the big earthen bowl, and the wok was being used to cook up the pig fodder. Ah Da hurriedly rose, cursing his old lady for not having roused him. She laughed, 'I was just thinking of calling you when you woke up.'

Ah Da said, 'I'm going to the rice depot. I'll come back and eat later.' As he walked out the door, he ran into the journeyman rice-flour-noodle maker, Old Flathead. His head was so flat, it seemed as if he couldn't possibly have much by way of brains in such a shallow receptacle. But the rice-flour noodles he made were delicious. Ah Da and Master Flathead exchanged civilities, and then accompanied each other to the rice depot.

The door was wide open. The two men stared a moment, and then ran inside to have a look, but they couldn't see any signs of burglary. They could only hear a strange humming groan from the machinery. When they looked, they saw the main electrical switch had been thrown on. Normally, the belts on the engine should have been going to and fro and up and down continuously. Instead, they just sat there, humming and quivering slightly. Ah Da threw the switch off, checked to see that the fuse wires were all okay, and then threw the switch back on again. The foot-wide belts lurched forward a bit with a sudden commotion, then stopped,

232

humming and quivering again. Master Flathead said: 'Belts are stuck. Let's have a look.'

Ah Da and Master Flathead weren't quite themselves for many days afterwards. Particularly since the situation got more and more sensational, and they unwillingly found themselves the two main figures at the very heart of the news. In the end, they themselves began to wonder if their own 'facts' and 'experience' were really true after having been repeated over and over. For, in the end, personal experience endlessly relived becomes yet another kind of dream.

And anyway, the whole affair was so dramatic, it was hard to believe it wasn't phoney. When the battalion commander had his potluck duck, it was destined to be his 'tail meal' – the 'last supper' conferred on condemned criminals. So the circumstances and incidents of this tail meal have since been grossly exaggerated by all concerned, including that famous statement of 'real know-how for making money', which has since been endowed with exceptional significance. The landlord went around everywhere describing the battalion commander's peculiar behaviour on that particular morning. 'He was in some awful hurry, ah, that's for sure!' He repeated his lurid description of that burst of loud footsteps until no one could possibly ever forget the peng-penging sound they had made. The paternal uncle was canonized a 'semi-immortal' who knew and could foretell the future, although, at first, it is true, the dream was considered some nonsense, or a trick. But then it became a story that people would recount to each other, for whatever it was worth. And at last, almost everyone believed that the dream affair was absolutely true.

Ah Da was left alone with a kind of pitch-blackness in his heart he could never entirely get rid of. He was convinced, from the beginning of the affair to the end, that his last throw of the switch had been a truly criminal act. For if he hadn't thrown the switch that last time, he thought, the battalion commander might still have had a chance. His legs became bowed from carrying around the dreadful weight of this awful secret, and he heaved sigh after groan. Only many days afterwards did he tell his family about it, weeping himself sodden in relief at doing so.

By the time he confessed his 'criminal act', the affair had achieved a status on a level with the summit of Mount Tai for loftiness, weightiness, and sheer renown. The immediate reaction of popular opinion was to the effect that Ah Da had merely been the instrument of heaven and had been impelled to throw the switch by dark, obscure supernatural forces. At the same time, it was pointed out that the battalion commander had once cheated Ah Da by docking his grain and money and had habitually ordered him around like a cow or a horse.

When Ah Da heard this, the burden on his conscience eased a bit, and his bowed legs even straightened out a bit. But he nevertheless felt a certain heartache. After all, even if the battalion commander had been really awful to him, he had never tried to take his life. Why did heaven permit him to throw that switch? Why didn't heaven get Old Flathead to do it? They had gotten along fairly well, for the most part. Ah Da occupied entire days with this kind of wild speculation and foolish fancy.

To put the matter simply, what had happened was that the battalion commander had somehow gotten himself entangled in the belt of the rice husker, and been slowly squeezed to death. This belt was the main conveyer belt connecting the motor to the machinery. For safety, there was a groove in the ground about as deep as the thickness of a bundle of rice stalks, through which the long belt passed, twisting and turning, before it was connected up with the other belts of the machine. Apparently, the battalion commander had stepped into this groove, perhaps while trying to clear away some obstruction, and had the misfortune to get caught in the belt. If there had been others around to help him, he might have got away with only a slight injury. But! Ah Da had overslept and left him all wrapped up in the belt for over an hour, with no-one the wiser. Of course, following his usual practice, Ah Da would not have come in to fuel the machinery until half past five, so that still would have left the commander wrapped up in the belt for nearly an hour.

As for exactly how entangled he was, what shape and posture he had assumed by the time he was found, and how people had managed to disentangle him, his wife never knew, and no one afterwards ever attempted to describe the scene for her. Only faintly did she remember, well afterwards, overhearing things like, 'Oh, he was stuck but good! Three people tried and couldn't pull him out. Had him all bound up like a tourniquet. We just couldn't get it off him.'

Later it seemed as if her spine had been frozen stiff, right down to the marrow. She had felt a kind of strength, somehow akin to a bitter and deep-seated hatred, confronted by the mutilated, deformed corpse of her husband on the ground of the rice depot. When she at last began to mourn, she trembled from head to toe. Shivering, though not really cold, she had one very strong impression. That was that she had not received any fair warning, not a single premonition of disaster. They had simply run up all agitated and shouted at her: 'Lianzhong Qin! There's been an accident at the rice depot! Lianzhong Qin, come quick, hurry!' Her family name was actually Zhu, and her given name Yuqin, but because so many women in the area had the same name, this was how she was always addressed.

She thought the rice depot had caught fire, and ran off in its direction humming two lines of a song that was running through her head. First she saw them clustered in and around the depot, thick and black as crows. Ah Da was sitting white-faced by the door, unable to weep, and Master Flathead, his ashen face askew, with his legs bent was trying to hold back the surging crowd. Packed into little knots here and there, suddenly people began shouting: 'Lianzhong Qin's here! Make way!'

Immediately, the crowd opened up, and people on both sides craned their necks to look at her. It was only then that it struck her that something to do with her had taken place. She looked at the heap of clothing on the ground. No. It was the twisted, mangled body of a man. She advanced

235

involuntarily, squatted down and removed the newspaper covering the face – her husband's face, with a macabre grin of excruciating pain and hideously bulging eyes. The blood brimming from the nose and mouth had already congealed. Blackness burst out from somewhere behind her eyes.

Of all the notions flying around inside her head, two stood out. She had been utterly forsaken by heaven; heaven, to her great surprise, had not even a slight twinge of pity for her; she had not had the tiniest premonition or advance warning. And then, of course, there were the funeral expenses. She had only a bit more than 180 yuan in cash, plus her grain ration. What to do? How to go on? Cry, of course one must cry. More than ten years of married life: sour, salty, bitter and peppery, and, in the end, no way to make head or tail of it all.

The question of how and where to lay out the corpse followed closely on the heels of all this. They couldn't very well do it in the rice depot, so they carried the body out. By custom, they should have carried it to the building where he had dwelt in life, but out of the ten or so households that shared it, every one had shut its doors tight. He had been, after all, an outsider, a stranger, and he had died a violent death. Who was not afraid of evil, demonic miasmas?

Finally they just laid him out in the empty space in front of the building. They couldn't even manage to borrow a door plank and a couple of stools, so they just placed him on the ground. After a while, the sun came up over Taimu Shan, the warm rays settled on the corpse, and the flies came trooping over, brigade after brigade. Only then did she realise the full measure of her bereavement. The corpse of her husband was not yet cold, and already the hearts of her neighbours had hardened. Her brother had been transferred to another area, and no one would lift a finger to help her.

At that moment, her son and daughter came running home from school bathed in tears. Lianzhong Qin hugged them, choking through her own tears, 'Get the bed board to lay out your pa.' Weeping profusely, they got it. Some said this really wasn't proper, but they helped the children get out the bed board and stools, and the battalion commander finally lay in state on a proper bier, or, anyway, bed.

When the paternal uncle at length showed up, he went up to the dead man and patted him, crying, 'Poor young lad, so devoid of virtue! Poor boy, now you'll be accountable!' The words and tears of the old vegetarian gentleman suddenly aroused recollections of the past which had all but faded from people's minds. Everyone looked on gravely, feeling suddenly solemn. Ah, in truth, 'the net of heaven has large meshes, yet it lets nothing slip through'.

Then Lianzhong Qin sank to the ground wailing, and everyone else stood around silently watching. Eventually, the commune armed forces department sent around a clerical worker, and the production brigade branch secretary came, too, to discuss what to do next. How much of the bill would be footed by which side was a matter of some contention. Since the battalion commander had left precious little behind other than his body, it wouldn't be right for Lianzhong Qin to use her own cotton padded quilt to cover him, for then it would have to be burnt. Thus, the production brigade would have to contribute one of the publicly owned quilts. However, they took out all the cotton stuffing and laid only the outer cover over the corpse.

After all, he had been a public figure of sorts. So the heads of the production brigade decided to allow him to lie in state in the brigade quarters and to assign militiamen to keep vigil beside his bier, to send him out in a fitting manner. When they thought about it, it had been for the sake of the production brigade that he had lost his life. Gradually, the necessary resources were found and the whole business proceeded as well as circumstances permitted. Every responsibility got assigned to some responsible person. The coffin, of course, presented a major problem. Eventually, the cost was defrayed 50 per cent by commune funds, 30 per cent by the production brigade's funds, and Lianzhong Qin had to provide the remainder.

Now it happened that during this same period, a small event, almost entirely devoid of significance was taking place. The battalion commander had been registered as a resident of the village surrounding the rice depot, Nine Well Village, and in the same village there lived an old cattle herder called Old Man Ah Zhong, who was good only for herding cows. He couldn't even transplant a rice seedling. He had one grandson, and he and his old wife would go around eating at their various sons' houses in turn. He had an arrangement with the villagers who had contracted for the cattle herd that he would herd them in exchange for a grain ration.

Old Man Ah Zhong was just shoving his way to the front of the line to have a good look at the battalion commander's corpse, all stretched out on his bier, when his youngest son came dashing up, shouting, 'Pa! Come quick! Come back and see what's happening!'

Ah Zhong thought irritably then that the cows were still in the pen, although it was already quite late. Actually, his eldest son had already hustled them off to the hills, and only the pregnant cow remained. It was well over a month overdue, and there was still no sign of labour. But now the cow was pacing in circles around the pen, mooing in a low voice, tears streaming down her face, body twitching in pain. The youngest son exclaimed, 'Two previous calves came without a hitch, and now this one goes wrong. And with the contract, we have to pay if something happens. Damn! All these inauspicious things going on today . . . '

The old man petted the cow's muzzle and she nuzzled his palm with her sodden nose. Then he took her home with him, and outside the pigpen put down some straw, where he made her lie down. The whole household was now involved, and the business of the battalion commander completely shelved. No one even thought to mention it. The old woman boiled up eggs in brown sugar, and poured the mixture down the cow's throat. Ah Zhong squatted on the rice chaff with tears dribbling out of his eyes, looking at the cow. The cow, in quiet agony, looked back at him with equally dribbling eyes. He began to pray, 'Lianzhong! Go in peace! Please don't take my cow. I've no quarrel with you, I forgot all that

238

long ago. Even that year when you wanted to fine me, and wanted me to sell my house to pay it, and then in the end only got 300 yuan out of me. Today you've had to pay over your whole life. I pity you, but, please, let the cow go. If the cow dies, how can we possibly pay it off?' He prayed over and over again.

Of course, at first no one knew about all this. But later it got around as if the spirits themselves had spread the word.

The battalion commander's son and daughter spent a sleepless night, and so did Old Man Ah Zhong and his family. But, in the end, visible heaven must be lit. The candles before the bier began to sputter out, and the cow's breathing was beginning to sputter now too. Her slaver was thick and white, and, beneath her, bloody water trickled down. Ah Zhong could no longer bear it. He stumbled to bed and lay down, his whole body throbbing with fatigue, his heart aching even worse. His grandson woke up, saw his grandfather slumped heavily on the bed and scrambled up to try to comfort him. 'Grandpa, let me rub your back, OK?' But Ah Zhong breathed through his nose with a despairing wheeze. The little grandson fell silent and then got quietly out of bed. In the muted, barely discernible colours of first dawn, a calf lay by the cow's side. The cow was alive, exhausted, utterly spent, but the calf was big and beefy-looking, both eyes already open.

'Grandpa! The calf's born!' It seemed that heaven and earth smiled on the Ah Zhong household, and they joyfully readied the cow for a proper 'post-natal month'[7]. Ah Zhong looked the calf up and down. It was a really robust little bull. Gradually, the day had lightened. The hair on the calf's body was now dry and formed thick whorls. It was a rare thing, such thick, curly hair on a newborn calf. But the moment the calf raised its muzzle to return his gaze, the colour drained from Ah Zhong's face. He trembled from

7. After childbirth, Chinese women generally spend a whole month indoors recuperating, during which they eat a special diet and observe a host of customs which vary widely from region to region. Of course, this is not normally done in the case of animals.

head to toe. He was tired, perhaps he was seeing ghosts, but right in the centre of the calf's forehead were two deep brown vertical marks, almost like a third eye, and an abrupt, jutting brow. The very image!

'Son-of-a-dog! Son-of-a-dog![8] Get the lantern!' Ah Zhong was shouting for his grandson, not even bothering to stand up, both hands pushing against the earth. As the news of the battalion commander's demise had spread the day before, the sensational, blood-curdling news spread with the broadening green hues of morning.

'Wang Lianzhong's become a cow and been reborn in Nine Well Village!' And all at once people were telling each other : 'On the calf's body there are whorls where you can read the characters "Wang Lianzhong"!'

'So no wonder the cow was so long overdue. She was just waiting for Lianzhong to snuff it!'

The narrow enclosure in front of Old Man Zhong's house was soon packed full of people. Ah Zhong's grandson, Son-of-a-dog, who had been the first to see the celebrated characters, held forth: 'Actually, it's not "Wang Lianzhong" meaning "loyal", it's "Wang Lianzhong" meaning "middle".'[9] Then careful research revealed that the battalion commander's original name had been Wang Lianzhong meaning 'middle', but that he had changed it to Wang Lianzhong meaning 'loyal' during the 'Three Unswervingly Loyals' campaign.[10] Naturally, this was considered even more supernatural.

How could they have thought up such a thing? After all, neither Ah Zhong nor any of his sons could read, at least that's what Son-of-a-dog said. People cast all doubts away,

8. In many areas of the remote countryside, it is believed that ugly-sounding names will repel malevolent forces from a child.

9. The two characters involved are pronounced exactly the same, but written slightly differently.

10. This was a campaign launched by the man who was then Mao's hand-picked successor, Lin Biao, a military strongman noted for his sycophancy. The 'Three Unswervingly Loyals' were: loyalty to Mao Zedong himself, loyalty to Mao Zedong Thought, loyalty to Mao's Revolutionary Line.

and afterwards some ten or 20 literate witnesses testified that, clear and plain, 'Wang Lianzhong' was written in the calf's hair. Later on, of course, the constant licking of the mother cow erased the characters in the whorls. But when the sun was at its height, and the light was bright, some 20 or 30 people saw it and testified with one voice that the calf bore a plain, unambiguous 'Wang' character.

Anyway, the most unmistakable sign of all was the calf's face: the brows, the cheekbones, the muzzle. Of course, it is only fair to say that the battalion commander had looked a bit bovine even in his prior existence. And then again, the face of the director of women's affairs looked remarkably rodent-ish . . .

And then, after all the tossing and turning and being looked up and down, the calf could not quite manage to stand up by itself. It bent its forelegs and, quite against its will, went slowly kneeling to the ground. Its arrival in this world must have seemed ominous even to itself, for tears oozed from its eyes. Subsequently, the tears and the kneeling too entered the supernatural canon, and were bruited far and wide. 'Wang Lianzhong assigned as a cow! Crying! Kneeling for forgiveness!'

'O divine retribution!'

'O karma!'

The divine fuss

It was one of those truly millenarian events, occurring but once in a thousand years. The creation of satellites, rockets, nuclear weapons and all that was nothing at all compared to the karmic transformation of Wang Lianzhong into a cow. This was divine punishment indeed. At long last, heaven was opening its eyes, Buddha was manifest, and the gods were almighty!

Since the battalion commander had been a bad man, Buddha and the gods would simply use him to issue a solemn warning to all mankind. The bitterness of the human past, seeping into the bedrock of human forgetfulness, may undergo a slow kind of desalinization, diluted with indifference and other cares. But Old Man Heaven has eyes. Heaven does not forget. And suddenly, the people of Taimu Shan remembered too. They seemed to remember days upon days of something very like slavery. Humiliation after mortification came bubbling and sometimes shooting up, like geysers out of cold memory. Yet, at the time, they had not considered it so very hard to bear. They had all found it natural enough. Ah, but now even the dim memory, only the memory, was intolerable!

For when you thought about it carefully, it seemed that all those years of sacrifice and pain were futile and pointless. Besides, now there was no one to accuse, and nothing to blame, and nowhere to complain. They were left muddling along in an elusive present. But the transformation of the battalion commander jerked at an intricate and slippery knot of memory; it must be carefully thought on.

Panxi Township had never before been so lively. Lively isn't quite the word. Along one road, three whole hamlets were enveloped in a mysterious miasma. People pushed and shoved at each other from morning to night, as if possessed. From every remote corner of the far-flung mountain districts of Taimu Shan people came down, breaking the clouds, spontaneously converging on Panxi. Group after group, they came hurrying to see the calf.

The inhabitants of Nine Well Village were perhaps the most possessed by evil humours. Every day they would lead out the cow and her calf, and put her in the best enclosure in the pasture for the people to see. Young blades provided a complimentary commentary for the benefit of the newly arrived. The calf was tossed to and fro, and examined by everyone until it was half dead. The mountain folk were utterly enthralled. They would hurl all kinds of abuse and threats at the animal, leaving both beasts trapped in an incessant, menacing human thunder all day long, until even at night they trembled and twitched nervously. Sometimes the mother cow and the calf would cling together, terrified, shivering and quaking. Finally, Old Man Ah Zhong and Grandpa Ah Yang, the old brigade head, wouldn't let anyone examine the 'Wang' character any more.

When they had finished seeing the cow, they would visit the shops and make purchases, or find some place to rest their feet. Every place a man might sit was soon occupied. Everywhere people were compiling a popular inventory of the multifarious nefarious deeds of the battalion commander's previous existence. Who could say that the bad things that he had done had not really all fallen on his head in the end? Everywhere there were men hawking and spitting, and women talking and talking some more. The audiences drew themselves into tight little circles, listening and listening again, untiringly to the same story a hundred times.

Even the sun seemed a lot friendlier. The sweat it now drew from the brow of men was the stuff of merriment and entertainment. But of course the jolliest sweat of all was that of the merchants of the village. Even peasants and other residents who had never tried their hands at commerce began to open shops. Day in and day out, the mill in the rice depot ground rice flour and turned out basket after basket of rice noodles. The horror in the hearts of Flathead and Ah Da had not faded, but they could hardly dwell on it, as they were kept busy day and night.

All along the street there were snack stalls, sweet-and-tobacco stalls, fried-bean sellers, deep-fried-dough-twist vendors, smoked-fish mongers, tea stalls, locksmiths, pot-menders, tailors and cobblers everywhere, anything to make a few kuai. Pedlars of rosaries, incense, candles, and sacrificial paper money did an even better trade. After all, how could you come all the way to this holy spot without making an offering? People prayed for happy, secure families, domestic bliss, rich harvests. Quite a few charitable offerings were made. Doing good must always pay off better than doing evil, at least in the long run.

But there were hawkers of nylon clothing and digital watches as well. Small-time booksellers, fortune tellers, diviners, kung fu fakirs, patent medicine pedlars and their

customers were tightly packed together. The varieties of
hawkers and vendors continued to gush forth in a bubbling
stream. Even the beggars came out in force. The local
cultural committee reacted swiftly and announced that films
would be shown day and night at the meeting hall, and, later
on, young men and women got to feeling spring-hearted and
frisky, and could be seen jostling each other back and forth,
all neatly decked out in their best. What with so many men
looking at women and women looking at men, they say that
not a few ended up going off into the little gulleys around the
village to cling to each other a little tighter.

And so it was that Panxi Township became a major tourist
attraction. Everywhere you looked you could see heads
bobbing up and down, and everywhere you listened you
could hear talking and laughing. And everywhere you could
see a kind of misty look in people's eyes. The mysterious
miasma of Taimu Shan seemed to mesmerize people in a
truly wonderful way. In fact, the events surrounding the
death of the battalion commander had generated a momentum
of their own, until the dispatching of his funeral was almost
ignored. While folk from all over circled the two cows and
stared, the remains of the actual battalion commander were
stuffed into a cheap coffin of thin planks and placed on the
floor of an office to await the memorial meeting and the
burial.

Sadly, not a single soul came to stare at the corpse. Once
having recognized his incarnation in the calf, they paid no
attention at all to the human remains. And those who had
actually known him in life were particularly obsessed with
the bovine apparition, seemingly a ghost in their very midst.
They kept remarking how this or that feature was like the
defunct commander, especially those two marks betwen the
eyes. That made them all cluck and stick out their tongues,
or else just hawk and spit in horror.

Neither the dead man's relatives nor those of Lianzhong
Qin attended the funeral. They were all afraid of becoming
another 'cow' for people to stare at. Not even Lianzhong
Qin's elder brother came. Those who had professed to be

the battalion commander's good friends in the old days were either out visiting relatives or simply not home, busily avoiding the whole business. Those who had been quite willing to throw their weight around with his in former times left not so much as shadows at his funeral. It didn't help; they were gleefully pointed out on the street anyway and given the treatment now accorded to his memory.

The memorial meeting planned by the production brigade also lost a good bit of its momentum, since it was now impossible to speak of the thing, even to cancel it. Those who were responsible for the actual details had to scurry back and forth like rats, furtively carrying out their duties. Heaven and earth seemed upside down in the billowing miasma that covered the village. People walked about in a daze, not knowing what to do or forgetting themselves entirely.

Anyone who had endured the slightest humiliation from any quarter could release his or her frustration right there on the street. It was a boundless miracle. But most remarkable was the number of people who it transpired had endured who knows how many kicks and punches from the dead man during the year of the 'Four Kinds of People' campaign.[11] One by one, they would emerge and sit in a conspicuous spot, greeting their acquaintances and buying fruit to munch slowly or yellow-tipped cigarettes to smoke. They did not bother to join the curses and threats; they simply sat there looking carefree and utterly at leisure. Their sons and daughters and grandsons and granddaughters, however, were out in force, cursing and threatening at the top of their lungs, and sometimes cursing the rich peasants for good measure.

11. During the Cultural Revolution, there was a recurrent campaign to stamp out 'four kinds of bad people': landlords, rich peasants, counter-revolutionaries, and 'rotten elements', or criminals. This movement was associated with the worst excesses of the period, and even spawned a counter-campaign that was launched in 1983 against those who had terrorized, beaten, slandered or bribed their way to power supposedly in pursuit of the 'four kinds'.

245

All at once there were impromptu grievance committees everywhere. People would pour out their past sufferings with copious tears and snot, and those who heard would recall their own experiences and be unable to hold back their own tears. It was even more moving and delightful than a night at the opera. When one group had finished listening, another would relieve them, asking the speaker to start all over again from the very beginning. The voice of the speaker mingled with muttered repetitions of the battalion commander's crimes and created an unprecedented aura of happy, busy hubbub.

'. . . all that rot about "revolution"! It was nothing but looting and plundering! Me and Ah Zhong once went up to Mayang with some wood to sell. Had to, back then, because the woman was ill and we needed money for medicine. That dog's son came and confiscated it and didn't give us a *fen* [one hundredth of a yuan] in compensation. And then two days later he sold it off to somebody or other himself. Only a tiger-wolf like that would get turned into a cow before our very eyes.'

'. . . remember that year he kept insisting that Ah Miao had a private family plot he was cultivating on the sly? Took a pig about this big and fat and led it off. As if he didn't want to eat it himself! Bandit! After he killed the pig he went and handed out some of the best bits among the production brigade, trying to suck up to the leaders. May those who ate it have it turn into tumours and rot their intestines! Ah, now retribution!'

'. . . he'd arrest anyone he felt like arresting, and lock up anyone he felt like locking up. If he didn't like your attitude, he'd just keep you and wouldn't let you go home, you'd just stay right there in the "study group" doing all the really tough jobs.'

'. . . so you die of hunger! Big deal! Doesn't count for so much as an ant's death. But when he wanted to eat, all he had to do was call a public meeting, and the militiamen would all fall in and get some. And where did it all come from? Doesn't it always come from us peasants? 360 days a year, and we'd give them a hundred of "voluntary" labour. And weren't those hundred days just so they could stuff their guts?[12] Oh, they had a good feed, didn't they? Well, today he's become a cow and he gets all this good hay he should be even happier! Ha, ha! Yeah, he knows everything now, just can't open his mouth and say it like a man. See? Still dares to look at me and moo! Ptui! Filthy animal!'

'. . . that evil creature kept saying how he didn't believe in the gods or Buddha and wasn't afraid of heaven or earth. He wasn't even afraid of going out and striking down the guardian bodhisattvas of Taimu Shan! Now who ever dared strike at a bodhisattva and got away with it? People like that must be born out of evil spirits! If they dare strike a bodhisattva, would they hesitate to beat a man? Ah, the black years! Digging up our stoves, taking our roof tiles![13] He really let those "Four Kinds of People" have it, didn't he? Didn't even let a man's virgin daughter alone. They all had to get down and crawl. Now is that any kind of a man? Why, he couldn't even stand to see a fellow try to have a proper wedding get-together. If you didn't send the gifts upstairs, he'd be sure to come around with that big bamboo pole and clear off all the tables for you.[14] Any family that started off with that kind of brutal entertainment could count themselves cursed for good. Didn't he just clean out that wedding over in Shuangping, though? Even the groom ended up in his "study group"! And all that stuff about "trafficking in wives"! Wasn't that how he got that wife of his? All you had to do was offend him once, and that was it

12. Apparently public meetings of the militia were paid for out of public funds. Peasants were at that time required to do periods of 'voluntary' labour for the state, and, as the peasants point out, this was the device by which the cadres were excused from productive work.
13. Roof tiles and stoves, the most expensive items in a peasant's home, could be confiscated to pay fines.
14. The Chinese government has waged a long struggle against exorbitant bride price and lavish weddings that has continued down to this day. In many areas, the principal expense of a wedding is entertaining the guests, so that a limit is placed on the number of tables a host may lay.

– no peace to the end of your days. He'd never pass up an opportunity to make trouble for you. Call you a counter-revolutionary, put you in a cangue [wooden collar] and hang a rubbish pail around your neck, seal up your place, fine the whole household, and if you didn't cough it up in ten days, double the fine. And then if you didn't pay up, he'd come by and ransack the house in person. Just think! How did we ever get by back then?'

Anyway, with all this pent-up suffering spattering like hot oil in a wok, the day of the battalion commander's funeral procession arrived at last. The armed militia received orders to take part in the procession with all their weapons. A clerk of the commune armed forces instructed them: 'Very bad business, these last few days. I don't want any of you getting caught up in these superstitious tendencies going around. I want you all to take a firm stand, got that?' The men nodded vigorously and then positioned their heads perfectly upright in a straight line. The branch secretary of the production brigade murmured, 'Ah, people are such low creatures! In all those spartan years, with everything kept tight as a drum, no one ever dared break out like this. But as soon as you give them a chance to breathe easy, look at the mischief.'

At length the coffin was carried out into the hall. There were even three or four wreaths of flowers, and on the wall hung a memorial of the dead man done on grid paper. Above that, there was a sheet of lined paper inscribed in big black characters: 'Comrade Wang Lianzhong Memorial Meeting.' On one side of the coffin stood the bereaved family, on the other, all the bereaved leadership. In front stood a line of armed militiamen, with a few onlookers standing here and there behind them. A tape recorder borrowed from the production brigade played funeral marches.

Gradually, murmuring and muttering from the common herd outside the door began filtering in, and slowly the mourners inside became aware of a mounting pressure.

'Pretty impressive. Well, after all, he was their battalion commander.'

248

'Such people don't deserve a good send-off. Serves him right he got turned into a cow.'

'Who's going to bring wreaths when peasants like us drop dead?'

Then whistling started up, shrill and cutting. 'Lianzhong Qin! How come you aren't wailing for your old man?'[15]

'Open the coffin and have a look at what's inside!' By now the crowd had become itchy and restless, spilling over into the meeting place, but no one dared try to disperse them for fear of what might happen when they actually came in contact with the funeral party. After a moment of silent tribute, the mourners made three bows before the coffin. With each bow, someone outside let out a yell.

The deputy battalion commander delivered the eulogy. Every time he said 'positive contributions' or 'ceaseless devotion in the service of building the militia', or something like that, the crowd outside would bellow. As for the whistling, it never let up. Then, when he came to a part that went, 'He unfortunately died at his post, with all attempts at rescue proving to no avail, at the age of only 39', Lianzhong Qin at last let loose a torrent of tears that would have wrested a river out of its bed and stirred up the sea. She collapsed limply on the coffin, senseless with grief, tossing and turning and slapping it with both hands, weeping until she seemed half dead herself.

Her outburst prompted the crowd outside to shove their way in at last, pushing the pall bearers aside. The meeting hall was seething like a wok of hot congee, and no one could see or hear distinctly for a long moment. The leadership shouted themselves hoarse. At length they called the militia to clear a path through the crowd and get a rope and some bamboo poles to carry out the coffin. The dead man's son

15. Bereaved family, and widows especially, are popularly expected to wail loudly and incessantly for the dead. This requirement is so pervasive that a recent editorial in a Chinese newspaper cited the use of tape recorders playing continuous wailing noises for the benefit of passers-by as one of the misuses to which modern technology was being put in the countryside.

and daughter helped the others to pull their mother to her feet, still struggling furiously. Thus, the coffin was eventually carried out the door.

But when they at last reached the outside, they paused a moment in shock. Who could possibly have imagined such a sea of people? They were packed into the little stream bed so tightly that water couldn't even trickle through. A torrent of people, now an uncontrollable flood, seething and bubbling with excitement. Those behind shoved and pushed those in front, those in front moaned and complained to high heaven. The hubbub seemed to intoxicate and derange the crowd.

'Look out! They're going to shoot!' The terrified message was conducted through the masses like a jolt of electricity. Someone's nasty idea of a practical joke, or a spur of the moment cry of desperation from the militiamen themselves, half crushed to death and pulled to pieces? All at once the whole mass of people disappeared like startled birds and frightened beasts, men and women shouting, screaming, weeping and fleeing in every direction, leaving shoes and plaited bamboo hats scattered all over the ground.

The coffin had been turned on one side, and people had clambered all over it, their feet breaking through the thin planks in two places. Lianzhong Qin was rolling on the ground, covered in dust from head to toe, like the White Haired Girl.[16] Her son and daughter, their faces blood-red with mortification, hissed at their half-crazed mother. But the torrent of people had subsided, and only a few were left watching the scene from afar.

The coffin was again lifted, and the guard of honour assembled. The battalion commander's son, carrying the memorial picture of his father, walked in front. Then came the daughter and the local director of the Bureau of

16. *The White Haired Girl* was an opera written in early 1945 by He Jingzhi and Ding Yi, and performed in Yan'an. The eponymous heroine runs away from a cruel landlord and lives in a cave, eating the offerings laid out for the dead in a temple. Her hair turns white from grief, but she is at length rescued by the legendary Eighth Route Army.

Women's Affairs, supporting Lianzhong Qin, who was almost bent over double in pain. Under the tersely barked orders of the deputy battalion commander, the procession made for the cemetery hill behind the village.

When they reached the mouth of the little trail that led up the hill, a mad peal of laughter came circling down like a ragged buzzard. A young man with a demented look appeared at the entrance to the trail, carrying the little calf. He held its legs together and swung it around, high above his head, laughing and jumping and calling out: 'Lianzhong Qin! Your old man's right here! He's been reborn!' It was the village lunatic of Shuangping, Ah Qing.

Eight years earlier, when a young man of 17, his family had fixed up his wedding, arranging a match with a little 15-year-old, a welcome addition to the overworked womenfolk of the household. On the appointed evening, Ah Qing bowed his thanks to heaven and earth and entered the bridal chamber, where, observing the rites, he at last could remove the red veil. The bride revealed had a blooming face and delicately painted eyebrows, and was clad in a red padded jacket. She had a fringe of hair which, exquisitely styled, broke on her forehead like a wave. Her face, in snowy whites and powdery reds, bobbed up ever so discreetly to steal a little peep at Ah Qing. Ah Qing was so excited he couldn't seem to catch his breath. He had never seen anything so beautiful, and it was a long time before he descended from his pinnacle of ecstasy and went down to toast his elders.

Now back then the production brigade regulations stipulated that wedding feasts could lay out a maximum of three tables, and every table over that limit was liable to a 50 yuan fine. Ah Qing's family, anxious to win respect at the wedding of their eldest son, had laid on 20 tables. The matter had been kept strictly secret, and the aid of the production brigade secretary had been enlisted. Wine was distributed to all the families in the village to drink, however, so in due course the battalion commander put in an appearance with his militiamen in tow, in order to strike a blow against 'Old Customs'.[17] Quick as a flash, five of the tables were uncovered and all the fish, meat, vegetables and wine carried off. In addition, a fine of 850 yuan was levied. Ah Qing got worked up and started cursing, but he hadn't got two words out when he found himself trussed up and led off. Friends and relatives were so terrified they jumped at their own shadows. By dawn the wedding was a shambles. The new bride spent her wedding night bawling that she wanted to die.

On the second day, a message was handed down to the effect that the fine had been increased, and the detainees would now be released only on the payment of 1,200 yuan. In the event of non-payment, the family of the groom would have to seal up their home and leave the village.

Now, it happened that on a previous occasion, the little bride had had divination lots cast, and these had predicted that she would share the fate of Meng Jiangnu.[18] So she now became convinced that she was accursed and that her wedding had offended some evil fiend. When no one was looking, she drank a bottle of 'Happy Fruit' [an insecticide] and died.

In an uproar, the entire village of the bride's family came running to the groom's house and filled it to the brim. They devoured three carrying-pole loads of white rice, and then threatened to take the in-laws out and lynch them. Eventually, the production brigade sent a deputation over to clear everybody away, and arrested the bride's elder brother and

17. A reference to the campaign against the 'Four Olds': Old Habits, Old Customs, Old Ideas, and Old Ways of Life.

18. Meng Jiangnu married the handsome Fan Xiliang, but he was forced to do slave labour on the Great Wall by the first Qin emperor, Qin Shihuang Di (221-207 BC). Fan died far away from home and was buried in a section of the Great Wall near Shanhaiguan, on the sea. Meng Jiangnu, the model of a faithful Chinese wife, searched for him for many years, and when she reached the portion of the wall where he was entombed, her tears washed down the wall and revealed his body. She killed herself by jumping into the sea off the eastern end of the Great Wall. (Suicide was a sign of virtuous widowhood in traditional China.)

paternal uncle. Then the production brigade of the bride's village sent over their militia to demand satisfaction, and the two sides proceeded to turn the world upside down and back again. In the end, the commune leaders had to step in and arbitrate the dispute personally. It was decided that the Panxi Township production brigade would release the detainees if Shuangping village would foot the bride's funeral bill to the tune of 200 yuan, with the groom's family agreeing to lay on a truly lavish ceremony. Since human life had been lost in the shuffle, the 1,200 yuan fine was cancelled and the groom was to be released and sent home. But any further disturbances, and the fine would have to be paid up.

By the time Ah Qing got home, his bride was already in her coffin. Perhaps it was from this point that his derangement dated. True, in his fieldwork and home life he remained as capable as ever, and no one ever heard him complain or fuss. But he began to suffer, so they said, from the obsession with women common to ageing bachelors. He simply could not bear the sight of a woman in a red padded jacket. And now he was 25 years old and still unmarried.

Holding the calf, he blocked the path of the funeral procession. He was beside himself now. They pursued him to and fro, trying to wrest the calf from his grip. The branch secretary began to bellow at the top of his lungs, 'What is this rebellion?! Ah Qing! Are you trying to get yourself killed?' At this Ah Qing at last let go of the calf and seemed to go limp. He fixed his eyes on the branch secretary and stared, then he began to whimper, and at length went up to him and began to tug at his sleeve, snivelling and giggling. 'How come she hasn't been reborn? Why don't you arrange to get her reborn too?'

Meanwhile, Old Man Ah Zhong came up and picked up the little calf, who was now trembling from head to foot. When Ah Qing turned and petted the calf, Ah Zhong pulled him off to the side of the trail and made him sit down. 'Look, your wife has turned into a fairy, see? That was heaven's decision. Now, if you're a good sort and work hard, there'll be lots and lots of good women under heaven for you, and you'll get one.'

Ah Qing lifted his head and choked on a sob. 'It's not right! It's unjust! All these years!' The guard of honour began to file silently past. At one moment, Lianzhong Qin seemed to come briefly to her senses; but the next moment she appeared even more confused and befuddled. She looked at Ah Qing with dark cavernous eyes, and turned to look at him again as she walked by.

A few steps beyond the mouth of the trail up into the hills, they came to the graveyard. The grave had already been dug. Suddenly a woman's voice filled the little clearing with an aria from a Siping opera. Yet on all sides, there wasn't so much as a human shadow among the bright grass and faded tombstones.

> These days, Fan Xiliang must mourn his Meng Jiangnu.

Even Ah Zhong and Ah Qing, far down the trail, could hear it clear as clear could be. The voice was pure, tranquil, and brimming with tenderness, yet her hearers went practically green with terror, and cold sweat began trickling down their faces.

> And returning home at last, does not see his wife's face at all.
> Weep, weep the Great Wall's length, weep all ten thousand li
> Still you shall not find the end of conjugal fidelity.

At that, a few of the stouter-hearted men shouted, 'Don't be afraid, it's only the madwoman!' And sure enough, the madwoman was lying inside the grave itself, laughing and belting out her arias.

Now, the madwoman was actually a woman of Pingnan, and had been singing the Siping operas native to her home town since she was a very little girl. Her husband had been a sidewalk tailor in Panxi, who had left long before to make his fortune, along with his father. In Pingnan, he had the fortune to meet this woman and marry her. Both of them were literate, and, indeed, theirs had been a love match. The young woman's name was Aimei. She had helped her husband return to Panxi and open up a tailor's shop, and together they had worked, eking out a living and writing their own opera libretti on the side. She was very gifted, and all that she daily heard and saw eventually found its way into her lyrics, fitting seamlessly into an opera aria.

Now, her little tailor had been a fair and somewhat frail fellow, the good-looking sort of model of refinement who, it was said, didn't have enough force of character to raise his voice in anger, and was generally considered kind-hearted to a fault. They had loved one another dearly and passed many peaceful days together. But, five years before, Aimei had gone home to visit her parents with their child. Missing her husband, she decided to come home a bit early.

There seemed to be no one around the shop when she arrived. In fact, the door was stoutly locked. Aimei undid the lock, using the combination known only to her husband and herself. As soon as she opened the door, Aimei's husband was done for. Lianzhong Qin's sister-in-law, the wife of the commune Deputy Party Secretary, and the little tailor were in there, nestled snugly inside one of the quilts. It came out that the upstanding wife of one of the outstanding leaders had determined to learn the art of sewing, and, under that pretext, had been visiting the shop every day, actually in order to see the tailor. The tailor was a soft-hearted sort, as we have said, and was apparently simply not up to resisting Madame Deputy Party Secretary's carefully woven blandishments and threats.

The Deputy Party Secretary had gone to the provincial capital for a half year of in-service training, and had been gone since well before Aimei's own departure. On the day they were so rudely disturbed, Madame Deputy Party Secretary was carrying around a four-month foetus, and, to make matters worse, the Deputy Party Secretary was due to return any day. As for the little tailor, he was utterly unable to face his wife, in-laws, parents and child, and, in addition was living in terror of the Deputy Party Secretary's wrath. Eventually, he took a stout bit of material and strung himself up. The whole affair was effectively hushed up and blew over.

Aimei was ill for about half a year, and later became rather demented, wandering around and crooning her operas. In her lucid moments, she would say that she herself had hounded her husband to death, but even in her wildest ravings, she would never mention the business of that other woman. Lianzhong Qin, for her part, had no reason to dislike Aimei, yet she had beaten and cursed her on several occasions. No need to describe a beating at the hands of Lianzhong Qin; they said that even the dogs dared not whimper after such a beating, and the battalion commander himself, in his former existence, had not been able to shout her down. Anyway, it was this Aimei who, at this moment, was lying in the grave, singing:

> Already I've endured three summers
> And nine winters searching for my own
> Never thinking once that on your grave
> Already this green lid has grown.
> Fan Xiliang, Ah! 'Twere better by far to have become
> A ghost with only the Wuding River for a home.

They pulled her out. She giggled indistinctly, then, pointing with an operatic gesture at Lianzhong Qin, asked softly: 'You're not going to beat me? You're not going to curse me?' She reached out and tugged at the white cloth on Lianzhong Qin's head.[19] 'So you're wearing one too! You're wearing one too!' Bluffing and cajoling by turn, they managed to pull her down the hillside, while the rest of the procession got on with its task.

> These days the Yellow River can wash nothing clean
> And meanders zig-zagging, from bend to bend
> And so long the bitter lament of Meng Jiangnu
> Can never be sung to the end!
> Fan Xiliang, ah! Heaven has called you back
> To exalt you, enfolded in stars, like the moon.
> May I not likewise call you back
> To exalt you and enfold you in my arms as a man?

19. White is the colour of mourning in China, and widows wear white turbans.

256

With these mournful strains, the coffin of the battalion commander disappeared into the yellow earth.

Great days in the mourning

When the branch secretary at last assembled a few cadres to look into the 'incident', they all felt uneasy about it. It was the old 'Four Kinds of People' sitting right there by the roadside and smoking that particularly disturbed them. And the sight of the sons and grandsons cursing and threatening the battalion commander was almost more than their poor nerves could take. Worse, as soon as they stepped outside of headquarters, they could feel the scorching radiation of stares. Nobody openly passed judgment, but it was undoubtedly being considered somewhere in their minds. All the pride had gone out of being a cadre; their stature had been abruptly cut down. They even seemed physically shorter, unable to hold their heads quite straight any more. Now they were utterly dependent on pleasant expressions and good tobacco to smooth over their dealings.

On the other hand, those cadres who had got on well with people rather enjoyed going out these days, and they particularly welcomed the reception the hill folk gave them. They would stand there on the street chatting with them; the hill people would slap them boisterously on the back and clap an arm around their shoulders, and they would reciprocate and exchange glances quite bottomless with meaning. So, among themselves, the cadres became divided over the whole affair. Those with something to be proud of were proud enough, while the indignant were certainly indignant. No matter what was being discussed, someone was bound to say eventually, 'Well, just try going out into the street and see what people say to that, eh?'

Because the whole affair had come to involve 'the propagation of feudal superstitions', a meeting was eventually held at the commune level, and all the Panxi production brigade leaders were summoned. They all sat there on the edges of their chairs, nervously smoothing their clothes with sweaty palms, discussing 'how to resolve this incident of superstition appropriately, but thoroughly, without exacerbating conflicts among the people.' Of all the participants at the meeting, none wanted to incur the wrath of the hill people, and they were all anxious to avoid the sort of thing that had taken place during the Cultural Revolution. Some of them, however, while trying to be reasonable and not wanting to give offence, gently reminded each other of their heavy obligations in educating the younger generation, and so forth.

Only the supply-and-marketing chief seemed happy about the whole affair. He suggested that a way should be found of increasing business hours, because the various departments under him were having a vigorous stock-clearance competition, and whoever sold the most would receive the highest rate of commission. 'When it's over, I invite each and every one present to come and take part in our award ceremony. The meal, of course, is on the house, and there will be a few other little nothings as bonuses too.' Here he made a little gesture, pinching the air with his thumb and first two fingers. At this the gloom over the meeting seemed to lift a bit, and a number of potentially profitable or efficacious suggestions were put forward for handling the business. At last, the head of the local school was called on to hold a meeting. On the following day, a big meeting was held at the school to forcefully oppose superstitious practices. Scientific knowledge and political attitudes were mentioned, and of course the obscure relationship between the latter and student test scores was not left out. Then it was announced that the two cows were henceforth to be exhibited for one hour in the morning and one hour in the afternoon, with opening and closing times to be strictly observed. Attendance at the showings by party cadre or militia personnel was strongly discouraged. Articles pertaining to superstitious practices were not permitted in the marketplace, although, of course, private transactions would not be scrutinized. Commune tractors and trucks would be permitted to carry passengers in their free moments. The young madman and madwoman would be sent to a health care centre for a free five-day cure courtesy of the production brigade and the local neighbour-hood committee. Mollifying and conciliatory gestures were extended on all sides, and people were exhorted to look only forwards.

On the agricultural front, the tea crop was demanding more and more attention, and many people felt impelled to return to the hills and work. The calf, for his part, had no reason to regret their departure; the whole affair had cost him a lot of heartache. The pedlars and shopkeepers, in the wake of the crowd, also diminished in numbers. The stocks of the supply-and-marketing division were practically gone. Those who received awards at the prize-giving ceremony cherished the fondest memories of the battalion commander, as the cadre who took part in the banquet attested at great length. All in all, the affair was wound up very well indeed.

At last, people stopped coming to Panxi Town altogether. Ah Da and Flathead no longer had to spend all their time steaming rice noodles. As they put it, 'Ah, the whole thing seems like a big dream!' But the true period of mourning was just beginning. The unhappiest of women was Lianzhong Qin, and the unhappiest of cattle was 'Lianzhong' calf.

Lianzhong Qin was no longer living in the room that she and the battalion commander had rented. As soon as the great storm blew over and the tide of people ebbed, the landlord had returned the eight yuan they had prepaid for the half year to come. He told her his second son was about to marry, the date had been set for the following month, and they'd be using the room right away. But he was willing, in compensation, to consider the last five months free of charge as well. Then he added a few words about how reasonable the battalion commander had always been while he was alive, and how bad he felt about his death, and so on. The landlord's wife then insisted on dragging Lianzhong Qin into their little place for dinner.

Anyway, they had already sent some presents over to the branch secretary, and had managed to persuade him to clear out half of a little room in the upstairs of the health station, where some medicines had been dumped in a big heap, and

Lianzhong Qin was to be allowed to live there with her children. They didn't even wait for her to express an opinion in the matter, but had an enthusiastic crew standing by to help her move. Some old newspapers were fished out from somewhere in brigade headquarters; these were used to wallpaper the half-room, and then an electric cord with a light bulb was hung up. The landlord and his family laid some little mud bricks at the foot of the stairs to make a small kitchen hearth. Then, quick as you can make five minus two equal three, the whole family was moved.

The landlord still felt a bit guilty about all this, so he sent over a little round wooden table and a crock of pickled vegetables as well. Casting their blinking eyes around the room when it was all over, Lianzhong Qin and her son and daughter found themselves sharing a room with a huge pile of unused medicines. And it was really very old, almost ready to cave in. The so-called 'upstairs' of the health station was really nothing but an attic, with only ridgepoles and clay tiles overhead, and absolutely nothing to divide the room off with. They put their bed down in their half, and found that they couldn't fit a single other person in the room. Lianzhong Qin ran to the grave of her husband, weeping profusely.

She went there every day to weep for the benefit of a perfectly heartless audience. She knew very well that the deluded and deranged people around her were making a major fuss about the calf, and she also knew that the supply and marketing division, the rice depot, and even the small-time pedlars and stall-keepers were making small fortunes out of it as well. She wanted everyone to know that her husband was right there in the hillside, not in the body of that calf. She made a point of never mentioning the calf, of never even looking at it.

Ah, but the days were difficult to bear, so difficult! The poor beast, from the time of its birth, had never known a single day of the sort of bovine life that is the right of every cow. It knew full well that men were its natural enemies. They beat it, spat on it, burned it with their cigarette butts, thrashed it with bamboo canes, and even pulled its tail. But the worst part was when they would start shouting, 'Kneel down! Kneel!' Then the calf knew it was really in for it; it had been taught exactly what this meant with thick staves and lusty strokes. Enduring countless blows and curses, it had long since fully grasped the dark significance of the word.

Ah, it was nothing but a humble calf, after all. It would hasten to bend its forelegs and kneel. And then came the order, 'Get up! Up!' And a downpour of lashes and blows followed. Instinctively, it jumped up. Then it was 'Kneel!' all over again, and, as soon as it did so, 'Get up!' The poor calf heard these two commands over and over again until its head was spinning and it trembled, wracked by coughing.

The spectacle made the folks very merry indeed. They guffawed their huge appreciation, and the more the calf trembled, the more they kicked it. And so it went. When one lot had their fill, another took their places, and enjoyed themselves even more hugely. Gradually, the calf began to comprehend that, although it had the body of a calf, it was not quite a calf. But it could not comprehend why its lot was so very bitter. It could not know for whose crimes it was a scapegoat, in whose place it was enduring the boundless, bottomless abyss of hell on earth.

After it had been weaned, Old Man Ah Zhong was unwilling to include the 'Demon Calf' in his contract. His old woman had been continually ill of late, and he thought perhaps her illness had been brought on by the presence of the calf. Nobody at all was willing to look after it, but eventually they managed to get an idiot to take care of it. This particular idiot was the son of a big landlord in Panxi. The landlord himself had been a man of no small refinement, and had a fine hand for carving seals, but he was unfortunate in his heir. The idiot must have been the reincarnation of some bandit or thief spirit; he would steal the very planks of the family house and sell them. It was always the same story: he would be taken in by someone in a gambling game, he'd steal, get caught, cry, get beaten up. When the battalion commander was alive, he had beaten him like a dog. And now 'Lianzhong Calf' had fallen into his clutches.

The idiot would gleefully beat the calf himself, and was glad to let anyone who cared to come and beat it as well, any way they liked. When the calf was hungry, it had to go off and forage for itself in the hills. When it was tired, it had to sleep in a disused lime kiln outside the cattle pen, for it was not allowed into the cowshed. If the calf ever stopped in front of a house, the householder would react as if it were a 'hungry ghost'[20] or a small-time demon, and come out screaming and shouting and thrashing about with a club to exorcise it. When people passed by, they would always walk around it in a big circle, mumbling a kind of incantation, 'O karma! O retribution! Who told you to be so evil in your previous life? In this one you are bound to suffer for your sins!' Even the local dogs began to look down their noses at it, and would turn and snap at it on the slightest pretext.

The calf must have felt it keenly, for it would often moo in a poignant fashion, but never daring to moo very loudly. All it had to do was let itself go just a little bit, and it would be sure to catch a filthy hiding from some passer-by. But the calf did not die. It not only stubbornly survived, it got bigger and stronger.

People noticed a defiant mood in Lianzhong Qin which made them even more resentful of her. 'So she thinks things are still the way they used to be, does she? Ha! Who does she think she's going to impress?' The nastier representatives of the younger generation would lie in wait for her when she went out to wash clothes or rinse her vegetables, and then drive the calf in front of her, thrashing and lashing the beast within an inch of its life, burning it with their cigarette butts, and kicking it until it rolled on the ground in agony. Then it was 'Kneel!' and 'Get up!' and so forth. And the idiot would

20. Those who die without heirs become 'hungry ghosts', because they have no one to sacrifice to them on feast days. There is a festival of hungry ghosts once a year, when the gates of hell are opened for two weeks to allow them to walk the earth in search of sacrifices.

yell: 'Wang Lianzhong! Bow your head! Bow!' And they would force its head down. The calf would go 'moo-moo' and start trembling from head to hoof.

Lianzhong Qin choked back her tears and paid no attention. But the idle and not-so-idle womenfolk would gather right outside the health station door, saying: 'Horrid creature! What's she weeping on that empty grave for? She won't give the living his due!' 'I'll say! That's her own husband in flesh and blood, for better or worse. And look at her! She just sits there and lets him suffer!' 'Ah, women! When a man dies, it's all over! Soon enough they'll be comfortably settled with a better one!'

Soon Lianzhong Qin took to trembling just like the calf. The same treatment befell her son and daughter, too. Wherever they went, people would point to the calf and say, 'That's your own pa, in flesh and blood! Look at you! Not only do you refuse to pay him filial respect, you just let him suffer!' They would come home in tears and tell their mother, 'The calf is really a pitiful sight. Suppose it really was Papa. How he would hate us!'

Lianzhong Qin considered the calf's plight. Could it possibly be true? Could it possibly be Lianzhong transformed? That night she dreamed that first the calf and then her husband stood before her, pouring out their suffering and bitterness. The next time she visited her husband's grave, she found the tears would not come. Her thoughts settled on the calf and lingered. Then she heard him calling at the foot of the hill, in pain. She rushed down the hillside shouting furiously at the little band of calf-beaters: 'I won't let you!'

She grabbed two of them, wrapping her man-sized hands around their wrists, and yanked them off their feet. The idiot ran away, terrified out of his wits and bawling like a baby. Everyone else stood there thoroughly stupefied, and gaped in wonder as she went over to the calf and began to stroke it. The calf looked up at its rescuer in astonishment. Its whole hide was covered nose to tail with all kinds of scars, scabs, cuts and bruises. Lianzhong Qin squatted down, threw her arms around its middle, and let out a moan of pain.

The next day, when the idiot was walking along the dirt road that ran alongside the brook, driving the cows along, the calf caught sight of Lianzhong Qin on the stream bank doing her laundry and recognized her as the one who had saved him the day before. He suddenly wheeled and ran down the embankment, kicking the water with his hooves, sending two snow-white plumes of water in her direction. Then he went right up to her and licked her hand. Silently, he looked at her while the tears oozed out, and then lowered his great horned head as if he wanted to rub it on her body. It was a sight that rooted everyone who witnessed it to the ground.

After that, Lianzhong Qin went to the hills to cut hay, and cut only the very finest. The calf had found three people in the world of men who could love him. He would look for Lianzhong Qin every day, waiting patiently for her by the bank where she washed clothes. If by chance she didn't come, he would start mooing loudly, calling her. The spectacle drew tears from not a few of the women, and occasional sighs from the men. They all began to curse the naughty boys who had beaten the calf so savagely. They cursed the idiot too, and the idiot began to beat the calf less often.

Lianzhong Qin threw herself utterly into her labours of love. She forgot all her shame, and was never in the least embarrassed to be seen taking care of the calf in public. The calf, for its part, drank greedily and ate ravenously. In her eyes, the snuffling nose and hunched shoulders reminded her only of the battalion commander's mealtime etiquette in his previous existence. The calf grew sturdy and strong.

One day, Lianzhong Qin got some wooden poles, bamboo and rice straw, and put up a little hut right by the back door of the health station. She led the calf to the little hut, gave it hay to munch at night, and hovered around looking after it. The calf, free of cares at last, managed to repress his gratitude, and gave her a confidential look.

The affair was bound to rouse public indignation. A widow, living alone, taking in a strapping young bull. Even if it was her own husband reborn, it wasn't proper. It wasn't decent. What was more, the calf was collective property, and was intended to plough for the whole village. Naturally, if a fair price could be negotiated, they might be willing to part with it, but it could hardly be let go for nothing.

Lianzhong Qin replied that if that was the way it was, she would have the calf to keep and honour till death did them part, even if she had to squander her whole family's savings. The people of Nine Well Village considered that the whole matter was quite improper any way you looked at it. They set the price exorbitantly high: 2,000 yuan. At this point Lianzhong Qin had only some 72 yuan to her name.

She began to appear more and more eccentric, trying to borrow money from everyone, even the production brigade itself. Of course, nobody dared to lend her a thing. They all advised her to give up the idea. After all, the whole thing was just superstition; it wouldn't do to behave as if it were really true.

She began to weep incessantly while watching over the calf. She ran around frantically entreating people at the production brigade and even commune level, and lobbied Nine Well Village from east to west to try to get them to lower the price. The final offer was 300 yuan, but there was simply nowhere that she might be able to scare up such a sum. She decided to go around with a carrying pole, selling rice and sweet potatoes. But staples were the least profitable form of commerce, and anyway her neighbours relieved her of the carrying pole and wouldn't let her do it. At this point, she had already sold her entire grain ration, and mother and children began the slow business of starving.

The women all thought this was really pitiful, and everybody began to say that Lianzhong Qin had really exhausted even the most exaggerated notions of wifely devotion. 'Ah Qin, look,' they said. 'So it was heaven's will that he should become a calf and plough the soil. If he's good and puts all the strength a bull can into his work, in the next life he'll be a man again. No one can flout the will of heaven.'

'No! No!' she cried, 'I want to take care of it. I won't let it suffer! If you mean well, lend me a bit of money and let me look after it.' And she sobbed bitterly. There was pity for her, but some of the less pleasant memories they had of the battalion commander were also revived. 'We had enough of his lot back then, all right. And if fate is against him, then fate is just!'

Against them, there were some who remembered that he had done some good in his lifetime, that he had once saved the village from a forced sale of 'Patriotism Grain'. 'Above him there were worse men; and above those, everybody was bad!'

'It's not people who are bad, it is the ways of the world that are crooked, and fate that is all wrong. Ai, those years!' When they thought things over in detail, by and by they began to feel a bit remorseful about the battalion commander.

Finally, the old production team head of Nine Well Village, Grandpa Ah Yang, gave the word: 'Sell it off.' Thereupon, the calf was dragged off to the street market over in White Jade to be sold; but of course everybody there knew all about the infernal calf and wouldn't have taken it for nothing, so it had to be taken back home. There was no help for it. It was decided to have its nose pierced and to keep it in production brigade headquarters to be harnessed for ploughing. Lianzhong Qin fell ill.

The day of the operation came, and everyone turned out in force to watch. The calf bellowed outrage, and tried to pull out the rope in its nose, but Old Man Ah Zhong's sons pulled it taut, and it stopped short in agony. Mournfully, but with a healthy respect for the rope, it made its way to the cattle pen. Where the road passed by the stream, it suddenly charged over the embankment and down to the water. But Lianzhong Qin was not there. The calf howled helplessly and the tears oozed out.

A quiet farewell

Lianzhong Qin was ill for a long time, and she seemed to age visibly. Her hair turned white, and her robust energy left her. She crouched over the counter in front of the medicine chests making up prescriptions, and everybody said she looked very poorly. She seemed to have forgotten all about the calf.

But it was on everybody else's mind, even if no one mentioned it. Everyone seemed to feel its presence, no matter where they were. Its very existence was like a dark and tragic melody that wounded men and controlled their lives the way the music controls the characters in an opera.

One day, Lianzhong Qin went up to the drying grounds with some herbs. The calf was there, in harness, ploughing an empty fallowed field for practice. Old Man Ah Zhong's son was lashing it, teaching it the steps, how to pull, how to corner, and so on. It already nearly had the hang of it.

Suddenly, Lianzhong Qin seemed to see through the illusory world at last. It dawned on her how horribly cruel it was, how tragic, to use a cow or calf to plough a field. Just then the calf caught sight of her and stopped in its tracks, watched her for a while, inclined its head, swung it slowly from side to side, and then lowered its eyes. With a great sigh, it seemed at last to have heard the will of heaven. Lianzhong Qin returned home determined to kill herself, but before she could drink the fatal 'Happy Fruit', she was discovered by her daughter.

Again, Grandpa Ah Yang gave the word, 'As long as the calf is around, we won't have a day of peace and quiet in this village. It's made enough mischief around here. If things go on this way, we'll all turn into beasts!' He issued top secret instructions to a select few, and one day soon thereafter, before the sky began to soften with light, the calf was loaded into a trailer that had been stationed well outside the village, and sent all the way to Pingyang to be sold.

Lianzhong Qin was still fast asleep. The calf in the trailer watched the familiar landscape, where it had suffered so many hardships, recede in the distance. In its dark, damp eyes, everything seemed newly perplexing and obscure.

The story of the battalion commander ends there. After the calf went, Panxi Township emerged from the mysterious miasma that had engulfed it. Even Lianzhong Qin put it behind her. People felt that normal sunlight and pure air had returned. The story of the battalion commander who turned into a calf got muddled and mixed with folk-lore, and was eventually served up for the edification of children.

There was one young person in particular who managed to turn the lesson to advantage. That was Papa Ah Gan's number four son. He was an upper middle school graduate who had had to return to his native village. That year, there was no market for green tea, and the various trade outlets open to the village wouldn't take the crop. The production team found they couldn't market it anywhere, but this youth had a friend in Pingyang who in turn knew someone who had a way of contracting various machines and equipment. So he took the tea over to Pingyang, and they processed it into jasmine tea.

The whole calf affair was very useful in this enterprise. During the days of chaos, when the leadership was completely distracted, he managed to get a business licence and set up the 'Pan-yang Co-operative Tea Processing Corporation'. Through various channels, the tea made its way to Hunan and Jiangxi. In the end, he managed to unload the entire crop, pocketed the net profit, and returned home in triumph.

Who could say for certain that his business would still be around in a year's time? Next year is next year's conditions, next year's weather and next year's political climate. Weather, land and men are all fickle. But this half year had been exceptionally instructive at the very least. By the time he returned home, the calf had already been shipped off, so he must have escaped the ill effects of the evil miasma surrounding the affair, and no one ever learned of his amazing achievement. Only the branch secretary and the treasurer said a few grateful words in thanks for relieving them of the unsaleable tea. He replied simply, 'The tea was no good. No one would take it. I finally sold it at cut price and took the loss.'

The branch secretary said: 'Just be more careful next time, son.'

9 | The spirit of the Ninth

Wuhan, 21 July 1986
Dear Dorothy and Burt,

My trip has been cut short and I have been returned to Wuhan, where I am supposedly confined. I was stopped right in the street as I was going through Shiquan, and my documents and bicycle confiscated. After phoning around, they decided to send me either to Ankang or Xi'an. I rather stupidly chose Xi'an, simply because it was in a forward direction. The police were actually fairly nice about it, congratulated me on making such good time, and assured me I could get the permission I needed to continue in Xi'an. I should have known better, I suppose. They shipped me and my passport separately to Xi'an, with my bicycle on the roof of a bus. My documents were returned to me in Xi'an, but I was instructed to report to the police. Stupidly, I did.

Then I was in trouble. They gravely informed me that I had made the most serious violations of the law of the People's Republic, that a *NY Times* reporter was currently in prison in Beijing for doing what I had done, and that I had to write a full confession. I confessed my ignorance and nothing else, and they accused me of having a bad attitude. The next day, though, they decided that my attitude had changed, and therefore they would not imprison or even fine me, but simply send me back to Wuhan with my bicycle on the train. I was supposed to pay for it all, of course.

Since I had little money with me, I was sleeping on the street, under an arch in the Ming wall around the city. That night, one of my fellow deadbeats stole my briefcase, which contained my bankbook, my freight ticket, a passport, and,

270

of course, cash. Now I was in big trouble. The police wouldn't believe that my things had been stolen; they considered it a ploy to try to avoid getting shipped back. They pretended not to know the name of the place where I had been robbed, and warned me 'not to make jokes with the law'. I grew pretty angry with this and compounded my bad attitude. They told me they would make a full report to the Wuhan Gonganting [Police Bureau], and they hoped they would deal with me accordingly. Meekly, and sick of the whole affair, I returned here, and am now awaiting trial. How's that for misadventure?

P.S. I have at last received permission to go on to Lanzhou, so I'm going to finish this and pack again.

4 September 1986

I got yours of 4 August only today, though I returned a week ago. For some reason, my boss locked it in her desk drawer. Then she lost the key. (You may remember that I have three bosses: my boss, my boss's boss, and my boss's boss's boss, only the last of which I get along with even marginally. And that is by virtue of the fact that we meet only when I am in trouble, or at banquets in my honour that I am required to attend; he apparently feels that the latter compensate for the former. Incidentally, as is traditional in foreign language departments, none of my three bosses speaks a foreign language, and in fact my immediate boss has lived in Wuhan for 30 years without learning either Mandarin or the local dialect. I frequently need a Chinese-to-Chinese interpreter.)

I have two unfinished letters to you, one datelined Golmud, and the second written on the train home. Both are seriously flawed by that cliff-hanging ending you so resent, a product, I'm afraid, of the whole post-natal, pre-mortal enterprise and the unfinishedness of it all. They are also handwritten and illegible, and mildly terrifying from a Jewish mother's point of view, so I will synopsize.

I didn't mean that everything was stolen in Xi'an. I lost one briefcase. This contained some very important

271

documents, my bankbook, my freight ticket for my bicycle, my customs declaration form, glasses, sketches, old passport, 'white card' (part of my residency documentation, which permits me to pay my expenses in 'people's money'), diary, *Conversations with Metal Mountain*, and a very good book on the Tangshan earthquake. But it did not contain all my money, which I generally carry split up; the bulk of that, in fact, I keep in a silk pouch in my crotch, a habit acquired from my pot-smoking days, when I kept my stash under my belt. I had also, stashed in various places on my person and in the baggage room in the train station: a filthy sleeping bag, a spare pair of glasses, a set of clothes, a bicycle pump, etc. So my return to Wuhan was not quite as bereft as it felt.

I finally got permission to leave Wuhan again from my boss's boss's boss. I don't know what he said to the cops, but it did the trick in about two days. I don't really care to know the details, but I received permission to go as far as Lanzhou, so I went to visit a friend there. While there, I asked the Xibei Minority Studies Institute if they were interested in having me for four or five years while I studied Tibetan, and they seemed ecstatic at the idea. Of course, they've never had a foreign student and didn't know the red tape it entailed, but I visited the cops the next day and they seemed to think it no problem. If that is so, then I think that is what I want to do. I have always loved Lanzhou – on the Silk Road, melons, tea, fruit, Muslims, Tibetans and Mongols, and the Midwestern unpretentiousness of the place. The programme they have there seems first rate: Amdo dialect Tibetan, Uighur and Mongol optional, and seminars in Tibetan, Uighur and Mongol history. The director said I could defray my expenses with summer teaching, and that he would personally ensure that any teaching duties I had did not interfere with my studies.

The Lanzhou police would not give me permission to bike on towards Lhasa, so I hitched to Xining. The Xining authorities seemed more enthusiastic over the idea, but I was now short on time and money, so I told them I might try next year. They did give me permission for a remote area on the border of Xinjiang, a Mongol area, to which I went. From there to Dunhuang, where Barbara was spending her vacation, was a two-hour bus ride, so I went and dropped in on her, just as she was strolling down the street to catch the bus out.

We spent a few days at the caves, sleeping in the dunes. One of the buses going out to the caves was driven by some Golmudians, who persuaded Barbara to accompany me to Golmud and Lhasa. Good job she did, too, because the first day out hitching we got stranded in a tiny Kazakh village called Akusai, and my throat got very sore. We decided to forget the hitching and bussed to Golmud the next day, where I checked into the army hospital. One of my tonsils had already burst, and my temperature was above 39. They put me on an intravenous drip for six or seven hours a day, and gave me massive injections of penicillin. This went on for five miserable days, with Barbara sleeping on wooden benches, emptying my bedpan, and carrying my IV after me into the men's loo when I was ambulatory again. I was a little worried about spoiling her vacation, and needled her about being a Chinese wife. She assured me that she was only being a surrogate Jewish mother, and not to get any ideas.

The hospital was rather typical of high-turnover Chinese hospitals: they examine you once, prescribe the cure, and do not bother to check on how you are responding. Barbara went on an anti-smoking campaign against one of the doctors who left my room littered with glowing cigarette butts, and she generally found the callousness and lack of hygiene deplorable; I found them understandable, considering. I still had a bit of a thick throat when I was discharged, but my stir craziness got the better of me and I did not protest.

Twenty-four hours later, on a truck bound for Lhasa, I was worse than ever. I got out near Tanggula and tried to persuade Barbara to go on to Lhasa while I headed back to Golmud, but eventually we decided to go on together. This was probably wise, since Lhasa today is far, far better equipped than Golmud. But between that point and Lhasa lay two days' journey, largely through 5,000 metre-plus passes. That very night, we made the Tuotuo river (4,800 metres), and we both felt awful, me with tonsillitis, and Barbara with a headache, shortness of breath and a racing heart. My heart started to race too, but the truck driver, being a Tibetan, kept going until two in the morning, not noticing that we were both prostrated. It was just as well he did, actually, because we stopped at Amdo, only about 4,000 metres up, and both managed to sleep there relatively comfortably. At noon the next day, we went through Naqu (Heihe) in northern Tibet. We both felt so much better, we decided to stop, see the temple, and check out the local hospital.

The hospital in Naqu was bigger and far less crowded than the one in Golmud, and they put me on injections twice a day, with no IV, leaving me free to wander around. We were a bit afraid of the police, since it is a closed city, but figured I could plead sickness. By coincidence, the day of our arrival was the opening day of the biggest horse-racing event in Tibet, which is held annually in Naqu. The horses were magnificent, but the event is not really racing so much as a series of contests – shooting from horseback, snatching a white scarf from the ground while galloping, etc. And a gigantic market, with maybe ten thousand people or more, a huge city of white and blue tents, many of them with the most fabulous Tantric designs, and yaks, horses, Khampas, firearms, all kinds of gewgaws of religious, secular and dubious origins. It went on for days. I missed the first day, thanks to my illness, but saw much of the second day.

I responded very quickly to the injections, and by the afternoon of the third day we decided to leave for Lhasa. We were stopped by the police, but the cop was barely literate in Chinese, and thought the medical papers I showed him were a letter of introduction or a travel permit. We hitched a truck to Lhasa, where I got very good treatment and recovered completely.

We had about six days in Lhasa, which was just enough to do the Jokhang, the Potala, and the two monasteries. Lhasa has changed so much! The western part of the city now looks prosperous and neat, like any other Chinese city: huge buildings of doubtful taste, giant avenues, even extremely crowded and fairly regular buses, unheard of when I first came to Lhasa. A plethora of merchants driving each other's prices down, with a cascade of goods (all from the northwest now – the Sichuan highway has been closed for many months by a terrific landslide near Linzhi that apparently killed many hundreds of people). Watermelon that cost 1.40 a *jin* [pound] when it first appeared in April 1985, costs about .40 a jin today. Local produce, on the other hand - beef and butter – has gone up a kuai or two. There is a huge granite square in place of the rubble in front of the Jokhang; it is in traditional Tibetan style, and very good-looking. The shops and houses around it are also granite and traditional. The filth of the Barkhor is now covered with granite flagstones, and there are sewers. Let the vicarious nostalgics bewail the lost dirt and diseases, the lost innocence, the lost infant mortality, of old Lhasa!

True, there is a big hotel, two in fact, one run by Holiday Inn, which will manage the thing for ten years on a hard currency contract, and supposedly make it profitable for China. But they are far from the Tibetan part of town, and relatively harmless. They are about 80 per cent full, too, which is a lot of foreigners (the Holiday Inn alone has 400 beds!). But anyone who imagines that Lhasa will stop being Tibetan because of 4,000, or even 40,000, foreigners has a very low opinion of what constitutes Tibetan-ness.

Incidentally, Tenzing, the owner of the Snowland, where I stayed, was the one person with criticism for the improvements. Even he lauded everything but the temple square. He admitted that everything of historic significance had been preserved, the stele to Wencheng [a Chinese princess who married the Tibetan king and converted him to Buddhism], and the prostration stones, the tree she planted, etc – but he regretted the walls. Interestingly, he blamed not the foreigners for the great changes, but the non-Lhasa Tibetans, including those from Qinghai. Tenzing is fanatically parochial, and was obviously bitterly displeased with my decision to study the Amdo dialect of Tibetan.

If anything, the horrors and wonders of the place were more horrible and wonderful to me than ever. Coming down the last valley toward Lhasa in the truck, I had tears in my eyes and could hardly speak. But because of the new religious freedoms, the gruesome side of the cult is now worse than ever. Many of the temples have taken their human bone artefacts out of storage; there was a gold-and-jewel-encrusted skull in the meditation room of the 13th Dalai, and skullcaps of serfs and bones from the 'human cornerstones' were displayed proudly on many altars. I was disgusted, particularly since the old Tibetan Revolutionary Museum, where you could see a collection of hands amputated from serfs, and talk to a young monk who narrowly escaped being buried alive as a human cornerstone, has now been dismantled and turned into a boutique.

But the paintings! Barbara is really into painting, and we spent practically seven hours one day doing the Jokhang as it should be done – inch by inch, with a flashlight and sketch-book. We took slightly longer on the Potala, Drepung and Sera, too. Both of us like the 'slice of life' paintings best, mostly murals that included the details of the daily routine – washing clothes, boating, hanging from cliffs, etc. She was always catching intricate details that I missed, such as deer and collar harnesses. Jokhang has a mural depicting a collar harness that is probably contemporary with the one Needham got so excited about in Dunhuang, and the depiction is quite explicit this time. But she still does not share my fine appreciation for the truly horrible: the disembowellings, the demons, the dancing skeletons, the seas of blood, heads and intestines.

On my last day in Lhasa, I finally got around to seeing my old friend Pei Zhuangxin, the painter. Liu and Pei are good friends of mine. Nick and I met them in Xigaze, but saw them again in Lhasa, and we correspond. Pei is probably the best-known painter in Tibet. He graduated from the Sichuan Academy of Fine Arts, where he still has many admirers, and settled in Lhasa about ten years ago. He is a brilliant portraitist and has had a furiously prolific year and has also collected some extraordinary thangkas.

When I met them, Liu was an accountant at the No. 1 Guesthouse (which is Chinese) in Lhasa, but she has apparently mastered enough English to be a guide with the Bureau of Tourism, which involves extensive travelling. She wants to be a writer very badly, and I think she deserves to be. She gave me a piece she wrote about Nick and me. It is almost completely apocryphal in places, particularly regarding me. I did little talking to Liu because she insisted on speaking English and I insisted on Chinese. I think much of her information came from conversations with Nick, who is given to embroidering the margins, and, as she points out, she cares far more for the people in the story than the ideas – or the facts. But there is a wonderful bit about a battered Tibetan wife who runs away from her husband and apprentices herself to an old cabinet-painting woman. Our Liu offers her husband's services as a painting instructor, and they talk about husbands, art, religion, hell, life, etc.

Anyway, we both ran out of money, and after six days (counting one in which we were both sick, Barbara from undercooked yak, and me from pork fat), we had to leave. Five days by bus and rail from Lhasa to here – even a year ago that was unthinkably fast.

But the great discoveries of the summer remain untold. While in hospital in Golmud I read a book by Zhang Xianliang, *Nanrende Yiban Shi Nuren* [Half of Man is a Woman] in three days. It was the first time I have really read a book in Chinese without noticing on every page that it was in a foreign language. It is strange and modern, the first really modern thing I have read in China. Supposedly about 'the formation of a materialist', a man who falls out of the Party, goes to prison, is sent to Ningxia, and slowly discovers that his salvation is – his damnation. That is, genuine

Marxism, which teaches him his place far more effectively than the variety he is used to.

In this book, which is part of an envisaged nine-volume cycle – the second part, I think – the hero, who changes not only his name, but his personality, his history and even his Marxism in every part, at last marries at the age of 39 a twice-divorced woman whom he once glimpsed naked while bathing in a stream in the wilds of Ningxia when he was at hard labour, and tried not to fantasize about for eight years. He discovers he is impotent, and he takes it out, not brutally, but slowly and far more cruelly, on his wife. Not reminding her of her past, but simply torturing her slowly about her present, and cutting her off more and more effectively from his 'intellectual' life. Instead he talks to a mule, Karl Marx, Chuang Tzu, and heroes from Song novels. At last, he drives her to threaten to denounce him, which gives him the pretext to divorce her and move on to better things. By the end of the book, a really devastating and hilarious portrait of a brutal, selfish, egomaniacal, but never macho, intellectual is complete: a man who ever divides the world into 'those who live by thought' and 'those who live by instinct'.

The book was quietly brought out by a little-known Sichuanese publisher, and has been denounced in the press for its explicit discussion of impotence and foreplay. But *everyone* has read it. Truck drivers in Qinghai. Train workers. Even herdsmen, for Christ's sake. One of my writer friends criticized it for being 'better sociology than art', and my intellectual friends, and many of my graduate students, find the style of the book strange. In contrast, most of the proletarians I talked to about it this summer said its most salient characteristic was *xianshi* – a Chinese expression meaning something like 'realism'. A funny description for a book full of talking horses and the like, but they are completely right and have apprehended its truly modern essence. It is modern not only because of its fabulo-realist, almost Garcia Marquez devices, but because, unlike other Chinese novels, it contains no descriptions of nature and no

278

poems and is uncluttered by the usual traditional-Chinese-painting style of 'literature'.

28 September 1986

I just spent five days in the mountain resort of Lushan, taking the waters and visiting the conference site where Peng Dehuai was disgraced – very sad. Since then, my asthma (yes, the doctors have now definitively diagnosed me as asthmatic) has beat a retreat, and I have no more bronchitis. Sore legs, though, from hiking so far through fen and stream with B. I don't know what 'asthmatic' means either. It seems to mean that colds are fraught with particular danger, and that I should find some more hospitable climate to live in, since Wuhan is famous for its bad humours.

On top of one of the higher cliffs in Lushan, there was an old man with a stuffed tiger, who rented it out to people who wanted to be photographed slaying a tiger with their bare hands on the precipice. Barbara stopped and was photographing the old man with his tousled whiskers, carefully folding the stuffed tail into a threatening position, only to have it drop back disconsolately between the beast's legs when he returned to his camera. As I was watching them both, I was hailed by a young fellow who said he was an artist lecturer at the fine arts academy here in Wuhan – his specialty was murals. We got into a kind of heated argument on 'art for art's sake', and I was treated to a free lecture on the subject. It appears that 'art for art's sake' is being established as a kind of dogma here, a slogan that fascinates people without making them think.

Without any decent figures, it is really impossible to speculate on how awful the 'free enterprise' system has been. But it has certainly wrought havoc in education, which is now generally considered to be a national scandal. The Party plenum, three months ago, went after education in the northwest in particular, and stated that education nationwide was the Achilles' heel of the modernization programme, a fact generally recognized by anyone connected with it. The requirement for schools to be at least partly self-supporting has packed classrooms, hiked fees, and resulted in students who half support themselves not only before but after they graduate. My own class has doubled in size this year, and, after repeatedly threatening to do so, I cut it in half and added 50 per cent more hours to my teaching time. So far, the students consider this a vast improvement. As for my graduate class, I cut it in three, and am still faced with classes of 28 students, which are little more than kindergartens, because no effort has been made to establish a common level, in the hope of packing in as many sources of tuition fees as possible.

Perhaps the worst 'reform' in our unit, the one I get bent out of shape over, is the way the audio-visuals are being managed. The audio-vidiots have at last built us a lab, which I requested a year ago, demanding that the department lend out tape recorders to all my students in its absence. So now we've got it – but there is no provision for recording. It is virtually nothing but a jack adaptor and 30 headsets, a way of making one lousy recorder do less than the work of 30. Actually, I often see students sitting around just listening to the recorder with the headsets off, since the sound connections are poor, and the headsets hurt their ears. It is open only six hours a week, but, since it exists, they no longer lend out the recorders.

Things are even worse with the fast copier. I am no longer allowed to use it, since all the students are charged fees to use it, and it was alleged (accurately enough) that I used my privilege to get my students around the fees. At the National Teachers Day meeting two weeks ago, I got up and pointed out a few of these problems. Uneasy laughter and a remark that foreigners have 'true hearts but quick tongues'. I protested in vain that education was potentially a highly profitable investment in its own right. The idea is, after all, to get rich *quick*. Well, that is some people's idea anyway. Elsewhere the idea is to allow some people to get rich first so they can teach the others how to stay poor. And ignorant.

The film series is now being run with no consideration for language teaching: they choose films that have Chinese

280

subtitles or are extremely popular, like today's *Love Story*, and next week's *Charlie's Angels*. By the way, I discovered the rather piquant fact that *Love Story* was one of the first books to be translated after the Cult Revolt. Jiang Qing [Mao's wife, then minister of culture] apparently loved it.

That said, I am really very happy with my main class. Last year I remarked wistfully that I would like to have an older, more elementary group this year, and that is exactly what they are. Great fun, and they are forcing me to undo and redo yet again certain teaching techniques that I had got into out of habit rather than concern for effectiveness. I would still like to murder my graduate students; perhaps it is the moral vacuousness of a transient two-hour-a-week relationship that permits such a violent and basically unfair prejudice. In any case, my bureaucrats do not actively obstruct me, as Barbara's do, and I feel fortunate indeed by comparison.

18 October 1986

Sunday morning. The housework is worked and we are recovered from last night at the Mass Pleasure Garden. They were showing *Liang Shanbo Yu Zhu Yingtai*, one of my favourite Yue operas, and one of the more modern and risqué ones. It has a sad ending, but one scandalous scene has the hero and heroine on stage alone together for practically 20 minutes, without even a servant between them – and on the eve of her wedding too.

The music was so modern it was made into a kind of 19th century fiddle concerto, very listenable, but the singing was so rousing it drove Barbara's two American neighbours out up to the disco hall, where they were gravely told that by recent decision of the municipal authorities all Wuhan dance halls were off limits to foreigners. (This is probably a reaction to the presence of large numbers of African students this year.)

Their objections to the opera seemed culturally hidebound to me, but I do remember that my own taste for opera was consciously and conscientiously acquired, and that I acquired it partly out of a deliberate revolt against a 'natural' preference for soft and melodious music that I knew was not at all natural. Yet you are wrong to assert that Chinese opera does not resemble any of my other interests; it is far closer to 'poor' theatre than any of the Western variants, and it is small wonder that Stanislavsky, Brecht, Grotowski, and even Charlie Chaplin were entranced by it.

Yet Chinese opera is not 'popular' music any more than Western opera is. It is true that during various dynasties common people knew the arias to various operas and sang them much as common people hummed Mozart in the 18th and 19th centuries. But it was largely a chamber affair; opera troupes were kept and traded by the very rich, and female impersonators had a sexual function as homosexual prostitutes that often eclipsed their artistic work and led to the general untouchability of actors as a social class. In addition, the language of opera is extremely refined and difficult to understand, and most of the really great works of Chinese literature, excluding the Confucian classics, have appeared in opera form; *The Western Chamber* and *The Peony Pavilion* appeared as operas at a time when it was forbidden to read them as books, and it is safe to say that more people are familiar with the operas than the books even today. The moral plays of Guan Hanqing during the Yuan, poems of the Tang, like *The Song of Eternal Sorrow*, all of these went into the making of opera and contributed to its monopoly by the literati. In the *Dream of the Red Chamber*, Baoyu sniffs at his grandmother's liking for rowdy operas like *Journey to the West* as vulgar and low class. He is rightly reprimanded by Baochai, who reminds him that much of the finest literature in China appears in opera.

It is not 'popular music' in the literal sense, either. Last night I attended a performance of one of my favorite Jingju operas, *Selling Water*, and was handed a questionnaire by some young opera students who are attempting to find out why opera, which has had such a resurgence among the elderly since the Cult Revolt, consistently fails to inspire the young, or even the middle-aged. The questionnaire was full of extremely profound questions, such as 'What do you think is the correct relationship between music and literature on the stage?' Consulting public opinion on such very artistic matters impressed me as unparalleled in the West. If opera is more 'popular' here, it is because people are expected to be more cultured.

I have found four Tibetan students to tutor me, but I'm waiting breathlessly for the textbooks. Any word from the gurunoid bookstores?

5 December 1986

My class is grinding to something of a stand-off. They are older, married, low-key, with a strong tendency to be lazy and think only about exams. I refuse to give exams unless forced to by the administration, and I do not enforce discipline. Given the size of the class, I am perfectly willing to have everyone talking at the same time. They do not grasp that there is a method behind this, and assume that I am merely soft. Matters are not helped at all by my colleague, who rules by terror. They are constantly skimping on my lessons on the grounds that there is an exam coming up in Mr Gu's class. I have explained many times that they should concentrate on learning, and exams will take care of themselves, and they say yes, that is all very well, but if we fail the work unit will criticize us and we will have to fork over three months' salary as tuition, because the unit doesn't pay tuition for those who fail. So, for the first time, I am faced with discipline problems – with a class of 40- and 50-year-olds!

Both Tibetan texts are here, and I am at them already. Thanks very much. As you say, they are not the latest method, but then even French, German and Spanish instruction is about 20 years 'behind' English language instruction – that's assuming you think the latest methods represent an advance. I myself have a very firm idea of what bad teaching is, but no very consistent idea of what is good teaching. Eclectic, as they say. At one time, actually, I was toying with the idea of translating one of the more advanced

English method books into Tibetan, but couldn't find a Tibetan who wanted to learn English; they are all into Japanese and Hindi.

You ask why write, if not for an audience of some kind? The things I write are solely for you. It is you who imagine they are of general interest. (Incidentally, the comment 'You should write a book' is something that almost every foreigner living in China hears from his/her relatives. Elizabeth, Barbara and I all get it regularly, even from the Chinese.) I certainly don't think my stuff is saleable. If you find anyone seriously interested in Little Liu's piece, though, let me know. There is a lot more, actually, and what I sent you, as you point out, was very rough. She writes well, though, and about far more interesting things than Nick and I do.

Well, I'd better get off the typewriter and attend to the slow collapse of my teaching efforts. Perhaps there really is no crisis, and I am simply undergoing my annual December 17th depression. I am not aided by the fact that Barbara is undergoing similar – her first Christmas away from home and she seems to find it a big deal.

13 December 1986

Two of my Tibetan teachers just left to go home to Tibet to pass their holidays. They were a delightfully pretentious pair who insisted they knew their language flawlessly, and when I asked them to write things down, they would make up their own characters. (Interestingly enough, they looked far more like Chinese characters than the Sanskrit-derived Tibetan alphabet.) And when I asked them to read, they would babble gibberish. But I did fill nearly half a tape with it, and, upon listening to it, I realized there is nothing but baby-talk in part of it, and the words to a Tibetan song in the other. I do not blame them in the least. After all, to the extent that I have learned any language, I have done so by pretending to do so.

Winter is on. Had a coal stove put in the classroom, which my students obligingly keep stoked with coal and sweet potatoes. People come in from the countryside selling coots and other waterfowl, and those few sleeping in the streets look like inside-out sheep in their sheepskin coats. Spring Festival will be a rather grimmer affair than last year, I guess. With the cold, the shortages, and the rise in prices, it is rather unfestive around here.

I think I am going to the northwest. Partly, of course, to go to Lanzhou to check on how my application to Xibei [Minorities Institute] is coming, and partly to scout around for possibilities for what to do in case it isn't. But I also hope to reach Lhasa and spend time with Liu and Pei. It was only with my second trip there that I stopped seeing it as purely different and exotic, and it was partly the time spent in the countryside before going there that triggered the realization.

But here is what is really on my mind. You may know that 9 December is the anniversary of the 1935 student demonstrations that demanded democracy, freedom and resistance to Japan of the Guomindang, who were then masters of China. On the first anniversary of this date, demonstrations in Xi'an led to the 'Xi'an incident'. Last year, the 50th anniversary, saw militant demonstrations by Beijing University students protesting 'economic invasion' by Japanese imperialism. There were many arrests, and some of the students are said to have been expelled and sent to Xinjiang.

This year is the 51st anniversary. Although the threat of invasion, economic or otherwise, is now more remote because, largely as a result of last year's demonstrations, Japanese advertising was taken off television for a while, the demands for 'freedom' and 'democracy', ill-defined and alluring, have come to the fore.

In the spirit of the 9th, students all over China have taken to the streets and to the walls. Big demonstrations were held in Beijing, Hefei and here. On the morning of the 9th, a rather smallish, planned demonstration was held at nine in the morning, and around noon a banner went up announcing a march to the Normal University through the Mapping and Surveying College beginning at 9.45. At 5.45, 10,000 students assembled. Two guardians at the Mapping and

285

Surveying College kept the gates locked, but the students managed to get around them here and there. Some of the banners read 'Reform thoroughly' and 'Demolish bureaucracy'. That is a good taste of the flavour of the movement: even-handed, even-metred, fairly even-tempered – and thoroughly abstract. At least at the beginning. The authorities apparently gave ground and hoped to encircle the new movement and attack during its ebb.

The next day, though, it didn't ebb. Around 80 posters have gone up in Wuda [Wuhan University]. 'Lapdogs' loyal to the authority-run Student Assembly have pulled down quite a few and pasted adverts for films and things over others. But others remain, and I have translated one here:

TOLL THE FUNERAL BELL OF DICTATORSHIP!
Or China Will Be Ruined!

On the contemporary world scene, Western countries have dashed unstoppably far into the lead. When we look at the map of Asia, tiny little Japan has re-emerged and is trying to re-establish the Greater East Asia Co-Prosperity Sphere, while South Korea and Singapore have come from a long way behind and are swooping by us into the future. But what place is there for our magnificent China? The best we can say – that of a beggar! And what is the reason? Are Chinese incompetent? Of course not! But we have inherited 9,000 years of a system of dictatorship.

From the beginning of Chinese civilization, at no time has it ceased gnawing at our nation's body. It has greedily ripped away our human rights, repressed our individuality and freedom, and heartlessly destroyed our creative powers. Even if a few years of progress has changed the broth, the medicine remains the same. The reform of the economy has encountered the stubborn obstacle of the political dictatorship.

The dictatorship has not only encumbered the economic development of our country, but also deprived us of our most essential condition of life – freedom, democracy. Without the elimination of dictatorship, China will never rise. The day when the Chinese people become fully human will never arrive!

How in this freedomless, undemocratic, so-called 'Ancient Civilization' can we speak of democracy and freedom? By the condescending favours of bureaucratic politicians? Enough! This is a false, false democratic freedom. They have fooled us for 9,000 years. This sort of 'slackening and tightening, slackening and tightening' of the reins leaves you numb and senseless. It destroys the spirit but whets the appetite. Freedom, that means our freedom. Democracy, that means our democracy. That which was stolen from us, we are now taking back! Let us believe only in ourselves; our salvation lies only in ourselves!

However, some have benefited, while others have lived so long as 'undemanding slaves' that their warm love of democracy and freedom has been extinguished. Among these we must include a few pitiful university students. Because of this, every true-blooded young person must come bravely out, organize, and stand together in solidarity. We must assume every constitutional right and exercise our liberties to the fullest, marching, demonstrating, and struggling bravely. We must even shed fresh blood to waken those who are standing but still asleep, and let the ideas of freedom and democracy take root and put forth shoots. Our China must rise and fight, that is the only way our history can guarantee our destiny!

Young people, compatriots, the great 9th of December has arrived. Let us be brave, brave again, and brave yet again! Let the funeral bell of dictatorship resound everywhere!

LONG LIVE THE SPIRIT OF THE 9TH DECEMBER!

That's it for now. I'll write you in another two weeks or so.

2 January 1987

I got your recent air-letter asking me to write one a week. I'll see what I can do. But don't worry. All the trouble seems to be over.

Did you ever read *Ten Days that Shook the World* by John Reed? He has an extraordinary solution to the problem of writing about a topic of tremendous objective importance, but irresistible to subjective involvement. He was not a great writer, but he did write a great book. I think perhaps it is one of the hallmarks of truly modern literature that great books may be written by writers of rather poor form. May I live to write one. Anyway, here is an account of the most interesting bit I saw on New Year's Day in Peking. I had gone up there to get some texbooks for next quarter, which I got, actually, so we're all set.

A NEW YEAR'S DAY SKETCH

By the time I reach Peking University on New Year's Day, night is falling thicker and thicker. Snow too. You look up and it pours down out of the stars. The Lesser South Gate, with its sheet steel guardhouse, stands in a grey glare, and students mill in and then fan out in twos and threes. Inside, the dingy dorm windows are brightly lit, and passers-by can stare right in, their gaze only occasionally hampered by dripping laundry. It is the Friday before examinations, and the apprehensive silence of unturned pages in the glare of unshaded reading lamps is palpable. But most of the passers-by are a relaxed, noisy lot, shouting and circling the buildings, still in twos and threes. Here and there, slogans are heard, but a lot of it is just rowdy shouting with a self-derisive ring: 'Long live democracy!' 'Forward! Forward!' 'Yaaa!' 'Wooo!' (We have done this before; you all know what we mean.) A young woman leans from a broken third-storey window, beating a metal dog-dish with a wooden spoon. A firecracker goes off, slightly muffled in the snow. In groups of down jackets and padded cotton army great-coats, they are coming out to march. Now there are moving clusters on every street corner, and broken lines forming in between. 'Excuse me, please. Where are we going?' I am not speaking figuratively. He smiles, 'That's difficult to say.' He isn't either.

'Go to the Big Character Posters!', someone says. Our cluster, perhaps a hundred now, stretches out an arm and makes for the posters. There are only a few there, pasted over the shreds of last night's crop. The propaganda statutes adopted in 1978 prohibited them, and the ones put up every day are safe only as long as the students are going to and from classes. The University security guards tear them down at night after the last students have turned in. At noon, they reappear in the glass display case in front of the post office.

'Look! This one's new!' Someone produces a flashlight. I expect them to copy it down in notebooks, but it's too cold to hold a pencil. A knot of arms holding out little tape recorders tightens around the three sheets of computer paper covered in small characters in a childlike hand. One student begins to read it into the tape recorders at the top of his lungs, just like a celebrity saying a few words at a press conference. Further on, there are three sheets of Peking University stationery with a *Song of the Peking University Students' Movement* on it, complete with music. No one pays this one much attention; they all know it.

Now there are hundreds gathered by the posters, and in the distance we can hear several thousand. The maleness makes it seem like a football crowd, but an orderly, good-natured one. They are shouting '*Hao!*' ['Good!' or 'Great!'] at some speaker I cannot hear. I time myself counting a hundred walking past, and the parade continues for 40 times that interval before I give up and follow it. 'Where are we going?' 'To see the University President.'

The Administration Building, like most of the University buildings except the dorms, is of an uncompromisingly Chinese beauty: clean white walls draped from a soaring crest of roof tiles, elaborate armatures that permit the decorated columns to bear the weight of the roof casually. The latticed windows, painted red, are now lined with students, including a blond American in jeans and a parka. In front of the doorway, three students with a banner of computer paper: 'Long live democracy!' The building is surrounded. We wait.

The snow thickens and above our heads someone prises open the window above the entrance. Two people venture out and a microphone descends on a cord into the crowd. The high-pitched voice of President Ding emanates from the loudspeaker in the evergreens behind us. I keep looking back, but the thousands are facing the microphone, not the loudspeakers.

'Of course I am willing to listen to whatever you have to say. And I certainly promise to get to the bottom of your grievances, whatever they are. So what I want you to do now is to go and – ' Something between a rumble and a roar breaks out. NO. ' – write out your demands and then we'll discuss them.'

'No, you don't!' 'Right now!' 'Let's talk now!'

'Well, of course we can talk now. You can stay here as long as you like. That's OK! But I'm afraid that if you don't write down your demands, I . . . won't be able to remember them.' An audible smile goes around. 'So write them down and give them to my secretary, and I give you my word . . . I give you my word that I'll have an answer for you within two hours.' Watches are checked: 'By 11.20, then.' The microphone goes back up into the lattice window and the President goes back into the building.

A short, round-headed student with a vaguely parted Beatle haircut and an undecided fuzz of moustache begins shouting from behind a sheet of paper into four or five tape recorders:

'Article One: Immediate, unconditional release of the students arrested today.

Article Two: A guarantee that those arrested will not suffer reprisals in any form.

Article Three: A full and truthful account by the news media of the events that have occurred today.

Article Four: Legalization of the Big Character and Little Character Posters put up by university students.'

'*Hao!*' The crowd stamps its feet with cold and enthusiasm, and a song breaks out, horrendously out of tune, from the students high on the hill facing the entrance. The *Internationale*.

290

Arise ye prisoners of starvation
Arise ye wretched of the earth
For justice thunders condemnation
A better world's in birth.
No more tradition's chains shall bind us
Arise ye slaves no more in thrall
The earth shall rise on new foundations
We have not been, we shall be all.
It's the final conflict, let each stand in his place
The internationale shall be the human race!

And then the national anthem. A tall, good-looking student is talking, his knitted ski-cap bobbing, his glasses slipping down to the end of his nose from time to time. His voice is calm and clearer than President Ding's, even without a microphone.

'The important thing now is to organize. We can't count on everybody coming out like this every time there's something to be done. I hope that . . . I hope every department will have a liaison person, someone responsible for keeping those involved in our movement informed, and keeping in touch with the movement centre.'

'What centre?' says someone behind me quietly, 'Who dares organize? We have to just keep shouting each other on as⁻necessary.'

The tall one pushes his glasses back onto the bridge of his nose. 'Look, as it stands now, we've got demands but no leaders. And without leaders, demands aren't much. You heard President Ding – he wants someone to present our demands in writing to his secretary. What demands should we present? Who will go?'

'Alright! You're our leader! You two!' Election by acclamation? That's what is happening; leaders are being tossed up rather than lowered into the crowd. He has only time for one little modest smile, and then it's down to work. First, he goes about establishing a list of all the arrested students. 'Does anybody know of anybody in your department who was arrested?' The names come in, 24 of them. Then he askes what demands they would like to raise.

'I'm tearing this paper up and handing it around. Does anybody have a pen? Write down your demands and give them back to me – to us. Raise anything you think just, but please, comrades, classmates, don't waste the struggle of your fellow students with unreasonable, impossible stuff!'

'Just your four articles!' 'Four articles!' 'Keep it simple or they'll just ignore them!' 'They won't remember them!' 'They won't understand them.' Another audible smile. But the tall one insists, tearing the paper and handing it out.

'Well,' says a voice, 'I think we ought to put a time limit on our demands. We say, you do such and such by such and such a time, or we'll do so and so. Otherwise, they'll take 30 years to answer us.'

'What time limit were you thinking of?'

'Tomorrow. Twenty-four hours. Otherwise they'll say, we'll see next year.'

'*Hao!*'

'And then, if they don't agree to our . . . you know . . . demands, then . . .'

'Strike!'

'We'll strike classes and exams!'

'Come on,' says the tall one. 'You're not really going to strike your exams.'

Now the round-headed one with a sharp voice come up. He has a torn slip of paper in his hands. 'The Central Government must recognize this whole student movement as legitimate!'

'*Hao!*' Adopted by acclamation. 'Yes!' 'Right!' 'Oooh, so right!' adds a squeaky voice. More audible smiles.

'A time limit!'

'Otherwise we'll . . .'

'No, I don't think that's a good idea,' says the tall one. 'That might be a very dangerous move.' Below the terrace, a knot of students starts dancing to shake off the snow and keep warm. They sing *Filling the World with Love*.

'Quiet!'

'Very well, then . . .' The time-limit faction dies down to a murmur, and the two leaders go inside bearing demands

292

on shredded slips of paper.

Then the tall one is back: 'President Ding is contacting the Municipal Bureau of Public Safety. His secretary says they'll have an answer within two more hours!'

'We'll wait!' But some of them shove off in the direction of the West Gate. There are about 500 left waiting. My socks are wet, but I stick around, stamping my feet. 'Are you a reporter?' one asks me, looking grave.

'No, I just came up from Wuhan. To get some textbooks,' I add hastily. There has been much made of 'outside agitators' on TV – a 'counter-revolutionary "People's Guard Party" ' discovered in Shanghai, and a 'hoodlum' from Guizhou unearthed at Renmin Daxue [People's University] in Peking.

'Oh, a foreign student.'

'No, I teach there.'

'Is there much of a movement?'

'Not at my place. I teach lower-level cadre. But we're right next to Wuhan University.'

'They had a demonstration.'

'Yes, one. On the 9th of December.'

'Do you ever have demonstrations like this in your country?'

'When I was very little, in the early Seventies. I remember them very well.'

'What would President Reagan do if there was a demonstration like this in front of the White House?'

'Bust people over the head and arrest them! Well, it depends, I suppose.'

'Depends on what?'

'On how many heads they had to bust.'

'How does this compare with the ones in your country?'

'Very similar. Not as many women here, I guess. And the posters are . . . sort of abstract.'

'What do you mean?'

'We had lots of different groups. Communist parties serving communism in every conceivable national cuisine: Moscow dishes, Peking dishes, specialities of Albania . . .

Everybody had their books chosen, their strategies worked out. But we spent a lot of time running around hiding our books and strategies, just shouting a few simple ideas to a lot of people. Shouting slogans, pasting up slogans, carrying slogans. Good slogans, some of them, but not deep enough. I think we didn't understand that it is the task of students and people out in front who have deep ideas to turn around and tell the people in back. Tell them everything. Deep ideas, too. But some people thought our workers were hopelessly far behind, and kept the movement to themselves until it was bought off and crushed.'

'We don't think that. We know the workers. The workers are right behind us. In Shanghai . . .'

'What do you think democracy is?'

'An abstract slogan. In my country it sounds just as hollow as "Continuing the revolution under the dictatorship of the proletariat" sounds in yours. What do *you* think democracy is?'

'*This* is democracy. We're doing it right now.'

Hours go by in vigorous, foot-stamping conversation. Students and topics wander around from group to group. The Western press is there in Russian-style fur hats. A short, pudgy supercilious American and a tall, solemn Frenchman. The American is saying, 'So, they've got their martyrs now. Pretty nickel and dime martyrs!' He doesn't wait for an answer but moves off to a group of students, now bristling sympathy. 'Oh, yes, we were right there on Tiananmen this morning . . . saw quite a bit, too, we've got real good footage of you people, real good. So that was your president, was it?' He is practising his Chinese. 'And what are you going to do now?' Smiles, no answer. 'Strike?' 'Maybe.' The Frenchman says something about deadlines and they disappear.

Now I can see the top-knot on the tall student's ski cap, bobbing like a buoy in the crowd on the terrace before the Administration Building's entrance. 'President Ding is contacting the Public Security Bureau at this very moment. His secretary says they'll have an answer very soon. And when our comrades, our fellow students, are released, if they are released, we will go to the South Gate and hold a big reception!'

'*Hao!*' We flap our arms and our breath smokes. The worse-off students, like the round-headed one, are slightly stiff in their padded cotton clothing, while the others move more fluidly in ski pants or tight jeans. Occasionally there are bluish flashes as students take pictures of the occasion. Then, suddenly, a brighter, scorching flash appears from the side of the building. A middle-aged bureaucrat stands by the window holding a 1930s-style camera with a huge parabolic flash attachment.

'What do you think you're doing?!!' For the first time, the crowd seems menacing as it moves toward him. The tall student steps up nimbly to speak:

'Don't be afraid! We're not afraid! Comrades, classmates, come on! We've got to believe in ourselves more!'

A voice at the back: 'You go ahead and believe in yourself, I'll be afraid!' The tall student smiles. Somebody shouts: 'Hey, mister! How about another shot?' But the photographer is gone.

More foot-stamping and arm-flapping. At last the round-headed one rushes up from the depths of the building. 'Good news! President Ding has just heard from the Public Security Bureau, and our classmates are being released at this very moment! All of them! President Ding has already sent a car to receive them! Let's go to the South Gate.'

'What? What about the other demands?'

'Well, I think that's nothing to do with President Ding. There's nothing he can do about them. You know we'll need to keep struggling.' This is from the tall one.

'The second demand! That much can be settled right here in the school!'

'Let him reply now! The second demand now!'

'No reprisals!' 'Article Two!' 'Article Two!'

'Very well,' says the round-headed one, 'I'll go back and ask right now.' He is back in a moment. 'I didn't see President Ding, but I told his secretary, and he said that concerning the second article, there's no problem.'

'No problem! What does that mean?'

'Make him come out!' 'Let Old Ding come out!' This time the two leaders are both gone a long time.

'Poor Old Ding! He's getting old and slow.'

'He's coming!' 'Oh, here he is!'

'Welcome, welcome!' A smattering of applause. This time I can see Ding's face quite clearly, a shock of white hair and a square jaw. There are only a few hundred of us left, and he addresses us without the mike. 'I have contacted the City Bureau of Public Security and they have assured me that the students are being released . . .'

'All the students? How many?'

'. . . students are being released. I've sent a car to meet them, but as it is snowing and the roads are bad, it will take some time to get there and back . . .'

'How many? How many?'

'I have a list of 25 names.'

'Twenty-five!' 'What about other schools?'

'I don't know anything about other schools. I only take care of mine. I can't be responsible for all the universities.'

'Article Two!'

'Now, as for your other requests . . . There are many things, as you know, that I don't control, outside this school. I can't run the news media for you, and . . .'

'Print it in the campus paper!'

'. . . and I certainly don't run the central government either . . .'

'*The Campus News*! *The Campus News*! Tomorrow!'

'Come on! That's not the point! Article Two!'

'Article Two! Article Two!' Now everyone has seen through Old Ding's diversion, and we are back on track.

'Well, now, as you . . . as for your second request, well, if the students have done nothing illegal, and broken no laws, I can assure you that . . .'

'Nope! That's not good enough! Demonstrating is illegal now!'

'Well, if they . . . well, when they come back, I will see

what I can do, do everything I can, and I assure you that what students do outside my school is of no concern to me personally . . .'

'Right,' says the round-headed one. 'Now, let's all express our thanks for all President Ding's help!' This time the applause is vigorous and very warm. Several students bid the president an affectionate goodnight. One who is a bit derisive is roundly censured by the rest.

The round-headed fellow looks exhausted but pleased. 'Classmates, it is nearly eleven. We can go home now and . . .'

'Go home?!'

'. . . or we can . . . go to the South Gate and greet our arrested classmates . . .'

'South Gate!' 'To the South Gate!'

'Alright, comrades,' says the tall fellow. 'But I must ask you not to leave the gate and block traffic in the street; this is a working-class neighbourhood and people have to get up early and go to work tomorrow.' The crowd agrees, or doesn't disagree, but when we reach the gate, two-thirds of the assembly continues blithely on into the street. The two leaders themselves stand in the gateway, or even outside it, rather than be left leading from the rear. Hours pass and even the snow slows down to a crawl, but the crowd has grown again to around eight or nine hundred, plus some on balconies around the gate. All the vans or official looking cars are stopped and peered into. Public buses are left alone, but a policeman on a motorcycle is stopped and questioned briefly. On a balcony, a student props up his ghetto-blaster, which blares out Beethoven's Ninth played by Von Karajan and the Berlin Philharmonic. Then – a small minibus. We stop it excitedly. This is it! Someone sets off a roman candle. 'What's he shooting that thing off for?!'

'Oh, it isn't them!' 'Well, where are they?' Every pair of headlights now creates a headlong rush into the street. Now and then, the tall one goes to the guardhouse and talks worriedly on the telephone. The crowd continues to grow; people are getting up faster than they are going to bed now.

At around 1.30, the tall fellow emerges from behind the
phone and takes off his ski cap for a moment. 'I've just
talked by phone to the guards at the West Gate. Two cars
went in a moment ago. Eleven of our students . . . our
fellow students . . . were on board.'

'What? Only 11? Why aren't the others being released?'

'Who says they aren't being released?' says the tall one
irritably. 'Wait and see!'

'Well, where are they?' 'Right there! There's one!'

'I never made it to the demonstration; I was arrested
before I ever got there.'

'How did that happen?' 'How did you get out?'

'Well, I guess we weren't really arrested. See, this guy
comes up and says he's a researcher for the Academy of
Science, and he'd like to know what the demonstration's
really about. I tell him, well, we're demonstrating for
democracy, and he says, really, well, come with me, and tell
me about it, and I say, well, I'm busy exercising a very
important democratic right just this moment, but, and he
says, I think you better come with me anyway, and I say,
what's this, you can arrest people, too, huh? And, well, that
was that, he took a couple of us off, told us we weren't being
arrested, they just wanted to have a chat about democracy.
But when we got there, there were a bunch of ordinary cops,
uniforms and all, and some of them swore at us, what the
hell do you goddam students think you're doing here, and I
said, you, look at you, you don't have any culture at all, you
swear and curse at people you don't know, you could at least
observe a modicum of courtesy. And then they didn't say
anything for a long while, and I got really hungry, and told
one of the cops . . .'

'What, didn't they feed you?'

'Well, they told us if we gave them some money, they'd go
out and get us some take-away scoff, but we didn't . . . and
after a while they told us the party was over and we should
clear off, so I came back here.'

One of the arrested students had gone home, found all his
room-mates gone or leaving to greet him by the South Gate,

and followed them. When he sees the whole crowd running toward him, he playfully turns to run away, but it is too late. In a moment he's riding on the crowd's shoulders, and flopping around helplessly. His every weary word goes into ten tape recorders raised to his lips.

'Yes, eleven of us . . . I don't know . . . I hope so too . . . yes, but not too badly, just slapped us around a bit . . . Well, then they said they hadn't really arrested us, they just wanted a chat.' He looks completely knackered, and can't seem to keep his torso straight; he keeps lying down on the bobbling heads beneath him. At last they set him down. He raises his hand – V! It disappears in a prairie fire of forked fingers: VVVVVVVVV! Two classmates lead him off, arms around his sagging shoulders.

Another arrestee appears, smiling even more shyly as the klieg lights have now arrived. More answers to the same questions. The answers are identical, but the crowd never tires of hearing them.

And now it's nearly three in the morning. The snow has finished falling and Von Karajan has completed his second or third performance – nobody is counting. Students are tramping home with eyes like headlamps and Beethoven's music, if not exactly Schiller's libretto, on their lips.

Beijing – wall posters, 2 January 1987
PLEASE REMEMBER THEM!
Some of us Peking University students who took part in yesterday's movement in Tiananmen had to pay out a bit of blood. The power of our classmates' demonstration has already forced our release. But let us all be sure to avoid a 'post-autumn reckoning'. For this purpose, we would first like to announce the names of the arrested students, so that they will all know that if their interests are made to suffer in any way, all of us will come out in a body in their defence.

We first announce the list below, in the hope that other departments will do the same:
Liu Ze, Department of Sociology, Class of 1985
Qi Jian, Department of Sociology, Class of 1985

299

Liu Gang, Department of Physics, Class of 1984
Yang Mei, Radio Department, Class of 1984
Huang Xingshou, Radio Department, Class of 1984

APPEAL
Fellow students! Yesterday the TV broadcast on the New Year's Day events in Tiananmen Square was heavily slanted in order to divide patriotic students, separate us from the people of the city, and prevent the facts and real similarities between the students and the masses from surfacing. We appeal to the University authorities personally to organize a Chinese-foreign press conference, at a suitable time and through proper channels, in order to let the full facts be known. We also appeal to all right-thinking Peking University students to come and support our proposal!

PATRIOTISM IS NO CRIME! STAND UP FOR WHAT IS RIGHT!

My tonsils are a bit inflamed again, so I have postponed my trip to Lhasa and may cancel. But my usual annual depression was very light, although I've been having a lot of nightmares.

Wuhan, 11 February 1987
I am back, tonsils and all. More of that in a moment; it was an interesting, and in some ways a fruitful trip, though not a very happy one. I did get in at the Xibei Institute in Lanzhou, it seems. And my health was perversely impeccable throughout, just to spite you.

I was pretty annoyed at your last letter, but since I am, at least from a literary if not a political point of view, in the wrong, and since I seem to be losing friends right and right, I will try to moderate my fury. Look. From a literary point of view, the thing I wrote on the Peking demo was undeniably too arty, and a little bit silly in places. I got carried away. I had this idea of doing something John Reed-ish, you know, permeated with the actual details and real feeling of

300

revolution, but had neither the talent nor the scale of events to justify it. One's reach should exceed one's grasp, particularly when reaching for the desk drawer.

But I do have something besides the feel of the demos to contribute, something above and beyond what you read in the press:

1) The students were not naive. Certainly they were less naive than the Western press condescendingly pictured them. (The press, you see, understands the 'totalitarian nature' of the regime, and assumes futility on the basis of its own prejudices.) And they were far less naive than the regime would like them to be. They understood not only the nature of their own regime (look at how they handled the delaying tactics of President Ding; at the businesslike way in which they raised demands and stuck to them even when the first one was granted; at the way in which they stood waiting until three in the morning for a release they were assured would take place, which they suspected might not; and how they recognized the pettiness of the last-minute switch of gates that robbed them of their triumphal reception, but not at all of their triumph). They also understood, in a highly sophisticated way, the limitations and powers of their movement as it is now constituted (look at the way they raised demands that were within the possible, but not at all obvious, look at how they avoided placing time limits, look at how they avoided concrete organizational measures, but nevertheless provided a kind of collapsible leadership just where and when it was necessary). The tall kid, anyway, seemed aware that it is a rather paradoxical stage of the movement: the elemental impulse toward freedom is national, but limited because too abstract. The concrete struggles are going in all different directions on a local level, but they are limited because they are local – and also because they are not really democratic: the only kind of democracy exercised is a very local, direct, exciting, immediate but disorganized, and ultimately unreliable, sort.

The regime is right on one point: this feeling of direct democracy did exist in the first stage of the Cultural

301

Revolution, and that alone shows that it is not necessarily either consistent, deep, or historically sufficient for a movement of this scope. There is present a rather complex tension – the need for organization, for communication with other layers of society and other campuses, for leadership, and, on the other hand, the advantages of not having any recognized leaders. This last factor is now quite evident. The response of the regime, in the absence of actual student leaders, has been to attack itself for being 'too soft on them'. No one, of course, remarks on the 'naivety' of a regime whose only response to the abstract demand for 'democracy' has been to launch a far more abstract campaign against 'bourgeois liberalism' with no apparent targets.

2) The students were not confused. At least not nearly as confused as the regime, which in turn is not nearly as confused as the Western media. But the Western media, rather than admit that they don't know what is going on, like to talk about what they do know is going on – in this case, the inter-party factional struggles, which are sufficiently unknowable quantities to allow the pundits to speculate with impunity. The confusion to which you refer, that 'conservatives' are supposedly to the left of the 'progressives', does not exist here. It is a confusion of the Western bourgeois media. Few of the students are very interested in the different factions of the Communist Party, particularly now that the few outcasts who sympathized with them are outside it. Few pretend to know which leaders are potentially sympathetic at the very top. Communist Youth leaders are considered opponents to a man, and act as such, tearing down posters and wrecking demos. That is all the students know and all they need to know.

The Western version goes something like this: There are two factions in the Communist Party. One is a conservative left-wing faction led by old farts like Peng Zhen and Chen Yun. These people point to the demonstrations and say, 'This is very dangerous, we must step on this, halt the urban reforms, be content with what little the reforms have accomplished in the countryside, etc.' The other is a progressive right-wing faction led by the late [i.e. disgraced] Hu Yaobang, and the not quite late Deng Xiaoping. They point to the demonstrations and say, 'Nah, we can live with this, this shows our China is a mature country, look how good-natured the demos are, etc.' Now, as the CP does not hold its factional struggles in public, it would seem this version is unfalsifiable. But it is obviously false. Deng led the attack on the democracy wall movement of Xidan [in 1978], and he is leading the attack on the current movement. In addition, no one tries to place the two technically most powerful men in China today, Zhao Ziyang and Li Xiannian.

The Chinese version of this two-faction party system avoids the left-right nonsense, and concentrates on the crucial trivia of age: a *Lao Benzi*, or 'Old Idiot' faction, and a somewhat more youthful faction led by the spring chicken Deng. In fact, at least in my opinion, there are as many factions as bureaucrats, and each responds quite pragmatically to events, only trying to anticipate attempts to exploit events made by other bureaucrats. But students, quite correctly, pay little attention to all this. They are not confused because they are not so naive as to think that it concerns them.

3) The demonstrations are not hopeless. They are an inexorable reflection of the rising level of culture, material and ideological, in China. In that sense, it is the regime's reaction that is hopeless. The regime is also trying to do battle with Western ideas on precisely the ground where it is most vulnerable – political freedom. This is because it has completely abdicated all struggles against the West in the areas of foreign policy, protecting China's independence from imperialist alliances, and has ceded far too much in the area of the national economy. Bourgeois liberalism exists; it is in the foreign policy and much of the economic non-planning of the Central Committee. The Shenzhen experiment is now universally recognized as a failure, the regime is in debt internationally and bogged down in the cities. China is facing defeat in Kampuchea and even along the border

with Vietnam. The bankruptcy of this bourgeois liberalism is being blamed on . . . 'bourgeois liberalism'.

The regime's reaction is hopeless, not the student movement. They are not hopeless because they are not so naive and confused as to imagine they will win everything today or tomorrow. In the minds of many students, the movement for democracy *was* democracy, and many of their demands centred around legitimizing and recognizing the movement as such because of this. The limited objects have in fact been achieved, and the whole country was forced to turn its political attention to this demand.

4) I am in complete sympathy with the demonstrations. There is a danger from the right, but nothing says that it will take a right-wing direction.

Back to my article. It was not really written for you, but for you and for Barbara and for the desk drawer. I was trying to write 'literature'. It was a big mistake. In my defence, I can only say that I am not surrounded by incisive political writers these days, but rather by artists, and I suppose I take on things through osmosis, without really examining them.

I spent most of my time in Lhasa with Liu and Pei. Liu has written another story. She has a great feel for the rather petty-minded alienation of the Han petty bourgeoisie. I think she probably gets a lot from her husband, who has a terrible case of it. He began to get on my nerves from the very first day, never allowing Liu to speak, and condescendingly fawning on her paintings. He is full of enthusiasm for almost everything, but has learned too well the fashionable superciliousness of foreigners, and knows how to wriggle out of the uncool expressions of commitment he often makes with a very cool, idiotic, and unfunny laugh.

Liu and I and Little Li, who is a painter in the Jokhang temple, went off to Samye temple, the oldest in Tibet, founded by Padmasambhava himself (the story goes that he had demons build it at night while men worked on it during the day). It is built in the shape of a mandala, with four gates, and once had four multi-coloured *tschorten* [stupas], one at each of the four points. Only the white one remains. Nice murals; not great, I guess, but very nice. Lots of line drawing, much of it very freehand and not perfectly proportioned, scenes of the life of Padmasambhava [founder and patron saint of the Red Hat sect of Tibetan Buddhism], very few Sakyamuni or Yellow Hat leader pictures, with their lack of action and maddening serenity. Instead, slices of the ordinary life (wrestling matches, bathing) and some wonderful stuff from the Kalachakra. Before his death, the Buddha Sakyamuni passed on the secret teaching of the god Kalachakra to some gods and sages assembled at his bedside, among them King Suchandra of Sambala, who took it home and had various commentaries and editions prepared. He also built a gigantic mandala in which the whole truth of the Kalachakra Tantra is said to be encoded. There is a mural of the Buddhist Armageddon in 2327 AD, when King Rudra Chakrin is supposed to lead the Tibetans against the Muslim Saracens, and establish the Holy Crusade of Buddhism. The painters, cudgelling their brains to do a science fiction mural set 500 years in the future, came up with something that looks almost 17th century: Buddhist warriors bearing flintlocks – the only firearms I've ever seen in murals here.

Samye is a minuscule town that lives entirely on religion; people say sutras when tidying up, going to market, or walking off for their morning crap – any time they're not actually using their mouths for other things. There was no place to sleep, so we put up with a richish sort of cadre who told us stories about the hermits walled into the caves up in the valley and tiger-spirits who sometimes spirit people away and wall them up. One of the stranger stories was about two Americans who had come to Samye about nine months earlier. The young woman had the young man wall her up in a cave to do a proper religious retreat, and he became a familiar sight in the village, where he bought tsampa to bring to her. For all our host knew, she might still be up there in the cave, for she was never seen in the village. He expressed the fervent hope that she had achieved enlightenment. I asked who was feeding her now, and our host said that after a few months of meditation, you learn to do with less and less food. In fact, a real lama never touches tsampa and lives on a kind of pollen cake from a plant. In the beginning he might eat ten of these a day, but he soon trains himself to do with less and less, until he only needs one a day, the size of your fingertip. I said yes, but what about this poor lady in the mountains, and he said, well, he couldn't find the cave, even though someone had pointed it out to him, and nobody bothered to go up there and look.

The next day Li and Liu went back to Lhasa, and I crossed the river again and spent two more days by the temple. When I got back to Lhasa, I bought a chicken and went to see Liu and Pei. Pei did two great paintings of me, and was going to give them to me. However, we fell out, and I doubt if we will ever be friends again. Liu said she is writing a book about alienated Hans living in Lhasa, of which there are many, who could leave if they really wanted to (the ones who really wanted to have all left), but something sticks them to the place. They hate it and can't bear to leave it.

'Like who?'

'Like Pei. Pei hates it here, and can't bear to leave.'

'What do you hate?'

'Everything. I hate everything.'

'He hates the fact that he gets criticized for going down to the countryside to paint, while they get offered cars and money to do it; he hates the fact that they get more than he does, simply because he's a Han; he hates the fact that they get all the banquets and travel opportunities and bonuses and commissions; and he hates the fact that if he were one of them he would be nationally famous, but he's not because he's Han.'

'Who are "they"?'

'The Tibetans.'

Well, I start to talk about reverse discrimination, and how it has become a racist slogan in the States. I say 'they' also have a huge illiteracy problem, only one university, which has just started up, and a life expectancy less than half that of the Hans . . .

'Good. They should all drop dead.'

Liu said quickly, 'I wouldn't go that far.' A long silence. There was nothing to be said. I got my stuff together to leave. They did not urge me to stay.

'Oh, actually, what I just said was a joke. Ha Ha.'

That was, incidentally, the first time that I've ever seen Liu really distance herself from Pei. She too has a rather dim view of Tibetans, says they are lazy and what not, but it is a sort of ignorant view of someone new to the place, not a deep-seated hatred like Pei's. I like Liu a lot and am reluctant to give up her friendship.

On the bus on the way back to Golmud (where you catch the train for Xining and the interior of China), this snivelling little Han shit turned to a Tibetan and said, 'Oh, are you drinking cow urine?'. He was assuming the Tibetan didn't know any Chinese, but in fact the Xiahe Tibetans from Gansu speak a dialect related to Amdo, unintelligible to other Tibetans, to whom they almost always speak Chinese. The Tibetan was a Xiahe from Gansu, was drinking top-quality Lanzhou brew, and was furious. The Han's friends intervened to prevent him from being beaten to a pulp. 'He was only joking. Ha ha.' The Tibetan ignored them and beat him to a pulp.

I think this is the end of my friendship with Pei. He is a stupid, philistine, racist bigot. What's more, he is a hypocrite, for he lives off the Tibetans, arts off them, worships their handiwork, and, of course, 'some of his best friends are Tibetans'. Well, I do not discriminate between yellow bigots and white ones. But I don't get it, how he justifies such absurd hypocrisy to himself, or if he bothers. How does he paint with such understanding and think with such petty hatred? Does he imagine that his supposed suffering during the Cultural Revolution justifies him in some way, as if the Cultural Revolution were the very last word in human holocausts? I am really fed up with him.

Classes start in a week, and I have lots to prepare, in addition to the translations to finish.

10 | Artists at home by *Liu Fei*

'When are you leaving?'[1]

'My plane ticket's for the 26th. There just wasn't enough time this trip.'

'You still want to come back, though?'

'Oh, I'm coming back. I want to do some really large scale sculpture in Tibet. Even if there isn't any money in it.'

'We'll pitch in and lend a hand when the time comes. Shit, let's do something really *wild*!'

'Yeah, there are some pretty nice spots here in Lhasa. Let's come up with something really good.'

'We could do a whole bunch of Tantric-style[2] modern men. To top them off, we could put big yak skulls carved with sutras on their heads.'

'Plenty of schemes to choose from. The trouble is, when you look at them closely, they won't pan out. I'd say the best thing we could do would be to find something that would cost us only for the materials. You know, pick any old place to do the thing.'

'Ah, then gloria to us in excelsis! Ever more! Ai, these last couple of years, the money you've made is all right. But just look at the toys you've been turning out. Come on, let's put together some real works of art.'

1. The first speaker is Liu's husband. The second speaker is a fellow-artist and friend from Chengdu.

2. Tantrism, usually associated with Hinduism, entered Buddhism in about the sixth century AD. It is a strong current in Lamaism, the Tibetan form of Buddhism. Tantric art features many kinds of figures, but the most famous are the erotic or rather morbid protector deities.

'To tell the truth, the money hasn't been exactly rolling in either. Just thinking about it makes me want to puke blood. Actually, I've been meaning to give the whole thing up and wash my hands for good for a long time now. So let's get things all set up, wangle ourselves the go-ahead, and then I'll come.'

'Eh. How much you got saved up now? Ten thousand?'

'Nah. My income's somewhere near that figure now, but the bank account's gone. Bought a couple of sticks of furniture, you know. Very pricey.'

'What, did you get a piano or something?'

'Mm.'

'What!? Who plays it?'

'My son. He's one and a half.'

'Hai! There's where you're making a big mistake. It doesn't matter who's playing it. The Renminbi is constantly depreciating now, you know. This could be a way of saving money, too. And think of all the metal and timber in it.'

'Actually, it was a real bargain. Got it for nineteen hundred. And it was really handy. The Emei Film Studio shipped it right to my door. Now, you know, the price is right through the roof. If you haven't got at least thirty-two hundred, you're out of luck. There are already folks offering me thirty-five hundred for mine. In another two years you won't be able to touch it for less than five thousand.'

'It's too tough to scare up money in Lhasa. Your "old man" here has been working in Tibet for sixteen years, and all I have to show for it by way of household goods is a camera and this rubbish around here.'

'Come off it! What about all the paintings?'

'What use are they? Can't get them into any magazines, and if I try to send them to an exhibition, I'll never get chosen. Selling them off is even more out of the question.[3] I just dump them all in here and watch them rot. Feed the

3. There are several options open to painters, almost all of whom work for the state. They may sell their work to magazines, which often reserve the back cover for paintings. They may send it to an exhibition ouside their own work unit, but for this they usually require permision from the

maggots. Let the rats build nests with them. I've applied for a transfer, even tendered my resignation a million times. Nobody cares. Got to wait until I'm old and toothless before I can move back home.'[4]

'I see you're still too "left" here in Tibet.'

'Change the channel, change the channel. Let's not speak bitterness today. Hey, want to come to Tibet to do business?'

'What business is there to do around here?'

'Aiya, you can hit it big with practically anything. Open a handicrafts shop, or a gallery. Your old man here's got the talent to rake the money right off the foreigners. This 203 kuai a month stuff won't even buy vegetables come winter. Look, there are ways of getting big money all around us. You could churn out Tibetan arts and crafts on a mass scale, for example. You know, like ceramic Buddhas or fake jewellery, beat-up scripture-book covers. All those ornaments and trinkets in the Barkhor these days are just like giving money to Nepal and India, right? Why should socialist Tibet have to import all that rubbish anyway? Besides, Demon Li's pottery just can't be beat. We can get him to turn out a little kilnful for us on the side, and that should make us enough to live in style for a couple of years at least.'

'And don't forget bronzes. All that stuff can be copied. It's really cheap to get bronzes "processed" in Chengdu these days. Only ten kuai a vase.'

unit first. Pei probably tried to exhibit outside the unit on a previous occasion without permission and was admonished for it. Finally, they may try to sell it. Several painters in Lhasa have made considerable sums, often in hard currency, by selling paintings to foreigners. This is now legal, as is exhibiting or selling outside the work unit.

4. If you are unhappy with your work assignment, or if you simply want to live in another province, you have two options. You can arrange for a transfer, which means applying to to another unit to take you, and persuading your own unit to let you go; or, you can simply resign and hope to find work when you arrive. (But your unit may not let you go.) Old people, on retirement, are usually allowed to return to their place of birth if they wish.

'And it's even cheaper if you do it by the batch. Nothing simpler than making that kind of bronze look old. Cut two holes, smoke it a bit, and it's an instant antique. And there's the money for the new camera lens, right?'

'Got to make sure you give a receipt, or they won't be able to get it past customs.'[5]

'Absolutely! These days every business in Lhasa is so short on stock, they're all collapsing in confusion. The old stuff in the Barkhor is practically sold out. Even donkey bags and horse bells have gotten to be hot items. What's more, the Central Committee is calling for the development of a "Third Front" of production.'[6]

'What, what, what? What's this about three, four, five brands of production?'

'Ah, it means . . . big money production! The whole key is being able to manufacture all sorts of native-style art stuff.'

'I heard somewhere that those bandits in Beijing just sell off the paintings for practically nothing, but on the other hand, they get quite a bit for pottery. Big hotels actually order the stuff.'

'Let me offer a little bit of useful information. Almost every foreigner that comes along would like to pick up a T-shirt that says, "I climbed the Great Wall" or something, for a souvenir. So, it's simple. We just get ourselves a block and etch an image of the Potala, and there we have it. We'll make a fortune.'

'Small-time stuff.'

' "Small profit, big turnover."[7] Every shirt costs three

5. That is, they will have to give the foreigners receipts or they won't be able to get the fake antiques through customs. Of course, they'll have to fake the receipts, too.

6. Agriculture is the first front, industry the second, and commerce is supposed to become the third.

7. When Tibet first opened up to foreign travellers in the late seventies, the policy was one of bringing in small, wealthy tour groups that were well organized. In 1984, Tibet was officially opened to individual travellers, and at the same time, nationwide, the slogan 'small profit, big turnover' was launched to try to gear tourism towards less organized and less wealthy groups. This was particularly important in Tibet.

yuan. After we print it up, we can unload it for ten. You know how many of the *Lao Wai* [foreigners] came this year? Fifteen thousand.'

'Well, the important thing is to get the art gallery set up. It might save a huge number of frustrated painters. Say, me, for example. First and foremost.'

'We could call it the Tibet Art Gallery. That has a nice ring. You know, there's a lot of interest in Tibet right now abroad. It might help promote international understanding as well.'

'We'll have a mask done all in bronze, and then we'll hang some bells and some bunting. The effect will be devastating.'

'And we can have revolving exhibitions. Right at the entrance, we'll have a huge photograph of the artist himself with his paw stuck out like this: "Ha-lo!" '

'Yeah, showing a couple of inches of filthy cuff!'

'And then in the summer at the very height of all the tourist madness, we'll do one for ourselves. During the off season we'll do them for the other monsters. Of course, at the door, we'll recognize only money, no faces. Makes no difference who comes.'

'Shit, though, we're buggered. What about the site. Is there a place?'

'Easy! There's this square office space by the Lhasa Exhibition Hall car park that's already been contracted out to somebody to use as a shop, open up a restaurant, or some kind of general store. Anything goes. So what's wrong with using some of our artistic creativity? Next year in February their contract's up. We can get the contract for ourselves. The rent should be about five yuan a square metre and half the profits, or else ten. Shouldn't be too much.'

'We'll pay ten. Don't haggle with the Exhibition Hall.'

'Only thing is, we're short of capital. We've got to get other people to invest.'

'How much do we need?'

'Oh, ten or twenty thousand, say.'

'No problem! I'll go back and scrape it together. I've got this friend who's stinking rich now. He's got a couple of hundred thousand at least, and he'll help us with no strings attached. Now, what about the taxes?'

'I think there's some kind of regulation that tourist-related industries are tax-free for the first five years of business. And some people say there is only a 5 per cent tax on merchandising anyway.'

'No sweat! We'll pay!'

'But then we've got to go through the Office of Religious Affairs, 'cause we'll want to produce some objects of ritual use.'

'Ai! No use us lot trying to get into high places. Morning till night I do nothing but fight with that crowd. Soon as I see a bureaucrat I feel like running. We'll have to find some clever, courteous fellow to do it, you know, one of these guys with a natural feel for business.'

'Isn't that friend of yours an official of some kind? If we could just get hold of the highest officials in the Autonomous Region, say X, or Y, and get them behind us, the rest would be in the bag.'

'What we need is somebody who has a real head for business, and a hand for bureaucracy, you know, somebody who won't back out and leave us in the lurch when push comes to shove.'

'That's impossible. I'd better take care of it myself, after all.'

'I wonder if we'll be covered by the state Patent Law? We ought to get a patent on our tank-top business.'

'That'd only help if somebody tried to copy us.'

'I'm not a bit afraid of copying. After all, each edition will be in our hands entirely. We'll change it any way we like.'

'Just wait till somebody tries to print up a Potala shirt. We'll have a Huanxi Porn Buddha all ready to go.[8] We'll make mincemeat out of them. And then there's bicycle rental. The ritzy places in Lhasa are already renting them for ten kuai a day. Any guesthouse where the workers can say

8. This really refers to the Huanxi Buddha, a Tantric deity depicted in the act of copulation.

so much as "Yes" or "No"[9] is getting filthy rich these days.'

'We'll rent them for five kuai.'

'Suppose we buy a hundred and get them reinforced. We could recoup the outlay in a month. Paint them all red and nobody will dare to steal them, not even if you beg them to!'

'Great! Then I'll just quit my job and become the new marketing director.'

'Okay. Sales Department and Office of Public Relations Manager.'

'First thing we'll do when we've got money is buy ourselves a car. So as not to have to beg everybody and their grandmother for lifts every time we go out to the countryside.'

'Right, buy a car. Go out to the countryside and start collecting stuff. I've always been really interested in collecting antiques; at last I'll be able to do it properly. I never wanted any children anyway; I'll just leave the lot to the State when I die.'

'Better still, you can leave this to me, right now.'

'How much does a car cost, anyway? Eighty thousand for a Toyota?'

'Nah. Twenty thousand. There's a kind of two-seater 0.7 ton pick-up. It'd be perfect for carrying goods. I can't remember the name, though.'

'We'll rent it out when we're not using it.'

'No we won't. We'll use it ourselves.'

'We'll offer free room and board to artists from all over the world. But of course they'll have to leave all their paintings here.'

'Good idea. Bed and board can't cost us much, and when the paintings start changing hands, they'll fetch good prices. If they don't have any paintings, we'll take all their sketchbooks and everything. Let them take photographs and then go back and try to publish in their own good time, [10]

9. In English in the original.

10. The speaker is assuming that foreign painters will want to publish their work in magazines, as they do in China. For this, a photograph of the work is sufficient.

or just show them to their friends and be done with them.'

'There are ways to make money everywhere you look. Sidewalk portraiture, you know, wearing Tibetan clothes, riding a yak, in a monk's cassock, or something. We could paint every wally who comes along.'

'And how about getting Jialin[11] to come out in flesh and blood and do his stuff right on the spot? That would be sure to drive the crowd wild. Business would explode. It'd be a wonder if we didn't make him carve till his hands were dripping blood!'

'We'll ask artists from all over the country and all over the world to come and exhibit. Exchange around a bit. Me, I'll first go to India, just to have a look around.'

'Get a cook, set up a sort of public kitchen, and never have to cook again.'

'You're a pessimist! By then we'll just stay in hotels. Toss out all those fancy chairs and tables. Put all our rubbish in. That'll really make the Lao Wai open their eyes.'

'I'm going to buy a game rifle. Hunt wild boars. Go to Ngari.'[12]

'Just get into straightforward arms trafficking and the money'd be even better. Or smuggle heroin.'

'Yeah, then you'd steal half the merchandise and be pilfering the munitions dumps one after the other.'

'I think it'd be better to get ourselves a couple of tanks. No, missiles. Aim them right at the Potala, blast a great big hole. Pick up a couple of really high-class Buddha images to take home.'

'Nah, that's a bore. We'll just stage an outright military coup. First of all, we'll occupy one of those hotels for top leaders, have a good feed or two in the mess . . .'

'Never wash dishes again!'

'Get the Dalai to come back and read us sutras.'

11. Jialin is a well-known sculptor in Tibet, an acquaintance of the two speakers.
12. Ngari is in the western region of Tibet, along the border with Nepal, Kashmir and Xinjiang. It is underpopulated and very wild.

'No, let's choose a new incarnation altogether!'
'No, *you* be the new Dalai Lama!'
'Ten thousand boundless longevities!'
'Bollocks!'

11 | Evil winds from the south

Dear D & B,

The class is off to a good start. My upper class is a good, well-knitted group with many different levels, but high morale. The grad students are a frightful pain. They steal my tapes, rip down my posters, cry when I yell at them in class; I am thoroughly fed up with them, and they with me, but we muddle on purely out of convention. For them, anyway, this is normal, but I find it very awkward. How do you teach people you hate?

I have translated a rather confused article about abortion and male responsibility. It came about like this: One of Pei's paintings was published in *Fujian Youth*, and the two editors responsible for that number came out to arrange things with Pei. They left a copy of one issue with him, and in it was 'Artificially Induced Miscarriage'. Liu read it and discussed it with the two editors, who offered to put her in touch with Tang Min, the author. When she told me about it, she and I wrote a letter to Tang Min together, which the editors delivered. You may wonder why I bothered. Well, she does raise some very interesting issues, even though she doesn't really know how to treat them.

And I now think there *is* a sort of Chinese style, contrary to what I said when you were here. Not that English writing is always rigorously linear, but it is not nearly as necessary that a Chinese writer stick to the point, particularly at the beginning of an essay. On the contrary, it is a bit like listening to a story teller, or reading Sima Qian. It begins with the title, then a few lines set out like poetry that are

317

practically unrelated to the title, then an anecdote that is only thematically related, etc. It is entertaining, but sometimes maddening, and it is the sort of thing the translator is not supposed to meddle with, since it is not at the semantic level. And from the point of view of discourse analysis, it is very interesting: the circling of the author towards his or her kill.

Barbara came by last night bearing gifts, having remembered that today is my 28th birthday and decided that Jews celebrate all their festivals the evening before. We teriyakied up some fish and drank a bottle of very good white wine which is presently being produced by the French in the Tianjin region. She also gave me a gorgeous hardbound volume of Chinese storytellers' morality tales. They are often about whores with hearts of gold betrayed by vicious intellectuals, one of my favourite themes.

The political reaction to the demonstrations continues apace, and is spilling over into a social reaction. The just-published unabridged version of *Lady Chatterley's Lover* has been banned, and the liberal editor of *People's Literature* purged for publishing a racist novel about Tibetans. This is hypocritical, since anti-Tibetan racism is rife in the official cinema, and I am bloody sick of all the 'anti-racist' portrayals of Tibetans as happy little dancing niggers. There is nothing quite so racist as the anti-racist garbage put out by the state. Interestingly, Zhao Ziyang is being set up as the Zhou Enlai of the new reaction: it is entrusted to him to make moderate statements and admonish people, telling them that the campaign must remain in the party, and not spread, etc. I believe, though, that the reaction is almost spent, since Deng has been reappearing on TV, and at a recent funeral it was reported that wreaths arrived from Hu Yaobang. The tell-tale slogans about 'bourgeois liberalism' are disappearing gradually.

That's really it for now. I have lots of other typing to do. We've published a journal rather along the lines you suggested when you were here – articles introducing various subjects to the non-specialist. It is very useful as a way of

318

getting them to read each other's writing, and also as a source of supplementary exercises, and practice in editing. Above all, I think it gives them a chance to stand back from their writing and see it without any obvious mistakes in grammar, so as to consider points of organization and clarity. I'm very pleased with the first issue, and hope to publish it bi-weekly or even weekly. I'm sending you a copy, since you were in a way its godmother. Lot of typing, though.

3 April 1987

I got a very long and very polite letter from Tang Min yesterday. She is ill in a hospital in Fuzhou, but she was kind enough to answer my letter and at least a few of my criticisms. She also supplied some details for a potted biography:

> Tang Min lives in Xiamen in Fujian Province in the Southeast of China. She is the fiction editor of *Xiamen Literature*, and she has published several short stories and non-fiction articles dealing with the oppression of women. These works have earned her the label 'witch' from her critics, but also evoked a nationwide response from Chinese women, and a much wider discussion of women's issues.

Yes, I suppose her article is the first time I have seen such things discussed in the Chinese press, but that in itself is not so noteworthy, since last fall was a time for first times of all kinds. What is interesting in her article is that it articulates the predicament of women in precisely women's confused, convoluted, self-contradictory terms.

My article on Chinglish has been published, along with a whole collection of even more unfocused and confused essays. My favourite one is called 'Written in Spring' and it is about flowers, male chauvinism, regrets about the University, and many other things. When I asked the author what her main point was, she said she didn't know. The Chinese typesetter, unfortunately, corrected the intentional mistake in *my* article, but he managed to compensate by

319

introducing a huge number of his own mistakes, so that most of it now makes absolutely no sense at all.

Jane Austen is becoming all the rage here. I read *Persuasion* in a fit of insomnia the other night. Much inferior to her other stuff – the heroine lacks all life and character. But, as always, there were one or two really priceless conversations.

10 April 1987

Sorry I don't really have time for a proper ten-page letter, but it is production time for our weekly science magazine here, and I have to proof it and type the results.

Today I got the dreaded letter from the Northwest Minorities Institute, telling me that the People's Congress, no less, vetoed my application on the grounds that the Institute wasn't good enough for me. They suggested that I apply to the Southwest Minorities Institute, which I have done, but I am not hopeful. I expect it will be rather like it was three and two years ago, and I will be looking frantically for a job to keep me in China right down to the deadline of my visa, which expires in June. I thought I could avoid all that by planning sufficiently far ahead. It seems I can't, because, after all, everything is easy until it is finally impossible.

Barbara is here. She is very tolerant of my typing mania these days; she sits quietly nearby and reads Gertrude Stein and Doris Lessing and always comments intelligently on my drafts, no matter how drafty the arguments. You are right, next year is pretty difficult to think of without her.

9 May 1987

I'm in the middle of washing clothes, preparing a qualifying examination for the MA candidates, moving my office and packing my things for departure within a month, God knows where to.

Barbara and I had a great time in Changsha – spent the better part of one day at the Han tomb of Mawangdui. It is as well preserved as anything in Egypt, the cloth and the lacquerware were actually far superior, and the corpse was in perfect shape. We were treated to a video of the doctors poking the 2,200-year-old flesh to demonstrate its flabbiness. But there is this extraordinary difference. The Egyptian culture is not around any more for comparison, whereas the clothing, the food, the games, the painting, the books, everything in Mawangdui, has a contemporary or near-contemporary counterpart. To look at the wine cups and be able to read the inscriptions, to recognize modern notions of fashion in burial garments 2,200 years old, to know the rules of a game buried before the first Roman emperors! The corpse itself produces a similar effect: staring into her face, she looks like the wizened old lady next to you. We know her name, her relatives, her habits, even what she liked to eat and drink (it appears, rather like my boss at work, that she was fond of muskmelon seeds). Prop her up in a seat on the No. 1 bus, and nobody would notice her until we got to the end of the line.

Last night was opera night. We went to a good Yueju, and had dinner at a Hunanese restaurant out of newfound respect for Changsha. B will be over in just a bit; we're going out for Korean noodles, and then stay home for *Dream of the Red Chamber* which is being serialized on TV.

About the future. I can't 'never mind about money'. I want to be financially independent – I'm bloody old enough. Barbara is doing the right thing; she's going back, going to earn enough money to put herself through the certificate programme and then come back. If I could bear it, I would do exactly the same But the thought of returning West is really nightmarish to me. I can't go back. I can't leave here. I don't want to. Suppose I can't get back? I was miserable there, and it has only gotten worse. I would be unspeakably miserable.

29 May 1987

I seem to have a job offer from Guangzhou Pharmaceutical College in Canton. This is quite firm; I'm to go there for an interview and sign the contract in three weeks. Apparently this is the work of my ex-student Peng. He is now working in Guangzhou, and it will be no small pleasure to be able to live near him again; he's a great bloke. Guangzhou has other attractions, of course, such as Cantonese. And since it is far more cultured and less proletarian than Wuhan, it is a good place to hob-nob with left-wing youth and artists, a great place to observe how successfully south China can be Hongkongized. Being in the centre of the 'evil winds from the south', it's a thoroughly petty bourgeois city in many ways. The food is really great, too. I have always liked Canton almost as much as I hate Hong Kong.

One of my students, Mr Chi Guoxiang, grew up in the part of Fujian where Tang Min did her *lao dong* [manual work assigned to intellectuals]. He says he never tasted rice until he was 14 years old, and that they got electricity – from a water wheel – only last year. They had to hike over 25 kilometres to get to a road where they would deliver their grain to the government authorities. Often they delivered too much and would have to apply for grain relief during the winter. The authorities, obligingly, would put grain aside for them, but then they had to go 25 kilometres out to the road to lug it back. A large number of the villagers had no land at all and lived by hunting.

Over lunch today we had an interesting talk about computer-assisted translation. I argued that it was a pipe dream without artificial intelligence, because computers go about translation word by word, and the result must be translated into grammatical sentences by a native speaker. Mr Chi argued that in fact there are a very small number of sentence patterns, and that these could be taught to the computer, so that the correct sentence pattern in the target language could then be chosen, and the correct words fitted into it. I think that assumes that sentence patterns in one language can be put in one-to-one correspondence with sentence patterns in another; that is an assumption which I do not believe holds very true even on the level of the word. The whole thing seems to rely very heavily on a rather shallow, purely rationalist view of language. When I think of

Tibetan, which has at least three entirely independent lexical sets, graded according to the relative 'honour' of the speaker and his interlocutor, I really have to accept that the empiricists were right. Languages are different.

July 1987

I have been to Guangzhou. I like the place and always have – Californian hedonism, Mediterranean epicurianism, casual dressing habits, and concern for money and self, but with certain odours that remind me of Honolulu. I got the job; it's a good one, high salary, pretty short hours. But lousy textbooks, which I am trying to change. The classes are too big, too. Older folks, half doctors and half teachers of various medical subjects, mostly from outside Guangzhou, so their English is (but only marginally) better than their Cantonese (which is non-existent). I am learning Cantonese.

The area around Peng's place is socially fascinating, an area of real nouveau riche peasants. You can see them in the most expensive restaurants: tan, dirt-ingrained bare backs, bare feet, squatting on chairs and playing noisy drinking games, squandering in an evening what it would take a month to make in Wuhan. They are, in many ways, human fossils: they have the same surname and worship at a temple to their grandfather, a minor noble in the Qing. But they also ride Japanese motorcycles strewn with good luck charms. The pictures of tubby boys put up in front of their doors to bring good luck show them playing with walkie-talkies and video cassette recorders, but the traditional pitches are still there: number superstitions, geomancy, etc. Housing, anyway, is not high on their list. Peng understandably turns up his nose at their houses, one of which he must rent for an exorbitant sum.

Barbara got a job offer in Macao, and flew down for an interview. It is a lecturer's post at the University of East Asia on Taipa Island. She spent two days there, fell in love with the place and took the job. Todd is arriving in Guangzhou this Sunday. I had originally arranged a job for him at the hospital of traditional Chinese medicine in

Nanchang, but it fell through at the last minute. I'm very worried about him, but I had a nibble for another job today. I'm not sure he has any money with him. If not, he can stay with me in Guangzhou for a few months. I have a very high salary now, 600 yuan a month, and I'll be able to save quite a bit. I think. Life in Guangzhou is really quite expensive.

Guangzhou, 1 August 1987

I'm doing something rather interesting here. I've got a job proof-reading the English in some computer software for Dr Zhou, Mr Peng's wife. There are three bits they are particularly interested in exporting – one on Chinese recipes, one on acupuncture, and one on tourism.

The one on tourism is by far the most problematic: badly conceived and organized with too little thought going into the inevitable competition with more portable guidebooks, and a text cribbed from a Chinese road atlas. I have been commissioned to write a guide portion for Xinjiang, Ningxia, and Tibet. I am also doing some of the most extensive translations I've ever attempted on the bizarre customs of the national minorities, and one of my ideas was to have a lunar calendar in the program, so the tourist would have a good idea when various folkloric events were on:

Did you know that the She of Dongbei dress entirely in fish skins, which are not only waterproof but very warm, that they drink a bowl of hot bear fat to keep warm before going on a hunt? That young Tong women bite their lovers on the arm to show unhealing, festering, deep love? That a Tujia serves his guest sour food and bitter wine over two months old with only one chopstick, to express his modesty and regret at not being able to entertain the honoured guest better? That the Kazakhs play polo with the carcass of a dead sheep, and the Dais cook rice and ferment wine in stopped up bamboo sections, etc, etc, etc?

Having to read large numbers of guide books for the software, I am thoroughly revolted by their racism, particularly of the one most popular among the hippies, the *Lonely Planet* series. And their Tibet guide, which lists Elizabeth as

324

a contributor, has several thinly disguised Nick and David stories in it. Sigh. I wonder if I will ever live down my roguish first trip to Tibet.

I have gleefully given up the option of accompanying Todd in his exploration of China, and am going to carry out my threat to stay put and study – teaching methods, Cantonese, translation, etc. Nothing stays where you put it in my mind these days.

8 August 1987

I got back to Guangzhou from Fujian some four days ago. There is still no news from you, but then I expect you aren't expecting me to be back so early. Somebody has to welcome the furniture that arrives in this empty flat, piece by piece, day by day. Anyway, I'm having a good time with Cantonese, Tibetan, and preparing the new quarters.

Tang Min and I hit it off really well. We cooked and talked about Chinese women and homosexuality, and whether or not early Chinese society was matriarchal and whatnot. The night before I left, she did something really strange. She sat down and read my palm for two hours. China is full of superstitions, and Tang Min's generation particularly has a very feeble notion of science. She told me she had read many other people's palms, including Ding Ling's. [Ding Ling was China's best known woman writer, sent to do 'labour reform' in the Great Northern Wilderness.] Tang Min met her several times and always speaks affectionately of her as 'The Old Lady'. She says the Old Lady was a barrel of laughs, which is not at all how I picture her. I had visions of that dour combatant against superstition sitting across the table from Tang Min, who gazed fondly at her lye-soaked, red-palmed hands.

But it was obvious to me that TM had never really studied palmistry, even as it is practised in the countryside. Not only that, but toward the end she hardly looked at my hand, and seemed to be more interested in Barbara, whom she has never met, than in me. I tried to tell her that she didn't really believe in palmistry at all, she was just exercising her

325

imaginative powers, making up people's lives as she imagined them, inspired by the lines on my hand much as I am inspired by the lines of her work I think I understand. She agreed that she didn't really believe in it. So, it was a pretext for a kind of intimacy that would have been far too rude without some kind of convenient pretext. *That* she didn't agree to.

Xiamen is a kind of cross between Washington and Hawaii. Clams, mangoes, the smell of tropical fruit and low tides. But it is also a special economic zone, and a kind of Waikiki Beach for the Hongkongese. Few people seem to be locals, and putonghua is more common than the local dialect, Minnanhua. Tang Min suggested that Todd and I rent bikes in Quanzhou and visit a tiny village on the coast, Chongwuzhen, where she had recently gone to participate in a ceremony commemorating the 600th anniversary of the city wall.

Chongwuzhen is in a county called Hui'an, where the people have a thing about the Tang and Song, which is when that area first became part of the Chinese empire. The women dress as they believe women did in those days, in huge cloth-draped triangles of hairdo, bright yellow straw hats, two-piece two-coloured tunics that do not quite cover the navel, silver string belts and bright blue pants. They have lots of gold teeth and flash them a lot, because they are pathologically shy until married and then very gregarious. The men look like ordinary men, in shorts and T-shirts, but one of them told me this was because men are allowed to dress 'fashionably'.

The town is surrounded by an ancient wall with four gates, and the wall is surrounded by a cemetery. The burial customs are perhaps designed to save land, because after a body has been buried a certain number of years, they dig it up and put the skull and bones in a big ceramic jar above ground, which they leave open for public examination. We saw two funerals, both of fairly old people, and another person who had just died being carried out of the house and loaded onto a tricycle, still in his wicker easy chair, and then covered with a cloth and driven through the street like a new refrigerator. Strange, wonderful place. There are temples every few hundred metres in the towns, and every few kilometres in the country. The nearby villages look very Cult Revolt, you know, monstrous Mao medallions built into every corniche, and cement exhortations left and left. But Chongwuzhen was positively feudal: yes, they think it's still the Tang or Song.

I always like Quanzhou, so we spent a few days there, too. It is a kind of feudal place, too. People there who have money do not spend it on food or clothing as they do here. Instead, they spend it on putting up beautiful houses, with orange, crab-shell coloured bricks, and sweeping eaves like wings. And then in marrying off their children. And, finally, on big jolly funerals, with gigantic rolls of blue cloth that stretch the whole length of the street the cortege is to walk. Quanzhou has a very relaxed atmosphere, like Xiamen, but for a different reason. Quanzhou is a special economic zone, too; if you want to open a factory and you don't want to have to meet state standards, you just drop a few gifts here and there on holidays, and you're all right. Also, the overseas Chinese community has huge, unofficially sanctioned influence in all things. In Xiamen all that is official.

Todd went up to Shanghai and I went back to Xiamen, spent another day or two talking to Tang Min, and then got on the boat and came back. On the boat I met two young sculptors from Jiangxi, one moving to Guangzhou, the other to Shanghai. They came by for lunch today, and we had a good laugh at my efforts to be hospitable in a practically empty apartment. They are good company, and feel a bit homeless and alienated here as well, so we stick together.

They gave me some photos of their work, which is terrific, but occasionally romantic. They are very influenced by Rodin. Rodin and Freud. I had protested against this current to Tang Min, saying that Freud was the old crap in a new, 'unrepressed' guise that had nothing going for it except a slight let-up in repression. She said, 'You don't understand. This is the first time in Chinese history it has been permissible to say sex is a pleasure and not a duty. Of course, it is only a foreigner who says it, but still . . .' Fancy that – Freud, the Masters and Johnson of China!

I also brought back some more Tang Min stuff to translate. There's one bit in particular I really like, a short story about this rather unpleasant village bureaucrat who never quite makes the switch from being an unpleasant Cult Revolt tyrant to being an unpleasant 'reform' tyrant, and dies trying to get rich in an obscure accident in a rice polishing plant. The peasants are very real peasants, and life is recognizably real life.

And here are some thoughts about the translation of the coarse language in 'Artists' you asked about. In translating expletives, I try to keep in mind, not the literal meaning but the impact and effect, to try to find an equivalent. This may seem difficult, because expletives often seem to have lost their literal meaning, e.g. 'bloody', or the force seems to have little to do with the meaning. For example, 'sod', which is a weak expletive, is semantically equivalent to 'bugger', which for some reason is stronger. Fortunately, the same variations occur in Chinese.

There are basically three expletives in 'Artists'. The most common one is *'ma de'*, which I translated as 'shit', and you changed to 'hell'. Now in fact, 'ma de' means 'your mother's', and Edgar Snow, who quotes Mao using it, translates it unambiguously as 'your mother's cunt'. But this is too literal, since it is really a very weak expression in Chinese, closer in force to 'hell' than 'shit', and many Chinese do not even consider that it refers to a cunt, although a moment's reflection shows that it must.

Note, too, that expletives are very regional in China; I have visited an area of Fujian where it is common to greet people of your village as *biaozi*, or 'son of a whore'. No harm meant. Then there is Pei's reference to himself as *Lao Zi*, or 'your old man'. In some areas of China this is a terrible insult, while in others it is perfectly innocuous.

In *Xi You Ji*, the Monkey King infuriates the Red Boy demon by telling him that he is his grand-uncle; elsewhere he belittles the various demons of heaven by saying they are only his grandsons; probably no sexual innuendo is meant, although the demonic reaction might indicate otherwise. On the other hand, at a recent football game in Wuhan, the Wuhanese crowd, known for their coarse language, taunted the referee by having one of their number ask, 'Who's the referee's father?', whereupon a thousand strong would answer, 'Me!' My knowledge of Pei, and the similarity of his language to Wuhanese, led me to believe that this kind of insult was meant, and Peng confirmed it, but it has been softened to 'your old man' in the translation, partly out of deference to other interpretations. Finally, the last two words of the story: '*aiqiu*'. This is one of those rare instances when literal meaning and illocutionary force are the same in both languages. It, or they, simply mean, 'Bollocks!' But when the story was published in Chinese, sadly 'aiqiu' was cut off.

It is really frustrating to have to begin all over again with Cantonese, and I'm having a hard time forcing myself to speak the stuff; it means reducing the intelligence of conversation to such a basic level, and anyway, I am really, as a Wuhanese, expected not to know it. Still, there is a bright young woman, Little Hong, here who is helping a lot. And before Barbara left, we would play drinking games in Cantonese. She will have to learn, you know, they don't speak anything else at all in Macao, save for a few thousand who speak Portuguese.

I think foreign languages in general are a bizarre pursuit to become fashionable, actually. It is one of the few fashionable things you can do that make you look like an utter moron nine times out of ten, and ten times out of ten for the first few years. Perhaps that's one of the reasons it's so unfashionable in the States, where people can't stand to look like morons, even if they can only avoid it by being morons. Not only does it make you look like a moron, it can make you look like a liar. I once told you that I went from pretending I understood to understanding in every language I ever learned, and I sometimes had to pretend for years before I actually understood. True. And I seem to be doing the same thing with translation, which is somewhat alarming. That is, I read through it, and I think I understand because I have 'guessed'. Actually, I have only imagined the story for myself, using some of the important words in each sentence as clues. Then I sit down and try to translate it literally, and come up with a quite different story. And then I sit down and try to translate it again, and come up with a third. Makes me think my comprehension is 1 per cent vocabulary and 99 per cent imaginary. Yet translation, whether for the desk drawer or for readers, is one of the least self-indulgent forms of creative writing I can imagine. As for the poor quality of the paper and typing, I apologize, but this unit is far poorer than the computer centre. I tried to buy a decent brand of paper in the shops, and this was all I could find.

Anyway, I'd better get to bed. My typing keeps the neighbours awake.

16 September 1987

Classes are underway, and very good fun. They are a really great lot, a bit weak in the ears, but with great mouths and minds, lots to say and the kind of explosive honeymoon of enthusiasm that one gets when one uses methods whose moment has more than come on a class that is feeling underused.

The bureaucracy has been serious trouble. Getting the key to the language lab was like pulling teeth, and when we finally did unseal the place (it had been sealed for a year immediately after being set up, for fear someone might use it and break the equipment), we discovered well over half the headsets out of order, and the tape recorders atrophied. I do not like language labs and am a militant member of a faction of language teachers which condemn the whole theoretical approach (a profoundly behaviourist one) behind them. But I want the bloody classroom, because I like to conduct my class in three places at the same time. And my students have very poor self-study habits: a lab might persuade them to spend more time listening and less 'reading'. Then there was the VCR, and that was still worse. I had to see the president twice, and get one person transferred to another job. However, this week we are mopping up the blood (not entirely that of mine enemies) and getting underway.

23 September 1987

Oh, shit. More writing about writing. I am simply too impatient to rewrite stuff. Still, some of the points you raise are very important, so I will try to get them out of the way.

Barbara actually raised the same stylistic criticism of 'Taimu Shan' (lack of pronouns over proper names) that you did. To me, though, it looks like a deliberate stylistic device. Tang Min deliberately never refers to the battalion commander by name at first, only by the purely arbitrary title he has assigned himself (later we learn that even the character for his first name was taken for political reasons). This is ironic because of course it is more respectful: superiors are not addressed by their names, although sometimes very important people are, say Mao or Deng. It is only after his name appears in the hair of the calf that it becomes generally known and used, a fact that expresses not only his fame but the contempt in which people hold him. Ironically, the man who always liked to be remembered would probably have preferred to have been forgotten. I do not object to using pronouns, of course, but would like to preserve all the intended ironies. I would suggest one 'battalion commander' per paragraph, pages 2-5.

Macao, 11 October 1987

Tang Min is now being sued by *People's Liberation Army Daily*, Madame Battalion Commander and two minor bureaucrats, as well as the Panxi County People's Government. The charges are criminal: slander, libel, using a real person's name without proper permission, and a more vague one about defaming Party officials. She has refused to back down and is going to fight it out in court. The case has already involved many of China's leading writers, and the

331

leading literary magazine on one side (defendant), and the nation's second most influential paper on the other.

Here are the facts, from what I have read of the documents. 'Taimu Shan' is a fictionalized account of actual events: Wang Lianzhong, the battalion comander, is the real name of a real figure who actually did almost all the things Tang Min ascribes to him. Tang Min, however, had already left the area when he died, so she had to rely on informants ('Ah Lu'). The authorities are understandably eager to know exactly who these informants are, and have arranged this suit in order to try to pressure Tang Min into revealing their names. So their first step, and this is rather unusual in China, since the first step should be to contact Tang Min's leaders, was to write a letter to the *PLA Daily* in the name of Madame Battalion Commander requesting an inquiry into the allegations Tang Min made against her dead husband. The letter was signed 'Zhu Yuqin', which, you may remember, was the BC's wife's name in the story. (But it was *not* the name of the BC's wife in real life.) It denied all the allegations of torture and wrongdoing (although it did not reply to them specifically), and centred especially on the contention, attributed to Tang Min, that her husband had been reborn as a cow. Of course, Tang Min did not actually make that contention.

The inquiry did not contact Tang Min at first, but tried to find 'Ah Lu', and recruit other people to testify against her (no one came forward). The results of the inquiry are very interesting. They state, falsely, that 'Zhu Yuqin' is a real name, and they include long quotations that are not quotations at all, but only the *PLA Daily*'s synopsis. They do not actually directly deny the accusations of graft and torture, they simply say he was a conscientious and painstaking worker carrying out somewhat misguided 'left' instructions from higher up. Very interesting. Then of course they assert that Tang Min is guilty of libel, slander, and uglification of the Party. I'm going to send you – after the trial – as many of the documents as I can get.

Why don't you look around for somebody who would be interested in publishing the lot? I don't oppose including stuff from my old letters at all. I just don't remember any of it and can't imagine how it would hang together. Wasn't a lot of it about old girlfriends? I'm glad you have time to paw over my stuff, but if it does get to be too much, feel free to drop it. Also, do submit everything to me for a final check, and remember that I have the last word.

25 October 1987

On 'Taimu Shan', first of all, I think we should think of another title, and I will accept bids from all quarters. Tang Min's original title meant something like 'metamorphosis', but it had a slight reference, in the second character, to a Chinese expression that means something like 'scapegoat'. Because I feel the story is a metaphor for the mindless euphoria following the fall of the Gang of Four, in which nothing really changed for four years, I changed it to 'Metaphor-mosis', but it's a bit hard to say, and too easy to confuse with the Kafka story.

The case is still unresolved, and must probably await the result of the 13th National Congress. Part of the process hinges on the question of whether the battalion commander had a copyright on his name. A law granting persons copyrights to their names was introduced in 1986, and has been tested here in Guangdong against several companies who used the names and photographs of babies on their chip packages without the permission of the copyright owners – the parents. But the law was introduced after the publication of the story, and explicitly does not apply to dead persons, so the battalion commander's wife (whose real name was *not* used) has to prove that she inherited the copyright. If she succeeds, I suppose it will be a very minor blow for women's rights, ironically against one of the few literary tribunes that Chinese women now have.

29 November 1987

This is my first week of the new class, and it's really tough. A masterpiece of bureaucratic organization. I have people who have never studied English in their lives (two) in the same class with half a dozen people who have studied for more than ten years, and two English teachers ('Oh, we're just here to listen', they told me. But it's a reading class, for God's sake, and they keep trying to talk to me when I'm helping the weaker students.) I feel as if I am simply being made into a babysitter for my boss. All these people put pressure on him to give them a class with a foreign teacher, and he obliged without a single thought about whether or not I could teach them anything. It's not the low-level students I object to at all; on the contrary, they show up and work their asses off. It's the high-level students who want to turn my class into a free-talk session. My boss says just teach and let the class haemorrhage – he thinks it will bleed out the weaker students. Wrong. The class is going to bleed high-level blood, starting next week.

There is a big campaign against traffickers in cigarettes going on. It would be nice if it were coupled with an anti-smoking campaign, but even without one, the rise in prices is sure to tell. There has also been a certain decline in the number of black market money changers on the street. Unfortunately, it is like rats: the periodic campaigns only last for the period of time it takes the reproductive cycle to replace them, and the black market breeds very fast.

All in all, things are not very merry right now. I haven't heard from either Barbara or Tang Min, and I am worried about both. Or you, but I know you can look after yourself. I guess what's really wrong here is that I miss Wuhan. And Barbara.

4 February 1988

News from here. My third molar went under the drill on Wednesday. It was only mildly unpleasant, but it had to be done three times. Apparently I hadn't developed a proper cavity, since my teeth are practically ironclad. Instead there was a diffuse malaise on the back of the molar overlooking the trench where the wisdom tooth once slumbered, its head in the gums. Malaise is terribly hard to drill out, and almost impossible to fill. He kept wrapping this kind of metal strap around the butt of the tooth, and filling it like a mould, and then it would all fall out as soon as he took the strap off. Finally he grunted his satisfaction with the result and released me, but the damn thing fell out mid-sentence in class this morning, just as I was explaining what metal fatigue was. I went back at noon and he did the whole thing again. Very painful this time. That must be good. My mouth doesn't seem to close the way it used to. Do fillings have to be ground down? I mean, should I start gnawing furniture or something?

The Guangdong Provincial Waiban is organizing a conference rather similar to the one in Wuhan that I wrote 'Shut Up and Communicate' for. Possibly even more idiotic. We've been invited to submit papers on one of four topics: teaching methods, aspects of linguistics, co-operation between Chinese and foreign teachers, and how foreign cultures differ from Chinese! I considered giving my famous Chicken Soup lecture, but since the mess from the conference is supposed to be printed and circulated, I decided to dust off 'Shut Up and Communicate' instead. Anyway, rewriting it was clarifying, since it necessitated rereading, which, as you point out, is something I never do. The original really was hopelessly diffuse. Back to work. Once more into the speech!

14 February 1988

I do not have naively linear notions of progress that entirely exclude curves, switchbacks, and even large circles any longer, but I do have a notion, or even an illusion of progress. I think, in fact, my model is linguistic. I do not imagine progress to be a time-linked quantity like motion or velocity at all; I think of it as linked to an endless progression of choices, like linguistic choices, each of which is made according to a whole range of limiting factors and

335

guiding purposes, only the least compelling and most general of which do not change. Thus progress is hardly ever consistently in one direction, and resembles a zig-zag drunkard's walk along a dizzying branching of roads. Such progress can really be measured only by how far you have come, and the question, 'Are we almost there yet?' is best relegated to the back seats of long car drives from my earliest memories. Still, no matter what notion of progress one has, one is always slightly fazed by the sight of one's own footprints in the underbrush ahead.

Where was I? Hong Kong. I left about two days after writing you last, I think. Caught a filthy cold, and then came down with bronchitis, and of course I couldn't afford to see a doctor in Hong Kong. While I was coming through customs, I met up with a little old lady from Jilin who was trying to find somebody who would fill out her forms – she was illiterate. I offered to help and was immensely proud of myself when I found I could do it easily.

A sad story, really. She came from a Korean village near the border with N. Korea, and her relatives had all been dying off before her, finally leaving her with only some rather distant relations who had emigrated to South Korea before Liberation. Of course she couldn't walk across two borders to get to them, so she got herself a passport (but no visa), and rode a train for a week to Guangzhou, whence to Hong Kong, whence to Seoul, etc. She was about eighty years old, you understand, totally illiterate in any language, rather weak in Mandarin, and with no Cantonese. She had huge shopping bags, stuffed way over the customs limit with white Kirin wine, an address she couldn't read, and no Hong Kong money. So I humped her bags and filled out her forms until we got to the Hong Kong side. The border guard wasn't particularly impressed, but waved us through.

There is an incredible xenophobic scare in Hong Kong now, and, as you can imagine, the immigration procedures for Chinese passport holders make the Heathrow gang look like a bunch of obsequious bellhops in a ritzy hotel. For nearly five hours we sat in a room waiting for her name to be barked in Cantonese. Then she was herded into a little chamber where she was fingerprinted and interrogated and her money taken. And then we waited another hour, and then it happened all over again. Finally, she did get a transit visa, but only after her flight out had been arranged and confirmed through a Korean travel agency in Wanchai.

During the agonizing waiting, the room filled with people from all over China in even worse circumstances. At one point, Ms Lu – that was her name – spotted two people similarly scratching their heads over the forms, and said, 'No, they couldn't . . . well, maybe, just let me see . . .', and, sure enough, they were Koreans, from a village not far from her own, also emigrating. Anyway, eventually we all got through. I took a lot of the liquor through customs for her; I don't know how she managed in Seoul. We got a train into Kowloon, where I got a taxi for them, and told the driver where to go.

By then it was time for me to find a bed, although I had hoped to get in, get my books, and get out in one day. I walked down Nathan Road to my usual flea pit, but as I was waiting for the elevator I decided, no, I couldn't face it. It was not the mere physical filth, you understand. It was the moral, social filth. That particular stretch of road is probably the only place on earth where males can experience anything like the sexual harassment of women in the Middle East. Everyone, everyone, absolutely everyone you see, from the chemist with his condom displays, to the newspaper sellers ('No, no map. You like fuck book?'), to the gay Pakistani jewellery store guards, with their suggestive stroking of their baseball bats, to the shills for the cheap flophouses, to the 'brothers' hanging out in front of the Chungking Mansions, to the endless arrays of pimps and whores in all shapes, sizes, shades and prices, everyone thinks he or she can make money off your cock. If you've got one, they can milk it somehow. Everyone is ripping off everyone else.

While walking down Nathan Road toward my haunt, I passed between three glowering cops and some whiteboy college Joe who was refusing to pay his taxi driver or something, and going on in the vein of, 'Go on, arrest me, then! I dare you!' I winced inside but dared not linger, and about ten paces further on I heard a sickening crash and looked back. One of the cops had grabbed the guy's neck under one arm, whirled it against the jewellery store grate behind him, and the other two were shoving at the body in an apparent attempt to collapse the neck. They then handcuffed the bleeding, unconscious, and possibly paralysed remains, and tossed them in the back of the taxi. Whence to jail, I suppose. Quite astounding. I had thought only Chicago cops had a bedside manner like that, and then only with blacks. I am now no longer surprised at the frequency of reports in the *Standard* or the *Post* that the Hong Kong police have apparently killed another one 'in custody'. What will we do with that lot when we finally get the place back? The agreement rather foolishly accepts the integrity of the police force, but surely a few hangings of these scum on purely legal grounds would be in order.

Anyway, the whole thing left me pretty shaken and I decided I couldn't quite face a night in the Chungking Mansions. I tried to find the Youth Hostel in Mount Davis, out in the country on the Hong Kong Island side, where I had stayed years ago when I really was a youth, and had gazed in awe at people my present age who were still doing the route. I couldn't find it, and instead ended up way out in the sticks someplace. I tried sleeping outdoors, but it was too cold, with me under-dressed, under-fed, and suffering from bronchitis, so I headed back to Kowloon. And now it was very late, and even sleazier than before, and the Chungking Mansions were full. Eventually I found an even worse hole for almost twice the price.

I woke up in the middle of the night with a migraine so severe I vomited, and felt weak the whole next morning. About ten, though, I decided I had to find the British Council or face another day in Hong Kong, so I went east and west and asked this way and that, and nobody, but nobody knew where it was, and it was listed in the Yellow Pages as being in a 'Commercial Building' which had no address. Finally, somebody at the Centre for the Performing Arts managed to find it for me.

They have a library, oh, yes. And you may use it if you are a Hong Kong teacher, preferably a British Council one, which allows you to pay a 50 dollar deposit and borrow three books for no more than two weeks. Tapes? Videos? No, I'm afraid the copyright laws would never allow such a thing, I'm terribly sorry. Alright then, what about your teacher training programs? Yes, they do have an excellent program for the RSA TEFLA certificate I want. But you understand that is for our teachers only, the ones working right here at our centre. I should have known. That way they can charge the teachers for their teaching simply by calling it training. Yes, I understand. One final question. How come you lot are so fucking useless and your counterparts in Beijing are so helpful and thoroughly conscientious?

Anyway, I had already almost entirely spent my Hong Kong money, nothing on food, nothing on medicine, just a night in a hotel, a few bus fares, and a boat ticket to Macao. For nothing.

12 | Translations and revolutions

Guangzhou, 22 February 1988
Dear Dorothy and Burt,

I still haven't had a letter from you since the ones from Burt that arrived the day Dorothy left. Yes, I know, it is simply the combined lassitude of the Chinese and Indian mails. But it bothers. I imagine your pearls accumulating in some dingy cell with broken windows, beneath an inscription scrawled by some newly-employed wag: 'Entropy of Information Rules OK'.

I am still not clear on the relationship between entropy of information and the other kind of entropy, but more of that in a while. It is chiefly the other kind around here. Spring Festival accentuated the falling apart of things with a wave of frenzied blowing apart that left seas of red paper clogging the sewers. The Cantonese enjoy Spring Festival so much they celebrate it five nights in a row, and then again fifteen days later. The first morning after, when you are trying to sleep in, the street-by-street lion dances start, a custom I would really enjoy if it weren't for the lion's apparent appetite for firecrackers.

I guess the most enjoyable part of Spring Festival is the huge flower markets on every street during the days leading up to the festival, and the kumquat plants and peach-tree branches in blossom being carried home everywhere for use as Christmas trees. Kumquat, which is a Cantonese word, is a homonym for good luck, and it is auspicious to have one in your home on Chuxi, that is, New Year's Eve. I managed to buy one for two yuan by finding a farmer whose kumquats were still green – gold is the colour of money, not green,

340

and green kumquats on Chuxi are said to be inauspicious. I also got a peach blossom branch, now busily falling apart in harmony with the rest of the universe, a chrysanthemum, a kind of purple cabbage-like flower, and eight narcissus bulbs, now busily dying on me. I have recovered from my bronchitis, but now my allergy is back. And elsewhere on the entropy front, my textbooks are nowhere to be found, and I must go to Beijing to try to get them. It is impossible to get train tickets, and I have no assurance of success even if I do.

And now to entropy of information: here is the retranslation of Liu's honeymoon journal. In the end, I really got into it. I could see and smell it all again. Her description of Sakya is a bit pale compared to the real thing, but she does very well on the shit-strewn truck stops where Nick and I and then Barbara and I spent so many days.

I am very glad I am not editing this book. One must have some organizing principle, not just an image of oneself one would like to project. The principles that spring to mind are all of a rather far-fetched kind of analogy. Transitions, yes. But my personal transition really has absolutely nothing to do with the economic transitions going on around here. They happened to be simultaneous. The more obvious far-fetched analogy is this: my coming to China was another step in my attempt to find something I could do in life which did not have a revolutionary purpose, my attempt to live without a revolutionary programme, discipline and enthusiasm. That is, in a sense, what an entire generation of Chinese of my age are trying to do now. But of course I have nothing in common with them. I am not doing this voluntarily, and I certainly don't believe that life without revolutionary purpose will accomplish anything revolutionary, or even worthwhile in a historic sense.

On another level, I was never sent out to the countryside, or jet-planed, or any of that. Yet perhaps there is a little something there. The other night I was talking with Peng and Dr Zhou about the early Sixties and the beginning of the terrible purges. Dr Zhou went on and on about how her family was purged; her father had to denounce himself, not for what he did, not even for what he thought, but for what he was. And of course when he had done so he was accused of insincerity (how can one sincerely denounce one's self for what one *is* without changing?). Dr Zhou could not bring herself to give the details of of his self-criticism, if there were any, but I think it had to do with his social background, and his ingrained petty bourgeois habits, vague accusations like that. Dr Zhou looked at me and said, 'I suppose none of this makes any sense at all to you.' I said, I think truthfully, that I thought I understood very well what it was like. She looked incredulous, but Peng, who knows a bit more about me, nodded in the darkness. Peng is the best friend I have besides you.

8 March 1988

I always put on a pot of tea before I sit down to scribble to you, and then I get so carried away it goes cold and 'dragon' and bitter. This time, though, in honour of a successful second class, I am steeping my prize 'Dragon Well', very expensive and difficult to buy in Guangzhou, so you must remind me not to let it go cold, no matter how I writhe and squirm in my scribbling. (Yes, I know . . . but isn't that the difficulty, really? The problems we discuss are moot by the time we have actually exchanged any ideas on solutions.)

I got your letter with manuscript on Monday, but then classes started in earnest. We are off to a very good start. Mostly women, quiet and determined, serious young wives and fiancées who couldn't care less about going abroad and have their minds so set on English they treat the 'topical' and 'general interest' settings as (what they are) mere opportunities for language practice, and (what they aren't) rather uninteresting except as a means to that end.

They are all in a state of utter bewilderment as to my goals in class; it is all they can do to keep their eyes on the teacher as he moves around so incomprehensibly, with the seats all facing each other instead of him. Keeping ears and mouths pointed in the right direction is quite beyond them. Today being our second day and International Women's Day, I started off with a story about Deng Yingchao. A few days ago, speaking at a memorial meeting for the 90th anniversary of Zhou Enlai's birth, she remarked that she was really fed up with reading in the foreign press all the references to herself as Mrs Zhou Enlai, or as Zhou Enlai's widow. No one in China knows her by those names, and they are not what she is called or is. Now, if she'd waited a few days to say that, at some IWD celebration or other, I wouldn't have thought anything of it. But I think it was very nice of her to say it on the 90th anniversary of her husband's birth.

Anyway, I made the obvious point about using Ms with women's names whether they were married or not, and how particularly necessary this was in our class, with its large proportion of women, married or not. Ms Wang, the political instructor, figured out what I was talking about towards the very end of my talk, and looked bored and seemed to say, yes, well, we'll go to a meeting on the subject this very afternoon, and now what about the lesson?

Sip. Shit, cold again. So you see I am not quite so fluent and articulate as all that; all this takes time, and the tea is getting cold apace. Perhaps I overestimate my own persuasiveness. I know that you are not always taken in, being a very critical reader of old letters indeed.

But Dorothy, there is so much rubbish in what I wrote in 1984. It is not your fault; I think you are doing a heroic job. I like the way you cut down the paragraph on the 'boums' in Nanning; if I remember correctly I wrote all kinds of rubbish about not really feeling superior because I had a real sex life, when obviously I really did. But I think you should explain that Millie is a dog, or else omit this obscure and not very funny joke. Note that I blame the tonsillitis on my dog-eating habits here, and on my arguing elsewhere – I get more hot air out of a case of tonsillitis!

And then my criticism of Chinese medicine is horrendously unfair and must be corrected. China has wiped out VD, leprosy, smallpox and many other scourges, and is making tremendous gains against malaria, schistosomiasis, encephalitis, etc, by using programs of preventative medicine unthinkable in the West. I based this purely on personal observation, and what had I observed back then?

The blame lies entirely on the 25-year-old me. Take the treatment of capital punishment, for example. In fact, I am not against capital punishment, and wasn't even back then. I am not particularly for it either; I don't believe in punishment in principle, simply because it seems to be ineffective in preventing crime, except in a few, mostly political cases, and I am almost always on the wrong side of these.

And then all this belly-aching over the permit system. Well, let it stand. But maybe a footnote is in order. Something along the lines of, 'The author now fully understands the restrictions placed on the travel of foreigners, at least in certain areas like Tibet, and abides by them even where he doesn't really understand them. Understanding comes slowly.' After all, we want to make it clear that I no longer hold such views. And then the racial segregation stuff. Again, I must give my 29-year-old law-abiding self equal air time.

The papers and television are full of the horrible attack on the Tibetan TV camera crew that was trying to film the *Monlam* or 'Welcoming Maitreya' festival in Lhasa. It was, by all accounts, a completely unprovoked attack, well prepared in advance. The leaders of the Party who were attending the ceremony were almost stoned to death in a room on the second floor of the Jokhang, and escaped, many badly hurt, from a window. Later, two policemen guarding the home of a Tibetan ganbu who lived near the temple were lynched.

Monlam was being held for only the second time since 1959. It was revived in 1986 thanks to the efforts of the Panchen and other pro-government elements in the religious hierarchy, plus pro-religion elements in the government. Why, then, the riots? Why now? Because if the pro-government elements get their way and there is a significant religious revival in Tibet, certain people will lose a lot of moral and material support. The older exiles will trickle back to die in their homelands and the young Tibetan militants will drift off to colleges in the US and never come back. The Tibetan feudal system will begin to thaw. There was a very simple way to prevent this from happening, and it was bound to occur to the lamanoids on the other side eventually.

The feudal system has been kept cryogenically preserved by the liquid nitrogen of Western liberalism. Last night, for example, I was reading an article by a bloke who claims to be a Tibet-lover. It was riddled with errors and exhibited the unmistakable mark of the writer who has arrived at his destination before he saddles his premises, a perfect example of the 'I know what I see' writing that is done by people who see only what they know. His kind of thinking is perhaps best illustrated by the matter of the toilets, about which he says, 'Just as the British brought free trade to Lhasa at the point of a bayonet, the Chinese have brought modern amenities, including a higher level of sanitation.'

When I first arrived in Lhasa, the streets were, as I said, banked with human shit and urine poured in a trough down the centre, less than a block from the Jokhang. In this filth, people squatted on the ground to sell bread, yogurt, and meat. The municipal authorities (undoubtedly Tibetan, for in this part of Lhasa non-Tibetans are not even allowed to own houses) were building outhouses in the area, and we foreigners were a bit surprised to notice that the Tibetans insisted on shitting in concentric rings outside the houses, while the Hans always entered them. Naturally we speculated on the reasons for this, and naturally hit on an explanation which seemed quite reasonable on the face of it: that the Tibetans were expressing their defiance of the Hans by trying to seal up the entrances to the outhouses in shit.

One night I discussed this theory with a rather anti-Chinese Tibetan I knew. He thought it was the funniest thing he had ever heard. Actually, he told me, Tibetans believe in a theory of medicine largely based on humours or vapours, and it is commonly held that smelling another person's shit is not good for you, so they prefer to crap

345

outdoors, or at least cover their noses and mouths when they do it indoors. However, they recognize the wish of the municipal authorities to clean Lhasa up, so they tend to congregate in the vicinity of the municipal outhouses. Well, that extra bit of knowledge makes all the difference; it enables the tourist to settle down, to put the numbers together into a sum, to take the sums apart into numbers, to change places and understand the true relationship between what you see and what you know.

So I've started writing letters to newspapers, in futile rage. It is a silly exercise, which I detest and hate myself for succumbing to. Yet I do it compulsively. I must say something: I suppose it all has to do with the struggle to fit into the 'little life' that I talk a bit about on New Year's Eve in Budapest. It was a kind of revolutionary faith that allowed me to put up with being put out of the Party; I was sure they would succeed even without me, perhaps especially without me. Then I realized that they wouldn't, even without me, yet I remain sure that someone will. In the meantime, how do I quench my own purely private thirst for politics? Ah, that is paradoxically a matter of self-indulgence, and not a political question at all. I am even inquiring about the possibility of casting an absentee ballot in November, for the first time in my life. I intend to vote Communist, whoever is running.

22 March 1988

The school is going through a paroxysm of reorganization. One of the students was expelled for hooliganism and two others severely censured for having women from outside the school in their dorm rooms after hours. (How could they? They have ten students to a room over in the dorms, you know. It must have been quite a conspiracy.) The head of the school is retiring. People are shaking their heads left and right, mostly right. My boss is so preoccupied with moral matters he has done nothing to answer my frantic requests for equipment, and it has been very difficult to get time set aside for the weekly films because everyone has been busy attending meetings during their spare waking moments. Particularly Ms Wang, the political instructor, who teaches Marxism-Leninism. She was supposed to be on leave, to study English, but her leave has now been cancelled.

Perhaps the worst off is poor Ms Chen. Her husband is in America, her son is in hospital, she has been forced to teach more than 18 hours a week, as well as raise her two kids and shop and go to more than 25 hours a week of English lessons. And yet she still finds time to write things like the following:

> Last weekend we went to Shangchuan Island in Taishan. We got some problems. The first, when we went to the beach we found we had been given a sun umbrella with a big hole and a soft holder, but we paid ten yuans for one hour to rent it. The second, when we rowed to sea, we found we had been given a broken rubber boat, but we paid 20 yuans for one hour to rent it. The boat got smaller and smaller and the water in the boat got more and more, we had to row back to the coast quickly. The third, when we went back to the beach and sat under the broken umbrella, we found we had been stolen the card of rent deposit of the boat and the umbrella, which costed us 100 yuans.

And you think you have problems!

28 March 1988

The pig that lives outside the back gate of the school just had piglets. At least a dozen of them. The natal cascade seems only to have increased her abdominal discomfort; she now actually drags her sagging belly along, hobbled with her own bulk, a groaning board on legs. But the piglets are adorable: curious and insatiable, remarkably intelligent and energetic. They remind me of my better students.

There is a programme on TV now about how to turn your pigs into money. It's called *The Money Tree*, and every week it features a super-peasant, one who contracted for perfectly incredible amounts of land and hired scores of field hands: a kulak, that is. Like the demobbed soldier who contracted for a gigantic tract of utterly undeveloped land, planted fir trees, and harvested the timber. He has reputedly made 4,000,000 yuan since the beginning in 1975. (But fir is not a crop that can be harvested from year to year; if he has made that much money, he must have stripped what was already there in 1975.)

Today a wall newspaper went up, *Volcano*, so named because of the sympathy the writers and editors have for the release of the pent-up tensions of geological and other sorts. It is basically full of thinly disguised sentimental pornography, almost like the gossip sheets we published in high school. Half a page was devoted to a long poem, unoriginally titled, *Oh, Little Girl*, or maybe *Ho, Ho, Little Girl*, after a song by the Sino-American pop singer Fei Xiang, renowned chiefly for the profile of his occidental nose. It is full of 'locked glances, empty of words' exchanged over the recumbent forms of the morning chemistry lecture. And then there was a long discussion that purported to be an oppositional document: it criticizes the authorities for their oft-repeated warnings that *tan lian ai*, literally, 'discussing engagement', what we might call courting or wooing if we weren't too hip for all that, can have an unfavourable effect on study habits. The author argued that not wooing can be even worse. I don't know. It's spring, but not even a slightly frisky sort of spring. The smell of sentimentality is a sickly sweet pall, like smoke from a crematorium. On my street there is a taxi parked, with pink-dressed nuptial dolls nailed to the sequinned fender like bagged deer.

3 April 1988

I just heard a disquieting rumour that my programme will cease to exist next year. Here we go again.

I'll get to the text in a moment. First, news and reviews. Hainan, as you may know, is being declared a province, and young people are flocking there for jobs, hoping that it will turn out to be something like Shenzen or Zhuhai. It is quite possible they are right, since the new provincial regulations are even more liberal: active encouragement of private enterprise generally, total freedom for capital, including foreign capital, to move in and out, and total freedom to import and export goods abroad, although there are some restrictions on re-export to the interior. (I expect at least part of the reason for the new status is to try to cut the Guangzhou connection that resulted in the re-export of huge numbers of automobiles from Hainan to elsewhere, a scandal for which several bureaucrats were executed.)

The exodus to Hainan is partly artificial; it is mostly not of people who cannot get jobs elsewhere. Every single one of them has a guaranteed job if he or she would simply agree to work in the state sector. They would not even need to go to the west, where they are most needed; educated labour is in a sellers' market in China today, and the recent NPC [National People's Congress] had to shrug off the desperate pleas coming from the western provinces for young talent to be sent there. China, they were told, was now democratic, and people could choose to go or not. Overwhelmingly, they have chosen not to.

In February, the Guangzhou papers began to publish appeals from the Hainan authorities trying to discourage people from showing up there without proper qualifications: the hotels and social services were packed to the gills with roast-mutton pedlars and key-chain sellers. Now they've gone a step further. The Zhujiang TV channel did a programme on the problem of unemployed college graduates (once a contradiction in terms) in Hainan; they interviewed a newspaper seller who was a graduate in Chinese from Gansu, and two university graduates who fixed radios, one a woman.

A strange business these memoirs of 1984. Virtually the same incident with the same moral is duplicated in letters in June and July, while a 'he' is changed to a 'she'. I doubt if this is due to your editing. It seems to me I must have made the incident up the second time, God knows why. I think what happened was that I started off to write about a French woman staying in the hotel, Christine, who was sort of a friend of mine until she made a horrible crack about how we should all be thankful to the Japanese occupation in Peking

349

for keeping down the population. She didn't understand why I considered such a remark too offensive to be funny, and we didn't get on after that, although she wrote me a few times and I answered her. Anyway, I started writing about her and seem to have switched to the Swedish punker without removing the 'last night' at the beginning of the sentence. I assure you, I didn't usually bother to invent the truth in my letters home. I hope this is an isolated incident. How bloody embarrassing. If I close my eyes, I can even remember hoping to impress Paul with my description of Christine, and then thinking of the Swede mid-sentence. Is it a real memory? Or more manufactured truth?

Particularly since there were a whole bunch of other incidents with similar morals I could have quoted had I known it would all come out in print: did I ever tell you about the time two foreigners tried desperately to get me to write 'I pissed on the Great Wall' in Chinese, so they could make T-shirts when they got back to England? I remember one of them was an elderly English lady. I told them I didn't know how, although I actually did, and I point blank refused to translate their demand to the desk girl in the hotel, afraid she would be offended. When I finally did ask her about it several weeks later, she thought the request neither particularly funny nor particularly offensive, just downright odd. Piss is not taboo, after all, nor is the Great Wall sacred. She was right. We were wrong, all three of us.

Barbara has gone to Taiwan for Easter. What divides us really is politics; she cannot understand why I can't stand capitalism. She can't accept the unfamiliar world (a rather frightening one sometimes) I live in, and I cannot live in the familiar world she accepts.

15 May 1988
Being without Barbara has heightened my tolerance and even my appreciation for all sorts of feminine and sentimental things. Partly it is the massive rethinking that always attends getting unstuck from one person and reaching out for others. You are really right, I suppose, loneliness is the

rule and not the exception, and it makes us realize what we have been missing – the normal extravagance of our sexual imaginations – and rediscover the delight of obsession. One is constantly imagining sexual dimensions to things and pursuing them with enough doggedness to discover, with amazement, that they often do exist: my students' insistent discussions of all aspects of marriage, the relish with which Dr Li enjoys the younger students' romanticism. (She is an obstetrician, and enjoys grossing people out. Today she offered to procure me human placenta and the scrapings of abortions, which, cooked in a soup, is a traditional Chinese remedy for asthma.)

Well, let me tell you about our class outing on Wednesday. We managed to get school funds, about 200 yuan, for the purpose, by agreeing to take along huge numbers of bureaucrats who also wanted to go. I was initially anxious lest they speak to my students in Chinese, or want me to lunch with them, but they kept off to themselves, getting carsick and littering and remarking noisily on the bad weather with the tremendous self-satisfaction of the confirmed pessimist – as well as spending the bulk of the funds they had allotted.

We went to Conghua, a funny kind of resort about two hours northeast of Guangzhou: a dam, a reservoir, and here and there those little cameos of canyons, a waterfall (artificial, of course), a bamboo grove, mountains and fog and pine and so on. Even a set of monkeys imported from Hainan, with the cages left open so they can wander the hills and fool tourists into thinking they were wild.

I sat next to Dr Li on the way out. Do you know, every single class I've taught in China has had a Dr Li, an older woman (for it is always a woman), full of things to say and quite powerless to say them, whose listening ability lags hopelessly behind, who eventually panics when she realizes that the other students are beginning to make sense out of the terrifying babble that surrounds her in my class, and who, at some point in class, bursts into tears. I asked the other teachers if this was a common experience, having a 40-

year-old woman burst into tears for no apparent reason, and they assured me it was unheard of. Yet it happens in my class every single term. I suppose I put too much pressure on them, and they put too much pressure on themselves. It is always an older person who is there 'on merit', that is, someone who has always excelled and been the best in the past, and suddenly finds herself at the very bottom, growing older and older, with no way of closing the gap.

The other day she sat in class with head bowed and I carefully worked around her, trying not to draw attention to her. Suddenly, during the pair work, she got up and rushed out. Mr Liu, who is the young 'reformer' (this word, so popular in the western media, actually means something like 'wheeler-dealer' to most Chinese, redolent of NEP-men, kulaks, and corruption), rushed out after her, and I followed after a decent interval. Poor Dr Li was disconsolate, and she said my 'kindness' made her feel even worse. Yet I know I am not guilty of any kindness, my quick temper is legendary, and it is my pressure to perform that she finds unbearable.

So Dr Li talked in Chinese. I checked to make sure the other students were too busy speaking English to notice, and then listened. She said, 'Do you know why there is a peak in sterilization every three years? Because there really never was a one-child-family policy. You do sterilizations after the *second* child. So they check on first births and return after three years or so to sterilize those who've had two.' She described taking part in the very earliest of the campaigns, back in the early Seventies. No, that early? 'Yes,' she said. 'The peasants, they called us the "castration brigade".' The Chinese term she used is generally used only for pigs and chickens.

'The things they said were so ugly! But look, they have seven, eight kids in some places, they can't feed them, they don't care if one dies, they just go ahead and have another.' This seems incredible on the face of it, but I know for a fact that what she says is true. One such village, a coal-mining town in Anhui that had been deliberately left out of the census and the birth control campaign, was reported on the evening news some two weeks ago. They had mothers with seven children, not one of whom could go to school or eat a full meal.

Why do they do it? 'For the money, of course. If you have one kid and she gives you ten yuan a month, that's nothing, but if you've got seven or eight, you don't have to work!' But at some point they must realize that there's no extra land for the extra kid to work, and that 'two hands are idle but the stomach is not'. 'Yes, but they don't know that. And it's a whole new problem, you know. There was no private land before. Extra kids were an extra burden on the whole commune. People still think that, well, you have an extra kid and the others eat a bit less, that's all, and they still grow up and work for you.'

Dr Li is pessimistic in the extreme. She believes that China cannot possibly support more than 1,300 million people, the population it is very likely to reach by the year 2010. The campaign to hold the population under 1,200 million is now given a very slim chance of succeeding, and the government has stopped talking about it. The latest article I read declared that the 'two-child limit' was reasonable and sustainable; actually, the same article said that peasants found it economically impossible to survive on only one child. We are in retreat.

I asked her if she knew the reasons for the defeat of the birth control campaign. Well, there is no national policy, only a crazy quilt of little village policies, for which she is a medical flunkey. Why is there no national policy? Why isn't there a single law that can be applied to town and country? 'I don't know! It is the Chinese way. Foreigners do, Chinese just talk about it.' I believe she is wrong to despair. The decrease in the birthrate worldwide is entirely due to China's efforts; China is by far the biggest success for birth control worldwide. 'Then the world is in for it, that's all,' she says.

We arrived. Fang Shangying, the *Lao Guniao* ('Old Maid', this is the rather nasty term used for 28-year-old women who show no particular interest in men) of the class, is grumpy and carsick, and we all bustle about, jostling her

353

and making matters worse. Then it's off to the lake, where I swim. No one joins me. I ask Lin Wei why not, and she blushes, well, '*mianzi*', that is, 'face'. What? She indicates a sign I had not noticed: 'Swimming forbidden. Swimmers are entirely responsible for their own safety.'

Then, the boum. Under a pavilion with upturned eaves, the students dance to disco-muzak and play party games: musical chairs, and then this other thing where you tie a balloon to your foot and then try to pop other people's balloons, and so on. The whole thing is enjoyed with riotous laughter, and those who lose have to 'do a programme', that is, sing a song, or do a comedy routine, or something like that. The other Dr Li, a 43-year-old surgeon with the PLA, loses a round of musical chairs and sings. We are astonished. He has a huge, professionally trained voice, and it leaves us momentarily moved and self-conscious.

Momentarily. Then the party games begin again. It is far sillier than the boum I described in Guangxi in 1984; the participants are five to twenty years older – and I am four years on. But what would we be doing if we were Western, pseudo-adult, supercilious, cool and half-sodden with alcohol? Finding pretexts, finding suitable excuses to rub against each other suggestively, or at least to express ourselves expressively. No, it makes sense to me now.

Ms Fang does not really take part, she just sits there and laughs. Her dignity, or at least her shyness, insulates her and her alone. Everyone else is required to participate, but the Lao Guniao is too respected. I wonder how that works. I remember how I was once criticized for not taking part in Party 'socials', and not getting socialized when I was in the Party. The 'socials' were mostly dancing to music I dislike in styles I never learned, but there was no attempt made to grant me special status, or to respect my preferences.

I think, actually, there is a difference. This class boum was not trying to socialize anybody. We were just finding pretexts for tossing aside mianzi and letting loose. That was something that did not happen at Party socials; rather the contrary, I was always aware that I was judged far more harshly at socials than in my political work.

On the way back I got into a long conversation with Ms Fang. She talked about her years in the countryside – she was of the very last cohort to have to do work in the countryside after upper middle school. 'We never talk about it because . . .' here she indicates the 24- and 25-year-olds in the class '. . . they would never believe us.' Ms Fang is 28.

Mr Liu is also of that cohort, but his experience is somewhat different. Ms Fang chose to go to a kind of 'work station' set up by her father's work unit, as a way of keeping the unit's children close to their parents. It was a barracks, built with unit money and given some land taken from the local peasants. They worked together as a team, unit leaders checked their production level, and they were allowed four days' leave every month or so to visit their parents.

Mr Liu, on the other hand, chose a real farm, where the workers were paid a wage. Conditions there were far worse, and the peasants hated them. 'Why?' 'Because we stole their chickens all the time!' Mr Wu laughs at this. 'Yeah, I have good memories of that. We used to steal chickens every night. Not just chickens, you know, vegetables, fruit, you name it. And swim during the day, too. We didn't get much to eat, but it was all right, didn't have any homework to do, lived away from our parents, you know . . . freedom. Nobody telling us what to do.'

Mr Wu is another different case. He grew up in a filthy, poor hovel in Hainan, the poorest part of the province. He lived hand to mouth, trading with the stone-age hill people of the interior. 'Back then the Miao had no cash, you know, and there was no way to sell things for money; we were the only way they had of getting money. We bought deer antlers and mushrooms, all kinds of stuff.'

Ms Fang received no wages for her labour, but it was not a big step to return to the city and the academic world, which she did after two years. 'I was sick all the time,' she explained. 'They made me look after the cows when I was sick, instead of planting rice seedlings and so forth. And that way, I could study. The only problem was, they were so big, you know, and when they decided not to listen to you, there was really nothing you could do. Once a cow went into the water and wouldn't come out. I just sat there until nightfall, waiting, and eventually it got out and went home and I followed. It got dinner but I didn't.'

Was it so bad? 'Yes,' said Mr Liu. 'No,' said Mr Wu. 'Yes,' said Ms Fang, 'The peasants hated us. We just took up their land, and didn't produce anything. Our parents had to send us money or there would be nothing to eat.' Well, what was the point? 'There was no point. It was the Cultural Revolution.' (It wasn't actually, she was talking about 1976-7.) 'They just wanted to get young people out of the cities, so they wouldn't do the sort of thing they do now.' (Incidentally, the peasants still hate us. Last night there were meetings all over the school because college students have been getting into brawls, not only with each other, but with local farmers near the swimming hole they frequent.)

You fret about my alleged slovenliness, but I am more worried about my tendency to be careless with money, and when I get around to holding a campaign, that is the tendency I intend to rectify. Ms Lin and I had a discussion about this. You would like Ms Lin, by the way. She got married in order to live alone. You see, she couldn't get housing from the school unless she was married, and she had to live with her rich father. So she married a student who promptly went off somewhere else to study, and managed to get a room of her own. It is an exposed brick hovel in the maze of alleys near here, but she has decorated it beautifully and spends all her time in it. Anyway, she still shares my carelessness with money; we sometimes lend each other meal tickets towards the end of the month. We trace it to our shared petty bourgeois origins: neither of us ever lived in a situation where Daddy wouldn't bail us out if we were really hard up. So we have rather similar attitudes towards cash: it is a kind of pocket money allotted by fate, nothing more. We sniff at those who plan their expenses; we are above that sort of thing, because others do it for us.

356

In my case, the school. I accepted the obscenely high salary here under duress, but with the understanding that I would spend about half of it every month on teaching materials that I knew the school would not provide. That was a mistake, not only in principle (because it's wrong to privatize education that way) but in terms of my own interests. I am simply not capable of budgeting, and I often end up spending far more than I should. I spent nearly 400 yuan on films last month, and have been living on Ms Lin's meal tickets for the past week.

28 May 1988

The news from here is of horrendous inflation and serious malnutrition developing among large sections of the 'intelligentsia'. University students now constitute the largest group of undernourished persons in China.

The figures just don't add up, when I come to think about it. When I arrived in China, four years ago, wages were about 80-100 yuan a month, and pork about 1.20 a jin. Today the figures are 100-120, and 5+ respectively. Vegetables have doubled, and even rice, which the government promised would never change when the country was liberated, has gone from 3.6 mao a jin to nearly 6. Now, as then, people spend about 80 or 90 per cent of their salaries on food. But how is that accomplished? Are people eating more rice and less meat? Are they living on savings? Are they eating less? Are we turning into Thailand or the Philippines, places with immoral material extremes, where less than nothing is invested in the future?

There is a talk show on TV now about teachers trying to find extra-curricular work to supplement their starvation salaries. This is now official policy, since the announcement at the NPC that intellectual salaries would not be increased no matter how bad inflation was. Education has entirely stopped in many areas of Fujian because so many teachers have started businesses and no longer have time to teach classes. In addition, there are several areas which have not yet begun the current school year because·of the shortage of text books; paper factories now have options on how they sell their paper, and none have chosen to sell to state-run textbook printers, who pay low prices. Official newspapers, including *Renmin Ribao*, have the same problem, but of course, more powerful backers.

Teachers in Shanghai sell ice-cream during class, and even in our school a host of little businesses have been set up on campus, including an over-priced ice-cream seller where the gate watchman used to be. The classrooms are becoming littered with ice-cream wrappers, and last Friday Ms Rao disappeared from the room every five minutes to get an ice-cream. Sigh.

There is a little ditty making the rounds that goes something like this:

Number One son yells,
Number Two son laughs,
The 'Neither Three nor Four' sons count their cash.
The intellectuals sit in their bridal chairs
Half-naked and in rags.

Number One is a popular expression for the proletariat, Number Two is the peasantry, and 'Neither Three nor Four' means those who speculate. Note that the daughters of the family have the highest ritual and lowest actual significance.

Yes, but of course this is a peasant country, and the reforms have undeniably profited many of the peasantry. Not as much as the 'Neither Three nor Four', but still. There are now many villages in China that are really well off, and China is a country of villages. However, the profit has stratified the countryside and produced big imbalances in the economy; rice is now a bit tight for the first time since anyone can remember. The problem is that farmers around Guangzhou have discovered they can make a big profit by growing groundnuts instead of rice, and exchanging ground-nut oil for rice in the city. They then offer this rice to the state as their quota of 'patriotism grain'. Of course, since the grain was bought in a state store, it has already served as another peasant's quota. But the obligation is fulfilled, and the peasant is free to sell the rest of his groundnut crop as he pleases.

News of Tang Min, too. Good news, actually. The court will hold two hearings around the 10th of June. The plaintiff will have the right to appeal to higher courts if not satisfied with the verdict, which seems entirely likely, since the court's preliminary investigation produced a huge stack of evidence proving that the story was completely factual except for two fairly minor details: it was not Wang Lianzhong but another ganbu who broke up Ah Qing's wedding, although Wang was implicated in the disposal of the takings; also, the little tailor was involved with the Deputy Party Secretary's wife, but committed suicide as the result of some money scandal. It was also determined that the plaintiffs would have to prove intent to libel.

5 June 1988

My students organized a little party. In fact, it was practically organized to death, but a jolly good show it was nevertheless. One of the sketches performed was about a middle-school teacher who cannot afford to satisfy his gluttonous offspring's penchant for ice-cream, so he calls in sick and goes into the ice-cream business himself. Because he is afraid of being recognized, he fails to sell the lot, and they have to eat the ice-cream for dinner. Encouraged, the lad asks if he can become an ice-cream vendor, too, but the father tells him firmly that the next day they are both going back to school where they belong, and leave business to the businessmen.

The two MCs tried to provoke a discussion after the skit, and, rather to their surprise, succeeded. Ms Chen, the biochemist, said she could no longer afford to clothe her two sons, and was planning to sell clothes. One of the eye surgeons said we should all be grateful to the government for this generous permission to moonlight ourselves ragged. Interestingly, it was the younger ones who were outraged and opposed to moonlighting, both on principled grounds and because they were, they thought, ill-equipped to compete (true). Ms Fang's generation believes it is just another diversion, like going down to the countryside was, and the younger ones said they were too shy to go about hawking things like the 'Neither Three nor Fours' do. Anyway, I think the sketch made a few people think, maybe for the first time, about what it will mean to have to moonlight in order to be able to afford to teach. Another sketch was about an attempt by some doctors to recruit patients for a hospital that had priced itself out of business. It was outrageous, and all the doctors who had gloated over the predicament of the teachers complained that their noble profession had been defamed.

Then the dancing. As you know, I am congenitally clumsy, and so unhip my pelvis barely shows up on X-rays. Normally, of course, I dislike all dancing, with the envy and mortification of the truly incapable. But my students were so . . . graceful, really. Beautiful. Particularly the mad Ms Lin, who is so ferocious that none of the men dared to dance with her, and she had to dance with her friend Ms He. Ms He agreed only on condition that she could be the man and lead, but there she was, in a white silk dress she specially begged money from her mother to buy, one limp-wristed, sweating hand on Ms Lin's back, which was arched like a bow. Stretching her finery like a string, Ms Lin whirled Ms He in tighter and tighter circles until Ms He collapsed, and Ms Lin stalked off to find a real man. The real men cowered at the other end of the dance hall, and danced with each other if at all. Why can't a woman be more like a man?

Dr Li (male) and I then did an English version of the crucial scene in the *White Haired Girl*, to huge appreciation. I sang Xi-er, the white-haired girl, and Dr Li sang Yang Bailao, my father. It is one of the few revolutionary operas that date from the actual revolution, and not from the Cultural one. It was composed in early 1945, and performed within three months in Yan'an, and then later in Shijiazhuang, near where the original story was supposed to have been set. The story and the music are based on Hebei folk tales and songs. It was put together by Ding Yi and He Jingzhi, who I suspect of being the actual historical person behind *The Yellow Earth*; he's a vice-minister of something or other today.

Snow and wind on stage; it is the bitter winter of 1937 in a particularly pinched and bitten portion of Hebei Province. The wind sneers at the rags of the poor, and snaps at the flesh that pokes through; the snow wraps itself around their dormant coal stoves and refuses to melt. Xi-er has been sitting mending rags for some time, and sings of the north wind and the snow, gazing expectantly towards the door, where the snow is drifting unprinted. Her father has been hiding from the steward of his landlord for a week; he owes some rent, and New Year's Day is the traditional time for the settling of debts. The door opens. Dr Li staggers in with a carrying pole, draped in an old rag I use to wipe the blackboard.

Dr Li: Selling dofu I have made
　　　　Money for this bit of flour
　　　　But I can't let the landlord know
　　　　So I'll keep it hid right here (points to his wallet).
　　　　Ah – keep it hid right here!

David: Selling dofu, making money
　　　　　With the money buying flour
　　　　　With the flour, we'll make jiao-zi,
　　　　　So we'll pass a happy New Year!

Dr Li: Other farmers' daughters wear
　　　　Lovely flowers in their hair,
　　　　But your dad's just too darn poor,
　　　　Flowers we just can't afford. (winking slyly)
　　　　Other farmers' daughters wear
　　　　Lovely flowers in their hair,
　　　　But your dad's just got two feet
　　　　Of red ribbon for your hair.

(Xi-er is overjoyed and dances around the stage, twirling the red ribbon in her hands and skipping.)

David: Other fathers give bouquets
　　　　　My pa's just too poor to pay,

> So he's got these two long feet
> Of lovely ribbon for my hair.

Dr Li: And I also got two door-gods for our door!

David: Door-gods!

Dr Li: They'll guard our home all the new year!

David: They won't let the devils in!

Dr Li: Door-gods, door-gods ride tall roans!

David: On our doors they guard our homes!

Dr Li: Door-gods, door-gods have big knives!

David: Keeping devils from our lives!

Both: Keeping devils, ah, keeping devils from our lives!

(This was later altered by some wag to 'Keeping David from our lives!')

I had to teach the last bit about the door-gods to Dr Li, because in fact he was raised on the Cultural Revolution version of the *White Haired Girl*, which cut out references to feudal superstition. Fortunately, I have a version recorded in 1959. It was a great success, particularly when Dr Li staggered on stage, bent beneath the carrying pole, and the whole audience spontaneously burst into the opening chords of his aria.

Enough. To answer your questions. Yang claims that I am going to be working here next year on more or less the same basis. On the other hand, he refuses point blank to give me a contract. I refuse to work without a contract, and am seeking another job. I don't know what is going on. Perhaps it is related to my denunciation of the school for its inability to deal with its own audio-visual department (which is controlled by a convicted criminal who uses the equipment for his own profit and amusement, and refuses to allow me to use it for education. The criminal in question is the son-in-law of one of the directors of the school). In any case, I am fed up with Yang, fed up with the hoodlums in the audio-visual department, and fed up with an administrative mentality that believes that problems are solved when people calm down.

I am giving a paper at the Provincial Conference on the Teaching of Foreign Experts (sic) next week, and it will be a good opportunity to plug for jobs. I already have an offer to be a translator in Shenzen, but I don't like the idea of giving up teaching. I am not too worried about it, and I hope you aren't either. I mean, if worse come to worst, I can be a bloody translator and learn some Chinese, or maybe even take some time off and learn to write.

27 June 1988

The plaintiffs did not show up for the 'Taimu Shan' hearing. The case has attracted so much attention that it had to be moved to another hall to accommodate the auditors. Students, artists and writers from all over China came, everybody but the plaintiffs. The reason given by their counsel was that one of their six lawyers couldn't be located. A strange excuse, but the case was adjourned to a later date.

Guangzhou is in the midst of a horrible economic shudder. Every day there is a new paroxysm of panic buying, particularly savage on weekends. Every morning, tight-lipped but intent discussions of the previous evening's purchases and the next month's likely price rises. Every Tuesday afternoon, the traditional time for 'political study' gives way to new and even more brainless ideas on how to while away the idle hours of physicists and biochemists by selling breadrolls and repairing the non-existent refrigerators for increasingly impoverished students. Here are Dr Li, Dr Li and Dr Chen discussing the anticipated price rises:

Dr Li: Hai! I wanted a bicycle. An old one would do! Nothing!
Other Dr Li: You mean the 'four famous brands'? Forget it!

Dr Li: Anything! There was nothing anywhere! Finally found a cruddy old 'Golden Lion' and somebody bought it right under my nose. Can you believe it? And he already had two.

Dr Chen: You'd be better off buying clothes, anyway. Clothes are going up in July.

Dr Li: Of course, everything's going up in July. Except maybe postage stamps. They haven't gone up since liberation.

Dr Chen: That can't be right. I figure that if they really were going to raise everything, they'd do it bit by bit. They certainly wouldn't advertise it.

Dr Li: They don't. Every day the bloke on TV says nothing's going up.

Dr Chen: Well, then . . .

Dr Li: Haiii! After all these years, you still believe what the government says!

Other Dr Li: Sssh! Remember, you're a Communist!

In fact, Drs Li are both Communists, while Dr Chen is not. But the whole thing seems to be orchestrated and carefully manipulated by the speculators and middlemen, while the government stands by helplessly wringing its hands. And here are Ms Chen, a biochemist, and Mr Pan, a physicist, discussing the pressure put on them to moonlight. They are trying to decide whether to ask me to cancel some classes, so they can study for an exam given by another teacher:

Mr Pan: No use. If there's no class, I have to tend to my business.

Ms Chen: Aiya! So you're in business, too.

Mr Pan: Why, what do you do?

Ms Chen: I have to sell *doujiang* [bean milk]. No one else is willing to do it, and because I'm head of my department, I have to make the doujiang, too. If we don't sell the lot, well, then, I suppose I take the loss. My boss asked all the other people to do it, and nobody was willing, but because I'm the department leader I cannot refuse.

Mr Pan: No. I know . . . I'm a head, too.

Ms Chen: Oh, what are you doing?

Mr Pan: Fixing refrigerators. Who will you sell the doujiang to?

Ms Chen: The students! But they don't have any money either!

Mr Pan: They don't have any refrigerators, that's for sure! But at least you stay on campus!

'Hainan Fever', the great rush for jobs I noted a few months ago is definitively over. Some 90 per cent have already returned home, while those who remain are living in abysmal poverty selling things to each other. Youths from Guizhou are high on the list of hangers-on, since Guizhou's richest prefecture, considerably larger than the whole of Hainan, has a net industrial product of 3-4 million yuan annually, compared to Hainan's burgeoning 6 million. For most of the northerners, though, the money has run out. Many of the despairing head toward Guangzhou, and then they really wash up, so I expect we may look forward to a mushrooming population of highly educated criminals and hustlers. And a lot of competition for the moonlighters.

Finally, there are no more wide-eyed stories on the farmers' news programmes about Super-kulak of Panyu County who contracted half the county and got the other half to work for him. On the contrary. The news right now is of the huge contracts in Sichuan (always the pacesetter) that are just barely eking out. There is a terrible shortage of fertilizers, for one thing, and for another, they try to work the land with so few workers that the crop is not sufficiently tended or weeded and dies. So the government is now trying to discourage the too rapid displacement of rural labour by attacking the practice of contracting an unworkably large section of land, throwing the peasants off it, and employing a few of their landless sons.

Oh, and I do have a gig here next year. They have complied with all my demands. My paper at the philistines' conference was a raging success: all the Chinese sought me out, and all the foreigners (some of them touting 'Christian-centred cultural studies', ugh) shunned me. I got four job offers on the spot, immediately after my presentation, and won an award. That encouraged the management to close with me, so I have another year at this place, which actually does ease my mind somewhat. I wasn't really prepared to move.

10 October 1988

Today I got a panicky letter from TM. The trial finally took place on 6-8 September, and the results were not exactly as foreseen. It appears that the court did, as predicted, establish that the basic facts of the story were absolutely true, and that TM had no malice towards the party concerned. I am not sure of the exact sequence of events from her letter, but it is clear that a large number of peasants gave evidence in her favour, and a number of university students were present and applauded her interventions, only to be quashed by the bailiffs. Thereupon, one of the nationally famous poets who had given evidence in her favour stormed from the court. Then TM gave a long summing-up in which she said, among other things, that Chinese writers were the most underpaid in the world (either not true or misleading, depending on what you define as a writer, and what you consider pay). She was then cut short by the judge, and she too stormed from the court. Being the defendant, she had no right to do that, and I'm surprised her lawyers didn't stop her. In any case, the judges were not amused, and told her that the matter of her contempt of court would be referred to a higher court. A month later, that is, a few days ago, she was informed through her lawyers that if she did not admit grievous wrongdoing before the upper court convened they would see to it she would be found guilty (of contempt or of slander?). The prosecution is asking for a prison term and a fine of not less than fifty thousand yuan, and her lawyers were told that even if she did admit 'extremely serious errors', the punishment would only be softened to a fine of about five thousand yuan. Tang Min considers, I think probably correctly, that a guilty verdict would make both her and her husband unemployable, and she would lose the ability to publish.

12 January 1989

Tang Min now says that she was ill, recovering from a miscarriage, when she left the court, and that she did later write an apology for leaving. She wrote me a letter explaining all this a few weeks ago.

The prosecution has yet to establish any conceivable motive for libel. Even if we assume that Tang Min made no effort to verify the parts of the story that are not strictly true (for example, the story of the tailor's death: in fact, he comitted suicide in a 'Mao Thought Study Group') and simply repeated hearsay, it would not be libel unless she knew it to be untrue and repeated it with the intention of damaging the plaintiff's character. (But the dead man is not the plaintiff; the plaintiff is his widow, who changed her name to Zhu Yuqin so she could bring suit!). The prosecution keeps trying to hinge its case on something called *sixiang fanzui*, or 'thought crime'. This could have worked twenty years ago, but they can't use it now; imagine what it would do to the fledgling legal profession to establish such a precedent. Also, they must show that the story had nefarious social consequences, but at least one higher judicial official has stated that the story, as a blow against the 'ultra-left' line of the Cult Revolt (it isn't, but he apparently thinks it is), has had very good consequences.

In short, it would seem that the prosecution has everything against it. Not so. They have very skilfully managed public opinion, and the widow Zhu, by judiciously holding up a picture of her husband in front of the TV cameras, theatrically bursting into tears, and screaming obscenities in her local dialect, has managed to portray an ordinary peasant woman unfairly victimized by a pointy-headed intellectual. Nobody seems to realize that the story is really very sympathetic to her. Or who or what it is attacking. If your sympathies are sneaking to the widow I think you should firmly rein them in. She is no longer a village woman; she is a powerful cadre in a county seat of some tens of thousands of people. This county seat, by the way, is a hotbed of corruption, being the capital of one of the province's poorest areas and just down the road from one of the country's richest, Wenzhou. The local bureaucracy, that great, sullen, counter-revolutionary force that has plodded on through man-made disaster after disaster, is solidly behind her.

Tang Min is certain that the verdict will go against her, and her lawyer seems to agree. I am not so certain. The court seems very anxious to get an out-of-court settlement, and save everybody's face. That would be the Chinese thing to do.

13 February 1989

He Shang was a television series broadcast last summer; was, because its scheduled rebroadcast has been cancelled, and it has for all practical purposes been banned. The title means 'River Elegy', and, as that indicates, it was the sort of light-minded, heavy-hearted pessimism of which angstful young intellectuals are so enamoured: the reason for the stagnation of Chinese civilization, you see, is not the imperialist development of the productive forces of the whole world for the benefit of the West, nor is it the heavy burden of over-population, nor the exhaustion or scarcity of the soil, because these real factors are not so changeable and more conducive to real pessimism. No. It is entirely the work of the Chinese national character. The problem is the way they think, as reflected in the national symbols they have chosen: the Yellow River, a capricious, silt-choked, ponderous waterway, given to floods and ill-suited to navigation; the Great Wall, a purely defensive, conservative structure, reflecting isolationism, smugness and a total lack of that wonderful, outgoing, friendly, entrepreneurial spirit of the West, so prominent in the Opium Wars; the Dragon, a species of dinosaur so extinct it never existed. If only, if only . . . we Chinese had national symbols and a national ideology that were not so hidebound, so reactionary, so atrociously passive and narrow, if only we had a national ideology that really conformed to the rousing enterprising spirit of the Third Plenum of the Eleventh Central Committee, etc.

Now, if the CCP contained any serious Marxists, it would have been pretty easy to dispose of this rather silly, anti-materialist stuff. Even the *Far Eastern Economic Review* did a pretty good job on it, pointing out that just like the 'rebels' of the Cult Revolt, and the tame critics of recent years, *He Shang* lashed only the ancestors and paid staunch lip service to the status quo. (It was for this reason that it had support at top levels, including, so they say, Zhao Ziyang.) But the CCP is Stalinist to the core, and Zhao Ziyang is on the wane because of the economic anarchy of last summer, so Wang Zhen was allowed to let fall, during the celebrations held to mark the 30th anniversary of the founding of Ningxia Autonomous Region, that he considered recent attacks on national symbols like the Great Wall and the Dragon to be attacks on the Chinese people and on Chineseness in general, cowardly and dastardly ones at that. And that was the end of the dastardly series.

Well. Here we have the philistines in full dress. The ban is thoroughly wrong, especially since it lends authority and an aura of importance and even originality to a series which in no way deserves such distinction, and it also stands in the way of exposing the real flaws. And on top of the ban, we now have a turgid campaign in the press against something called 'cultural nihilism', no names named, nothing specific or useful or even critical in the usual sense, to further confuse matters. This is a time-honoured technique for engaging in artistic and cultural struggle that was pioneered by Yao Wenyuan in his critique of *Hai Rui Dismissed from Office* (which sparked off the Cultural Revolution), if not before.

The tendency to take the opposite position to that of the bureaucracy, whatever it may be, is a rather healthy one for

369

young Chinese intellectuals, though of course facile and self-serving for non-Chinese journalists. I only wish there had been more of it in evidence during the recent riots in Nanjing, when the government unambiguously sided with Chinese students against the Africans. But this attitude shares with the bureaucracy a common assumption: that the poverty and backwardness of the country can be blamed entirely on the incorrect thinking of the people. Then the struggle to modernize the country is not at all a class struggle, or a political struggle, or even fundamentally a material struggle; it is simply a matter of thinking correct thoughts and imbibing the marvellous magical medicine of capitalist management practices compounded by Lee Iacocca and Donald Trump. Maoism is not so very incompatible with *Fortune* magazine, not in the long run.

Which brings me, of all places, to Shenzhen, where I have just been doing research for the *Rough Guide*, for nowhere in China is there a place where the belief that you can alter your economic and social being by merely adjusting your thoughts (so very flattering to the young intellectual's self-esteem) is so strong. And nowhere more pathetic.

The first scene is a rather expensive restaurant by the seaside in Shekou. (Cheap restaurants are very hard to find in the Special Economic Zone, and I have just cycled 40 kilometres without breakfast.) The waitress is flustered when I address her in Cantonese and replies in English.

Me: Your English is better than your Cantonese. You must be from the north.
She: Yes, I'm from Lanzhou. Well, not from Lanzhou, but I went to the University there.
Me (abashed; I thought only America had college-educated waitresses): And how long have you been here?
She: A year now, I guess. I taught in Lanzhou for about three years after graduating, and then got fed up, so I up and quit and here I am.
Me: Oh. How did you get residence here? I mean, do you have a temporary residence permit, or what?

(Residence permits for Shenzhen are very hard to get, rather like green cards in the United States. It is, however, fairly easy to get a temporary permit that entitles you to starvation wages and immediate deportation when your contract is up.) *She* (more abashed and slightly worried; who is this guy, an agent for immigration control, or what?): I don't have one, actually. I just came and settled. And, well, maybe in a month or two I'll get a temporary one. I hope.

Me: Yeah? Well, how is it? Do you like it here?

She: Oh, of course. Why, it's much better than Lanzhou.

Me: Better than teaching? Really? Why?

She: Oh, you mean that. Well, I guess not. But, of course, the money . . .

Me: Is the money that much better?

She: Well, not really. I mean, I made about 80 yuan a month in Lanzhou, and that wasn't enough, I couldn't save anything. Here I make about 400 a month –

Both of us together: – and that's not enough and I can't save anything!

She: Plus, you know, rent is terribly expensive, especially when you don't have a permit and have to sublet from someone who has. But I don't go out much. We work all the time, and when I finish I don't even have the energy to read.

Me: So why is it better, then?

She: Well . . . the weather is nicer. And Lanzhou is so polluted. But which do you like? Have you ever been to the north?

Me: Yes, and I like Lanzhou. I mean, here life is so inconvenient. If you're very rich, well, it's okay, but so is it anywhere. Take just now. I was trying to find a bike repairman to raise the seat of my bike, and there wasn't one for four kilometres, just petrol stations and big factories. And no small restaurants for ordinary people, just this place. And tonight I'll stay in my hotel room because there's really nothing to do here in the evening that costs less than 100 yuan, right?

She: You can watch TV. Hong Kong channel.

Me (thinking maybe I won't stay in after all): Don't you ever

371

miss Lanzhou? Longju and teahouses? 'Dragon Eye' tea? Sheepskin coats?

She: Oh, no. I'm really from Changsha anyway. And besides, here we young people have no one to tell us what to do, we are free to be creative and to work to the best of our abilities. Not like up north. Here people are much more open-minded. What you say may be true, about the cultural life. But what difference does it make if I have no time? Sometimes, though, I think if I could go anywhere and do anything, I would leave here.

Me (glancing at the lights of Hong Kong visible across the water, fairly certain what she is going to say): Where would you go?

She: Guangzhou!

Well, there are plenty of people in Guangzhou who'd trade their residence permits for hers, as soon as it comes through; most of my colleagues would kill for a chance to wait creatively on tables and fold napkins to the utmost of their abilities.

The next scene takes place in the Shenzhen museum, where I'm busy imbibing production figures from graphs and displays. The museum is, along with the library, a perfect symbol of the place: a tall, four-storey building with three glass lifts whizzing from the crow's nest to the hold, a corridor snaking around a huge impressive open pit – everything, in short, except for contents. It's virtually empty. Understandable, I guess; history began here ten years ago. There are no visitors, either. The admission charge is two yuan, and the Shenzhenese, as the guide explains, don't go out much: 'Not like us northerners. Why, in Nanjing I went to museums every Sunday.'

Me: Yes? How long have you been here?

She: About a year and half.

Me: Do you like it?

She: Oh, yes. Up north, you know, there is so little freedom to do things. People are so conservative. You can't use your own abilities. Here there are so many new ideas.

Me: What kind of new ideas?

She: I mean, about management. You know, up north nobody works hard because they don't have to. But here there is a kind of lively, creative management outlook; it motivates people.

Me: For example?

She: Well, we learn the new management techniques from abroad and apply them flexibly.

Me: Really?

She: Sure. You know, the rest of China is very jealous of us. But we make more money because we earn more. We work harder . . . and we have an inspired way of thinking about the economy.

At this point I put it to her that they make more money because they are heavily subsidized by the government, not only directly, but through being allowed to engage in speculation and profiteering strictly forbidden in the rest of the country.

She: There is something in what you say. But trade is also a form of construction, you know.

Me: Speaking of construction, how is Shenzhen getting along with the freeze on capital construction? Is that going to affect things here?

She: No. The last part of 1988 (when the freeze was in effect) was even better than the first, and 1988 was our best year ever.

Me: What about industrial shutdowns?

She: Oh, that was due to lack of raw materials. We don't have that problem in Shenzhen.

Me: How's that?

She: We . . . have connections.

Of course they don't have these problems; they cause them. In point of fact, Shenzhen was at the centre of a vast network of *guan dao*, the wave of bureaucratic profiteering that is seriously referred to in the press as 'bureaucratic state capitalism'. When the rest of the country was experiencing a serious contraction of production in order to combat the overheating of the economy, Shenzhen was having its best year ever. And while the rest of the country sacrifices real production in order to counteract the distorting effects of the phoney, unproductive sectors of the economy – the *pibao gongsi* ('briefcase companies', set up for purely speculative purposes), the hoarding and profiteering and inflationary 'expansions' – Shenzhen is sacrosanct.

I never did find out exactly what this 'flexibility' that she kept talking about as the key to Shenzhen's 'inspired economic thinking' was. But she did mention short-term contracts, and how they have helped ensure a cheap and docile labour force for the increasing flight of Hong Kong capital across the border. Hong Kong steadfastly refuses to allow in Chinese labour, despite its acute labour shortage, so various companies, including the Hong Kong-owned ones, are voting with their well-heeled feet and setting up in Shenzhen, where a strange utterly polarized society now exists. The contract labourers from Shantou, Meixian, Hunan, Shandong and Hui'an Xian live alongside the 20,000 or so original residents, who, by dint of their rights to land, have all become coupon clippers, rentiers and factory managers, burning money every night in the five-star hotels. There are big Sanyo factories in Shekou, too, with armies of young women workers with thick Hunan accents, like a whole Hunanese village erupting from the factory gates at the sound of the whistle. Asbestos shanties spread like lung cancers around Shekou, Shenzhen and the other manufacturing centres of the SEZ, and everywhere there are big red paper posters advertising help wanted from the floating labour force.

Back in Guangzhou the mood is very *fin de siècle*. All the guidebooks quote the old saw that everything new starts in Guangzhou. They don't mention that it gets old and falls apart first here, too. I remember when I was in Hainan back in '84 they had to schedule regular daytime power cuts in order to free up the grid for industry. They seem to be doing the same thing in Guangzhou now. There is hardly ever power in the middle of the day, when I have to use a tape recorder or video in class.

During the evening blackouts, an eerie sort of anarchy prevails, a kind of verbal looting by young thugs hanging out in sidewalk restaurants, talking about it but never doing it. None of the traffic lights work, but the traffic flow doesn't seem markedly more homicidal than usual. The nightly news, when there is power, carries stories of an anti-corruption drive, but they defeat the purpose of reassuring the public. One was about a cadre who exposed a racketeering superior and was expelled from the Communist Party. Another about a racketeer who was fined two months' salary and his unit fined about 10,000 yuan for half a year's profits totalling half a million yuan!

And now the reasons for the sudden tabling of reform for the next two years become obvious. They have little to do with the gross deformations of the economy; many of those deformations are the goal and not the side-effects of reform: inflation, unemployment, liberalized enforcement of tax regulations, 'incentives' for racketeers and profiteers, 'big business' and 'little government', all good IMF, Reaganite, Thatcherite slogans. The real reason, one suspects, is that we are now emerging from the biggest strike wave in anyone's memory. The other day, the head of the All-China Federation of Unions gave an interview during their national conference in which he blamed the strikes on 'bureaucratic management', an obvious attempt to put a pro-reform twist to the movement. The biggest strike he cited, however, in Xiaoshan City of Zhejiang, was over bonuses, and the longest, some 1,100 workers on strike for three months, was over something called 'workers rights'.

Like you, I am a real pessimist. I think the real problems are not susceptible to easy political solutions: the scarcity of land, the surplus of people, and above all the strangling grip of imperialism on world capital markets. But it was those problems, not the phoney solutions, that, as you put it,

375

'initially bound (me) to China and the Chinese'. And even if I had to live another year in the full blast of the evil winds, I couldn't share your type of pessimism. After all, I don't think the current (stalled and partially repudiated) reforms are anything but a few people getting very rich. I don't believe they are a revolutionary or counter-revolutionary transformation of the whole society.

I never believed there was anything particularly socialist about most people staying poor, as I made clear in my early, horrified letters when I first got here. I have faith neither in poverty, nor in getting rich, neither in the reforms, nor in the temporary repudiation of them. Where my pessimism parts company with yours is not here but abroad. I can't believe the imperialist stranglehold will last; it can't go on. The imperialist democracies are not getting rich by producing wealth; you and I both know that is Thatcherite cant. They are getting rich by impoverishing their own lower classes, and particularly the lower hemisphere of their planet. Even assuming, as you do, that that won't lead to a revolutionary explosion and will simply proceed apace until the vast majority of the planet is starving to pay for their Marlboros and Cokes and Toyotas, a parasite that kills the host organism must itself die. And then China, which has been struggling with real problems and not purely artificial ones, will inherit the earth, an overcrowded, poor and messy place.

China is the future: it is more crowded, more cultured, less private, less individualized – and, despite everything, it does work. It is, despite the terrible poverty, a higher stage of civilization than Thatcher's Britain, just as France in the late 18th century was a higher stage than Britain, although far, far poorer, and in some ways more violent and cruel. I believe the same thing holds for most of the struggles China faces today, and that is one reason why, no matter how horrid and inflationary things get, I'm staying. China represents the future.

13 | Things fall apart

Guangzhou, 12 March 1989

Dear D & B,

Thanks for forwarding the money. The day I dispatched Liu's hoard, martial law was declared in Lhasa. I saw film clips of the riots on the nightly news (there is certainly no 'news blackout'; Lhasa has been the major story for over a week now). The riots were concentrated at the eastern end of the street where Liu works. The big granite buildings on Jokhang Square, built by Fujianese stone cutters when Nick and I were there, have been largely demolished. Li, the painter who accompanied Liu and me to Samye in '87 (and who has spent all his life in Tibet and worked on murals in the Jokhang), lived in one of those buildings. Also, the restaurants and shops owned by Muslims and *getihu*, or private businessmen, were looted, gutted, and often burnt level with the pavement. A pogrom. I can't see any way out except this: the Dalai Lama must come back and take up the place of the dead Panchen himself.

The latest scam here is no scam at all: Guangdong is allowed to play the black market quite legally. Major companies, as in Shanghai, are allowed to change hard currency earnings into RMB at the black market rate, in addition to not having to turn any over to the state. Well, that means they can use their cheap source of RMB to outbid their neighbours and to buy up produce from Fujian, Guanxi and Hunan, export the lot for still more foreign exchange, and so on, ad infinitum, ensuring that the super profits do not trickle down, or in, and starving the neighbours of foreign exchange.

377

The interior provinces, in turn, are resorting to 'trickle out' economics. In addition to exporting their produce to Guangdong, they are exporting huge numbers of thieves, pimps, whores, beggars, and 'unproductive' pedlars and service people. Seriously, this is *the* social problem in Guangzhou, and it is talked about in the same tone as last summer's inflation.

27 April 1989

As you must know, there's a lot going on. It's much bigger than '86, and it's going to go a lot farther. There are rumours, rumours everywhere. Ms Lin told me yesterday that Beijing was under virtual martial law and the big armed division numbering 20,000 that is used for drowning unrest in bloody rest has been moved in. Today that appears to be rubbish. But there are new open letters and new 'big character posters' daily in our college, of all places. Equality. Freedom. 'Seize equality and struggle for freedom!' 'When will the real educational reform come?' And today the workers have joined in, 100,000 in Beijing.

However much I like the sound of it all, I have lost much of my enthusiasm for the student movement after Nanjing [the anti-African student agitations]. The main student columns in Beijing have slogans and demands that are even more minimalist than the vague niceties of '86: 'Dialogue with Power.' 'Stop Corruption.' 'Reform Thoroughly.' If the regime would merely agree to the extremely modest demands being put forward, the student movement would quickly succeed to death. Only the utter intransigence of the regime will prolong it. (Incredibly, the regime has even refused the demand for a 're-evaluation of Hu Yaobang', choosing merely to ignore his supposed mistakes; thus the official propaganda is considerably *less* critical than the students'!) Already the government has declared that the aims of the CCP are the same as those of the students. Very possibly true. They are both unpleasantly anti-socialist and pro-Western, and neither has confronted the only foreign models that would be helpful here: the USSR and Hungary.

378

Imagine it, the whole country is on the verge of rioting, and the only issues the students dare raise are 'dialogue' and 'Hu Yaobang', two utter non-issues. A friend of mine just came back from Beijing and Xi'an and told me about the riots in the latter (thousands of young lumpens burning cars and buses), and the sit-in in the former (clouds of small character posters in English and Chinese being carefully copied by students around the Monument to the People's Heroes). The student movement is bound to start ebbing after May 4, but the underlying social unrest?

13 May 1989

Neither Liu nor TM have yet acknowledged the money or the publications I sent them. I don't think the money matter is serious; I sent it via the Bank of China, and I have receipts. However, Lhasa is still under martial law, Liu's street was one of the centres of the rioting, and TM has legal difficulties to attend to. It is worrisome.

There is no smarm here about 'capitalist work ethic'; the ideology of capitalism here is unabashed laziness and unbridled greed. There may be unrest in China, but Guangzhou is fat and lazy. And poor and lazy. My students, who are so utterly destitute that nearly all their salaries must go for food, and who must beg from their parents to add to the minuscule wardrobes they must spend half their waking hours washing by hand, are some of the laziest and most sluggish I have ever taught. It isn't the laziness of the capitalist non-work ethic – the knowledge now enjoyed by Guangzhou's getihu that they will get filthy-rich without having to produce wealth – or even the selective hustle of the corrupt and bribery-prone elements of the bureaucracy. There just doesn't seem to be anything at all that motivates them. The sullen apathy of the seriously malnourished, maybe. I've noticed that a steady diet of canteen food has a bad effect on me, both mentally and physically, so I make it a rule to cook on weekends. But they do not.

Yet things are happening even here. There has been sharp criticism of the Party Secretary for his very dubious activities in the name of reform. An open letter, run off by an anonymous in the computer department, is making the rounds:

Comrade Party Secretary:

The democratic review is about to take place. Please therefore address the following matters as they deserve in your work report.

1) After the meeting on the mobilization of education reform, that is, after the Central Committee called for an increase in open and aboveboard dealings, you suddenly abolished the college leadership open house day. Does this or does this not constitute ignoring our Party's mass line policy?

2) During a certain discussion meeting, upon hearing a teacher criticize your work, you instructed the lower ranks not to be 'too arrogant'. Doesn't this indicate that you lack the breadth of spirit and frankness required of a Party Secretary? You then went and abolished the system of holding discussion meetings altogether. Were you afraid of people's criticism?

3) As head of the College Trades Union, do you assume responsibility for the fact that in more than two and a half years no form of meeting whatsoever has been held, and no explanation given? This is a clear violation of the State Council of Education Educational Trades Union Representative Council Articles of 1985, Article 4, 'Provisional Regulations'. Doesn't this imply you are not willing to push forward the democratic administrative system of founding an academic council? How can this inspire confidence? Do you still believe that the qualifications of a Party Secretary include the ability to organize and coordinate the interests of all sides, or not?

4) You often occupy the Crown automobile for your personal use, but you refuse to lend it out for the use of other personnel of our school. What does this show?

5) At a meeting on housing allocation, you contested the right of a teacher to a larger and better flat in order to allocate it to

your son, although he in fact works for another unit. And you asked others to take smaller rooms. Is this the kind of attitude the Party Secretary should have?

6) During a meeting on remuneration (which did not go through the new Academic Council. Is this proper?) you increased your own share some 60 per cent. But most cadre, teachers and workers got increases of around ten per cent. Is this the spirit of 'crossing a dangerous strait together', the spirit of the Central Committee? (One must point out that since we are not a private enterprise, you are not a contractor who has taken risks. Is taking that much more justified?)

7) During the last trip by the Public Health Department to Hong Kong on business, why did you, who do not work for the Public Health Department, insist on going? Is this or is this not an unhealthy tendency?

8) Although you apparently have no controversial plans for reforming our work, you have issued quite a few circulars on the subject. Does this indicate that you lack the necessary ability? Or is it that you are basically unwilling to make a start? Don't you think you have talked enough, given that the things you should have accomplished have rarely been accomplished?

9) In the recent business of the refrigerators, our college lost about 200,000 yuan (that is, our capital). Do you take responsibility for this affair? In an institute of about 800 people, that is equivalent to about 250 yuan less in pay per person.

10) Where do you think our institute is at in the reforms? We all know that, according to the upper echelons, 'teachers are the crux of the reforms'. Have you paid any attention to this? We think that what you pay most attention to is whether or not teachers put in an appearance at your fixed weekly political study meetings. Do you think this is the way to stimulate enthusiasm for reform? Doesn't this eloquently testify to the limitations of your policies and principles?

A youth who hopes for a flourishing college

A few notes for the uninitiated: The Party Secretary is a consummate Party hack with no credentials for educational work whatever. He does not have any academic post, but maintains his very considerable power over the the school solely by virtue of his Party post. Now, according to the separation of Party and state, a principle established at the 13th Party Congress (but paid lip service to long before), people like him should not exist. Oh, he does have one other post. He is – don't laugh – our trade union leader!

The 'remunerations' referred to are a bit puzzling unless you know that since the big reforms I talked about a while back, a very large part of a teacher's income depends on how much money his or her department has managed to scrape up through money making activities on the side. For example, Ms Chen, the biochemist, having lost out on her doujiang venture, turned to selling foetal liver cells to hospitals, and made quite a killing. However, when the money at last trickled down to those who had made it possible, it worked out to ten or fifteen yuan a head. The thing is that the money is distributed by and often to the leaders, neatly defeating the utterly spurious rationale of the reform, which was to fire the ground troops with enthusiasm and self-interest. The Party Secretary, who to my knowledge has not fixed any refrigerators or sold any doujiang, has clearly qualified himself for a large share of almost all the profits.

The business of the refrigerators was a straightforward exercise in bureaucratic speculation. The PS apparently thought the school could turn a quick profit by importing refrigerators and reselling them to remote areas of Guangdong. The product turned out to be hopelessly inferior, and most of the units didn't function at all, making them unsaleable. The resulting loss is, as the writer points out, a spectacular dent in buying power for the average teacher, representing over a month's salary. The fact that this sort of thing is probably illegal has not come up, but I'm pretty sure it is. I wonder what real capitalists, let alone real educationists, would make of all this. Pathetic, isn't it?

So what happened? Well, meetings were held. The target of the letter got up and acknowledged that the substance of the letter was true and challenged the audience to try to do something about it. And that was it.

Then the demonstrations began, and posters went up on the *gaolan*, the bulletin board: 'When will real education reform arrive?' (Cor, you'd think they'd had enough of that one!) 'Struggle for democracy, seize equality!' Equality! There's a new one. We didn't hear that in '86. Freedom and Science don't have the same electrifying effect on me that they had in 1919, when the May 4th movement broke out under Li Dazhao and Chen Duxiu, so I was sitting here watching a cobweb catch flies while Ms A sat opposite me last night talking glowingly of things like 'press freedom' and 'multi-party system'. But equality! That's my slogan, that's the one I want to march behind, that's the slogan for the students who have been pauperized by the getihu and the speculators. It's the slogan for teachers and workers, and even for the lumpen elements in Changsha and Xi'an who went out and started looting to try to raise the train fare home. Equality! If the student movement will get behind that one, they will face a working class with open arms.

I'm afraid there is some way to go before the students really get behind it, though. The truth of the matter is that the Beijing student movement is not terribly democratic, at least not in the sense of being representative. Symptomatic, yes, but representative, no. Their tactics and their slogans all indicate a pressure movement, anxious to be kept informed, consulted, dialogued to, thrown scraps, and tolerated, but not anxious to take a really active part in economic affairs. Which is too bad. We badly need someone to step in and give the economy some direction; there is a planned economy still, but no plan any more, and the longer we delay the stronger become the forces that would like to see the whole thing go up in one big bang of enterprise and price reform. Those forces hardly have the interests of education and social progress in mind, still less the working class.

Yet I wonder. The fact that 100,000 people, many of them unemployed workers, staged illegal demonstrations, not once but twice, and less than a dozen people were injured, is incredible. And already, before explicitly social demands were raised by the movement, the government has taken steps to reverse the 'optimum deployment' policy (that is, making unproductive workers redundant) in an attempt to keep the unemployed off the streets. Everyone except the students seems to know what is really at stake.

I think the workers were more anxious to embrace the students than vice-versa. The students are extremely anxious to separate themselves from any incitement to strikes. Of course, they immediately repudiated the riots in Changsha and Xi'an, and so do I, but I know that a student movement that does not at some point embrace social unrest is doomed to fail. Or rather 'succeed'. The current student movement as of now has no goals different from the stated goals of the CCP. Many of their leaders are Communist Youth or Party members, in contrast to 1986. They march, sometimes cynically, but sometimes not, behind banners that say things like: 'Long live the correct leadership of the CCP'!

The demonstration here in Guangzhou, a largish affair that occupied much of Jiefang Beilu on the night of May 4, chanted the bizarre slogan 'Long Live Chairman Mao, Long Live the Communist Party, Long Live Democracy'. This was a tongue-in-cheek answer to Zhao's half-hearted endorsement of the demos that was utterly lost on the bystanding workers, and initially quite lost on me. The student leaders have been quite good at sticking to the constitution and trying to force the authorities to do so too by example. Yet the lack of an independent programme, which is bringing them closer to the CCP and apparent victory, is going to cut them off from the masses and any hope of real victory. The difference between the student movement and the CCP is that the students are sincere and behaving in an orderly fashion, while the government is in chaos, preparing a rotten compromise, but unsure just when and how to go back on it.

Yet these differences are not as great as they appear. The absence of any programme two years after the '86 demonstrations indicates a certain amount of cant on the part of student leaders, a willingness to sacrifice real movement for the sake of a large movement that really isn't moving. And of course there are lots of Communists who are seriously concerned about the state of the country and with the students. Dr B tells me, 'They were right in 1919; they are just as right today.' But everybody now knows that the social situation in China is explosive, and nobody wants more Changsha and more Xi'an.

Hu Yaobang is a strange sort of hero for a student movement, unless you understand how utterly friendless Chinese intellectuals now feel, surrounded by a rising tide of nouveaux riches, and hemmed in by a virulently anti-intellectual bureaucracy. Short, inarticulate, and given to grandiose pronouncements made on whirlwind tours, he had apparently promised too much to too many people on too many occasions, and these promises were stored up for use against him by that great Stalinist Machiavelli, Deng. The '86 protests were a good pretext to get rid of him, that is all. There were rumours that Hu had wanted to make a comeback, but had refused the partial rehabilitation that was offered, and that his death on April 15, during the plenum, was partly due to exertions on this score.

At any rate, he was missed. Just after his death, posters began to go up at Renmin Daxue [People's University] and a few other places, and the student protests began to take shape. They were incredibly effective in anticipating the moves by the bureaucracy to hem them in. When Tiananmen was sealed off for the funeral, the police arrived on the scene to discover that they would have to lock in about a thousand students. Also, the Autonomous University Students' Federation replaced its odd UN Security Council-style structure with a more democratic one that takes decisions by majority vote, so that, when, on 4 May, Beida and Qinghua, the two most prestigious schools, tried to veto a march, they were forced to participate by majority vote.

Beida and Qinghua are rightly considered the two most conservative schools. They are science and technology-oriented, with relatively few of the history, philosophy and social science students that normally provide the catalyst for demonstrations. The most active schools seem to be the Shifan Xueyuan, that is, the Teachers' College, and Renmin Daxue (it was the students of the latter, Renda, who tried to storm Zhongnanhai [the government leaders' enclosure] on the evening of 18 April). One pundit in the *South China Morning Post* pointed out that one of the reasons for their incredible bravery was that, as China's future teachers, they had very, very little to lose.

To me, the most ominous development is that the student movement, instead of raising truly radical social demands, is simply becoming more strident and 'self-sacrificing' in the peculiarly Eastern way – white headbands, hunger strikes, spectacular suicides and bloodcurdling oaths about dying on Tiananmen. This false radicalism is of course much easier than organizing so that the real enemies do the sacrificing, and it also corresponds quite neatly to the utterly desperate position of the Chinese teacher, particularly the humanities teacher. Why not starve to death on Tiananmen? It is only more public than doing so in a stinking bachelors' dorm in a middle school in Hebei. False radicalism, but very seductive, combining Zen ideas with the slogans of Patrick Henry, along with extraordinary programmatic timidity.

When Ms A told me breathlessly, 'On the day of Hu Yaobang's funeral, ten students went and kneeled on the steps of the Great Hall of the People to present their petition, and some of the onlookers wept,' I said, 'So what?' Ms A said, 'You don't understand, because you are a foreigner. In China, you kneel only to the Emperor. To kneel shows . . . well, imagine the level of desperation to which the students had been reduced, imagine the humiliation they are willing to endure.' And this is supposed to be a democracy movement?

Now, here are some questions posed by the student leaders in the 'dialogue' held between them and Yuan Mu and a few other bureaucrats:

386

Q: Yesterday, during the demonstration of 100,000, the people of Beijing saw us, some marched with us, many gave us water and bread, or stood on the rooftops chanting 'Long live the students'. Some were in tears, moved by our militancy and patriotism. Doesn't this show that the masses of China are behind us?

A: I think I already answered that question. No, it does not.

Q: Given that Hu Yaobang was a brilliant leader who made outstanding contributions to reform and had a very positive role in the leadership of the country through a very difficult period, is it not unusual that no mention should be made or reason given for his sudden resignation in January, 1987, and this more than two years after the fact and now that he is dead? Does this or does it not indicate an abnormal internal life in the Communist Party?

A: (after considerable circumlocution): It does not.

Q: Who is the biggest speculator in China?

A: (laughter and visible contempt for the questioner).

At first I was a bit thrown by that last question. How could anybody know that? They don't usually advertise. But in fact it was a very pointed reference to the son of Deng Xiaoping, who was severely crippled by Red Guards during the Cult Revolt, and now heads the federation of the handicapped. He also heads a company heavily implicated in the largest single bureaucrat-speculation case uncovered to date.

The contempt and condescension of Yuan Mu for the students was even clearer at a press conference given for the students the next day. He ridiculed their effrontery in demanding to meet with officials of higher rank than his august self (he is only a mouthpiece with no power), and repeatedly told reporters how much he personally loved and cherished the little students. And he was talking to a group of students he had handpicked himself!

The real student organization, the Autonomous Federation, which was thrown up during the protests, remains unrecognized and 'illegal'. The government has disingenuously refused to meet with it for 'fear of sowing discord' in student ranks. Upon hearing this, the 'legal' student leaders, who overwhelmingly sympathize with the movement, resigned. It is essential for the Autonomous Federation to achieve recognition, at the very least. Otherwise the repression will be terrible. Let's have more talk of that and less of leaving their corpses on Tiananmen Square!

20 May 1989

Since Wednesday my classroom has been padlocked, with the following notice, which I scrawled in explanation: 'In solidarity with the Beijing strikers, there will be no English class today.' Nevertheless, as classes begin and other students organize for marches on the provincial government, I stand outside the classroom to hand out homework and talk politics.

Today especially. Last night, at about one o'clock in the morning, when my flat was still full of students, 'important news', that is, bad news, was announced. ('They always announce "important news" late at night', remarked one student.) The army has marched on Tiananmen, the government has forbidden further hunger strikes and demonstrations, and the students have tried to call off the hunger strike – unsuccessfully. This morning Zhao Ziyang is absent, and posters up all over the school, which were first dismissed as rumours, telling in detail how he delivered six suggestions for dealing leniently and in a peaceful manner with the crisis, and was accused by Deng of splitting the Central Committee; whereupon, he resigned.

It is raining, and a 46-year-old physician has cycled all the way across town in the downpour to attend a class I will not hold. I feel a bit embarrassed as he climbs the stone stairs, past walls fairly sloughing off the coloured paper of democracy. 'Bad news, Dr A,' I tell him, meaning the class. He looks up and I see his face is soaked. 'My heart is black,' he says, his voice breaking all over the place. It's not the rain and it's not the class. 'My China,' he says. The other student who has come is a cardiologist and an officer in the PLA.

388

There is a certain humour in the hostility with which Dr A greets his classmate, and Dr B is sheepish. When I talk to him, he looks at the floor, but Dr A looks at the peeling wall posters and weeps unrestrained.

(While writing these lines, I am listening to a maddeningly placid bovine creature read out the declaration of martial law in Peking by Chen Xitong.)

Where to begin. A week ago, I guess. It was a bit irksome for us in Guangzhou to watch the hunger strikers in Beijing assemble with white headbands reading 'Mourning for the Nation' that Friday afternoon. Not just because of the well-known Cantonese love of a good feed, but because the movement was so slow in arriving here. We were still in the very cheerful initial phase, the 'festival of the oppressed', and people were taking to the streets with an almost hippyish nonchalance. The first demos here were small and not much noticed by anyone. The first one to reach a thousand was the Zhongshan University march on May 4th, and that seemed to be about half policemen.

The first really big ones were jolly affairs, with ten thousand students chanting 'You poor, hardworking cops' at the green hordes who good-naturedly directed traffic for us. Even Ms C, a grim-faced young woman from Xinjiang with ample experience of the '86 demos and their aftermath, said, 'We've been under for so long it feels good to let go and not worry about the consequences'. The bloodcurdling oaths to fast unto death struck us as almost killjoy.

(It's pouring rain. Our school's contingent just left for the provincial government building in the first really illegal march. It was both big and angry. The student strike, which was at barely two-thirds strength before the interdiction of student strikes, is absolutely total today. I ran into one teacher who normally has a class of 200 on Saturday morning; today, exactly one showed up.)

Our own institute, Guangyao, was the very latest of the late. It really wasn't until the third day of the strike, when fifty students had collapsed from the fast, that anything

substantial went up on the bulletin boards. Even then, as Y
pointed out, it was more poetical than political:

TO THE HUNGER STRIKERS OF BEIJING
You are our true warriors.
You are giving your lives for the awakening of the masses.
You have brought the sweet dew of freedom, equality and
democracy to the parched land.
You have turned a fresh page of history.
Some say this is fomenting chaos.
Some say this is all a plot.
Some say you have been duped.
Some say you are naive and childish.
But that is the deception.
That is the plot.
That is the unwillingness to look reality squarely in the face.
That is the unwillingness to see people as they are.
Engels said it long ago: 'Where has there ever been a great
historically progressive step taken without a huge historical
disaster?' From disaster to awakening, from misfortune to
prosperity, the responsibilities of our generation can no longer
be postponed. Your warm blood has fertilized and shaken the
thousand-year-old tree to its roots. The corrupt and withered
leaves have been shaken to earth. It is the swan song of the old
world and the herald of a new epoch.

On Tuesday some agitators from Qinghua arrived and made
contact with our students. They put up several posters that
said 'Guangyao Students, where were you?', referring to our
absence from the demonstrations in front of the Provincial
Government. They also put up this little leaflet, hectographed
some days before in Beijing:

A WARNING TO PATRIOTIC COMPATRIOTS
Beloved compatriots, when you hear the broadcasts that label
the broad mass movement of university students as an incitement to chaos, when you read the reports that describe the
savage repression unleashed by the Xi'an police as 'protecting
public order', you will surely be shocked by the boundless gall
of the government. When the government handpicks a few
obedient students to take part in the so-called dialogue of
29 April, while the students' real representatives present

preconditions that are scoffed at by the government, the government adds the insult of 'muddle-head' and 'fomentor of chaos' to them, and foists an illegitimate student organization upon us.

Before a government like this, we are momentarily powerless and helpless. How can weak students hope to react? We understand, however, that the development of the nation, the purging of bureaucratic rottenness and the conquest of democratic freedoms cannot be left to the initiative of others; it all depends on us. Although we have no other channels open in our dealings with this bone-gnawing government, we at least have our own flesh and blood, our own necks and heads to lay on the line, to push for the people's interests. We are ready to sacrifice all for the interests of the nation.

The participation of 400 students of various colleges and universities in Beijing in the hunger strike in Tiananmen demonstrates how we reject the label of chaos and articulates our demand for dialogue. The broad masses of students have responded to us, but the hunger strike is not a goal per se, it is only a way to honest dialogue. We are forced to carry out actions like this, and, on the other hand, to send our people out to spread the news of this movement, to organize students and student movement guards to keep order among our pickets and to protect the health of the hunger strikers, especially in the event that police violence should take place.

Compatriots, society is the common property of everyone. The nation belongs to us all. If we don't say this, who will say it? We are willing to give our blood and our youth to awaken the people.

'We want no condescending saviours to rule us from their judgement halls . . . Let us all decide for ourselves!'

Qinghua University, 13 May

This went up on the 16th, along with a call for a strike, which Ms C and I and a few other teachers heeded that afternoon.

(They are broadcasting and rebroadcasting Li Peng's speech to the assembled cadres and military men. Yang

Shangkun is going on and on about the terrible inconvenience he experienced trying to reschedule the various events for the welcoming of Mr Gorbachev. Ms C snorted: 'He's a foreigner; this is our country, and we can do what we feel we need to do.' I agree. But also, one of his complaints is that it took him an hour and a half to get to the airport because of the marches. Shit, that's what it normally takes, unless you're an official.)

We then went down to the Provincial Government. I was amazed. It was already as big as what I saw in Beijing in '86, and a lot more militant. The headbands read 'Elegy for the Nation', and the mood of the hunger strikers was made even more sombre by the fact that the Chinese sit-in, or *jingzuo*, apparently forbids speaking. Of course, most of the slogans were on the order of: 'Down with bureaucracy, up with democracy!' But names were being named: Deng Pufang, the son of Xiaoping, and two sons of Zhao Ziyang, among others. 'Free speech! Free press! Rule by law, not by man!' 'Support the hunger-striking heroes!' And best of all: 'The anti-bureaucracy inspectorate should not be under party members of the same rank as those it inspects!' So it's not all abstract.

That night on the tube, the press began to shift away from the government and broadcast mostly appeals to the government to agree with the just demands of the strikers. The other government influence on the nightly news was rather indirect. The horrid Women's Federation under the wretched Kang Keqing put out an appeal that went something like: 'Dear, dear sons and little brothers, your big sister and your mummy are so worried about you they weep over the stove; they're preparing a big meal for you to come home to. Please, please join them, etc, etc.' Nothing to indicate that many of the strikers are women. Actually, there was a poster that played exactly the same theme from the other side when I got home:

FORGIVE ME, MOMMA!
Momma, you always said to me, 'You must study hard! Don't get involved in any rough stuff!' You also told me not to be

taken in by strong prejudices, lest there be 'accounts to settle in the autumn'. [This is a reference to the practice of disciplining unruly students by assigning them to disagreeable posts in faraway places when they graduate.] You also told me that Chinese people are always pleasant to your face, but ready to stab you in the back, and that 'the revenge of a gentleman may last more than a decade'.

But, dear momma, when you see that a thousand or more students have collapsed from hunger in Beijing, when you see that on the wrappings on their heads are written the words, 'Mama, I don't want to hunger strike, but . . .', when more than a million people are on the march, and more than 20,000 right here in Guangzhou . . . Dear Mom, can't you understand your son – a member of the protest contingent. Momma, forgive me!

The next day was the day we all marched, and the school took part as a body for the first time. It was also the day the workers of Beijing joined the protests, Gorbachev remarked that reform in the USSR had 'hotheads' too, and joked that maybe Shevardnadze, the firefighter flown down to Georgia during the unrest there, could be made available on loan.

There wasn't yet an established branch of the city-wide strike committee at our school that Thursday morning, and I wasn't sure if there really would be a strike, so I got up very early, around six, and went out to read the big character posters that had gone up in the night. No mistake: a strike and a big march. I told my students and, on their initiative, we put together a small contingent, with English slogans and copies of the *Internationale* to sing in English. In the middle of the preparations, one of the Party leaders who has authority over me came charging up and told me to stop. I said I couldn't teach during a strike, and that I thought it would be good if I went along with my students. He said they 'couldn't accept' what I was doing, and I said I 'fully understood' that, and that was that.

And then . . . the Party Secretary who I wrote about at such great length last time (did you get that?) threw his weight behind the march! In retrospect, this doesn't seem so astonishing. There was already a certain precedent in Beijing, and, as Ms C points out, a motive: 'When students are thinking about Deng and Li Peng, nobody is thinking about the Party Secretary. When I tried to raise the issue of his conduct during the demonstration, everybody said I was muddling things up!' But as far as I know, it happened at no other college in Guangzhou. One minute we were waiting interminably so we could set out on our march, and the next minute all the well-known leaders of the Party and the Youth Section were running around with bull-horns, getting everyone into line, lending us an enormous silk banner with the school name on it, arranging a march route with the police, and even sending one of the ambulances after us with drinking water. It was a performance that left us stunned, and even a little bit grateful.

The march was a dream – *all* my students went and practised their English as they never did on picnic or at the beach. We were hailed as heroes by the students, and even cheered by the workers whom we tried to get to join the march. There was time to shout ourselves hoarse, and time to talk Trotsky and Permanent Revolution and Bourgeois Democracy, and time to drink tea and eat *yang mei*, the sort of sour plum that Cao Cao [c. 215 AD] would simply describe to his troops to get them to salivate. We were copiously photographed; our contingent appears prominently on the bulletin board even at this moment, though for some reason the only thing that indicates my presence is a shot that sort of shows my nose sticking out from behind a beautiful young woman in floppy sun hat and conscientious expression.

We marched from about 10 in the morning until 7:30 at night. There were over 30,000 people by the time we got to the Provincial Government, and they had to put us in a kind of holding pattern, because unlike Peking, Guangzhou doesn't have a big square near the main government buildings. Many of the best slogans, unfortunately, were eight-character puns of the sort you find in Chinese classics, but don't translate very well. Not a few of them were directed at the leaders, but my favourite simply read: 'Budget for 1988: Education = 20 billion; Public expense entertainment = 80 billion'. In Guangzhou the main thrust of the demonstration was, rather characteristically, economic. But it was the right kind of economics, whereas the Beijing demonstrations were the wrong kind of politics, so much claptrap about 'democracy' and not a word about what people really need to do with it.

(Typhoon force winds have struck Guangzhou, and the only other news, besides the continuous reading and rereading of Chen Xitong's first three martial law edicts, and the replaying of Li Peng's drooling law-and-order speech, is a warning to all units to carry out the established safeguards against typhoon weather. At this moment the students are somewhere in front of the Provincial Government, huddled against the onslaught, bracing for the worst. I am debating whether I can make it down to the canteen for lunch, or if I should just heat up something from the fridge.)

For a day I was right there with everything I love best: talk, demonstrations, China, beautiful women . . . I was ecstatic when I went home and took a shower under cold, cold water. Then I turned on the TV. Things in Beijing were already very, very bad.

One of the most touching moments came when Qiao Shi and Hu Qili went to the hospital to interview some of the collapsed students. One of the students was feeling a bit lively, so he sat up and asked permission to make a little political speech. He then told the camera that the student movement was not anti-communist and upheld all the ideals of communism. As he saw it, there were four major problems before China today, and not one of them was really being addressed: 1) population; 2) energy shortage; 3) poor education; 4) economic chaos. He hoped the Communist Party would stay in power, but for that to happen they would have to clean up their act. Then he turned to Hu Qili, who has at least one son involved in corrupt practices, and asked if he agreed. Hu and Qiao both said they did, and he sank back on his pillow and closed his

395

eyes. I am not so naive. I cannot seem to close my eyes, but he did touch on something real, something one rarely sees in the big character posters or the endlessly repeated videos of the pronouncements of the big characters of the current drama.

The next day, rumours were everywhere, some on Hong Kong radio and in the bourgeois press. The BBC said Deng had resigned (from what? the Military Commission?). The General Trades Union Federation was threatening a general strike if the government didn't give in. The army officers in Beijing had all signed a letter saying they would not use force against the students. Deng was moving in 30,000 troops from outside the area. Much of this later turned out to be true, unfortunately not the bit on the Beeb.

As I was walking back from a meeting this morning, I saw D's latest contribution. It's one of the best and most comprehensive, so I will give her the last word:

AN AUTOCRAT'S CHINA
From 1988 until the present, China's economy has reeled from crisis to crisis. Unable to avoid borrowing from abroad, prices have soared while money depreciated, factories have had huge outlays and minuscule profit margins, energy is short, transport strapped, staples tight, population exploding. Every sort of crisis has been compounded, even a flood of fake and inferior goods in the market place. China's education system, long in an all-round and total state of collapse, has left teachers disgusted with teaching, students disgusted with study, illiteracy way, way up, schools operating on 'voluntary' contributions, and a large number of teachers forced to give up their profession just to be able to make a living.

Chinese political life is the scene of an all-round and pervasive rottenness and corruption, a system of autocracy, nepotism and bribery. Graft has tainted people once thought to be far above it, and irresponsible elements steal the wealth of the nation for personal gain. Because of corruption, the nation's defences have suffered terrible losses along the border with Vietnam, soldiers and generals are inept in the Sino-Indian border conflict, and the entire armed forces seems to have gone into business. The navy smuggles video recorders, the air force smuggles brandy and cigarettes, and the infantry is in close combat on the construction front. The armed police speculates in automobiles.

The moral force of the nation has been deeply corroded, and the heartless and incessant pressure of events has forced every person to wear a mask, assume a servile posture, and pretend. All of us seem to have developed split personalities. People have become egotistical, selfish, and utterly oblivious to the public good, so unconcerned that children have fallen into water and been allowed to drown before many onlookers. Hooliganism and murder go unnoticed, or anyway, unchecked, and people have become so cynical at any expression of goodness that all humanitarianism has lapsed. The long dictatorship has slowly eradicated all virtue from the hearts of the people and created a skin on their faces so thick it cannot be penetrated by gun or knife. The situation is grave. In the past year many layers of government have been saying that, on one front after another, there is no way out.

Can it be that China cannot be saved? No! To say that is to comfort the bureaucracy and the thoroughly corrupt, and to allow them to get away with not even attempting to solve problems. So what is to be done? We need democracy. It is the only weapon that can destroy the autocratic system and the whole range of its corrupt outgrowths. The basic meaning of democracy is that the people themselves should take charge of the administration. If powers must be delegated to a certain group of individuals, this group must be freely elected by the people.

Right now, the general quality of our people is low, and it will require great effort to overcome this obstacle, but this fact cannot be used as an excuse to oppose democracy. We have quite a few intellectuals, ordinary citizens and party members who are certainly no worse than the citizens of other democratic societies. As the urbanization of the population became a serious trend in 1985, the government began to promulgate measures to prevent peasants from entering the cities. In fact, these measures were meant to prevent them from raising their cultural and political status. The purpose was simply to continue the system of autocracy. Because of the restrictions on much of the population in the countryside, the growth of democracy there has been severely checked, and peasants have provided the bulk of the soldiery.

Freedom of the press is an essential ingredient of democracy. The two cannot be separated. Journalists should be the straightforward and honest spokesmen for society. Now they have become mechanized purveyors of lies. We must above all demand freedom of the press.

To solve the transport crisis, we need money. To solve the food shortage, the pressure on the environment, pollution, and the population problem, we need money. But only the government has this kind of money. Where has it all gone? Into the pockets of bureaucratic speculators, into the coffers of leaders with power. The result is that reform has gone back and forth, and the only ones to profit consistently have been the bureaucrats, big and small. This is not the reform we wanted.

A philosophy of human life and equality is the only ideal solution. Although the level of knowledge among people and their contributions to society may vary, the significance of each life is the same. Everyone wants the right to a life of beauty.

Intellectuals are the guardians of society, the spokesmen for the nation. Science and technology are needed for social productivity, and productivity is the measure of the social system's worth. Respect knowledge and talent! Long live democracy! Long live freedom!

(The tight-lipped lady is back reading the martial law edicts. The typhoon will last another two days at least. And then?)

27 May 1989

It's not like anything you've ever seen, or I've ever seen, or anyone in China's ever seen. Here it is, a week after martial law was declared in Peking. There are still posters up all over the school, ruminations on the link between overpopulation and basic democracy, caricatures of Deng

398

Xiaoping as a blood-sucking, bridge-playing vampire, Li Peng as a rubber stamp, and even an elaborate imperial lineage showing exactly whose sons are involved in which profiteering firms in Beijing.

The class strike ended on Wednesday [24 May] and no one doubts that the reaction is setting in, but there is still a whiff of the ozone in the air that mobilization of the masses creates. Nor is it confined to our school. On Beijing Road there are computerized *dazibao* [big character posters], xeroxes of the Hong Kong papers' coverage of the demos (much more thorough than we get, what with the martial law administration), and hundreds of little couplets like the New Year's couplets people paste on their doors: 'We eat, we clothe ourselves, but we have no freedom and no democracy!'; 'Deng Xioaping, you're old!'; 'Li Peng, get down; Wan Li, come back!'; 'Clean out the rubbish!'; 'Citizens of Guangzhou, thank you for your support!'

The week-long sit-in at the Provincial Government is basically over, and the hunger strikers are eating again, but every half hour, activity stops and ears wave in the direction of Hong Kong for the latest rumours. We have heard hundreds, all virtually devoid of fact, but we never tire of hearing them: 'Two hunger strikers dead!' – 'Zhao Ziyang is out!' – 'The Party is getting ready to call the whole thing counter-revolutionary!' – 'Deng has said he never wanted to send in the army!' – 'Li Peng was the true scapegoat; Deng feinted with Zhao in order to sacrifice Li' – 'No, wait . . .' Absolute rubbish, most of it. But with the military sitting in every TV and radio office, there is practically nothing else to listen to.

It's too early for the reaction. There will be one, and it will be very profound. Because the mass movement was of such a sudden and spontaneous character, there is very little organization to sustain it through the ensuing weariness of the masses in the onslaught of official reaction to come. Li Peng is not stupid, merely a narrow-minded empiric, devoid of vision, who identifies socialism with his personal dictator-ship, and does not shrink from teaching the masses utter disgust for both. He knows that his only excuse for his actions before the Party and the people is providing stability and calm, which not a few workers and peasants might welcome after several weeks of apparently fruitless activity. If he starts the reaction too early, it is bound to provoke the masses anew, get caught up in the receding wave of mass protest, and renew the barely papered-over breach in the party, as well as piss the army off no end. He is not stupid enough to start it this week. Maybe next week.

There are heated debates about the constitutionality of Li Peng's martial law order. It is true that the NPC [National People's Congress] is supposed to be exclusively empowered in this regard, but actually the Standing Committee can exercise this power when it is not sitting, and I suspect there is some clause that says the Department of State can too, because it was they who declared martial law in Lhasa.

There is also much speculation on the fate of Zhao. Two posters declare that he has resigned from the secretaryship of the Party, and even describe in detail how he presented six points for dealing with the demos to the Politburo, only to have them rejected by someone standing in for Deng. Then he resigned. It is very plausible, and there are several details that convince me. Zhao did not appear at the meeting on Friday the 19th when Li Peng and Yang Shangkun announced an imminent crackdown to an overwhelmingly military audience. His last appearance was in the wee hours of Friday morning when he tried to persuade hunger strikers to give up the strike. His voice cracked and he choked back tears at several points; worse, he began his speech with the fatal words, 'I didn't come down here to apologize and ask for forgiveness', an unmistakable hint that he did.

His last really official televised appearance some days earlier was also significant. He was talking to Gorbachev, and remarked, seemingly out of the blue, that Deng Xiaoping was a leader of such extraordinary character that, by secret decision of the 13th Party Congress, he was to be consulted on all important matters before the highest bodies of the party, even though not officially a member of them.

Now, I remember that at the time there was a certain amount of talk that such a clause was a condition of Deng's 'retirement' and, anyway, everybody has long known that nobody dares clean the toilets in the Great Hall of the People without asking the Old Man first. So it was a bit disingenuous of Zhao to tell Gorbachev he was letting the cat out of the bag. But why he should choose to do so at that moment was a bit puzzling until it was explained to me by my students.

The official reason for not dealing with the eminently reasonable demands of the students (now acknowledged as such by the government) was that the regime was too busy with Gorbachev. The real reason, as everyone knows, is that the Politburo is not allowed to disagree with itself in public, and it was deeply divided. And why should it be deeply divided, with Zhao firmly in command, both in title and in fact? Because there is a sixth geriatric member of the Politburo, and he was not pleased by the conciliatory stand Zhao was advocating. By drawing attention to the doddering shadow behind him, Zhao was clearly placing blame for the disunity on Deng. No dialogue took place because Deng was afraid of it degenerating into trialogue, or, worse, a dialogue between Zhao and the students, with the Old Man talking to himself and Li Peng off in a dark corner of the Great Hall.

The general view is that Li Peng, eminently qualified by bureaucratic temperament, brutality and cynicism for the historical role of Cavaignac [French war minister who put down the working class unrest of June, 1848], lacks the intelligence and inspiration, and is basically too timid to resort to force on his own. His Friday night speech, which is being 'diligently studied' and 'whole-heartedly supported' by everyone from the governor of Guangdong, Ye Xuanping, to the Retired Cadres Club at our school, was a bad one; that in itself means nothing, since he didn't write it. But he hadn't even read it before the meeting. His intonation in several places was wrong, and he even read 'April' for 'May' when discussing the demonstrations.

401

More of the Byzantine and utterly tiresome struggles in the Politburo in a moment. Let me tell you my story and give you a kind of worm's eye view of events. I will begin my recitative on Monday of this week. One of the New Year's couplets was a poem by the Hungarian poet-patriot Sandor Petofi:

Life is exquisite
And love is more so
Yet now in freedom's name
We may let both go.

Not all are of this quality. The posters reserve their full venom for Deng, the presumed inspiration of the uninspired and uninspiring electrical engineer. Yet Li too is given his due. There are several posters that have the format of mock film advertisements, or student recruiting posters: '*Bloody Despotism*, starring Li Peng'; '*Autocracy for Beginners*, taught by Qin Shihuang [the first Qin emperor, with whom Mao had liked to be compared]'. There's even an elaborate Freudian analysis, blaming Li's violent, anti-social tendencies on his loss of a father-figure (he was orphaned at three), and an unfulfilled rebellion against his adoptive father (Zhou Enlai).

There are posters about Deng Yingchao [Zhou Enlai's widow], too. She is said to have threatened to leave the Party if the troops fire on the students. Why she should say such a thing to Hong Kong reporters is not a question that occurs to us; it is all over the school, with posters that say things like, 'When the Son is Unfilial, the Mother Sheds Tears'. The next day, a letter from Deng Yingchao warning against rumours is read over TV and even the campus loudspeakers. It is, however, generally sympathetic to the students. There is also a poster quoting a leader of the 38th Army stationed in Baoding (one of the groups called on to enforce martial law): 'Whoever fires the first shot, I will shoot personally'. True? Who knows?

There is a new signatory to the posters, something called the 'Autonomous Student Assembly', an officially recognized branch of the city-wide strike committee. It is not an elected body, and it is not recognized by either the school administration or the official Student Assembly, though many members of the latter are sympathetic to it. I am pleased; it means the strike now has some form of organization. It is also good for me because, by participating in the strike, I have been forced into a kind of leadership role I don't want and can't take. The ASA posters are not propagandistic, but agitational and to the point: big march on Tuesday night.

Naturally, I'd love to have gone. The march on Thursday [18 May] was one of the happiest days of my life. I know, I know, history is not so simple, and it never fits into the palm of your hand. I am in a foreign land, and very much aware I am not really a part of this, much less leading it. All I feel is that extraordinary euphoria of seeing all about me people who, for a brief moment, are not the passive dough of politics, who are doing the kneading themselves for once. It is the greatest happiness I have ever known, because to me political life has been mostly the process of watching things fall apart and analysing them. And now, momentarily, people are creating themselves as political creatures, all over and at once.

But I couldn't take part. The edicts have been very careful to spell out the main task, which is to separate 'a tiny handful of fomentors and plotters' from the broad masses of patriotic students. (I think I mentioned that in the Chinese press 'a small number' means one to ten thousand; 'a tiny handful' means ten thousand to a hundred thousand; and 'a very, very small minority' means a hundred thousand to a million. The current phrase is *jishao shu jishao shu*; that means 'an extremely small minority of an extremely small minority' of bad people are 'plotting to deny the leadership of the CCP and socialism'.) How wonderful for them if one of these should turn out to be a foreigner! I stayed home, bitter, on Thursday night. And it was big, about 400,000 by the radio's account. I could hear it all over the city.

That was the march. The student strike did not fare so well, at least not at our school. About half the students were out when the strike was at its peak, and easily 90 per cent had returned by Tuesday. I even suggested that they should call it off, though, of course, until they did I would observe it. They said our school would 'lose face' with the city-wide strike if they did. On Tuesday, the official Student Assembly put up a dazibao announcing partial restoration of classes. On Wednesday, the Autonomous Assembly called for restoring all classes. Nothing is more demoralizing than a partial strike or a trickle-back.

On Wednesday morning I had a little tiff with my boss. You see, I put up a dazibao. It was quite innocuous and it was in English, mostly to urge my striking students to keep up their English during the strike, and also making the obvious point about the necessity of English for any kind of serious open intellectual policy. But my boss accused me of interfering with China's internal affairs, and then said I had disobeyed the constitution (which had an amendment tacked on by Deng in 1978 abolishing the previous constitutional right to write dazibaos). I pointed out, a) the innocuous content of my dazibao; b) the fact that it was in English and directed at my students, like many other announcements I have put up; and c) the fact that the administration itself has been putting up dazibaos to counter the student ones on a regular basis. (There was even a kind of dialogue going between the Autonomous Assembly and the Retired Cadres Club when I last looked.) My boss smiled and said, 'Well, when you get out of class, we'll talk some more.' I went over after class, he didn't bring it up, and the dazibao is still there. And they were very pleased that I was back at work.

Wednesday was a very optimistic day. Everyone was certain, from the Hong Kong broadcasts, of course, that Li Peng was finished and that Deng was determined to sacrifice him to save his own skin ('I never agreed to send in the army!'). I wasn't so sure, but it was quite certain that martial law had been an embarrassing failure, and it was hard to see what would happen next. Y, on the other hand, was darkly pessimistic when I talked to him; he was certain of imminent defeat.

It was clear that the energy of the movement was slowing. The dazibaos were not appearing as thick and fast, and the sit-in in front of the Provincial Government shrank and finally packed up. On Thursday my students came to class bleary-eyed and very depressed. Hong Kong radio was reporting that a letter from three departments of PLA general headquarters was preparing the ground for declaring the entire movement counter-revolutionary, and Zhao was definitely out. Li Peng also appeared on TV again, smiling and confident, much to the students' distress: 'He looked profoundly happy. Not acting. Like he knew he'd won. Like a bureaucrat back in office.'

The reaction was gathering pace, too. After their disastrous attempt at stamping out the dazibaos on Sunday, which had resulted in a blizzard of posters from the Communist Youth leaders denouncing the 'anti-poster Mafia', the administration had changed tactics and begun copying out important speeches and articles and posting them up as dazibaos. They also reconnected the loudspeaker system, unused since the Cult Revolt, to broadcast political messages. Meetings were held, and teachers who had been too sympathetic to the strike were criticized; everybody was warned against taking part in any further marches and urged to 'diligently study' Li Peng's slavering speech. Ms G was especially criticized for not using her influence to 'control' me. Ms H was completely demoralized: 'We have no hope for this government.'

It's funny. During the height of the dual power in Beijing, when the government held the outskirts and the students and workers held Tiananmen, it was easy to tell who was holding the broadcasting studio at Chang'An Dajie Tele-communications Building. One day they played a good half hour's coverage of all the demos, and read letters begging the government to agree to the students' demands, gleefully announcing the formation of a broadcasters' contingent in the demos, along with journalists, foreign affairs service people, CITS [China International Travel Service] and even State Department employees. The next day it was eyes on their typed-out martial law edicts. They didn't even look at the cameras. I wasn't the only one who noticed; everyone did.

The anti-poster Mafia is at work again, and another copy of the PLA letter to the suffering soldiers of Beijing has gone up – with some sardonic student comments on it. But the reaction is definitely on the way.

30 May 1989

I have written Tang Min twice and Liu Fei once, to no avail. Come vacation, I will go out there in person and see what's up.

For the most part, the level of political sophistication among the students is infinitely higher than that of the Party, which for nearly a week has been bellowing that the hearts and minds of the students are pure and patriotic, and their intentions are wonderful, and indeed identical with their own, and it is now necessary to drown the whole thing in blood. Peng Zhen last night made a speech that consisted of one enormous logical contradiction ('they have good intentions and no good can come of that'), and actually made Li Peng look sincere. At least he is quite forthright about identifying socialism with his personal dictatorship.

The quality of the big character posters has risen enormously this week. Today, two went up refuting the claims of the central government to 'unity and stability' by pointing to its total impotence in the face of economic anarchy, and contrasting it to the well-ordered and disciplined activities of the two May 4th movements: 70 years ago and today. An even better one dealt with Peng Zhen's speech and discussed to what extent the bureaucracy serves the interest of the people, and to what extent the current movement does. And here is some historical background, from yesterday's poster:

WARNING! BLOODSHED IS UNAVOIDABLE!
The anti-autocratic and anti-dictatorial movement inspired by the Beijing students seems to have come to a quiet conclusion.

In reality, however, this is but a period of calm before a still greater storm. The students sitting in on Tiananmen Square have taken an oath: unless they reach their goal, they will not surrender. Obviously, the democratic structures centred on the student movement and the ruthless dictatorship of the Li Peng regime stand in a mutually exclusive relationship. The result of the struggle between them is awaited by the whole world.

Let us examine a few pages of history; the bloody lessons we find there may shake us to our senses. From the time of the Opium Wars, when the West forced open the front door of the feudal system, a vision of democracy has filtered into this autocratic land. The democratic spirit gradually arose in our ancient people, and knowledge accumulated bit by bit. Thus the great life and death struggle between democracy and autocracy began.

The Rongcheng Reform [of 1898, the so-called 'Hundred Days Reform' led by Kang Youwei during the reign of the Emperor Guangxu, a liberal who toyed with the idea of constitutional monarchy until arrested by the Empress Ci Xi] may be called the first struggle between democracy and feudalism. Then the democratic forces were very weak, and the 'Six Gentlemen' paid for Ci Xi's conservative reaction with their heads. At the time of his death, Tan Sitong said: 'The evolution of every nation takes place through bloodshed. If China today has none who have given their blood for this evolution, she cannot prosper. Then let Sitong be the first.'

The Xinhai Revolution [the 1911 revolution led by Sun Yatsen, which established the Chinese Republic], when democratic and warlord forces contested for power, resulted in the repression launched by the restorationist faction of Yuan Shikai, against which Sun Yatsen was powerless. The struggle cost not a few fighters their lives, which they freely contributed.

In the May 4th movement, the students led a patriotic movement on an unprecedentedly grand and vigorous scale. The warlord regime of Duan Qirui abolished their student association, put it down by brute force, smashing the student march. Nevertheless, broad masses of students across China made their unquenchable patriotic spirit felt.

407

During the period of the KMT dictatorship the policy of 'One Party (the KMT), One Ism (the Three People's Principles), and One Leader (Chiang Kaishek)', was forced upon the country. Despite this, student movements continued, and continued to frustrate the efforts made to crush them. We will not forget the Zhenzhu Bridge Incident, nor the December 1st incident, nor the Xiaguan Incident. As Li Gongpu and Wei Yiduo wrote in *The Altar of Freedom*: 'What is it we desire? First of all, freedom. In the second place, freedom. Finally, freedom again!' Both of them were slain by Chiang Kaishek.

In the first period of Liberation, when our country had the outward appearance of freedom and democracy, the NPC was the highest authority in the nation. But then in 1966, the feudalist-restorationist Cultural Revolution broke out and created more than ten years of hardship and turmoil. The personal dictatorship of Mao Zedong reached new historical peaks. All who resisted or pointed out the damage to the country it was causing were killed. Think of Liu Shaoqi, Peng Dehuai and Zhang Zhixin; remember how they died!

Now the government is of the familiar type again! It is again 'One Party (the Communist Party), One Ism (Socialism) and One Leader (Deng Xiaoping)', the unbreakable net of absolutism. On the 26th, Li Peng wrote on behalf of the Department of State enforcing martial law in Beijing to reveal the true face of this new warlord regime. He doesn't know or care about the warm feelings of people all over the country for our movement; he says he simply needs military force.

Compatriots, remember the lessons of history. Dictatorships have always murdered to protect their bloody grip on power. The struggle against them, the struggle of democracy and dictatorship, has always meant the sacrifice of fresh blood.

Today they meet again, as they did in the Rongcheng Reforms. To avoid the defeat of the Hundred Days Reform and the vacillation of the Xinhai Revolution, we must seek again the spirit of the May 4th movement and not forget the lessons of the past ten years. With the wounds on our bodies, we cannot wait. Our movement is a true warrior for the people. Perhaps this is the last time our movement must prepare for total sacrifice, for the nation and the people. It will crush the semifeudal autocratic system to the earth. It will begin a new democratic page in the long history of China.

But the enemy is the oldest system of despotism on earth. Although it has failed miserably to rule the country, it is still capable of ruining and oppressing it. It cannot be soft or peaceable. It will not go quietly. Like all dictatorships, it will have its last frenzy. So it must call in the army, declare martial law, try to isolate the students, black out the news, stifle popular support by every conceivable method, bare its teeth and claws . . .

WARNING! BLOODSHED IS UNAVOIDABLE!

5 June 1989
First of all, I'm in no danger personally, so don't worry. Of course, there is the future. Nothing will ever be the same here now, and it's entirely possible that all kinds of things will happen – some of which may affect my job. But that's the future. Now for now.

Yesterday morning, as I was leaving for English Corner with a couple of students, my eye caught a dazibao on the student dorm wall (the ones on the gaolan have been torn down). It said that 50 people had been killed by the army in Peking. Another said the death toll was 200. Then we ran into a march. The head banner bore a big black swastika and the number 500. I began to think, is it possible?

No. Impossible. Not even Li Peng could be so stupid. After the huge outpouring of energy, the workers and students were tired, almost thankful for the respite afforded by martial law. If the regime did nothing to provoke them, they might just possibly go away. Or so a bureaucrat would think, being naturally prone to mental laziness himself. The longer they wait, the longer they do nothing, the stronger the regime is. Start a fight now, and the whole nation will see who is really responsible for 'fomenting chaos'.

But that morning I had had a discussion with Ms X that

disturbed me. She had just got a letter from Peking in which her classmates described a new kind of organizer and a new kind of organization. Suddenly, things were being organized immaculately, not with the rough democracy of the students, and paid for with remarkable quantities of cash. Her correspondent concluded that the student movement had become yet another pawn in the power-play between two, three, many factions of the bureaucracy – probably between Zhao and Li. I had rejected the notion out of hand. A movement of a million people is not a pawn; on the contrary, the bureaucrats must themselves react to it. The most they can hope to do is to try to use it post hoc. They could not organize it, much less manipulate it from behind the scenes.

Yet, there was no other explanation possible. In a struggle with the masses, the bureaucracy would be happy to sit and wait, confident of the eventual fatigue of the people, if only from their experience of the past few weeks. Only a threat from another bureaucratic faction could produce a sudden frenzy of homicide. There was terrible tension underlying everything we did that day – yesterday. Was it true? Was it true? We ran into two more demos, each one had a higher death toll. But it was only when I got home and listened to the Beeb that I was sure.

It's true. The pictures are all over the gaolan this morning. Corpses and rivers, rivers of blood. A dazibao describes the video made from Hong Kong TV, showing the students being crushed in their tents by tanks, a woman being reduced to hamburger by tank treads, students linking arms, singing the *Internationale*. Line after line of students, linking arms, 'It's the final conflict', mowed down by peasant soldiers who probably wouldn't recognize the tune even if they could hear it over the screams and gunfire.

A strike. The students have blocked the two bridges over the Pearl this morning, and classes are shut down tight. An appeal for a city-wide general strike has gone out, and the news that it has been heeded in Macao. Only the workers, only the workers can save us now.

410

9 June 1989

Guangzhou is quiet again. The schools are empty; the students decided to empty them in protest and to prevent arrests. Those that were prevented from going home to their parents by the government or by the many transport stoppages are being housed off campus by classmates. My own school has sent out written pleas to them to return, but threats are being made and no guarantees of amnesty proferred. On the contrary, the group of workers we saw demonstrating down by the bridge a few days ago has been taken into custody, according to yesterday's paper. No one in his right mind will come back now. The gaolan has a number of pro-government dazibaos on it, and a firm note prohibiting any further ones. Any students or teachers who defy the new regulations, adopted verbatim from those in force at universities in Beijing, will be very strictly punished. But the army is probably not coming here, since there is really very little reason for them to do so.

Today my boss told me that my application for a further contract was denied by the foreign affairs bureau. This means I have no job for next year, which hardly surprises me after the last few weeks. I'm going to try to get one elsewhere, but of course I may fail. If so, I will go first to Macao and then try to get a boat to Taiwan. And wait.

I have letters from TM and LF. Both have received the money. TM adds thanks for publication and publicity, and some horrible stories of the crushing of the student movement. Her brother went to Beijing right before the bloodbath, and she herself was an important spokesperson for the students of Fuzhou. She is probably in big trouble. Her case has been referred to the highest court without the lower courts having passed sentence. It is not a good time to be awaiting a supreme court verdict.

Postscript

Since the last letter and the first edition of this book, much water has passed beneath the bridge. Tang Min is in prison, and I have lost (twice in one year!) my right to stay in China. Yet now, more than a year and a half after the last letter was posted, I find that this story still has that unfinished, I'll-let-you-know-as-soon-as-I-know, cliff-hanging quality that so frustrated and tantalized the recipients of these letters.

Shortly after I posted the last letter in this volume I was offered a job at Xiamen University. Arriving in Xiamen, I found that Tang Min had finally been allocated a flat, a "room of her own" to write in. (She had previously been denied one on the grounds that her husband had no residence permit for Xiamen and the municipal authorities didn't want to grant a room to a "single" woman or a female head of household.) Six months later she was allocated a year in prison for writing "The Mysterious Miasma of Taimu Shan" and began serving her sentence immediately. She had, despite the problems caused by her botched abortion, managed to become pregnant, but she miscarried in prison.

As for me, I was soon informed that my job was being "cut from the budget" along with about 60,000 university students—part of a thinly disguised package of reprisals against the whole of tertiary education by the new regime of militant ignorance. With only two days notice, I had to leave behind my friends and my home (some 260 kilos of books and other fond impedimenta now sitting in crates somewhere in Xiamen). The day she took me down to the docks, Tang Min faced me with the severe look of a dissatisfied reader and asked me about my plans for the future. I had to give her what has become the watchword of the bureaucracy in this miserable "planned society" that has now given up the pretense of planning. "Mingtian zai shuo ba!" ("We'll discuss it again tomorrow!") And we had to laugh.

Three months later, I received an invitation to teach at Guizhou University; I returned to China in November 1989. Tang Min had not yet been arrested and I visited her briefly on my way to my post. At one point I mentioned her impending prison sentence. She smiled thoughtfully and patted the pink blanket on her bare apartment floor that served as a bed. "I bet there are good things to write in that place."

I was again denied the job. So I traipsed around northeast China in search of another and was eventually thrown out of the country in mid-February 1990, after a farcical investigation by local police in a minuscule town. They couldn't think of anything better to charge me with than returning to try to get back into teaching, which they decided was illegal on a tourist visa. They were wrong; I appealed, successfully, but face is a very important commodity for the police, and I had to leave anyway. I then went in again on a tourist visa, determined simply to spend my time in my room translating Tang Min's published works. I was immediately shown the door again and this time I was denied a new visa.

"Picking up a stone to drop it on your foot" is how the Chinese press disapprovingly speaks of Western attempts to isolate China in the wake of the mass murder of June 1989. I agree with them; China is its own market, and can easily live without the West. Oh, I like the idea of China finally kicking the foreign cigarette habit, stopping its new opium trade in Japanese consumer goods, avoiding the Third World debt trap; but that is of course not going to happen. On the contrary, China will manage to drop its stone and eat it too. They wanted Western European "modernization" without Western "liberalization," and they shall have the iron fist of Eastern European economic collapse without the velvet "liberation."

Sanctions are not going to protect the rags and tatters left of China's national market and social services; if they were,

Western governments would be dead set against them. I believe that Chinese people have more to give us than we do them. They are now facing up to the problems the Chinese bureaucrats, and we in the West, are busy ignoring; the problems that hunger striker in May saw from his hospital bed: population, land scarcity, scant resources, lousy education.

The Chinese were busy facing up to them in the year before June 1989. Before it all happened many of us, me included, felt bitter and conscientiously pessimistic, unshakably confident that our world was at last definitively crumbling and there would be absolutely no one to pick up the pieces and do something with them. Yet after it happened, with weeks of televised torture and fink hotlines, maddening buzzes of lies and cynical half-lies, I left China a sworn optimist.

Tragedy, yes; we must have tragedy, though the student movement had more than its portion. I think of it as happening in two waves: one abstractly "democratic" and student-centered, rather like the first demonstrations in 1986 or the occidentophilic "revolutions" in Eastern Europe, and the second forthrightly anti-corruption, anti-nouveau riche, massively proletarian, and tragically belated. The student movement was already defeated, suffering from too many heroes and not enough leaders. One must have both.

That day in June when troops were running wild in Beijing murdering heroes, some of my students and I visited the Peasant Studies Institute in Guangzhou, where Mao once taught. One of them drew my attention to a photo of the communist pioneer Li Dazhao, hung above his last words: "The greatest moments of human life are inevitably imbued with sadness. It is no accident that the most beautiful natural scenery is found in stark and harsh mountain regions, nor that strong and even violent music strikes the deepest chords. What is great in life always comes with terrible sacrifices, with tragedy." Brave words. But real leadership means being as economical as possible with tragedy.

Will there be real leaders? Will there be people who can avoid the tragic blunders of 1989? Will there be leaders who can make a new movement, act as a tribune for the whole

414

people and not simply a petitioner for the disenfranchised intelligentsia, who can reach out to workers and poorer peasants and through them right into the army itself? Oh, yes, I'm sure there will be. I think I've actually met some.

I thought there was something indecent, not to say insane about this feeling of optimism tempered by tragedy, yet when I discussed it with Chinese friends, I found a lot of people shared it.

Chinese Friend: "Well, it was kind of *liaobuqi* (amazing), wasn't it? I mean, we all felt it coming, that some sort of explosion was inevitable. But who'd have thought it would come so early? Sometimes I would think to myself before, maybe when Deng dies. . . . Who'd have thought it would happen while he was still alive? No matter how bad things get, it won't erase the memory of how wonderful it was."

Me: "For you and for me, perhaps. You and I didn't lead it, and we didn't get killed or wounded. Those people are all dead, in exile, or in prison. Nor are we the ordinary folks, the workers who took the brunt of the. . . ."

Chinese Friend: "*Aiya*, the most *liaobuqi* of all were the ordinary citizens. Nobody protected them. Nobody even led them. But there they were, in newsreels from Taiwan and Hong Kong, running out in the middle of the night, in boxer shorts and barefoot, or taking off their high heels to run faster. To protect the students. Nobody protected them. They knew nobody would. Suddenly, out of the blue, people take to the streets and everything is different. Then the next day, the tanks take to the streets and everything changes back again. The people who led it and organized it are gone, and the ordinary people who did most of the suffering see only that it's all back again. But me, what I remember is that it all changed, overnight. It really did happen."

Mingtian zai shuo ba.

December 1990

Index and glossary

() indicates additional information or comment; [] alternative or translation

416

417

Index and glossary

Guangzhou [Canton] 322, 323, 324, 363, 374, 379, 411
  demonstration 384
  Pharmaceutical College 321, 389
  social problems 378
guanxi [connections] 45
Guanyin [Goddess of Mercy] 148
gui-ding [regulations] 30, 46
Guiyang (Guizhou) 26, 32, 33
Guomindang [Kuomintang, KMT] 36, 114, 285, 408
Gyangze (Tibet) 137, 139, 145

Hai Rui (1513–1587) 28
Hai Rui Dismissed from Office (1962 play by Wu Han) 369
Haikou (Hainan) 27
Hainan Island 27, 28, 348, 374
  exodus to 349, 365
  scandal 349
Han dynasty (206BC–220AD) 14, 16, 122
Hangzhou (Zhejiang) 33, 43, 44, 148
Hans (ethnic majority) 16, 26, 40, 50, 128, 133, 306
Hanshui River (Hubei) 206, 212, 218
He Jingzhi (1924–) 250, 360–61
He Long (1896–1969, CCP general) 114
He Shang 368, 369
Hong Kong 1, 19, 20, 22, 24, 34, 39, 69, 105, 189, 336, 337, 339
  immigration procedures 336
  police 338
Hongkongese 147, 326
Hongwu (1328–1398, Ming emperor) 45
housing 17, 18, 32, 46, 84,
Hu Qili (1929– , CCP ex–leader) 395
Hu Yaobang (1915–1989) 303, 318, 378, 379, 386, 387
Huaisheng mosque (Canton) 20, 43
Huangguoshu Falls (Guizhou) 26
Huanxi Buddha 151, 313
Huazhong University of Science and Technology [HUST] (Wuhan) 182
Hui (Muslims) 50, 51, 75
Humble Administrator's Garden (Suzhou, Jiangsu) 38
Hundred Days Reform (1908, [Rongcheng Reform]) 408
hungry ghosts 262

Imperial Palace (Peking) 18, 47
India 137, 144

inflation 357, 363, 377
Inner Mongolia 13, 16
Institute [Beijing Institute for Cancer Research] 76–7, 85, 86, 94, 95, 100, 111, 149, 198
International Women's Day 343
Internationale 291, 393, 410
Islam in Quanzhou (Fujian) 39

Jan[et] (author's stepmother)
Jataka [stories about Buddha] 56
Jews in China 186
Ji Gong (song from TV series) 213
Jiang Qing (1913– , Mao's wife) 28, 89, 186, 281
Jianguo [mandala murals] 139, 162
Jiaohe (Xinjiang) 64, 66
Jiaqing (1522–1566, Ming emperor) 212
Jiayu fortress (Gansu) 57
Jiefang [Liberation] trucks 131
Jinan (Shandong) 136, 172
Jokhang temple (Lhasa, Tibet) 135, 276, 345
  Square 377
Journey to the West (novel by Wu Chengen 1500–1580) 64, 93, 125, 193, 203, 282
Juvenile Delinquent (film) 203

Kalachakra Tantra 305
Kang Youwei (1858–1927, reformer) 407
Kangxi (1654–1722, emperor) 55, 212
Kashgar (Xinjiang) 40, 53, 55, 60–62
  market 62
  people of 63, 64
Kazakhs (ethnic minority) 59, 61, 324
Ken (author's brother) 200
Kham (Tibet) 114
Khampas (people from Kham) 115, 174
Khan, Genghis (1167–1227) 16
Khan, Kublai (1215?–1294) 16, 18
KMT *see* Guomindang
'Kongji Lama' 144, 145
koubba [grave] 28, 61
Kunming (Yunnan) 27, 34, 38, 52
Kuomintang *see* Guomindang

land contracts 347
language teaching 87–89, 102–103, 109–110, 185–186, 199, 201, 205, 280–281, 283, 319, 330, 334, 342
Lanzhou (Gansu) 59, 128, 272, 371, 372

Index and glossary